RIGHT TO ROCK

RIGHT TO ROCK

The Black Rock Coalition and the Cultural Politics of Race

MAUREEN MAHON

DUKE UNIVERSITY PRESS *Durham and London 2004*

© 2004 Duke University Press. All rights reserved.
Printed in the United States of America on acid-free paper. ∞
Designed by Rebecca M. Giménez. Typeset in Scala by Tseng
Information Systems. Library of Congress Cataloging-in-
Publication Data appear on the last printed page of this book.

FOR MY MOTHER, MARY,

AND IN MEMORY

OF MY FATHER, MAURICE

CONTENTS

ACKNOWLEDGMENTS

"Loneliness is such a *drag*," Jimi Hendrix once pronounced. And writing, a solitary pursuit, can be a lonely enterprise. Mercifully, friends and colleagues have been with me through the long process of bringing this book on black rock to closure, preventing me from feeling too lonely, lonely, lonely. I was fortunate to start this project at New York University in an environment where mixing anthropology, media, and research in the United States seemed to make sense. Kamau Brathwaite, Donna Buchanan, Manthia Diawara, Barry Dornfeld, Steven Gregory, Fred Myers, Tricia Rose, Andrew Ross, Bambi Schieffelin, and Connie Sutton introduced me to a broad range of perspectives and have been superb intellectual and professional mentors. I owe a very special thanks to Faye Ginsburg who was, from the very beginning, an engaged and demanding advisor whose commitment to taking art and activism seriously has been both formative and inspirational. Deborah Elliston, Amy Empson, Brian Larkin, Meg McLagan, Robert Moise, Tony Rossi, Lotti Silber, Marilyn Thomas-Houston, Deborah Thomas, and Erica Wortham gave me excellent moral(e) support at NYU. I thank Patsy Asch who graciously provided my housing during my fieldwork in Los Angeles and Steve Feld for his encouragement along the way.

My colleagues at Wesleyan University and UCLA have provided stimulating environments and community. I especially want to thank Karen Brodkin, Carole Browner, Mickey Davidson, Ann duCille, Susan Hirsch, Jay Hoggard, Jeff Kerr-Ritchie, Cheryl Keyes, Liza McAlister, Claudia Mitchell-Kernan, Harryette Mullen, Sarah Ohly, Gayle Pemberton, Renée Romano, Ashraf Rushdy, Kate Rushin, Mark Slobin, Valerie Smith, Besty Traube, and Jennifer Tucker for their camaraderie. Sandro Duranti and Richard Yarborough have been especially energetic supporters of my research and fun to hang out with; they also have shared their ideas about music and politics and helped me work through my own. Thanks to Renée Romano and Laura Helper who read and commented on various drafts. I'm especially grateful to my colleague Allen Johnson for his incisive reading of the manuscript and his valuable suggestions at a critical moment. Thanks also to Antero Garcia, a UCLA undergraduate, for his assistance with the discography.

The staff at Duke University Press made putting the book together a pleasurable experience. It has been enormously fun to work with Ken Wissoker, who approached this project with a buoying mix of from-the-heart enthusiasm and firm editorial guidance. Two anonymous readers gave the text a thorough and thoughtful review and their comments led to significant improvements.

Lee Baker has been a dear friend with an unlimited supply of positive energy. Patrick Dodd brought glorious *couleurs*. Chris Pfaff got things started by giving me clippings on the BRC, digging up the names and phone numbers I needed to get connected, and insisting that the whole project was a good idea. Ned Anthony provided companionship, intellectual challenges, and got me closer to appreciating Led Zeppelin than I ever thought possible. With their expertly timed phone calls and witty e-mail messages, Daphne Brooks and Judith Casselberry pulled me through the last stages of writing with my sense of humor and my spirit intact. They have been way more than generous with their warmth, insight, and ability to make me laugh. I value their friendship. Also, of course, thanks, Mom.

My greatest debt is to the members of the Black Rock Coalition in New York and Los Angeles. They welcomed me into their communities and made it possible for me to "do anthropology" on their organization. I am grateful for their interest in my project and for their willingness to help me every step of the way by providing phone numbers, newspaper articles, photographs, and above all their music and stories. Earl Douglas, Don Eversley, Rob Fields, Beverly Jenkins, Bruce Mack, Konda Mason, Beverly Milner, Jimmy Saal, and Greg Tate made important contributions to the research and smoothed the way considerably. A heartfelt thank-you to Bill Toles for his help in the field, for reading and commenting on early drafts, and for many great conversations about music and just about everything else. Vernon Reid has my lasting gratitude for believing in the project and for supplying healthy doses of his irrepressible wit. Pictures may well be worth thousands of words and I thank Andrea Clarke, Don Eversley, David Fiuczynski, Michael Hill, Bruce Mack, Tracie Morris, Tori Ruffin, Jimmy Saal, and Bill Toles for helping me locate photographers and for generously sharing their personal BRC archives. Mia Friday deserves special recognition for saving boxes of materials from the early days of the BRC and Living Colour *and* for taking the time to sift through them with me on an autumn Sunday afternoon. I am deeply grateful to Lian Amber, Drew Carolan, Janine da Silva, Giselle May, and Lamar Thompson for going to a lot of trouble at the last minute to supply me with photographs and for allowing me to reproduce their excellent work here.

Parts of the text of chapter 2 appeared in *American Ethnologist*, 27 (2): 283–311. Funding from the National Science Foundation Pre-Doctoral Fellowship for Minorities, a Small Grant from the Wenner-Gren Foundation for Anthropological Research, and a Ford Foundation Dissertation Fellowship made it possible to do the research and get the ideas onto the page. Funding of another sort came from my parents, to whom I dedicate this book. Their cautious belief in the civil rights dream and their understanding of how to deal with its realities helped me make it this far and, on an even more practical note, they were the first people to play records for me.

ONE

RECLAIMING THE RIGHT TO ROCK

I certainly didn't go in thinking that this was going to end up being some sort of organization. It really started out more like a griping session when it all began. But we all met afterwards and soon we were meeting on Saturdays every week and the meetings got bigger and bigger. And the talks would be more and more amazing. We would talk for hours, sometimes going long after the meetings were over.—BLACK ROCK COALITION COFOUNDER KONDA MASON, *BRC NEWSLETTER*, DECEMBER/JANUARY 2000/2001

We really started out as a way to air out certain gripes that people had about the "glass ceiling" in music for Black musicians. Particularly instrumentalists who really wanted to stretch out and were being told by, let's say the "R&B" side of the industry, that "Black folks don't wanna hear loud guitars" and feeling the response from the rock 'n' roll side was that "Niggers can't play rock 'n' roll." What started out as a bitching session, really became more about a proactive and developmental approach to the issue, which was, instead of talking about how we're locked out of the Master's house, why don't we just build our own?—BLACK ROCK COALITION COFOUNDER GREG TATE, *BRC NEWSLETTER*, FEBRUARY 2001

The idea of getting all these odd, misfit, iconoclastic, rogue artists together was just a very interesting thing. It kind of formed, in a way, a community of difference. These were all people who marched to the beat of their own drummer. And it was just heavy. The thing about the Black Rock Coalition was that it became an

IN THE FIELD

During most weeks in the 1990s, you could find black rock musicians playing sets in downtown New York's bars and clubs. For example, early in June 1993, people gathered for a party at the Pink Pony, a bar located on Ludlow Street in the Lower East Side of Manhattan. This was a celebration of the release of the seven-inch single "Springtime" by local favorite Faith, a Black Rock Coalition (BRC) band led by Felice Rosser. The Pink Pony is a relatively small space with vinyl-covered stools, Salvation Army decorations, and oversized tables with mismatched chairs. In the rear of the bar, a makeshift performance area has been fashioned against the back wall for the band's short set. Copies of the single and cassettes are on sale at a small table, but on this hot summer evening most people pay more attention to the complimentary drinks. The crowd, which conspicuously includes filmmaker Jim Jarmusch (who gives Felice a warm hug and kiss), is a youthful mix of blacks and whites, of men and women, many of whom I've seen or met at BRC meetings.

Outside at almost 9 PM it's still light. The sidewalk is packed with black and white musicians and fans who have spilled out of the bar to seek a breeze. It's like an impromptu street party, and I mill around with the rest of the crowd. "Oh, blacks playing rock? I've never heard of that," jokes a dreadlocked black man in a Jimi Hendrix T-shirt who invites me to see his rock band play later in the month. A black guy who says he lives near the Pink Pony tells me that he came over because he saw the crowd of black people—an unfamiliar sight in this neighborhood—and decided to check it out. I talk with Marque Gilmore, a drummer who's in at least three BRC bands. Dreadlocked, bespectacled, and bearded, Marque wears loose-fitting, hippie-ish clothing, silver rings, a leather bracelet, and at least one earring. His typical greeting is to place his right fist on his heart, bow his head slightly, and smile.

"This is a great night," I say.

"The vibe is real positive," he agrees. He surveys the crowd and pronounces: "Columbia couldn't, *couldn't* get with it, Spike Lee couldn't get with it, 40 Acres and a Mule couldn't get with it, so Faith did it on their own. And this is excellent."

Faith rocks at CBGB. Rene Akan (left) on guitar and Felice Rosser on bass, performing at a 1992 showcase for Spike Lee. Photo by Giselle May.

Marque's reference is to the failure of Columbia Records to okay Spike Lee's decision to sign Faith to his imprint.[1] They weren't prepared to take a risk on a black rock band led by a rocking black woman. Tonight, the Faith faithful have met to celebrate the band's decision to take things into their own hands and to produce and distribute their single on their own. The back of the bar is packed solid with eager listeners, and soon I'm in the thick of the enthusiastic, jostling crowd. Felice, Faith's leader, songwriter, and bass player, stands tall at center stage wearing a silver, spangly tank top and black jeans. In the 1980s she had played in a group with artist Jean-Michel Basquiat, but now she is leading her own band. Felice is flanked by her bandmates, black male guitarist Rene Akan and white male drummer Patrick Seacor. She adjusts her microphone, plays a few test notes on her bass, and then tries to quiet the crowd with a matter-of-fact "We're Faith." Marque subverts this low-key effort from the back corner of the room. Standing on a chair holding a poster twisted into a cone, he takes over as master of ceremonies.

"Do you all know why we're here?" he shouts through his makeshift megaphone.

An affirmative murmur rises up from the crowd.

"Do you all dig Faith?" he calls.

A louder affirmation comes as the reply, but Marque cups his hand to his ear.

"I said, *Do y'all dig Faith?*"

This time he gets the enthusiastic response he desired.

"We're all here to congratulate them—"

"Yeah!"

"—for doing what had to be done—"

"That's right!"

"—even though the wrong-headed said it couldn't be done."

More cheers and a round of applause. Felice smiles and then Faith plays.

They start with "Springtime," the single we're celebrating. After the first song, Felice takes a moment to say a word or two about "all the people who said 'you can't' and 'you shouldn't try' and 'don't even bother' and 'you're not going to be able to' and 'it isn't going to happen.' You know, it's best to ignore them." This brings another cheered affirmation from the crowd. "It's best to ignore them," she repeats. Then into another jam, "Commercialized," a song that will be included on *Blacker Than That*, the BRC's CD compilation which is itself an effort to independently produce and distribute black rock.

Faith's music has the grist and glimmer of the late 1960s vibe that the early 1990s can't seem to get enough of. Felice's sensuous bass lines and the rich musings of Rene's guitar intertwine with and are propelled by Patrick's hand drum beats. Felice's alto voice is sultry, intense, and compelling. She makes me think of Nina Simone in a reggae rock context. On this evening, Faith is playing to a friendly crowd. These are fans and friends who have been supporting the band over the years. At one point, an older black woman pushes her way through the crowd and makes a space for herself right in front of the stage. Once there she proclaims, "That's my kid!" and points to Felice who laughs in reply. For the last two songs Felice brings Diana Baker, who recently left the band, to the stage. Physical opposites, petite Diana and statuesque Felice sing their harmonies beautifully; both women are effervescent. In the crowd, people dance and clap. A tall black man stands with his arms upraised, index fingers extended from fists. A black woman in front of me lets go with a joyous dance. Felice's mother disappears from her ace vantage point for a moment but returns quickly with a friend in tow. This is Faith. The evening winds down after five or six songs and then the band steps out of its cramped performance space and mills back into the welcoming throng as re-corded music takes up the sonic slack. Faith and most BRC bands, like most unsigned rock bands in general, did the bulk of their performing in the live local music scene. Among the things that kept them going, beyond the sheer love of playing music, was the dream that they could make it big.

LIVING COLOUR

Back in 1989, the 24-hour music television station MTV started play-ing a video by a black rock band called Living Colour. The song "Cult of Personality" was a mid-tempo blast of rock with a catchy hook and up-front guitar licks. The song featured a guitar solo that culminated in rapid-fire arpeggios and then twisted into a thrashing freak-out. The lyrics warned about the seductive trap of the mindless adulation of charismatic leaders and the risks of negating one's own beliefs in order to follow someone else. Echoing the names mentioned in the song, the video featured black-and-white footage of Benito Musso-lini, John F. Kennedy, and Martin Luther King Jr., as well as crowds of people at political rallies and public appearances of the Beatles. These archival images were intercut with scenes of the band perform-ing the song on a soundstage. Decked out in brightly colored gear, the drummer, bass player, and guitarist (whose instrument was decorated with red, green, and blue paint) played with a fierce and infectious energy. The singer wore a fluorescent yellow tank top and shorts and had rainbow-colored strands threaded in his hair. His insistent vocals interwove with the guitarist's responses and rode on top of the steady, stomping bass. Among the lines that leapt out were, "When a leader speaks that leader dies," and, maybe more significant to the overall message, "Only you can set you free."

MTV put "Cult of Personality" in heavy rotation. The television ex-posure, coupled with glowing write-ups in the mainstream music press, including *Rolling Stone*, the American rock bible, helped make Living Colour a familiar name among the rock cognoscenti. An invi-tation to open for perennial English rockers the Rolling Stones on their 1989 "Steel Wheels" tour solidified Living Colour's legitimacy as a rock band and helped launch their own successful national out-ing as headliners. The success of Living Colour—the band's platinum album, three Grammy awards, and inclusion in the rock canon of the early 1990s—would have been a coup for any young rock band, but it was particularly remarkable that things had worked out for an all-

Part of the publicity campaign for Living Colour's first album, *Vivid* (William Calhoun, Muzz Skillings, Corey Glover, Vernon Reid). Photo by Drew Carolan.

black rock ensemble. Until Living Colour's arrival, black rockers had not been a part of the mainstream music scene since the halcyon days of Jimi Hendrix, who died in 1970. In fact, by the late 1980s when Living Colour released their first album, *Vivid*, African American musicians had been relegated to rhythm and blues, dance, and rap music. The prevailing view was that no one—not black audiences, not white audiences, and not black musicians—had an interest in black rock.

Living Colour challenged this notion, both through its forceful rock sound and through the comments the band members made in the press. The foursome of guitarist Vernon Reid, drummer William Calhoun, bass player Muzz Skillings, and singer Corey Glover always brought forward the issue of race, and they talked openly about the constraints placed on black musicians because of racist perceptions that informed music industry executives' concepts of "appropriate" black music. They also talked about their experiences as a black rock band: how in the early days audiences assumed they were a reggae act and how they had to win over skeptical and sometimes verbally abusive white clubgoers who didn't think that blacks could rock. Most of the articles about Living Colour described bandleader Vernon Reid's long struggle to get a record deal and be taken seriously as a rock performer. Usually, they pointed up the role that Mick Jagger played in convincing label executives to sign the band. The articles almost always mentioned the BRC, the musicians' organization that Reid had cofounded in New York in 1985 with artist manager Konda Mason and *Village Voice* writer Greg Tate. Their goal in forming the organization was to bring together musicians and their supporters so they could begin to address the music industry's resistance to black rock. For the average fan, the existence of the BRC and its critique of music industry racism may have been of passing interest, but for African American rock musicians and fans, the organization was a revelation. The cause the BRC outlined resonated deeply because it challenged the commonsense views of race and music that had long frustrated African Americans involved in rock. Living Colour was the exceptional rock band that got a major label deal, made it onto the mainstream airwaves, and played at major concert venues on the national circuit. Its success demonstrated to bands like Faith and the other black rockers who participated in the organization that it was possible to make it in a context that for the most part denied and discouraged black rockers. The BRC, the organization that had supported Living Colour's rise, provided a structure and context through which members could affirm who they were as black rock musicians and begin the arduous process of reclaiming for African Americans the right to rock.

BLACK ROCK

Living Colour *rocked*. This was an unexpected characteristic for a 1980s, all-black band, but one they shared with fellow black rockers Bad Brains and Fishbone. What set Living Colour apart was their connection to the BRC, a consciously created community for African Americans involved in rock. This was the network of people who had come together "to get Vernon's band a deal," as long-time members often put it, back when Living Colour was playing low-paid gigs in New York City's downtown rock clubs. Media coverage of Living Colour and its surprise rise often seized on the novelty of black rockers and then picked up the rhetoric of the BRC to explain that black rock really wasn't new at all. Newspaper and magazine articles would remind readers that rock 'n' roll's original architects were African Americans like Little Richard, Ruth Brown, Bo Diddley, Etta James, and Chuck Berry. They would explain that the contemporary view of rock as music made by white people for white people was shortsighted and, as the existence of Living Colour and the BRC proved, inaccurate. For me, an African American fan of rock who was accustomed to and tired of the notion that rock was music in which black people were not supposed to participate, the coverage of Living Colour and the burgeoning black rock scene it grew out of was riveting. It was the first time I had seen a sustained discussion of race and rock in the mainstream press, and the things BRC members were saying and doing piqued my curiosity. Eventually, my pursuit of a doctorate in anthropology was the opportunity to go beyond reading articles and begin actually talking with coalition members about their involvement in music.

I learned that "black rock" was a flexible musical category that for BRC members was capable of encompassing what they referred to as "the total spectrum of Black music." The category black rock was a direct challenge to the narrow understandings of black cultural production that dominated decision making in the music industry and people's everyday thinking. In addition to being an aesthetic category, "black rock" was also a political concept, one that BRC members developed to articulate and legitimate an aesthetic position that racialized thinking had rendered incomprehensible. These African American musicians were traversing musical terrain in ways that were unusual and disruptive. Their music represented a breach of the racial etiquette that keeps black Americans confined to a limited set of separate and unequal positions and practices that are widely understood to be appropriately black. In short, black rock was a critical intervention into what was for black musicians an impossible situation. As I became immersed in the specificity of BRC members' concerns and experiences, I began to see that their particular situation was part of a larger and long-standing problem that went well beyond the realm of music: the refusal, disinclination, and inability to deal with the breadth and complexity of contemporary African American people and culture. BRC members frustrated simplistic understandings of black people. They were proudly and adamantly black and yet they did not fit the dominant, flattening stereotypes of blackness. Quite simply, they embodied the diversity of African Americans usually absent from the onslaught of media representations and academic discussions that so often highlight the distressed poor, the drug-addled, the violent, the highly sexed, the long-suffering, the religiously devout, the good-time partyers, and, occasionally thrown in for variety, the middle-class professional. Young, well-educated, middle class, bohemian, and involved in a putatively nontraditional form, black rockers consciously eluded the available boxes for black people. Rather than apologetically go away, they struggled to create a space where they could express themselves in ways that resonated with their own experiences and sense of identity.

The animating force behind this study is my fascination and frustration with the impact of racialized thinking on the ways most people in the United States categorize beliefs and behaviors. The stereotypes I listed above are so strong that, having stepped outside of them, BRC members couldn't simply play their music. They had to organize a social movement so they could do so. This situation demonstrates that popular music is an arena where questions of identity, authenticity, and taste intersect with race in especially vivid ways. An exploration of music highlights the strict and rarely questioned definitions of acceptable black cultural expression and reveals the ways marketing practices, popular culture images, and everyday discourses structure understanding of what constitutes appropriate blackness. With these interests in mind, I did not set out to write a history of the BRC or black rock. Rather, I discuss the cultural productions and cultural politics of the BRC in order to illuminate the ways its members produce, perpetuate, and challenge understandings of black identity and black culture. I argue that the demographic specificity and similarity that contributed to BRC members' coming together and sustaining an organization for almost twenty years is crucial to the way BRC members understood and addressed the constraints they faced in the industry and the skepticism they sometimes encountered in friends and family. BRC members had come of age in the late 1960s and early 1970s under the influence of a heady mix of civil rights and Black Power politics, Black Arts Movement poetry, innovative music, integrated education, and middle-class status. These features shaped who they were, informed their aesthetic and political issues, and led them to a shared set of concerns about how to negotiate art, politics, and identity in the post–civil rights era. *Right to Rock* explores the efforts of black artists to expand the limited definitions of black identity and the consequences of their actions while examining the persistence and mutability of racialized structures, ideologies, and practices in the United States.

BLACK AUTHENTICITY AND DOUBLE-CONSCIOUSNESS

Addressing the relationship between aesthetics, racial authenticity, and racial identity is central to the BRC's project and, therefore, to my study. In the post–civil rights era United States, an interest in rock music marks an African American as someone who has either misunderstood which music is appropriate for his or her consumption or has abandoned black culture by investing in what is perceived as a white music form.[2] Musical preference is a loaded marker of difference that distinguishes BRC members from the black identities they are expected to hold. Here, music genre becomes a symbol of outsider status, a tool for policing racial categories, a way of attacking the absence of authenticity, and an indicator of familiarity with contemporary black cultural norms. Significantly, one does not have to be African American to classify the tastes of African Americans; indeed, a number of BRC members had white music executives confidently tell them that their music was "not black enough."

Concepts of black authenticity, which are central to these classifications, suggest that practices and beliefs that fall outside certain parameters are not "really black." Although the term authenticity denotes real and natural, our understandings of what is and is not authentic are based on assumptions that have been produced over time and that can change according to history and context. Authenticity is far from natural; instead, prevailing views of what is authentic become naturalized. We construct authenticity and we depend on it to evaluate the quality of art and the integrity of people. A useful category, authenticity promises certainty in otherwise ambiguous processes. In the United States, understandings of black authenticity are buttressed by what anthropologist Renato Rosaldo characterizes as a tendency to "conflate the notion of culture with the idea of difference" (1993:201).[3] In fact, marking difference from the Anglo-American mainstream is a common way of defining black cultural identity and informs post–civil rights era identity politics (Omi and Winant 1994). Blacks and nonblacks assume that sustaining authentic black culture, especially in an increasingly if imperfectly integrated United States, requires maintaining separation from other contaminating cultures. In short, "real" black culture and "real" black people must be really different, elaborating and guarding practices recognized as authentic through processes of "cultural protectionism" (Gilroy 1993:96).

Some notions of black authenticity are uncritically connected to long-standing stereotypes that position blacks as being spiritual, sensual, and artistic, but also predisposed to criminality, poverty, and other pathologies.[4] Assumptions about class status are embedded in images that frame a poor or working-class position as part of authentic blackness and suggest that "there is a correct formula for Black identity that should in some way address working-class politics" (Boyd 1997:22). In such an environment, asserting a black middle-class perspective can be interpreted as ignoring the economic, educational, and social marginalization of poor and working-class African Americans. It is evidence of a lack of concern about "the race." The roots of this tendency may be in the late 1960s black political discourses that characterized middle-class African Americans as assimilated, self-hating "Negroes" and contrasted them to progressive, independent "Blacks." Liberated from the damaging effects of Euro-American middle-class culture, "Blacks" embraced a "pure and uncompromising" blackness and were committed to fighting for "the people," in other words, the black poor and working class (Van Deburg 1992:54; cf. Harper 1995; Kelley 1994). This marking of intraracial difference depended on a claim that "Blacks" were more authentically black than "Negroes." The habit of making this kind of assertion—African Americans colloquially refer to it as acting "blacker than thou"—persevered into the 1990s and contributed, I suspect, to the BRC's decision to call its second CD compilation *Blacker Than That*, a title that suggests play with and against dominant expressions of black identity.

Although concepts of black authenticity have changed over time, they are embedded in a vision of black identity as an essence, a static category that transcends time and space. Describing the complexity of contemporary black identity, cultural studies scholar Stuart Hall argues that black identity is both a state of being and a process of becoming. One is black not simply because of ancestry or phenotype but because of practice and consciousness. This perspective reminds us that blackness is created, enacted, and produced through the choices we make (Hall 1992:220).[5] In the post–civil rights era, African Americans contend with the on-the-ground reality of black heterogeneity, white assumptions of black homogeneity, and black claims of unity that often demand uniformity. Recent interrogative book titles like *Am I Black Enough For You?* (Boyd 1997) and *Are We Not Men?* (Harper 1996) give an indication of the defensiveness that accompanies the expression of diverse black identities. As a consequence, it becomes necessary for black Americans and scholars who write about us to reiterate what should be obvious: that there is no single black identity shared by all black Americans, that black Americans are not a monolithic group, and that multiple, even contradictory, versions of blackness coexist. Depending on the context and the objectives of the people invoking it, blackness can be a politicized, artistic, historical, or strategic identification that reflects the multifaceted ways African Americans construct identities and understand themselves.[6]

The persistent debates about black identity indicate the extent to which it is a mutable and contested category, one that different groups — whether they be radicals, conservatives, or rockers — struggle to define and defend, often in terms that advance and legitimate their positions. BRC members worked to expand what can count as black art and black identity, while negotiating the persuasive terms of black authenticity. BRC members insisted on the heterogeneity of black experience and identity, proclaimed their openness to nonblack influences, and embraced what they considered the distinct qualities of blackness. Often, they challenged essentialist discourses about African Americans by invoking antiessentialist ideas. At the same time, they asserted black identity in ways that depended on the dominant terms of black authenticity. In examining their productions, I am concerned with understanding BRC members' strategic uses of black authenticity in order to explore the ways they negotiated dominant paradigms of African American identity in relation to their aesthetic commitments, personal experiences, and social contexts.

Black rock musicians put a post–civil rights era spin on longstanding debates about black identity and the position of blacks in the United States. It does not seem possible to discuss these issues without reckoning with the century-old formulation of African American scholar and activist W. E. B. Du Bois. The situation of BRC members is exemplary of the condition Du Bois called "double-consciousness." In his much-cited 1903 reflection on the question of African American identity, Du Bois asks how blacks can, at once, be "American" *and* "Negro" (1989:3). Black Americans, Du Bois argues, are historically and sociologically an inseparable part of U.S. society, but racism marginalizes us from the American mainstream (187). As a result of this simultaneous belonging and not belonging, black Americans are unable to achieve "true self-consciousness" and instead experience a "peculiar sensation" (3). "This double-consciousness," Du Bois explains, is a "sense of always looking at one's self through the eyes of others, of measuring one's soul by the tape of a world that looks on in amused contempt and pity. One ever feels his twoness, — an American, a Negro; two souls, two thoughts, two unreconciled strivings; two warring ideals in one dark body, whose dogged strength alone keeps it from being torn asunder" (3). Du Bois recognized that one challenge for African Americans would be to create a political and ideological climate in which it was possible to share in the opportunities the American dream promised without assimilating to dominant Euro-American norms, many of which disparaged black people. He recognized that black Americans have to fight part of this battle against racism and exclusion on the terrain of identity—at the level of consciousness—where so much damage had already been done. Throughout the history of the United States, Du Bois argues, every black American has struggled to "merge [this] double self into a better truer self" and to draw on the resources of both Euro-American and African American cultures (3). In Du Bois's time, efforts to achieve the true self-consciousness he idealized were thwarted by entrenched de facto and de jure racism. Black rock musicians discovered that a version of the situation Du Bois described in 1903 continued to exist in the mid-1980s.

At the turn of the millennium, as in Du Bois's era, addressing the relationships between black and white identities in art or social analysis is still controversial. Mainstream U.S. culture pressures people to choose one category—black or white—to categorize everything from individual identities to cultural practices to musical styles. Cultural studies scholar Paul Gilroy, for example, observes that "occupying the space between them or trying to demonstrate their continuity has been viewed as a provocative and even oppositional act of political insubordination" (1993:1). The BRC's activities disrupt the comfortable categories of black and white. They force us to acknowledge the black influences that shape forms and practices defined as "American," a term that often connotes "white." Rock 'n' roll music, a quintessential American form, is American music precisely *because* of its mixed black and white (or African and European) roots. Historically, however, African Americans and African American culture have been constructed as outside of the U.S. nation and society. This is true in spite of their impact on "American" culture.[7] Rather than capitulating to one-sided constructions of an authentic black identity or an authentic rock musician, BRC members responded to what I see as their contemporary condition of double-consciousness through their insistence on the legitimacy of black rock, a seemingly oxymoronic genre that links "black" and "white" categories.

BRC members routinely noted that they did not see their musical tastes as being in conflict with their blackness even though they knew others did. Identifying as black rockers enabled them to negotiate tensions between the expectations of both black and white communities. Geoff, a bass player born in 1954, explained the purpose of the BRC: "For me, it's an outlet for black musicians who had the same problem I did in high school: you couldn't play for black kids *or* for white kids." Geoff told me about the responses he and his black friends encountered when playing in a high school rock band:

Now the problem [was] . . . that we were playing rock 'n' roll then. . . .
We listened to Motown and all the other quote unquote black music
back then, but we were also listening to Led Zeppelin and Grand
Funk Railroad . . . and I dug all that stuff so that's the type of
thing we were playing. . . . But the problem came in that we really
couldn't play for any of the events in [our black] neighborhood because they didn't dig the rock music. I remember even playing on
one event . . . and everybody in the audience is saying, "Yeah, these
guys are going to be hip," and then we break out into this heavy
metal kind of rock 'n' roll. . . . These people were looking at us
[like], "What are these Negroes about?" And when we would play
with the white kids, they just didn't respect us. The only thing they
wanted to hear us play was "I Wanna Take You Higher" [by Sly and
the Family Stone]. . . . So I was kind of caught in the middle between
two worlds, so to speak.

Since 1985, BRC members have promoted an alternative black
sound and vision, creating a community where musicians like Geoff
could feel at the center instead of caught in the middle. Over the years,
they have advanced a cultural critique that challenges contemporary
racial common sense and used their music to present alternatives
to dominant images of black people.[8] Working together, they excavated and celebrated African American cultural contributions, all the
while insisting that "rock and roll is Black music and we are its heirs"
(BRC 1985).

THE CULTURAL POLITICS OF
RACE AND REPRESENTATION

The BRC started because some black cultural activists were sick and
tired of being sick and tired. Moved by their frustration with the rigid
category "black music," Reid, Mason, and Tate invited friends and colleagues to a Saturday afternoon meeting where they could discuss
the challenges African American musicians were facing in the music
industry and the local rock clubs. Among those present were musicians, aspiring and current music industry personnel, journalists,
poets, videomakers, visual artists, and supporters of the arts. All were
concerned about the pigeonholing of black artists. The first meeting
generated energy and hope, convincing participants that it was worth
getting together again. Meetings continued through the fall and word
began to spread that young black artists and musicians were gather-

This photo of some of the BRC's core members appeared alongside a 1986 *Essence* magazine music column about the new organization. Clockwise from upper left, Bruce Mack, Steve Williams, Naja Noon, Jared Nickerson, Tracie Morris, Vernon Reid, Konda Mason. Photo by Drew Carolan.

ing on a regular basis to talk about things that mattered. The wide-ranging discussions incorporated the sharing of stories about how individuals got into music, commiseration about the challenges they faced as aspiring professional musicians of color, exchange of information about performance opportunities, and debates about local and national politics. These meetings were a cornerstone of the BRC. The face-to-face gatherings allowed people coming from similar socioeconomic backgrounds and sharing similar artistic and musical interests — "like-minded people," as BRC members put it — to find each other and establish professional and personal connections.

Working from these lively conversations, participants analyzed the relationship between race, identity, and music and began developing critiques of the racism and stereotypes that operated in both the music industry and in the commonsense assumptions of black and white Americans. Before long, they had decided to call themselves the Black Rock Coalition and secured status as a 501(c)3 nonprofit, tax-exempt educational organization. The coalition has never had a paid staff and has always operated with volunteer labor. In keeping with the rules of nonprofits, the BRC has a board of directors and a national president. Both the New York and Los Angeles chapters have an executive committee consisting of an executive director, secretary, and treasurer; directors of operations, publicity, marketing, communications; and an orchestra director who is in charge of coordinating BRC ensemble performances. During the period of my research, the BRC had a national membership that ranged from 250 to 400 individuals—the majority of whom were men—and 50 member bands.[9] Member bands must be led by an African American or Latino, but musicians and nonmusicians of any race can join the BRC on an individual basis. In short order, members of the BRC had gone from talking about their concerns to doing something about them. They introduced their perspective into the New York scene with the Drop the Bomb party, held irreverently on December 7, 1985. This was the first of dozens of events that have, over the years, made the case for the legitimacy of black rock. BRC members produced parties, band performances, educational panels, and a public radio show through which they highlighted and celebrated their music. Following her move to the West Coast, Konda Mason launched a Los Angeles chapter in 1989 in collaboration with musician Rayford Jarvis and activist Mary Alice Bailey. Black rockers based in Los Angeles who had been following Living Colour's stratospheric rise were primed to support their own local BRC, and after several well-attended general member meetings, the Los Angeles BRC had its public launch with a fund-raising concert, "All Is Not Quiet on the Western Front/Black Rock Coalition Invasion Part Two," in July 1989.

Playing rock was something BRC members were passionate about, and playing rock was something BRC members were told they shouldn't do. For BRC members, then, music was not simply an artistic form in which they had a professional interest. It was a site of ideological and social struggle over the categories and conditions that defined them as African Americans. BRC members used music, media, performance, images, and rhetoric to articulate their vision of black rock, challenge existing racial hierarchies, and assert alternative representations of African American identity and culture. BRC members were also invested in the forces they sought to change. They had been influenced by dominant images of black identity and culture, of artistic success, of race and power, and of gender and class. Throughout, I pay attention to these dynamics, noting the ways BRC members operated within and were shaped by mainstream institutions and ideologies and describing the strategies they used to challenge them.[10] Race mattered to BRC members because it was a salient category through which they identified themselves—they were black and proud—and because their blackness limited their participation in their chosen profession. A critique of racism was part of their musical and political project. At the same time and by necessity, they made a race-based claim for the right to rock.

The BRC activities that I focus on are what anthropologist Steven Gregory has described as "the social processes through which relations and practices of racial subjugation are contested and politicized" (Gregory 1994:35). Gregory is among the scholars who analyze the persistent but changing influence of racism in the post–civil rights era and stress the importance of historicizing race as a category and racism as a practice.[11] In spite of legal integration, affirmative action, and the emergence of a black middle class, the period when the BRC formed was marked by the perseverance of institutional and individual racism. African Americans felt the entrenchment of racism in the difficulties they had securing bank loans for housing, advancing in employment beyond glass ceilings, preserving affirmative action, and avoiding police harassment (Lipsitz 1998). The 1980s also saw the backlash against the Civil Rights Movement's political gains for African Americans, a trend most clearly marked by the widespread support of President Ronald Reagan's racially charged rhetoric and actions.[12] BRC members put race and racialization in the foreground because to downplay them would have meant ignoring their daily reality. BRC members organized according to their ascribed racial category and their chosen racial identity to combat the limitations on black participation in rock, to express themselves artistically, and to define themselves personally. *Right to Rock* describes the ways the BRC's project enacts a cultural politics of race and representation.[13]

The BRC's focus on the music industry is significant since historically music has been a central African American contribution to American culture and a medium for emotional and political expression. Stereotypes of blacks as natural entertainers and highly musical folk with lots of rhythm have been shored up by the long line of talented and successful African American musicians. The BRC demonstrated that even a career in music was circumscribed by race. It is easy to accept blacks as musicians, but the image of a *rock* musician is, for most Americans, a white man with a guitar. Jimi Hendrix is the exception that proves the rule. BRC members could never take for granted the right to perform the music of their choice. Instead, they had to justify their projects and constitute a context for their enactment. All of this draws attention to the fact that the music industry's racialized market niches have influenced the ways many Americans understand racial identity and indicates the reason BRC members saw the music industry as the primary target for their critiques. When BRC members perform black rock, they are doing more than making music; they are also using music to produce, promote, and contest definitions of blackness. This practice of representation is an important part of cultural politics precisely because representation is not simply a way of reflecting reality, but a way of creating it.[14]

People who have been marginalized from institutional power frequently use popular culture forms and media technologies to make representations of their groups that counter negative images, the absence of images, and images produced by outsiders.[15] Anthropologist Faye Ginsburg uses the term "cultural activism" to highlight the relationship between representation and social action and describe the cultural politics of people who explicitly link aesthetic and political agendas (Ginsburg 1997). For BRC members, cultural activism allowed members to define who they were as black rock musicians and to expose the way the category black music perpetuates de facto segregation at record labels, in the airwaves, and in everyday life. Faced with definitions of "black music" that excluded the music they were interested in, BRC members used concerts, panel discussions, recordings, and Web pages to make visible and audible — to *represent* — black rock, the category that mattered to them.

As BRC members challenged definitions of black authenticity and expanded the possibilities of black cultural production, they were by necessity involving themselves in public conversations about culture and identity circulating in the black public sphere. Loosely defined as a mix of formal and informal institutions that include black-owned media, civic organizations, churches, entertainment centers, and businesses that cater to black constituencies, the black public sphere is a site in which discussions related to black themes occur and circulate. The black public sphere parallels the dominant public sphere, sometimes intersecting with it, sometimes challenging it (Appadurai, et al. 1994, Neal 1999).[16] During the 1990s, the high visibility of black Americans on television, in movies, and especially in

D-Xtreme, Brooklyn's "Slam-Funk Posse." From left, Bryant "Beezo" Kimber (raps and vocals), Mark "Kumasi" Rogers (vocals), Mike Machado (drums), Fritz Reid (bass), Stan Brown (guitar). Photo by Lamar Thompson. Courtesy Donald Eversley.

music led some scholars to talk enthusiastically of this black public space. We should be careful, however, not to confuse the visibility of African Americans in the mainstream media with African Americans having extensive decision-making power and economic autonomy therein. The institutional infrastructures in which many of the most widely available contemporary articulations of blackness occur are neither owned nor controlled by African Americans. This situation influences the ways black people and culture are represented and also informs the choices practitioners make about the types of media they use, the content they include, and the modes of distribution they select. Furthermore, the black public sphere is itself a site of internal struggles that result from differences in power, access, history, and interests of the parties involved. BRC projects in New York and Los Angeles were in conversation with and in some cases challenged dominant views of blackness and also those that circulated in the black public sphere.

Here, I should make the (perhaps obvious) observation that in addition to writing about BRC member practices of representation, I am engaging in the practice of representation. Talking about the BRC means talking about black middle-class Americans, a group whose existence is barely reflected in contemporary anthropological literature. This absence is in keeping with the discipline's focus on the

An early promotional piece for Marque Gilmore's Blue-Print. Marque is in the middle of the bottom row, holding his Chapman stick. Photo and design by Lamar Thompson.

black poor and working class (Szwed 1972) and the field's general lack of attention to U.S.-born middle-class groups (Nader 1972). As a result, "underclass" communities of African Americans have received most of the attention in social science literature and represent authentic black identity in most mainstream imaginings (but see Bell 1983; Gregory 1992, 1993, 1998; Mullings 1997; Pattillo-McCoy 1999). My interest in representation is also a response to the invisibility of black rockers that I perceived during the years that I worked on this project. Typically, when telling nonmusicians about my research, I encountered a kind of confusion that was at once instructive and disheartening. When I said, "I'm conducting fieldwork with black rock musicians," people often misheard me. "Rap musicians?" they would clarify. "Jazz musicians?" I admit that I don't always enunciate, but the part of the utterance that got lost was always "rock," a word that didn't make sense alongside "black." Although some people would respond by naming Jimi Hendrix, Lenny Kravitz, or Living Colour to confirm that they had understood what I meant by black rock, most tended to fall back on more familiar black genres, chatting amiably about jazz, blues, and rap. Another reaction was to express surprise that I was writing about people who were currently active. "Oh, they're still alive?" was a not uncommon rejoinder. This response crystallized the fact that when black rock resonated, it was located in a hazy and re-mote past. I pursued my research not simply because I wanted people to know that black rockers existed in the present or because the BRC's activities made for an interesting case study on cultural politics. I have written *Right to Rock* because the aesthetics and politics informing "black rock," the concept that BRC members champion, underscore the need to expand our views and representations of African American music, people, and culture to include a much more complex and compelling set of possibilities.

DOING FIELDWORK

"I see," Vernon Reid said slowly, "we're anthropology now." It was one of our first extensive conversations and I was describing my research and explaining how it differed from that of music journalists who had written about the BRC. As we strolled along St. Mark's Place in Manhattan's East Village, I told Vernon that as an anthropologist, I would be doing a long-term study, not a quick set of interviews. I explained that my research method, fieldwork, was a bit more extensive and intensive. For me, "doing fieldwork" meant engaging in participant observation, conducting life story interviews, and collecting BRC documents and materials. Throughout *Right to Rock*, I include illustrative passages from "in the field" like the one that opened this chapter to offer details about the BRC project and the creative work of BRC members. I draw these scenes from the field notes I took during the two years I carried out fieldwork in New York City and Los Angeles, the two cities where BRC chapters are located. In both cities I conducted research at clubs, studios, bars, cafes, and restaurants and also learned from conversations on the phone and via e-mail. This was my way of observing and participating in the BRC's production of a black rock scene and learning about the inner workings and public projects of the musicians' network that had supported Living Colour's rise. Fieldwork entailed spending time with BRC members, reading the monthly BRC newsletter, listening to the weekly radio program on New York's WBAI-FM, attending meetings and panel discussions, and going to events like Faith's party at the Pink Pony. Over the years, I saw numerous band performances at clubs like Wetlands, the Cooler, the Mercury Lounge, and the Knitting Factory in New York and Club Lingerie, The Troubadour, and the Coconut Teazer in Los Angeles. Most weeks, I was able to see several BRC bands, usually in audiences that included other BRC members. I circumscribed the unruly ethnographic terrain of New York and Los Angeles by focusing primarily

on activities related to the BRC. I spent most of my time at BRC performances and events, although I occasionally went to members' homes
or workplaces. Over time, it became clear that BRC networks extended
into friend and kin relations, ultimately fortifying the organization
where they had been nurtured. Of course, BRC members had lives and
interests separate from the organization and black rock and while I
learned about their other trajectories, I do not emphasize them here.

I conducted fieldwork with members of the New York chapter from
May 1993 to March 1995 and with Los Angeles members from March
to May in 1995. Although I would have had access to meetings and
members without officially joining the BRC, I paid the $25 annual
membership fee to demonstrate good faith. After a few months as a
member, I was faced with a dilemma: members of the executive committee had asked me to serve as secretary of the New York BRC. My
consistent presence at meetings and my obsessive note taking had
not gone unnoticed. After discussions with my dissertation advisors
and a conversation with Greg Tate, I decided to accept the position,
reasoning that it would be difficult to refuse it while continuing to
hang around. Tate had chuckled when I told him what his colleagues
had asked me to do. "They've chosen the perfect person for the job,"
he said. "Actually, it's an inspired choice. It's the work nobody likes
to do and you're already doing it." As secretary, I took notes at meetings; wrote, typed, and distributed minutes; coordinated and scheduled meetings; and handled correspondence. Accepting this position
alleviated my concern that I was merely taking information without
contributing something to the BRC and gave me a more clearly defined
place in the organization than the murky category "anthropologist."
True, many members were familiar with anthropology, having taken
a course or two in college. In my favorite form of acknowledgment,
vocalist Dean Bowman would occasionally sing me the melody line of
Charlie Parker's "Anthropology." Sometimes, members would comment on conversations or occurrences and note that they would be
good material for my project. Still, I suspect that my research seemed
a bit mysterious. While they were accustomed to journalists spending
time around the organization for interviews that led to articles published in newspapers and magazines, I did not go away and it was a
long time before I wrote anything.

When I was deciding whether to agree to be secretary, Tate tried
to put to rest my fears that general members would limit what they
said to me because of my involvement with the executive committee.
He assured me that the informality of the organization and the per-

sonalities of BRC members would militate against this. "In any other organization," he said, "it might be a problem, but everyone in the BRC is so critical anyway—no, it won't stop them. Are you worried it will affect *your* ability to be critical?" I was. Anthropologists depend on trust and rapport to conduct fieldwork and this raises concerns about bias and objectivity. All of us face a challenging set of conditions: Fieldwork depends on establishing close interpersonal relationships with one's subjects that can result in an anthropologist having "feelings of solidarity and obligation" toward them (Dornfeld 1998:25). While it would be impossible to do anthropological fieldwork without some degree of rapport, too much connection with, too much indebtedness to, and too much idealization of one's interlocutors can seriously skew research (Bosk cited in Dornfeld 1998:25). Being a so-called "native anthropologist"—someone very much like the group being "studied"—adds an additional set of concerns about one's ability to successfully conduct research (Gwaltney 1981; Kondo 1997; Messerschmidt 1981). My racial, generational, class, and educational similarity to BRC members coupled with our shared musical and political interests made me sympathetic to their cause, maybe too sympathetic to be adequately analytical, some skeptics might argue. Here, it is worth noting that recent commentaries reveal that many "outsider" anthropologists also experience a strong identification with their subjects. These scholars pay attention to the ethnographer's position as researcher, analyst, writer, and advocate (Dornfeld 1998; Marcus 1998; Feld 1994; Myers 1994; Turner 1990). They recognize that gaining access to their subjects may mean taking on roles that intensify and complicate field relationships. "One not only becomes part of the process one is trying to record," anthropologist Terence Turner observes, "but directly affects it in numerous ways, some intended and some not" (Turner 1990:10). In this period after the critique of anthropology (e.g., Clifford and Marcus 1986; Marcus and Fischer 1986; Rosaldo 1993), it has become difficult for any of us to claim to be fully "objective" observers.

Acknowledging that our positions influence how we experience and interpret social phenomena has strengthened ethnographic research and writing. Every anthropologist has to take note of his or her position in relation to his or her subjects over the course of a field study, and it's helpful to convey some of this information to our readers. While I recognized the similarities between myself and BRC members, I was acutely aware of differences. I was not a musician or industry professional and had neither the aspiration nor the talent to become either. Reversing the traditional anthropologist/informant status hierarchy, BRC members were generally more mobile than I, traveling regularly to Europe and Japan and within the United States in order to perform. Meanwhile I, a barely solvent graduate student, stayed home. Overall, they were better connected to media, entertainment, and performance outlets and personnel than I and knew how to exploit these channels. I was a few years younger than the majority of BRC members and only had secondhand knowledge of key cultural and political reference points that they had actually experienced. Finally, I was a female researcher working with a predominantly (but not only) male organization. BRC men dutifully helped me by participating in interviews, suggesting other people I should consult, and reeling off lists of artists whose music I should listen to. Still, I was never one of the guys. While my gender circumscribed aspects of my research with men, it helped me establish connections and rapport with BRC women. Although women comprise a small segment of the BRC (roughly 20 percent), they have played important and visible roles in the organization. Konda Mason was a cofounder and was a guiding force behind the launch of the Los Angeles BRC. When I was doing my research, both the East and West Coast chapters were headed by women, and women have usually held committee leadership positions. The combination of my insider and outsider status shaped my interactions with BRC members, informed the questions I asked, and influenced the ways I have interpreted my findings. I doubt that every member will agree with everything that I have written here (that would be way out of character for BRC members), but I hope that they will see the logic of my arguments.

The second main component of my research, life stories interviews with BRC members, has enabled me to incorporate multiple voices and viewpoints. The stories I collected through formal interview sessions recorded on audio tape and in informal conversations with members have contributed significantly to the way I frame my discussion. Throughout *Right to Rock*, I quote extensively from these interview transcripts in order to document the similarities and differences among members. The life stories offer illuminating data while giving a taste of the voices of BRC members, testifying to their personalities, wit, and insight. I conducted twenty-eight tape-recorded interviews with a cross section of the New York and Los Angeles membership. In selecting interview participants, I tried to reflect the BRC's gender, age, geographic, and vocational variation and included longtime and recent members, more and less active members, and musicians and nonmusicians. I conducted interviews in one or two sittings that lasted from one and a half to five hours. Frequently, interview participants added material to their stories days or weeks later, concluding observations with a statement like, "This is the kind of thing I was telling you about in that interview."

In working with these interviews, I follow Faye Ginsburg's (1989) approach to analyzing the life stories of activists and focus on the ways members use their life stories to construct and affirm their identities against a social and historical context that frequently denies their validity. As BRC members told me about their backgrounds, they also analyzed them in ways that enabled them to negotiate and make meaningful apparently contradictory experiences: for example, being black and American, being black and listening to rock, and being black and middle class, but pursuing a "bohemian" path. Their stories connected individual life cycles to historical circumstances, situating the speaker and demonstrating the logic behind his or her choices (Ginsburg 1989:134). I discuss these stories in detail in chapter 2 and draw on them throughout the book. Two caveats about these life stories: like any interview data, they were shaped by the context under which they were elicited (Briggs 1986). Because I stated my interests in certain general themes—race, music, and identity—participants were likely to tailor their remarks to address these concerns, even though our conversations were open-ended and often wide-ranging. Participants also may have highlighted or exaggerated certain points in order to fit what I seemed to be looking for. Another concern is that BRC members have told parts of these stories many times before—to each other in meetings and to journalists writing about the organization. There is again a risk of exaggeration, embellishment, or mythmaking here as speakers may emphasize certain features to fit their perception of what an interviewer expects to hear from a BRC member. Reflecting on our interviews once they had ended, a couple of members commented that they were "like therapy." Others used the interview as an opportunity to let off steam, and I collected several heartfelt rants along the way—some of which I have included in the text. To offset the possible skewing these tendencies may cause, I have included numerous and lengthy excerpts from different speakers. BRC member life stories are part of an intellectual process that anthropologist John Gwaltney argues is critical to the survival of all black Americans (1980). He observes that African Americans depend on an ability to produce "indigenous analysis" in order to make sense of living in the United States, an experience dominated by the central paradox "of being separate yet inseparable from the fabric of American life" (xxviii). The life stories of BRC members and the BRC's activism more broadly are eloquent examples of this process.

The third component of my research was a BRC "archive" that I accumulated through member donations and my own collection. This included coalition newsletters from New York and Los Angeles; *Ravers*, the BRC's occasionally published arts review; newspaper and magazine articles about the BRC and BRC member artists; BRC band press kits and fliers promoting club dates; CD, cassette, and video recordings of BRC artists; and videotapes of BRC member appearances on network and cable television. This body of materials was invaluable to my efforts to trace history and networks and to characterize BRC productions.

THE POLITICS AND POETICS OF BLACK ROCK

In *Right to Rock*, I describe the ways members of the BRC used their cultural productions to critique the limitations placed on African American musicians, describe the institutional structures and power struggles in which BRC members are engaged, and examine how their public statements and activities affected the social and aesthetic terrain. Throughout, I examine the economic, political, social, and aesthetic dimensions of black rock. The music BRC members produce in live performance at local clubs is both a creative expression and a social process that involves the formation of social relationships, the construction of identity, and the articulation of broader values and ideologies.[17] In chapter 4, I describe how these different facets of music making come together through a focus on BRC member performances in New York rock clubs. Through a discussion of these shows and an analysis of the BRC Manifesto, the organization's founding document, I consider the culturally activist practices and discourses through which members inserted black rock into the public sphere.

BRC members seeking to go beyond the local context by interacting with major record labels were reminded that mass-mediated music is simultaneously a commercial and an artistic form. Above all, the recording industry is a profit-centered business where tensions emerge as people negotiate producing profit and producing art. In chapter 6, I focus on the political economy of the recording industry, paying particular attention to the ways the politics of race have intersected with the development, production, and consumption of popular music. What I call the "racialized political economy" of the music industry—most clearly marked by race-based genre segregation—has had a decisive effect on African American participation both as performers and executives. Responding to the limits of the mainstream industry, a number of BRC members turned to alternative methods for circulating their music. In chapter 7, I discuss BRC member involvement in independent or "do-it-yourself" productions and examine the ways members used self-produced recordings and public access cable television programming to disseminate black rock.

Although unique for its focus on rock music and the workings of the music industry, the BRC is part of an African American tradition. In forming an organization to address the racial limitations they were encountering in their chosen profession, BRC members were continuing the long-standing African American practice of forming associations around social, political, and cultural concerns. Historically, these community-based clubs and organizations have enabled members to meet, talk, promote events, and address issues of social and political interest (Drake and Cayton 1993:688–715).[18] The linking of art and activism that the BRC enacts echoes the connections between artistic production and racial identity that characterize the Harlem Renaissance of the 1920s and the Black Arts Movement of the 1960s. And, as an organization for black musicians, the BRC recalls the Association for the Advancement of Creative Musicians (AACM), a Chicago-based organization formed in 1965 to support and showcase musicians and composers like Muhal Richard Abrams, Anthony Braxton, Lester Bowie, and members of the Art Ensemble of Chicago, all of whom were expanding the jazz idiom. In fact, many BRC members described the AACM as an example that inspired the formation of the BRC. In the first part of the book, I discuss the organizational aspects of the BRC. In chapter 2, I consider the factors that facilitated members' ability to work together in an activist organization and describe the similarities in race, class, generation, education, and music taste that linked BRC members. In chapter 3, I discuss the meetings through which BRC members identified commonalities and consolidated their organization. I show how they used conversation to define themselves, forge connections with one another, articulate the BRC's mission, and lay the groundwork for their activism.

While socially conscious organizing provided a framework within which BRC members could produce their music and is a focus of this study, it is the music itself that is at the center of the BRC. The form and content of rock 'n' roll, R&B, soul, funk, and reggae attracted BRC members as they came of age in the 1960s and 1970s and influenced the music they eventually produced. The hard rock associated with the 1960s counterculture incorporated calls for social, personal, and sexual liberation with political critique—especially of the war in Vietnam. The presence of these ideas and the challenge that the rock scene presented to the mainstream helped forge a link between rock music and freedom from individually and socially imposed strictures. Performers like Bob Dylan, Janis Joplin, the Grateful Dead, and Jimi Hendrix communicated this spirit in their lyrics, music, dress, and performance styles. This period also saw the efflorescence of self-contained black and integrated bands that influenced BRC members. During this golden age, James Brown, George Clinton's bands Funkadelic and Parliament, the Isley Brothers, Sly and the Family Stone, Stevie Wonder, Santana, War, the Ohio Players, Earth, Wind & Fire, and Mandrill played R&B, rock, and Latin grooves. They also created funk, the polyrhythmic form characterized by foregrounded, danceable bass parts, percussive horn blasts and guitar lines, and vocals that together conjured up the sonic atmosphere of a great party. While good times were at the heart of this music, the songs conveyed a considerable amount of social consciousness. The Isley Brothers's song "Fight The Power" was a propulsive reminder that "We got to fight the powers that be." Sly and the Family Stone moved from the celebration of "Hot Fun in the Summertime" to the caustic warning of "Don't Call Me Nigger, Whitey." In the song "Chocolate City," Parliament offered a clever exposition on urban black political autonomy and white flight to the "vanilla suburbs." Meanwhile, Funkadelic took on music industry common sense in "Who Says a Funk Band Can't Play Rock?!" During this period, spoken word artists the Last Poets and songwriter Gil Scott-Heron commented incisively about the political and social conditions of black Americans. Reggae's Bob Marley and the Wailers articulated and raised "third world" consciousness with a resonant perspective on colonial oppression and the need for rebellion. By the 1980s, BRC members were watching the careers of inventive African American guitarists like Sonny Sharrock, Jean-Paul Bourelly (who was a BRC member), and James "Blood" Ulmer, who released an album called *Black Rock* in 1982. Also during this period, black rock bands like Mother's Finest with its fierce metal funk, Fishbone with its ska inflections, and Bad Brains with its brilliant melding of hardcore punk and reggae came forward and provided inspiration.

Like most American teenagers developing an interest in music, BRC members spent hours in their bedrooms, basements, and garages tuning into FM radio and listening to albums by Led Zeppelin, Jimi

Hendrix, and Funkadelic over and over and over. They played air or real instruments, sometimes smoked weed, and usually imagined what it would be like to be onstage. Music was becoming an important part of who they were, and their attraction to the form influenced their decisions about playing an instrument, which instrument to play, how much time to spend practicing, which people to hang out with, and what career path to follow. They responded to the era's musical richness and breadth by infusing their own creative work with these tendencies. When they began their professional encounters with the music industry in the mid-1980s, however, the tolerance for the variety they had grown up with was out of fashion. Ironically, BRC members who had been shaped by the 1960s rhetoric of rock and freedom were being stymied by formal and informal music industry rules that said blacks did not play rock. Outlining their position and mission in the BRC Manifesto, they resisted changing their sound to fit popular definitions of "black music" and rejected charges that their rock-inflected music was "inauthentic." Instead, as they explained it in the manifesto, they formed "a united front of musically and politically progressive Black artists and supporters" to promote and sustain "the total spectrum of Black music" (BRC 1985). Their goal was to participate in the music that had become a defining feature of who they were as artists and individuals.

While attention to sociological and political aspects of music is necessary to make sense of the BRC's project, in *Right to Rock* I am also interested in aesthetics. In chapter 5 I develop a musical and ideological definition of the genre "black rock." Basing my analysis on BRC member recordings, performances, and comments, I discuss the qualities of the music and performance styles that for BRC members counted as black rock and the performers who counted as black rock musicians. Aesthetic values are distinct from sociological issues, but because of the dominance of racialization in music and the dependence on authenticity to understand black cultural production, the political and the aesthetic aspects of black rock are closely linked. To define black rock is to address the question of musical genre, both in terms of sound and in terms of music industry marketing decisions. Here, it is important to point out that although jazz, rap, and rock represent three distinct genres, the musicians associated with the BRC have enthusiastically blurred these boundaries. In the early years, the BRC counted among its meeting-goers and participants in early shows members of the M-Base Collective, a loosely organized alliance of jazz musicians that includes saxophonists Steve Coleman

Pianist Geri Allen was among the New York musicians who joined in the early conversations about music that launched the BRC. Photo by Lamar Thompson.

and Greg Osby, pianist Geri Allen, vocalist Cassandra Wilson, and guitarist David Gilmore. Guitarists Vernon Reid and David Fiuczynski and bass player Melvin Gibbs played with jazz drummer Ronald Shannon Jackson's ensemble the Decoding Society and guitarist Kelvyn Bell performed and recorded with alto saxophonist Arthur Blythe. Bell, Gibbs, and Reid had also played with Defunkt, trombone player Joseph Bowie's jazz funk experiment. BRC members had connections to rap, too. Bill Stephney, who attended early BRC meetings and who was a producer for rap group Public Enemy, invited Vernon Reid to play on "Sophisticated Bitch," a song on *Yo! Bum Rush the Show*, Public Enemy's first album. Public Enemy's Flavor Flav and Chuck D appeared on *Vivid*, Living Colour's first album, and rappers Queen Latifah and Doug E. Fresh contributed to their second release, *Time's Up*. Living Colour's second bass player, Doug Wimbish, played in the Sugar Hill Records house band; with drummer Keith Le Blanc and guitarist Skip McDonald, he performed and arranged music on recordings by Melle Mel, the Sugar Hill Gang, and Grand Master Flash and the Furious Five, the first nationally released rap music. Early BRC bands like Michael Hill's Blues Mob, the Deed, P.B.R. Streetgang, Blue-Print, J. J. Jumpers, Eye & I, the Family Stand, Shock Council, the Bus Boys, 24-7 Spyz, Blackasaurus Mex, Civil Rite, and Total Eclipse engaged in the genre-bending and blending that became a hallmark of the organization.

While the sound of the music plays a key role in assigning it to a genre, the race and gender of the performer can also affect the way music is categorized or whether an artist is able to secure industry support in the first place. In chapter 8, I consider the impact of race and gender on the ways black women and men participated in the production of rock music and examine issues of sexism, masculinity, and authenticity both in the music industry and in the organization. In chapter 9, I continue the exploration of the effect race has on rock performers through a focus on Jimi Hendrix, the signal black rocker. Fans, the music industry, and Hendrix himself manipulated his image in ways that both downplayed and accentuated his blackness. I discuss these processes and also consider the ways BRC members relate to Hendrix as a black performer who symbolizes creative freedom and the potential of black rock musicians.

Throughout *Right to Rock*, I have tried to convey the sound, flavor, and the feel of the music as well as BRC members' interactions with it. To give a visual supplement to these verbal descriptions, I have included photographs of BRC bands and members and reproductions of BRC-related artwork in order to indicate the choices they made when representing themselves. Music is a slippery cultural form whose multiple meanings cannot be pinned down. Listeners in-

Guitarist Jean-Paul Bourelly, funky and futuristic. Photo by Lamar Thompson.

terpret the combination of musical sounds, lyrical content, and performance style in many different ways depending on their social position and the contexts in which they hear the music. My task here is to describe black rock in terms of musical materials, performance styles, and cultural politics. This is an exercise in translation from the language of music and performance to that of speech and the written word and, as in all translations, some aspects of the original version will be lost. I also found that I could not talk about black rock without letting myself slip in some indication of the pleasure it gave me to experience it. I realize that this connection puts me at risk of being something of a "fanthropologist" and I note it because it is the position from which I experienced and thought about black rock.

A NOTE ON NAMES

When the coalition was founded in 1985, the term black, not African American, was in common use. While some members disliked the term "black rock," finding its redundancy offensive, other names like "black alternative music" were equally unsatisfying. Some used "progressive black music," but most continued to use "black rock" as I do in the text. In naming the groups referred to in this study, I use the terms African American, black American, and black interchangeably, and the terms white and Euro-American interchangeably. I do not capitalize the words black or white, but in quoted material, I preserve the author's capitalization of these terms.

In depicting events that occurred in the field and presenting life stories, I have changed identifying details and used pseudonymous first names to protect the anonymity of participants in accordance with the agreements I made with the members who participated in life story interviews. In cases where I have excerpted from newspaper or magazine articles in which members were identified by name, I have used real first and last names. Similarly, in discussing bands and band personnel, I have preserved real names. These artists— Living Colour, Faith, Screaming Headless Torsos, Me'Shell Ndegé-Ocello, Sophia's Toy, and Civil Rite to name a few—are among the many BRC members who put themselves forward on the public stage, and it seemed appropriate to pay tribute to their tenacity by naming names when discussing their inspired performances.

TWO

THE "POSTLIBERATED GENERATION"

I was a total rebel, total radical. . . . My high school . . . was predominantly black, had just turned predominantly black. . . . It was during a time when rhythm and blues and doo-wop and all that type of music was popular in the black community. But I was [the only black kid in my high school] listening to Hendrix and Led Zeppelin and Janis Joplin and Cream. And my room by that time was painted black and I had black light posters everywhere. I was riding the tail end of the hippie sixties thing and was becoming real serious about playing an instrument. —JESSE, A LONG-TIME BRC MEMBER

The people who came to the early BRC meetings found a critical mass of young African Americans who had attended integrated schools where they were taught the standard curriculum, learned the complicated ways race worked, and got an introduction to the fun and foibles of sex, drugs, and rock 'n' roll. These were people who were deep into music. They listened studiously to the radio, amassed considerable record collections, and followed the careers of their favorite musicians in the press. They devoted time and energy to music education—through school programs, private lessons, and informal playing with friends. They were the ones who routinely disappeared into convenient corners in their households to practice their instruments. A number of BRC members majored in music in college, immersing themselves in learning their craft and in some cases dropping out once they had only academic requirements left to fulfill. Others followed academic majors and completed their degrees. All of them made sure that there was room for music in their lives. These are some of the main factors that brought BRC members together at the early meetings and have kept them together over the years.

In spite of the similarities, differences in background and trajectory shouldn't be glossed over: most grew up in cities, but some were raised in suburbs; most went to public schools, but many had some experience with private education; and the majority, but not all, grew up in two-parent households. While the main thrust of the BRC was to serve those who were making a living as professional musicians, some members were amateurs who had no intention of quitting their day jobs. Over the years, BRC members discovered and discussed these features. They were the subject of freewheeling conversations at the early meetings and a way of identifying connections, comparing differences, and bonding in the process. By witnessing member interactions and conversations through my everyday involvement in BRC meetings and events, I learned about many of these commonalities. For example, I hadn't been hanging out with BRC members for too long before it became clear that most were both black *and* middle class and that nearly all had been involved in the desegregation of education. Still, this was a piecemeal way of getting at important demographic and ideological information. To be more systematic and comprehensive, I interviewed BRC members. In this chapter, I draw on these interviews in order to explore the depth, breadth, and significance of these similarities and trace the ways members explained their connection to black rock. In the life story narratives they shared with me, members outlined and condensed details of their lives and talked about the reasons they had joined the organization. In many cases, BRC members were using these stories to "reframe experiences they originally felt were dissonant with social expectations by constituting them as new cultural possibilities" (Ginsburg 1989:143; cf. Giddens 1990). In their stories, BRC members consistently drew attention to the specificity of their economic and social status, their educational experiences, and the impact of the historical moment in which they were encountering music on their political and artistic pursuits.

Influenced by discourses of both integration and black pride, BRC members produce what cultural critic and BRC cofounder Greg Tate calls a "postliberated black aesthetic" (1992:200). Borrowing from Tate, I refer to BRC members as part of the "postliberated generation." Born between the mid-1950s and mid-1960s, they grew up in the post–civil rights era of legislated racial equality, had access to institutions that previous generations of African Americans might not have dared to imagine, and developed a set of creative and political predilections specific to their generation. Among these was an interest in embracing and performing rock. In many cases, however, they found that the people around them were reluctant to accept this choice. BRC members were told—by friends, family, and music industry representatives—that they were not "acting black" or, worse, that they were "acting white" (cf. Fordham 1996). Through their involvement in the BRC, members of the postliberated generation encountered and reassessed the artistic movements, political struggles, intraracial debates, and class issues that preceded them (Mannheim 1952:293).[1] They incorporated and revised definitions of "authentic" black identity, responded to discussions about the potential problems and rewards of integration, and defended the logic of their involvement in rock on the basis of both creative freedom and racial birthright.

The post–civil rights era marks a division between the generation of civil rights activists and supporters and the generation of their fortunate sons and daughters. Those who attended the early BRC meetings in New York and Los Angeles were not the architects of civil rights agitation, but its beneficiaries. They entered adolescence in the ten-year period after the movement's victories were concretized in the Civil Rights Act of 1964 and the Voting Rights Act of 1965. This period was marked by efforts to desegregate public education, and many BRC members were on the frontlines of that often fraught process. The material and ideological effects of civil rights legislation and educational policy changes intersected with other factors that influenced BRC members as they embarked on their secondary education. These were the days when Black Panthers were advocating autonomy within black communities as well as armed self-defense, writers associated with the Black Arts Movement were conceptualizing a black aesthetic, antiwar protesters were challenging traditional notions of citizenship, and a counterculture was celebrating sex, drug, and musical experimentation. The Civil Rights Movement emphasized black belonging to the national fabric, arguing for equal citizenship rights under the law, integration, and the similarity of blacks to whites based on shared Americanness. By the end of the 1960s, the Black Power Movement had come into ascendancy with a focus that accentuated the distinctiveness of African American culture and identity. The shift from a dominant black discourse of integration to one of separation was taking place as BRC members entered adolescence. Difference was viewed as a positive force and the revolutionary concept that "Black Is Beautiful" permeated the media and the arts.

Similarity in race, generation, class, and education along with an active interest in music were the key factors that brought members together and shaped their cultural productions. One of the ways BRC members talked about this historical moment was by describing their memories of the music that accompanied these social and political shifts and their own growing up. Typically, they would list favorite bands, a process that marked the specific period in which they were encountering music and also illustrated the range of influences—musical and otherwise—that shaped them. Fondly recalling the musical textures of the 1960s, Patricia, a music industry professional born in the mid-1950s, described the era for me:

> My mother was heavy into music all my life. I lived at the record player. . . . I know the lyrics to all the old songs . . . because my mother played them. . . . I remember the first record I ever got. Ah, girl, it was Otis Redding's "Dock of the Bay." And "Try a Little Tenderness" was on the flip side of that single. . . . I had this little record player, almost a wind-up sucker. And we played it over and over and over. Otis Redding—that was the man to me. That's who got me. I wanted to be Otis. I knew every song, every lick in every song, every "Uh!" I loved him. . . . Preceding that was of course Bobby Bland. [And] we were listening to Lady Day [and] Sam Cooke. . . . That was also during the time when Motown was strong. All the guys in the neighborhood thought they were either the Temptations or the Miracles. Of course, I was Diana Ross. . . . But simultaneous with that . . . there was no such thing as "black radio" and "rock radio." There was just radio. There was one station and along with Motown would be Led Zeppelin, would be Iron Butterfly, would be—it was all one thing. So you listened to everything.

The influence of parents, siblings, and friends made a mark on the listening habits of BRC members. In another typical example of the musical paths of BRC members, Paul, an entertainment professional born in 1959, explained:

> I had a pretty wide range of influences in terms of music. . . . Besides whatever my peers were listening to, I was listening to whatever [my older sister] was listening to. . . . She was into the Beatles and the Rolling Stones and that kind of stuff. So even though we lived in a black neighborhood—and I think this is something that is pretty common in the background of BRC people, most of whom lived in black neighborhoods—. . . [we] grew up listening to all

Melvin Gibbs and D. K. Dyson of Eye & I. Photo by Lamar Thompson.

kinds of stuff. I think sometimes people are amazed at these black people who were listening to all kinds of stuff. But . . . I remember [a BRC member] pointing out . . . a picture of Huey Newton at his stereo in his house about to put on a Bob Dylan album which is a completely believable kind of scene because I remember those days. I was a kid at that time, but I was in that kind of a progressive, political, sort of countercultural, black kind of environment. Black hippies, if you will. [I was] also influenced by going to mostly white schools and also going to mostly white summer camps and youth groups and things like that, so I was exposed to a whole range of stuff and I think all the black stuff just came very naturally just by being black and living in that neighborhood.

Paul went on to describe his record collection: it included white artists like Roxy Music, Emerson, Lake and Palmer, and Yes as well as black artists like James Brown and the Isley Brothers. These listening habits reveal the kind of crossing back and forth experienced by many, black and white, who came of age in the late 1960s and early 1970s. Paul points out that Huey Newton, the consummate black radical, crossed racial boundaries in his music listening in a way similar to BRC members. This black rock story was shared—in the original version and in Paul's retelling—to remind the listener that African

Wayne Livingston's Shock Council. From left, Craig Neal (bass), Wayne Livingston
(guitar and vocals), and Ray Reid (drums). Photo by Lamar Thompson. Courtesy
Donald Eversley.

Americans can and do go beyond black borders of music, culture, and
politics. In the late 1960s and early 1970s when BRC members were
coming of age, this kind of crossing was becoming more common
and it contributed to the race, class, and generation specific political
and cultural consciousness that BRC members developed. Being part
of the postliberated generation influenced the identities they formed,
the music they produced, and the cultural politics they enacted.

RACE, CLASS, AND CONSCIOUSNESS

When I told one long-time BRC member that one of my research goals
was to identify common features that brought the membership together, she observed, "Well, just about everyone is middle class." Defining the "middle class" in the United States with any precision can be
difficult, and the project is complicated when attempting to pinpoint
a "black middle class," a fuzzy and mutable category whose definition
depends on often subjective interpretations of economic status, ideology, behavior, and identity politics. Because of the inescapable connection between class identification and perceptions of loyalty to the
black community, marking African American class status is as much
a political move as it is a demographic one. As I listened to BRC mem-

bers from similar economic backgrounds use different terminology—working class or middle class—to define themselves, I was reminded that there was more at stake in these categories than describing how much money one's parents earned or in which neighborhood one was raised. Historically, African American middle-class status has been connected to ideology as much as (if not more than) economics. Currently, in a context where being working class is often interpreted as being authentic and being middle class can be read as trying to escape one's roots, claiming black middle-class status is a loaded act.

Few BRC members could be considered part of the entrenched, old-money upper middle class that E. Franklin Frazier excoriated in his 1957 book *Black Bourgeoisie*. Often their parents came from working-class backgrounds and had migrated to urban centers in the north and west from the South and the Anglophone Caribbean to take advantage of World War II and postwar desegregated employment opportunities. Usually, they aspired to middle-class status. Geoff, born in 1954, described his upbringing in terms that illustrate these tendencies:

> I grew up pretty much in a black neighborhood of a larger suburban town. . . . It was like one of these all-American cities, blah blah blah . . . and it's very, very kind of middle class. It was one of the top ten school systems in the state and as such my parents moved there in a kind of postwar type of baby boom thing that they were about. Now, as I say, I grew up pretty much in a black neighborhood. So I'd say up until the fourth grade, I just knew black people, but still not stereotypical black people. Not that *I* think there's a stereotype, but a stereotype that some people think. [The black people I grew up with were] not urban, not inner city. [They were] very much middle class where the fathers went out to work and the moms stayed home. Whereas my father—and maybe one other father—was in a white-collar job, pretty much it was a blue-collar type of a neighborhood, but we all kind of lived a white-collar life.

Here, Geoff struggles to articulate what was distinctive about his community without falling into the trap of stereotyping black identity. His neighborhood was black, but it was not populated by the black underclass, the group that dominates social science and popular understandings of blackness. His comments draw attention to a number of features of black middle-class life. For example, economic advancement was not easy for blacks in a segregated, discriminatory marketplace. Further, segregated housing made it impossible for middle-class blacks to physically separate themselves from working-class blacks by establishing middle-class neighborhoods. Instead, the different classes lived side by side. Also, class variations within extended black families often meant that many middle-class blacks were quite close to the working class through connections to siblings or parents. In African American communities, symbolic criteria like education and respectability have been more critical in determining middle-class status than more objective measures like occupation and income (Gaines 1996:16–17; Giddings 1984; Higginbotham 1993). Consequently, Geoff could describe his neighborhood as middle class even as he points out that the majority of families were blue collar.

Geoff's perspective is rooted in a long-standing African American tradition of defining a person's class not according to profession or income, but "by a pattern of behavior expressed in stable family and associational relationships, in great concern with 'front' and 'respectability,' and in a drive for 'getting ahead' " (Drake and Cayton 1993:661–62). Steady employment in a blue-collar job could lead to middle-class status and what Geoff calls a white-collar life. Galvanized by postwar efforts to desegregate the public sector, the majority of BRC parents became civil servants. For example, after World War II, efforts were made to integrate New York's city government offices and positions. The parents of many BRC members (and my own parents) took advantage of these more equal opportunities. Only a few BRC parents worked in the private sector, which remained segregated, in the north and south, well after the passage of Title VII of the Civil Rights Act of 1964, the first federal law desegregating all places of employment. By the mid-1960s, most BRC members' parents had established themselves professionally and started families. Their jobs included the military, health care, public school teachers and administrators, social services and transportation employees, small business owners, and domestic workers. While many of these jobs were not middle-class professions, they allowed families to achieve home ownership and financial stability and to live comfortably on a single income.[2] A number of BRC members' mothers were full-time homemakers for at least part of the time they were growing up. From the African American point of view, all of these conditions were clear markers of black middle-class status.

When practiced before Black Power activists emerged in the mid-1960s with assertions of black self-determination and a critique of integration, this focus on upward mobility may have been criticized, but was nonetheless understood. Indeed, the rhetoric of the Civil Rights Movement highlighted the assimilability of African Americans to the white mainstream by understating the cultural differences between black and white Americans. By the late 1960s, in a period of increased black cultural and political nationalism, however, the influence of Black Power discourse led a new generation to interpret the principles of the Civil Rights Movement as subordinating black culture to dominant white institutions and practices. They were exemplary of the problems inherent in integration. Geoff offers his own critique of his parents' assimilationist aspirations in his derisive "blah blah blah" aside, distancing himself from the "postwar type of baby boom thing that *they* were about." In this rapidly changing context, middle-class striving was associated with "selling-out" and to identify as middle class took on a negative meaning; meanwhile, working-class status signaled a commitment to black culture and community.

Nearly all BRC members described their upbringing as "comfortable" and regardless of economic circumstances, parents' occupations, and homeownership, they were raised with a similar set of values. So, while some defined themselves as "very middle class" and others identified as working class, all members noted the efforts their parents made to create stable home environments and to instill in their children a sense that they were capable of achievement. This was true in single-parent and two-parent households, in urban and suburban neighborhoods, and whether parents were blue-collar or white-collar workers. Consistent in the life stories were recollections of being taught that with a good education and persistence, they could be successful. This perspective echoes traditional black middle-class uplift ideology (Gaines 1996; Higginbotham 1993). Significantly, the legal victories of the Civil Rights Movement cleared the way for these achievements as, for the first time in U.S. history, a critical mass of African Americans began to gain access to integrated education and desegregated opportunities.

By the 1980s, it had become a sociological commonplace to talk about African Americans who shared many economic, education, and, increasingly, neighborhood features with white middle-class Americans as a "new black middle class" (Banner-Haley 1994; Cose 1993; Landry 1987; Tatum 1987; Wilson 1978). When acknowledging these important economic advances, it is also crucial to attend to what anthropologist Steven Gregory calls "the *changing* significance of race and class" in African American communities (Gregory 1992, emphasis added). Gregory warns against treating the middle-class status of blacks as an unproblematic indication of freedom from the barriers of race. He argues that this view "not only minimizes the effects of con-

temporary racism on all classes within the African American population, but also fails to take account of the diverse ways in which race and
class intersect in specific sociopolitical contexts" (Gregory 1992:257;
cf. Pattillo-McCoy 1999; Wilson 1978). In the post–civil rights era,
race *and* class continue to influence political organizing and identity
formation among African Americans. This occurs not in spite of civil
rights legislation, integration, and affirmative action, but within the
new social and economic conditions they have created. The identities
BRC members construct and the issues with which they contend reflect this intersection of race and class.

GETTING EDUCATED

The life stories of BRC members indicate that their race, class, and generation together with their education led to certain experiences and
disposed them toward certain practices and aesthetics. All of the BRC
members I spoke with talked about their experiences with integration
in public and private school contexts. Here, they met people from a
variety of racial, ethnic, and class backgrounds and began to incorporate materials that reflected their cross-cultural encounters. These
forays into desegregated arenas were not without racial baggage, and
members also remarked on their encounters with racism and bias.
During our interviews, they highlighted the impact of being in what
were often newly desegregated spaces where they learned firsthand
about white Americans. Their desegregated education afforded them
what Bourdieu called "cultural competence"—the knowledge of what
to say and do in a given situation—and "cultural capital"—knowledge, influence, and power based on cultural rather than economic
resources (Bourdieu 1984). In spite of the benefits that accrue to
African Americans conversant with mainstream practices, many BRC
members were critical of the processes through which they achieved
their knowledge. They deconstructed an education that emphasized
assimilation to middle-class Euro-American norms while marginal-
izing African American culture and history. Their experiences with
integration led many to place an increased value on blackness and
black culture, even as they enjoyed and benefited from exposure to
a range of nonblack forms. This mixed background influences their
cultural productions.

Identifying the link between mainstream educational attainment
and mainstream social and economic success, African Americans

Felice Rosser and Bruce Mack on a break during rehearsals for the BRC Orchestra's Motown Love Songs performance. Photo by Janine da Silva.

have long viewed education as central to upward mobility, social equality, and inclusion in the United States.[3] The first major legal victory for desegregation came in *Brown v. Board of Education, Topeka, Kansas*, a case related to public schools. The Supreme Court's 1954 decision to strike down legal segregation of the schools was a first critical step in making all racial segregation illegal. It was followed by Title IV of the Civil Rights Act of 1964 which included in its provisions the desegregation of public education. In focusing on school desegregation, I do not intend to suggest that this was the sole issue or outcome of the Civil Rights Movement. Rather, I highlight this battle because of its significance to BRC members evidenced by the fact that the issue of school integration was a recurring theme in the life story interviews I conducted with them. The opportunity to be involved in school desegregation was primarily available to African Americans whose parents had the ideological disposition to seek out newly de-segregated jobs, schools, and housing. For most BRC members, the encounter with integrated education was a result of their parents' concerted efforts to secure for them the best education possible. Some parents took their children out of inadequate local public schools and placed them in private schools or in superior public schools located in distant neighborhoods. Such individually focused efforts were complemented by collective initiatives. For example, Geoff, who grew up in the Northeast, noted that his parents were part of a group of African Americans who brought a desegregation suit against the local school district. As a result, Geoff became one of a handful of black students in a white school and began living what he called "a two-level life." "I didn't want to be left out, so I made myself deal with these people [at school]," he explained. "But I also understood that because I was the only 'spot' in the class, as it were, I wasn't really—you know what I mean. I wasn't really taken in and made to feel as comfortable as I would, say, back in the neighborhood. You know, with the fellas and stuff." Geoff attempted to forge the interracial alliances that were touted to be one of the positive results of desegregation, but these connections did not always come easily. Mandated school desegregation did not eradicate racism.

Although my casual conversations during fieldwork indicated that BRC members shared similar class, education, and family backgrounds, it was still arresting to hear the echoes of perspectives and experiences in formal interviews with BRC members. In New York, with the exception of a few who had moved to the city to pursue careers in the arts, most had grown up in the New York Metropolitan area. In Los Angeles, only a few members were California natives; most members had moved to Southern California from the South and the Midwest after completing high school. Most members grew up in urban areas and lived in mostly or all black neighborhoods. Those who were raised in suburban neighborhoods, usually younger members, lived in integrated or predominantly white neighborhoods. Although some attended private schools, most BRC members went to public elementary and secondary schools and frequently were involved in integrating them. I estimate that over three-quarters of the membership have attended college—a testament, perhaps, to their parents' emphasis on education. Of this group, approximately two-thirds graduated. In our interviews, many of my informants called attention to their formal education, developing a race and class analysis to discuss their experiences in integrated school settings and to interpret their responses to the situations they encountered. Many of these stories are interspersed with sarcasm and joking, perhaps to alleviate frustration or anger, possibly to draw attention to the absurdity of race in the United States. Neither entirely bitter nor laudatory, their stories represent the complexity of postliberated generation life and demonstrate the connections between education, class, race, generation, and identity.

As anyone who has gone through adolescence in the United States knows, "fitting in" is a major concern for most American teenagers. The difficulties escalate when racial difference comes into play. Mark, a guitarist born in 1955, used a discussion of the band he played in as a teenager to describe the way integration influenced his neighborhood and the New York City high school he attended in the early 1970s:

MARK: [The bandleader] wrote straight ahead rock stuff. . . . There were these bands that just did nothing but rock. Just turn it up and go for it from note one.

MAUREEN: Why was that? Or, it wasn't strange for all of these black [guys to be playing rock]? Because this was all black folks, right?

MARK: This was all black folks, yeah. It's because they went to school with white people. We were generally in mixed schools. I know [at] my elementary school, I was one of the few black people in my class. The elementary school around my neighborhood was changing from German and Polish to black and Hispanic when I was growing up and by the time I reached high school, it had switched over. When I first moved there, it was an equal mix. They hadn't begun to run yet. Or they'd run, but they weren't running fast.

MAUREEN: [laughs]

MARK: And, uhm, the high schools were all predominantly white. [He pauses to consider.] Yeah, I think all were. . . . The junior high schools, some of them were black or predominantly black, but the high schools were, I think, all predominantly white, at least . . . or very well mixed. Because they really shuttled you around.

MAUREEN: Oh, is that how they got their school populations?

MARK: I think so. . . . They zoned the schools so that the people mixed around. . . . There was always like a culture clash between black folks and greasers and Jews and—That's one of the first places I really discovered that white people don't really dislike us, they dislike everybody. They dislike each other. I mean, cause greasers didn't like the Jews, the Jews didn't like the Germans, the Germans didn't like the Polacks, you know what I'm saying? And we were niggers. But so what? Nobody else liked anybody, either.

[We both laugh.]

MARK: And in there, you always had friends among all these different people who liked the same things that you liked and it didn't matter. So, like you had a good friend who was a greaser, you know, with the jacket and the hair. And a good friend who was, maybe in science class, something like that, one of the Jewish kids. And you had a Hispanic friend. You know, there were always friends that you had separate from whatever the group was all about. And then after a while, all the heads were heads, didn't matter who you were. [*laughs*] . . . New York is so democratic.

At his New York public high school, Mark found himself in the thick of local interethnic politics. As Mark's comments about his changing neighborhood imply, upward mobility for white ethnic New Yorkers meant leaving neighborhoods and schools that were becoming "too colored" (i.e., black and Latino) for the greener (or whiter) pastures of the suburbs (cf. Brodkin 1998). In the 1950s, New York City's white population had already begun to decline, dropping by 800,000; at the same time, the black and Puerto Rican population increased by 700,000 (Ravitch 1974:261). Those who remained in the city battled it out and, as Mark notes, forged individual alliances across racial and ethnic lines based on shared interests, whether that meant music, science, or drugs. The efforts to integrate New York City schools started in the 1950s and included the formation of a Board of Education Commission on Integration in 1954. The Supreme Court's *Brown* ruling was directed at states that prevented interracial education by constitutionally or statutorily mandating the separation of the races in public schools, but Northerners seized on the ruling as an opportunity to attack the de facto segregation of schools that resulted from segregated neighborhoods (245).[4]

In New York, the achievement of integrated schools was complicated by the city's changing population and the exodus of whites remaining in the city from public to private schools (Ravitch 1974:246). By the late 1960s, African American and Puerto Rican students had become the majority in the public school system (331). Still, there continued to be enclaves of predominantly white schools. Sharon, a music industry professional born in 1964, drew on personal experience to critique the procedures taken to integrate schools and the assumptions underpinning them:

SHARON: I went to . . . kindergarten through fourth grade . . . in my neighborhood. . . . Then the city got this bright idea that they needed little smart black children over in Forest Hills and they put us in this program at [another public school]. . . . So they took me [and my three friends] . . . and they bussed us too far away for a ten-year-old to travel to go to elementary school to Forest Hills where we were able to mix and mingle with the natives [*laughs*].

MAUREEN: [*laughs*] With the natives of Forest Hills, Queens.

SHARON: With the natives of Forest Hills. But I enjoyed it, I had a good

Tracie Morris in performance at the BRC's Isis Show at CBGB. Photo by Janine da Silva.

time, I don't regret it, I had a good time. I just did not like that it wasn't a share-and-share-alike program. . . . [They sent us] over into this other neighborhood and they didn't send anybody back. So there was no cultural sharing. And so I had to go to their ghetto, but they couldn't come to mine. That's the only thing that I really dread about that whole bussing thing. I don't mind bussing . . . but if it's not a two-way street, it's not necessary. I can learn right where I am.

At the time of the interview, I appreciated Sharon's wisecrack about mixing and mingling with the natives and took it as her playful nod to me, the anthropologist. Considering her comment in relation to other BRC member narratives about integration, however, I realize it was not simply a joke for my benefit, but a pointed analysis of the experience of being bussed. Some of the ideals informing integration do have an anthropological tinge: by communing with whites, blacks would be able to understand "their culture" and would be better equipped to succeed in it. Perhaps this is a post–civil rights era twist on the traditional anthropological mission to study others for scientific purposes. What is significant about Sharon's critique of her forced fieldwork is the observation that it was "not a two-way street." The project of integration was not meant to train nonblack students in the ways

J. J. Jumpers at the ʙʀᴄ's Isis Show at ᴄʙɢʙ. From left, Jonathan Floyd, Eric Armstrong, Kellie Sae, and Jared Nickerson. Photo by Janine da Silva.

of African Americans (although this occurred informally). Rather, in the integrationist project, unlike anthropology, validating the culture and practices of the nondominant group was not the focus. This oversight, underlined by calls for multicultural education in the 1990s, revealed the primary agenda of integration to be assimilation of African Americans into the white mainstream. As people influenced by black pride sentiment and identity politics of the late 1960s, Sharon and other ʙʀᴄ members viewed this marginalization of black culture as an especially egregious error. Their own cultural productions are far less one-sided, drawing on multiple influences and revealing the "cross-breeding of aesthetic references" that Greg Tate celebrated in his characterization of the postliberated generation (1992:207).

These forays into the mainstream resulted in cross-fertilization that the architects of integration might not have anticipated. David, a guitarist born in 1954, explained how his parents insisted that he stay on a rigorous academic track throughout elementary school and junior high. This led to his acceptance to Stuyvesant, one of New York City's specialized public high schools. Specialized and magnet schools were viewed as a stepping stone to admission to a prestigious college and offered courses of study that were unavailable elsewhere in the city. Ideally, these new curriculum options would encourage black, white, and Latino parents to transfer their children to desegregated schools (Orfield 1993:247). David recalled:

> Stuyvesant High School was on the Lower East Side . . . and this is 1967, '68, '69 when the Fillmore East and the Lower East Side and the Love Generation and the Black Panthers, *all* that stuff, was happening and I was right down there. Student rebellion and stuff. It was near [New York University] and the Village. So I got involved in all of that. And I had a friend named Andy who went to Stuyvesant who lived [on the Lower East Side]. So after school we used to hang out at his crib on Fridays and we'd walk down to the Fillmore East. . . . We all were into trying to learn guitar.

At Stuyvesant, an integrated school environment put David in contact with other students who were fascinated by the burgeoning counter-culture of the late 1960s and drawn to the Fillmore East where musical acts, including Jimi Hendrix, performed. Ironically, David's arrival at Stuyvesant, an educational institution intended to launch students into mainstream success, occurred at a historical moment when young white Americans were questioning mainstream values. Even as David and other future BRC members were acquiring cultural capital through their education, the dominant cultural milieu encouraged them to challenge the assumptions underpinning what they learned in school. In David's case, this accidental intersection confounded his parents' efforts to inculcate him with the mainstream education and values that would enable him to secure a good middle-class job. Ultimately, he followed a bohemian path, formed a band, and became a professional musician.

Although the majority of BRC members grew up in black or predominantly black urban neighborhoods and experienced integration at school, a few lived in predominantly white suburban neighborhoods, another post–civil rights era phenomenon (Cose 1993; Landry 1987; Tatum 1987; Wilson 1978).[5] Patricia described her family's move from a black urban neighborhood to a white suburban one:

> Now mind you, we were in the suburbs, but on the outskirts of the suburbs; we were just barely in there. Like right on the other side of the street was [the city], but we were in. And there was a huge gap culturally. All of a sudden I was "a nigger." I had never heard that. . . . Even though we were in [the suburbs] with all these people who were wealthy, we were not. We were still struggling and on the [margins]. . . . I had new friends who were white and Jewish. [Be-

fore], I didn't even know what that was. Had to. There was no black people in town.

The clarification that her family was in the suburbs, but "just barely in there" and that her family was "struggling" is another example of African Americans attaining aspects of middle-class status without being fully middle class according to mainstream definitions. Moving to the suburbs was a step up from the perspective of blacks in the city, perhaps; but for white suburbanites, Patricia's family was still on the outside. Particularly significant to Patricia was the social status she was ascribed as an African American in a white community:

> I always did well in school. I was this, that, and the other in the school when I left [the city] in the fifth grade. So when I moved to [the suburbs] in the sixth grade, they immediately put me in the dumb reading class and in the slowest this and that class, math, everything. I was just appalled. I couldn't believe it. I was with these people who were just so, I thought, inferior to me. [*laughs*] Who were these white children who were calling me nigger? So it was an interesting time. . . . There were like two black kids in the whole school. It was a trip. Anyway, I learned how to do the white people's game and how this thing worked and learned how to deal with them, because I didn't have a clue when I started. You know, I was a kid then, too, I just wanted to play and I wanted to be accepted.

Patricia's time in the trenches of predominantly white schools left her with an unromantic take on what she was taught: "I learned how to do the white people's game." Patricia's comments, like those of other members, acknowledge the extraordinary burden that was placed on African American students who were suddenly ambassadors to uncharted and often unwelcoming territory. Although black students had been brought into predominantly white schools to achieve greater equality of access and opportunity, they were still racially marked. For example, Patricia, along with some other members, recalled being tracked into remedial classes. The gap between attending integrated schools and feeling fully accepted at the schools is a recurring theme both in the narratives of BRC members and in those of other members of the postliberated generation.[6] Still, these stressful conditions did not deter black parents from seeking integrated education for their children. Their expectations, along with those of educators and legislators, were great, but young African Americans who integrated schools were, as Patricia reminded me, just kids who wanted to play and be accepted.

The perception that one would receive a higher quality public school education in an integrated setting was instrumental in creating the movement to integrate New York's neighborhood schools. It also influenced the decision making of some African American parents who made sure their children attended an integrated school, even if it meant bussing. James, born in 1961, analyzed his public school education taking into account the intersection of race and class. Here, he explained why he and his siblings went to elementary and secondary school in Bensonhurst even though they lived in Crown Heights.

JAMES: The junior high school slated for our district had such a tremendous reputation for violence . . . my mother was clear: she'd go to jail first before she'd send us there and she kept us out of school. By hook or by crook she got us to go to schools in other districts. But my mother sent us [to the other schools] believing we'd get better educations in white communities than we would in our own communities. [This] didn't work. The idea was—I was thinking about this this morning—the idea was that if they were teaching their own children, they couldn't *not* teach us the same information.

MAUREEN: Right.

JAMES: Which wasn't the case because what they did was, once [we] got off the bus they were tracking us.

MAUREEN: Oh, so the black kids were all—

JAMES: Yeah, were all being tracked through all these remedial courses. . . . What was happening was [our] parents never took into consideration the issue around class which I think is a large issue out there in Bensonhurst. . . . The kids I went to school with, their parents—who were my parents' peers—were working-class people as well, kind of struggling to attain some foundation. The thing is that it was much more assured for them. And a lot of the kids I went to school with, the kids were first generation Americans. A lot of the parents didn't speak English, they spoke Italian. . . . And the school system was so bad—even back then—and the teachers were so piss poor, *nobody* was really learning anything.

And it was interesting because . . . I could compare that to my best friend and the education he was getting in Huntington, Long Island, because his family fled and went to Long Island. . . . We were definitely reading different books. And I think their studies were more advanced out on the Island. The structures of the system are different there. So [by going to a white school outside our neighborhood], we didn't necessarily learn more. They took whatever measures they could to certainly *not* teach us more. I was almost tracked, actually. . . . My parents believed we were getting better educations, but that wasn't the case. Not at all.

James's mother did not anticipate the use of segregating tactics like tracking where minority students are placed in remedial classes—a fate James avoided because of the intervention of a concerned teacher. The effort of James's mother is notable because it is representative of the seriousness with which she, and other African American parents, regarded education. For James, attendance at the school meant getting a particular kind of education both inside and outside the classroom. It was through his Italian American and other white ethnic school friends that he was first exposed to rock and punk—on record and in Manhattan's downtown clubs—in the late 1970s.

As James's comments indicate, school desegregation took place in a context where race and class continued to operate. Anna, who was born in the early 1960s, compared her elite, white college to her white, working-class high school:

Even though I was always in . . . advanced classes [in high school], I realized how deeply inferior my education was when I got to college. [This also happened in] high school because I went to an integrated high school, which was very racially charged, in a white neighborhood. So I started to get an indication [then], because I saw a lot of stupid white children who knew more than me and it would really frustrate me because . . . I knew they weren't smarter than me, they just had access to better education. That used to really upset me because . . . in certain ways I couldn't compete with them even though I knew I was as qualified, if not more so. . . . College just concretized those misgivings I had. . . . I just realized how poor the education was. . . . I would go into these literature classes—I was always a big reader—and [the white students] would just say stuff, just mention things that I had never even heard of. Just mention. And I was always in the top class [of my high school].

Anna's comments demonstrate the link between cultural capital and class. She poignantly describes her frustration at the realization that she had not been exposed to the books, authors, and ideas that her classmates would "just mention." The "white" schools that Anna,

James, and other African Americans attended were often in working-class neighborhoods and were subject to inequities related to class difference. In the United States, where class is rarely acknowledged directly and whiteness is associated with high status, it is understandable that African American parents would assume that predominantly white schools would provide a good education and overlook the fact that the working-class whites served by the schools were, like working- and middle-class African Americans, marginalized from the mainstream.

Class and cultural capital operated in different ways for different BRC members. Paul, who attended one of New York's specialized high schools and an elite college, pointed out that his middle-class background and the fact that his parents and siblings had attended college gave him an advantage in the college search process:

> I was really up on the whole college thing which was good because I did not get very good advice in high school and this is a common problem, I think, for black students. Either [teachers and guidance counselors] aim you low or they just don't know themselves. . . . I think it's of some relevance here because I think a lot of people that were maybe the oldest people in their families or whose parents didn't come from a college background did not get good advice . . . and were not directed to the right places.

Paul pointed out that few parents of his black peers attended college; this, coupled with the racialized expectations of what black students should do in terms of higher education influenced the assistance parents were able to offer and the advice school officials gave. He recalled being discouraged from applying to Ivy League colleges because his teachers believed he would not be accepted; he applied to the "difficult" schools, supported by his parents who insisted that he aim high. Paul's comments reveal the extent to which racialized thinking can be an impediment, even in situations geared to countering the effects of racism.

BLACK LIKE THIS: INTRARACIAL DIFFERENCES

A number of BRC members drew attention to differences between themselves and their black peers. Many noted the ways the cultural capital and competence they acquired through their education constituted them—both in their own minds and in the minds of their peers—as "different." This placed some of them in the betwixt and between position Geoff described as being "caught in the middle between two worlds." For many, the recognition of intraracial difference was more significant than questions of interracial relations. Consciousness of differences between themselves and whites coincided with jarring contrasts between themselves and other blacks. As indicated by the persistent concern over black authenticity, there is more than one cultural system to which African Americans are accountable. Contact with white communities was a highly charged symbol of difference within black communities, and in some cases BRC members were marked because they attended distant, desegregated schools. As a result, they confronted contradictory standards for success. Frequently, the markers of mainstream cultural competence they were attaining at school were understood by black peers as signs of abandoning African American identity—in other words, as indications of "cultural *in*competence."

Musical preference is often a way of making a statement about identity, and many members noted that difference in their musical taste mattered to their peers. In the following exchange, Andre, a guitarist and bandleader born in the early 1960s, evaluated the personal and professional repercussions of his musical choices:

MAUREEN: When you were growing up, did you encounter resistance from black people who found out you were playing rock? I mean, did they think that was weird, or—

ANDRE: Oh, yeah . . . Well, you know, all my friends, they still joke about it today. And I started getting less and less calls for R&B and jazz stuff because they're like, "Oh, you're playing that rock shit now." . . . I think that when I was a kid and I was listening to Led Zeppelin and stuff I would get that a little bit. But some of my friends, I turned [them] on to it and they were cool with it, you know. So yeah, not so much—I wasn't chastised or harassed or anything [*laughs*] or run out on a rail. . . . It was more of a working thing with the R&B stuff.

For other members, however, negotiating intraracial distinctions was a central and challenging part of their school experience. Discussing the move from a private elementary school to public junior high in Brooklyn, TJ explained:

[It was] a big transition. Actually, the area I went into also had people that came from a lot of [housing] projects so they went into this school, also, and this was actually my first real involvement with people from projects—I'm not saying people from projects are any particular way. But they tend to be a little more out there than [*he pauses*] people from my private school, anyway. So it was a situation where I had to learn to deal with them. Got into a few fights. One of them especially used to love to pick on me. But after a while he learned to respect me because I would fight back. We never became friends or anything. . . . My junior high school was right across the street from my high school . . . But again it was still a mixture of people . . . you had Jamaicans, you had Haitians, you had American blacks, you had Jews, you had Italians. . . . And when I started playing football . . . when you got on a team, you got more personally involved with different people. So again, I met different people of different races and everything and you tend to find in actuality people are people. . . . It's a matter of how they're raised and what their personal beliefs are.

As he spoke, TJ framed intraracial and interracial differences in terms of culture—what he saw as important was not so much race or ethnicity, but the values and beliefs that one has been raised with. He struggles, like other members, to talk about class and education distinctions among blacks without appearing to disparage "people from the projects," but he does distinguish himself from them; they have different cultural capital from middle class identified African Americans (some of whom may reside in projects). The integrated environment of a public school put TJ in contact with a variety of people including other blacks who were quite different from him. To borrow Sharon's terms, his "mixing and mingling" led to a worldview that is more broad and inclusive than the perspectives of whites and blacks who have lived more fully segregated lives.

Yvonne, a vocalist born in 1964, explained that having piano lessons from the time she was six years old and attending an elite private high school in Manhattan distinguished her from other children in her black working-class neighborhood. Reflecting on her mother's opinion of the high school, Yvonne observed:

I think she was into the fact that I was getting a private school education and she thought that . . . I was more like [the private school students] than I was like the kids that were in my neighborhood and in that regard she was absolutely right. Because I had always had problems in my neighborhood with kids who were neighborhood kids. You know, every year my mom used to take me to Rockefeller Center to go ice skating and then we'd go and see that corny-ass

Christmas show, every year. And the other thing we used to do on Sundays after church: we would ride the number two bus down Fifth Avenue and we would go to every museum, *every* museum.... And after we left the museum we would walk down to Lincoln Center and see some kiddie puppet show there. But that's stuff that my mom did with me all the time and those were things that other kids in my neighborhood did not do. So when I would get home and say, "I'm learning Mozart and Beethoven and my mom took me to see *Swan Lake*," they would be like, "What are you, you freak?" [*laughs*] "You're not black." All of that bullshit. So it was a safer environment for me to be in [*laughs*] I think than to go to public school.

In giving her piano lessons, sending her to a private high school, and taking her to museums and even Radio City Music Hall's "corny-ass Christmas show," Yvonne's mother, a single parent who held a blue-collar job for much of Yvonne's life, was attempting to expand her daughter's cultural capital. These forays into Manhattan's visual and performing arts arenas exacerbated differences between Yvonne and her neighbors, highlighting the kinds of intraracial variations that are not always acknowledged in discussions of "the black community."

In many cases, the self-consciousness that resulted from the not fitting in that many BRC members experienced as teens became a basis for articulating their identities. Jesse, born in the mid-1950s, offered a jocular reminiscence about not belonging to the mainstream of his predominantly black high school:

JESSE: I was pretty much a social outcast and I dressed funny, you know, faded jeans, headband. If you looked in the dictionary under "black hippie," that was my picture there. And there were one or two people like me. We kind of hung out together, went down to the park and smoked dope which was like the weakest dope in the world, you know, but we were hippies and we didn't care. And I remember one day coming to school—and I always carried my guitar with me. You know, one of those kids who always has his guitar, wasn't playing it or anything, just has to have it with him, let people know I played the guitar. I remember walking past what was then called the Black Studies Room . . . and I heard somebody playing . . . the piano part to "In-A-Gadda-Da-Vida" [by Iron Butterfly], the organ solo part on the piano. I said, "This is cool, this is cool." I went in there. It was Andrew.

MAUREEN: [*laughs*]

JESSE: Andrew, jamming away. [*He sings part of "In-A-Gadda-Da-*

Vida."] I said, "I know that tune, man, I know that tune." I pulled out my guitar and we started jamming.

Jesse mocks his pose as the guitar-toting, dope-smoking, rebel black hippie and marks his relief at connecting with others like him. Meeting Andrew, who remained a close friend and who first told Jesse about the BRC, is an event Jesse recalls with an enthusiasm that is echoed in the stories other members tell about finding like-minded associates through the coalition.

In some cases, learning behaviors that were marked as racially different became a source of conflict for BRC members and their black peers. Angela, who was born in the early 1960s and who grew up in a Midwestern town during the 1970s, described how her music taste separated her from the town's growing black community and caused alarm among family members:

ANGELA: I really got into rock just probably—honestly—by the old association breeds assimilation. . . . I was surrounded by Caucasian teenagers who were listening to that and I dug it. . . . I had grown up on that kind of music. . . . I was not into soul music or funk. The only time I really heard funk and soul was when I [visited] my father's side of the family, his brothers and sisters. . . . The few black kids that were going to [my] junior high, they didn't think rock was weird because they were listening to it, too. It wasn't until I got into high school . . . [that] I started meeting up with a lot of black kids who were into funk. That's when they thought I was a total alien. I mean seriously. I caught hell.

MAUREEN: What did they do?

ANGELA: First of all, they called me all kind of names: "White Girl," or [they would say] "You like that white boy music." They put me down because they thought I couldn't dance. . . . That's a funny story in itself. . . . Like I said, I would go to my aunts' houses and they would be listening to funk and they used to watch *Soul Train*—I used to watch *American Bandstand*. . . . One day I was just dancing—probably arrhythmically—and my aunt looked at me and she went to my mother. She said, "You know, we got to get some rhythm into Angela. She dances like a little white girl." [*laughs*] . . . She was that concerned that I had no rhythm. So she taught me how to dance to funk. Yeah, she did.

An integrated context expanded the repertoire and interests of some members of the postliberated generation, but this was hardly a neutral process. Even the decision to watch Dick Clark's *American Bandstand*, the music show targeted to white teenagers, instead of *Soul Train*, Don Cornelius's black response to Clark's program, was significant. The fear that "association breeding assimilation" would have damaging, long-term effects was real enough for Angela's aunt to make a special effort to "get some rhythm into" her, and by so doing, reconnect her to appropriately black cultural practices. Presumably, this was a valiant effort on the part of an aunt to prevent a niece from being permanently scarred by integration. Angela's story underlines the fact that authentic blackness, a state of mind often perceived to be the natural birthright of all African Americans, is in fact a set of behaviors that people construct and reproduce over time. If Angela's affinity for white cultural productions demonstrated that she had not properly learned blackness, her aunt's reaction indicates that it is possible and preferable to correct the problem—no matter how belatedly—in order to guard against being left out of the African American mainstream.

BRC member narratives of their postliberated experiences with educational and musical integration underscore the interplay of race, class, and generation and contextualize their eventual participation in the coalition. These stories also draw attention to the competing demands African Americans face in the post–civil rights era. On the one hand, their blackness limited full acceptance by whites in situations where integration did not eliminate racialization. On the other hand, some blacks felt that their association with what were perceived to be white institutions and practices compromised their blackness. Their participation in rock may have marked them as unusual or outsiders, but the BRC gave them a space where they could set the terms of the debate and be insiders. Among the things for which the post–civil rights era is noted is a persistent if subdued racial tension and stark differences in the ways black and white Americans see the world. One point on which mainstream blacks and mainstream whites seemed to agree, however, was that black rockers were playing the "wrong" music. It was the coexistence of this prevailing view and young African Americans who refused to accept it that led to the formation of the Black Rock Coalition.

THREE

SATURDAY GO TO MEETING

I was lying in bed one morning, depressed, not knowing which way I was going . . .
And I was thinking, "What the hell am I going to do?" And Vernon called me that
morning . . . And I'll never forget . . . we just started complaining about the business and the music industry and why this band never got signed because of the
bullshit. And of course *he* was totally on the fringe and we just started complaining
about stuff and decided, "Why don't we just hold a meeting and talk about this?"
And got Tate on the line and Tate called some of his friends, I called some of my
friends, Vernon called some of his friends and we had our first meeting down in
SoHo which turned into the Black Rock Coalition, essentially. . . . And then life
began—again. Because that was just an amazing time. That was September 1985.
It was like a miracle happened. It was like light at the end of the tunnel.—KONDA
MASON, COFOUNDER OF THE BRC

The meetings Konda refers to allowed friends and associates to talk
about the position of African American musicians in the recording
industry. Before long, they had talked an organization, the BRC, into
existence. Speech in the form of jokes, conversations, pontifications,
and debates is central to the organization. Many BRC members told
me that speaking with others and hearing what others had to say were
the aspects of the early meetings that kept them coming back. Mark
explained:

> I heard about Greg Tate and Geri Allen and a couple of other people
> getting together and they were having these conversations about

music. I showed up for one of these conversations and there were about thirty people in the room. And it was like thirty *deep* people. And the conversation was like—these some gabbing folks. These some learned, gabbing, opinionated folks. And there was Vernon Reid who was the most opinionated and the most gabbingest of all of them. So I went and I went to a few meetings and then I joined. It became the BRC.

Through face-to-face discussions, participants recognized common backgrounds, interests, and frustrations. Over time, they produced their organization through spoken and written discourses that enabled them to define themselves, forge connections with each other, articulate their purpose, and lay the groundwork for their activism. When attending BRC meetings, people found camaraderie among a network of African Americans who shared rather than questioned their interest in rock. Describing the first meeting of the Los Angeles BRC, Angela recalled:

That meeting was so packed it took two hours just to get through the general introductions . . . but no one cared. Everyone was so jazzed about it. . . . I think that first meeting must have lasted four and a half hours. And everyone was totally enthused and I think most of us were just mentally just falling into each other's arms. Like, "Kindred black people. We're not alone." So that's how the first meeting was. Super satisfying.

Meetings were the site where important connections were forged (Myers 1986:431) and were essential to the emergence of the BRC as an artistic, intellectual, and activist network.[1] In this chapter, I focus on meetings in order to introduce some of the issues that concerned members and to demonstrate some of the interpersonal dynamics of the BRC. During meetings, African American musicians, artists, and supporters discussed issues, made plans, and reveled in the joy and relief at finding "like-minded" black folk. The BRC was created through such interactions and over time it has been perpetuated by the relationships and alliances that developed out of these exchanges. More than business-related events, meetings—BRC and otherwise— are processes through which people constitute organizations and networks, give them meaning, and connect them to other social worlds (Schwartzman 1989:11; cf. Myers 1986). By discussing experiences, feelings, and interests, the people attending these talk-laden meetings discovered what they shared as postliberated African Americans. As they verbalized concerns about black identity, described their involvement in black rock, and expressed a desire to challenge the existing categories of black music, they brought into being an organization dedicated to supporting these interests. Meetings are also the place where members talked publicly about what the BRC was or should have been, described its value, articulated what it meant to be a member, and critiqued the organization's failings. Through the lively exchanges that characterized the meetings, participants identified common ground, negotiated a shared identity, mediated group values, and sustained relations (Myers 1986:431). In the first section, I demonstrate some of the ways BRC members used talk at meetings to define themselves, address problems, plan projects, start and settle arguments, and to create a community. I have drawn from the notes I took during twenty-four BRC general member meetings and developed into field notes immediately after meetings ended. I have rendered speech as closely as possible to that of the original, although only some of the content is directly quoted. For this reason, and also to highlight the performative quality of these exchanges, I have represented speech as dialogue but without quotation marks. I present a composite meeting that follows the structure of a typical BRC general member meeting and includes the kinds of questions, complaints, debates, and comments that regularly occur. In the second section, I focus on how conversations produced and sustained the BRC.

IN THE FIELD: DEEP TALK

The BRC's East and West Coast chapters did not have offices and depended on alliances formed with other cultural organizations for meeting space. Early New York BRC meetings were held at Just Above Midtown (JAM) Gallery, which represented African American artists David Hammons and Lorna Simpson and was at the time the only black-owned gallery in SoHo. Tate had worked with JAM's owner Linda Goode-Bryant and used his connection to secure the space. Later, meetings were held in Harlem at Frank Silvera Writers' Workshop, an organization supporting African American playwrights. In Los Angeles, several early meetings were held at UCLA under the auspices of political science professor and BRC supporter Frank Gilliam. In 1993 when I was conducting fieldwork, New York meetings were held at Manhattan Center Studios on 34th Street near 8th Avenue. The building housed a grand old ballroom for live music performances and state-of-the-art recording studios. The BRC held its meetings in which-

ever nooks and crannies of the building were available: a small performance space, a large meeting room, or even the ballroom itself. Arrangements for meetings were made through two BRC members who
were on the studio's staff. These members also helped friends, many
of them BRC members, secure free or cheap rehearsal space at the
studios. When I was conducting my fieldwork, general meetings were
held on the second Saturday of every month and were led by one or two
members of the executive committee on a rotating basis. Meetings
were scheduled for 2 PM, almost never started on time, and usually
ran beyond the two hours for which the BRC would reserve the room.
Even after they had to leave the meeting room, members continued
to talk, carrying their conversations downstairs into the lobby when
the weather was bad or out onto 34th Street in front of the studios
on pleasant afternoons. On meeting days, I rarely made it back to the
subway before 6 PM.

A mix of formality and informality characterized meetings. Usually
chairs were arranged theater-style in several rows facing a table and
chairs where the executive committee members who led the meetings
sat. The neatly ordered seating arrangements and the clear demarca-
tion of leadership were undercut by the relaxed attitude of the meeting attendees. They sat in one seat while stretching a leg or arm over
another, chatted together while someone else officially had the floor,
and warmly greeted one another with handclasps and "Whassups?"
as latecomers strolled in. Every meeting had the same format although the content and flow varied widely according to the number of
people and their energy levels. First, there were introductions. Next,
the meeting leaders described projects they were working on and upcoming events. Finally, they opened the floor for discussion. The liveli-
est parts of every meeting I attended occurred when members became
engaged in conversations about industry issues, organizational direction, and current political and social concerns. Meetings included
"plenty of kvetching," as one member put it, but also allowed time for
discussions that ranged from problems individuals had encountered
with specific clubs to sharing information about rehearsal space to
conversations about local politics, contemporary race relations, and
current trends in film and music. Occasional special guest speakers—
respected avant-garde musicians like trumpet player Lester Bowie
and composer and cornet player Butch Morris as well as an audiolo-
gist—made appearances. Meetings I attended during the mid-1990s
featured discussions about rap and censorship, personnel changes at
major labels, MTV, and the status of specific black rock bands in rela-

Keeping the movement moving, the New York BRC's Executive Committee in 1989. From left, Steve Williams, Janine da Silva, Jared Nickerson, Donald Eversley, Greg Tate, and Tracie Morris. Photo by Lamar Thompson. Courtesy Donald Eversley.

tion to record labels and audiences. A great deal of time was devoted to comments about BRC members who had signed recording contracts, were in the studio, were on the road, or had received media coverage.

These freewheeling conversations were the centerpiece of meetings. Meeting attendees filtered in and out of the room according to their work and rehearsal schedules. In my experience, no more than a quarter of the people at any given meeting were women and nearly all attendees were black. Members received information about the date, time, and location of the meeting through the newsletter, and long-time members knew that the second Saturday of the month was meeting day. Meeting information was also provided on the BRC hotline. Generally, the BRC depended on word of mouth to bring nonmembers to meetings. One did not have to be a member in order to attend general meetings. In fact, the meetings were viewed as a recruiting tool, and members invited people who they thought would be interested in joining the BRC.

In the exchanges I discuss here, Beverly Jenkins, the New York executive director, Bruce Mack, the national president, and Jimmy Saal, the New York director of operations, were meeting leaders. Beverly got involved in the BRC when her business partner Bill Toles pulled her in as the tour manager of the BRC's black rock festival in Bari, Italy, in 1991. In addition to working full-time as a stage manager in Broadway theaters, she managed spoken word artist Samantha Coerbell and with Bill Toles comanaged bass player Me'Shell NdegéOcello. Bruce had participated in the first New York meetings and his band P.B.R. Streetgang was one of the first to join the BRC. Jimmy, one of a handful of white members, had joined in 1987. He learned about the organization when the Good Guys, the Richmond, Virginia-based black rock group that he managed, was invited to participate in a BRC event; over the years, he became a consistently involved and committed BRC member.

Although many people attending already knew each other, meetings always started with introductions. In turn, each member gave a brief biography that included his or her musical interests and activities, the length of membership in the BRC, and any projects they were involved in. Introductions allowed participants to place themselves on the cultural, musical, and political map and to identify other members with overlapping concerns. Introductions were also starting points for digressions. At one meeting, for example, Gregory Amani, a new member in his early twenties, introduced himself and his concerns:

GREGORY AMANI: I'm a bass player and my band is called Urban Nature. We're sort of a thrash-funk thing and we'll be at CBGB this Tuesday. I always wanted to be a part of something like the BRC because I think what it's about is cool, but I think the BRC should really be working to promote live black music. Rock music—
BEVERLY JENKINS: That's what we do.
GREGORY: Well, that's cool. Because my band—we're all brothers— we have to struggle double hard when playing a "white" venue. The audience will not give us props straight off. It's like we have to work extra hard to get them to say, "Hey, you guys were cool." We played at this club in New Jersey and it was like—man. You know what Spike Lee said about being in Indiana to watch the Knicks play the Pacers? He said, "I felt like I was at a Klan rally." That's exactly what it was like.
BRUCE MACK: It's true. But what we really want to be doing is educating our *own* people about rock and the history of our music. Get them involved in what we're doing. You can think about why we're the Black Rock Coalition. "Black Rock" is redundant as we all know. The name is a play on the ignorance of America. We're dealing with a lot of ignorance so we have to think it that way. Education and re-

education. I think of rock as a rubric in which we want to be able to play at *all* levels. I've been putting together a program for schools — public schools — that would try to do this.

GREGORY: That's great. These kids need to know about bands like Living Colour and Bad Brains.

BRUCE: Right, but you can't start there. You have to begin by tracing the history back to the blues and go even further like to field hollers or spirituals and all that. And then teach some blues scales and begin to show the connections.

GREGORY: Well, whatever you have to do. Because it needs to be done.

TOMMY: I teach fourth graders in Harlem and I'd like to work with you on the thing in the schools. And try to get the kids and parents interested in it.

BRUCE: Cool. The thing we have to remember is that the change we're all hoping for is not going to take place while we're sitting at this table. It'll be a process that has to take place over time. But it has to be initiated by those of us sitting at the table who are old enough to be viewed as "elders" by the young kids, fourth, fifth, and sixth graders, but also who are able to communicate with them. This will be like mentoring, passing on information, doing it in the tradition, the African oral tradition with us acting as griots.

From here, the digression continues with another member picking up the theme:

WILLIAM: We rehearse in the projects out in Hempstead, Long Island, and the kids there are all into hip-hop beats. At first, they were suspicious of the guitars and amps and said we were playing "white people's music." But they started to listen to the music, because our rehearsals were happening regularly. And eventually they started getting into it.

Building a black audience for black rock was a concern of many members. They recognized that while the genre of their music might dictate a white audience, their race suggested that they should develop a black following. Furthermore, many black rock musicians *wanted* to develop and expand black listenership for black rock, encouraging African Americans to see rock as a black cultural production and black rockers as operating within a black artistic tradition. Talking about theory and practice, registering complaints about difficulties, and making suggestions for handling them are typical of general meetings. There is business to take care of, but in the minds of the meeting facilitators, the most important project is to get members talking to each other.

When introductions end, executives give an overview of BRC-sponsored events and other activities that may be of interest to BRC members. This is also an opportunity for the pooling of information about hospitable performance venues. In addition to the money and equipment, musicians take into consideration the club's atmosphere and how its staff treats performers, especially black performers. They try to avoid places where there is a feeling of distrust or fear, a "funny vibe" as Living Colour put it in a song that described the persistence of not-so-subtle racism in the Reagan era. BRC members, like most African Americans, have encountered that funny vibe that tells them they are not really welcome at a store, a restaurant, or a club. Rock venues that do not want to draw black audiences or develop reputations as "black clubs" will refuse to book black bands; in other cases, once having booked them, they mistreat them by refusing complimentary drinks to band members (a standard courtesy), severely limiting the number of guests they can bring in, or being unhelpful during sound checks. Many of the problems BRC members face with the clubs are not racial, but the same ones encountered by all but the most well-established musicians:

GERARD: The problem with the small clubs is that what they do isn't strictly illegal.

[*laughter*]

JIMMY SAAL: Not strictly *illegal*.

GERARD: Just barely legal.

TJ: But you know, the way I think of it is, it isn't all about money. There's playing for publicity or visibility and then there's playing for money.

RALPH: I'd like to do both at the same time.

[*Someone mentions the name of a club.*]

GERARD: They're one of the better ones when it comes to paying people.

TJ: When they finally book your gig. They'll pay you, but getting them to book you is like—You know, you call and they say call back and you call back and they say call back later and they move your dates around and all.

GEOFF: I have a connection to some clubs in New Jersey, so if you want to gig there, give me a call. The owners are cool and you *will* get your money. And you'll get some new people to see you.

Rock musicians who need the clubs for visibility usually have little recourse when they are not paid. Local bands rarely sign contracts, and some club owners "adjust" verbal agreements to compensate after the evening's earnings have been calculated and deemed lacking. In this kind of situation, musicians need to know and circulate information about which clubs treat them fairly and which clubs rip musicians off. A sense of humor is a valuable resource, and members joke about the conditions even as they attempt to address them. While the BRC has not managed to change the ways clubs treat all musicians, executive committee members are careful to negotiate for fair deals and try to get agreements in writing when the BRC stages performances at local clubs.

At meetings, the leaders do not introduce issues in a fixed order, but there is a hierarchy in the ways meetings are run. Executive officers present topics, call on people to speak when discussions become more heated, and keep an eye on the clock; they also answer questions, sometimes with the help of other members. Still, the meeting leaders encourage members to speak up with their concerns and complaints, occasionally asking questions to generate these. Most members—especially long-time ones—bring their challenges to the floor and insert their opinions, often without regard for *Robert's Rules*. Discussions are a composite of interjections and responses. An exchange about BRC members Michael Hill's Blues Mob, Sophia's Toy, and Me'Shell NdegéOcello, all of whom had recently been signed to label deals, led to a debate about the role of the BRC:

BRUCE: You need to maintain your identity, even after signing. You have to stay strong even after signing.

BEVERLY: *Especially* after you're signed. Just because you're signed, doesn't mean you're cool like that. I mean, it took a long time to get Me'Shell signed. People wanted her to wear make-up. "Does she have to look like a boy? Does she have to sound like a boy?" The thing about the industry is that they want to change people to fit a fashion that's going to change.

DELANEY: Exactly. Exactly.

BEVERLY: They mold everyone, and then you can't tell them apart. No one stands out.

DELANEY: This is what I'm talking about.

BEVERLY: It's ridiculous: they see you, they sign you, then they want to change you. You know. You get in there and you have to be careful not to get awed by all that power.

BRUCE: Right, everyone is ready to write you a check or whatever.

JIMMY: But, you know Fishbone, they maintained their integrity all down through the years. They're a great example.

DELANEY: Yeah, but their labels keep dropping them.

BEVERLY: Me'Shell was fortunate because she had a lot of BRC folk in the band and working with her and they were surrounding her and supporting her. Some other people might have been like, "Well, why don't you just sign?" "Sign to anything." You know? But she had people with her who were about challenging the industry to see things differently. You just have to stay strong.

JIMMY: And wait for the right deal.

MALIK: But what's the BRC's role as pressure group? Can't you do something to push record companies to sign black rock acts?

JIMMY: Well, I don't know how we—

MALIK: I think direct confrontation is the key.

JIMMY: But we have no leverage. They don't care about us. Just think about what happened with Faith. Spike Lee was ready to sign them to 40 Acres and a Mule Music. Everything was ready to go. But when the package got to the top of Columbia [the parent label], the man in charge said no way. He wouldn't support it.

[At this point, there's a general grumbling and uttering of "Damn" and other expressions of disgust.]

MALIK: Still, the BRC could do something. Write letters or something.

JIMMY: Yeah, but what's the point in doing that? Are we going to threaten not to let them sign any black rock bands? I mean, come on.

BRUCE: The important thing is to build a BRC listener base, being strong in and of ourselves.

Mention of the success of one band brings to mind the always present concern about the prospects for black rock bands generally. Bands talented enough and fortunate enough to spark industry interest like Michael Hill's Blues Mob, Sophia's Toy, Me'Shell NdegéOcello, and Faith often had to contend with attempts to refashion their black rock into a sound that the label executives considered more immediately sellable.[2] While it is difficult for anyone to get a record deal, the situation is especially tough for black rock bands because the label can always invoke the logic "black rock won't sell to whites because it's black and it won't sell to blacks because it's rock." BRC members are aware of these problems but are not in agreement on how to address them. During the time I was researching the BRC, fighting the battle

Guitarist Kelvyn Bell playing in the ʙʀᴄ Orchestra's P-Funk/Art Ensemble of Chicago Songbook performance at Wetlands, 1990. Photo by Janine da Silva.

at the level of record labels was rarely discussed as a serious option. Jimmy's response to Malik was typical of the organization's decision makers; a grass roots protest effort did not make sense. The general focus, instead, was on building an audience base, proving that there was a market for their music. To a certain extent, the success of Living Colour and Fishbone challenged the negative perception of black rock and increased industry openness to nonconventional black musicians. Some members, however, believed industry executives viewed these bands as flukes or novelties and still did not aggressively pursue other black rock bands. Others warned that the 1995 break-up of Living Colour would discourage labels from signing other black rock bands, taking the demise of the band as a sign of the failure of black rockers. Finally, there was a general feeling that music executives will not respond to charges of racism or pleas for inclusion. They want to see the earning potential of bands. As one member commented at a meeting:

CARLA: With the music industry, the only color is green. If you can show them you can sell, they're interested. New bands have to sell hundreds of records on their own before they get signed. You have to show the labels what you can do.
[*There are sounds of agreement from the crowd.*]
DAVID: That's true up to a point, but in my experience, race is always

A flier promoting the Los Angeles BRC's annual birthday tribute to Malcolm X.
Courtesy Mia Friday.

an issue. We can't forget that and most people at most labels won't
let us forget it anyway.

VOICE IN THE BACK: You're right about that.

While some in the meeting greeted calls for a more radical response to the record industry with supportive comments, most people
seemed to follow the focus that the BRC leadership took: show the
industry that there is an audience for the music. Members talked
through the pitfalls of agitating and the problems of remaining silent.

Building an audience happens over time and may seem invisible, especially when compared to the staging of a protest. The majority of BRC members, however, follow this slower road in word at meetings and in deed as they promote their bands. Meetings did not always produce consensus about what action or position the BRC should take and members were not in agreement about all things BRC. As a couple of long-time members told me and as I saw during my fieldwork, there was a tendency for folks to disagree frequently. Ideally, though, the participation in meetings sustains a more general agreement that the BRC serves a purpose as a location where black musicians can discuss the things that matter to them. Audience was a big concern for most performers. Here, vocalist Sophia Ramos raises the issue:

SOPHIA RAMOS: I think one advantage my band has is diversity. Our audience is all kinds of people. It's college kids, it's yuppies, it's people from where I'm from.

JIMMY: We have to know who our supporters are so we can tell the record companies who keep telling us that there's no audience for black rock.

RICK: The other thing we need to do is to get our own people to shows. The BRC has become a Downtown Thing. We need to be doing things up in Harlem, Brooklyn, and the Bronx.

SOPHIA: I did a show up in the Bronx a while back and the kids were really into it. But then afterwards when they talked to us, they asked all kinds of naive questions like, "Do black people play music like this?"

UNIDENTIFIED VOICES: Oh, man.

JAN DA SILVA: You know, it's ironic, this whole conversation, because it's the same one I would hear at meetings five years ago, and I'd hear it eight years ago. I mean, I began getting involved because I read about the BRC in *Rolling Stone* [Fricke 1987]. Some of the people they interviewed in the article said that they wanted to see more black people coming out to their shows. I thought I should go down and support these brothers so I wrote down the names of the bands mentioned in the article and then I looked for ads for their shows in the *Voice*. That's how I started going to shows.

MATTHEW: That's how it should be. We should be supporting each other. My band plays around a lot and I hardly see any BRC folk out in the audience. We should be at each other's shows. But I'm guilty, too. I mean, I haven't gone to see your band. [*He gestures to TJ.*]

TJ: You should, man.

Many members were sensitive to the fact that fellow members did not attend their shows and, like Matthew, were critical of this lack of support. Most, however, were more concerned with broadening their fan base. For example, guitarist Kelvyn Bell, leader of Kelvynator, told me, "When I look out into the crowd, I don't want to see a single familiar face. I want a room full of strangers." The concern about bringing more African Americans to black rock shows—which many band members expressed—did not result in BRC events being planned in black neighborhoods. The interest in developing a black audience for BRC shows did lead to a greater effort to advertise BRC events in black media and to promote them to audiences of other African American artists, particularly those involved in the spoken word poetry scene of the early 1990s. Reaching out to this audience meant including poets in BRC shows, a practice that also went a long way toward increasing on-stage female participation in BRC events.

Getting work done requires, of course, the active participation of the membership, and early in the research process, I learned how volunteers are made when they do not already exist. While waiting to see what happened when Jimmy and Beverly made a request for help on a project, I was transformed from observer to participant:

JIMMY: We want to get the BRC and BRC bands involved in shows in the city during the summer. You know how there're all those free summer performances in the parks?

GERARD: Yeah, like Summerstage.

JIMMY: Yeah, there's Summerstage in Central Park although that's probably the hardest one to get on because they usually want national or even international acts.

BEVERLY: But it's still a possibility.

JIMMY: Right, but we're still thinking more along the lines of parks like Prospect Park and Fort Greene Park in Brooklyn and—I don't even know the parks in Queens . . .

BEVERLY: Right, and places in the Bronx, too.

JIMMY: So we need someone to find out what's out there and how to get on the bills. You don't have to have any experience with bands per se. Just need to be able to research the ins and outs and then give us the information so we can publish it in the newsletter and let the members know.

There was a pregnant pause after Jimmy finished the description. No one was prepared to volunteer to do research.

JIMMY: It's not a thing that will take a lot of time—just a few phone calls to the right people.

Everyone waited for someone to agree to help on the project. Just as the concepts "research" and "no experience" began to click in my mind, Jimmy looked directly at me with a big cartoon grin.

JIMMY: Actually, we were thinking of you.
MAUREEN: Oh.
JIMMY: Like I said, it's not a lot of work and it would be a big help.
MAUREEN: Uhmm . . .
GERARD: You should do it.
JIMMY: So just think about it. And let us know.

The preceding was a simple and public way to get a relatively new member involved in the action. I could have helped the process by figuring out that the job description was custom tailored to me and volunteered on the spot. In the end, I did take on the park project. I had been attending general member meetings and executive committee meetings on a fairly regular basis for four months, listening attentively, watching things happen, and taking notes. It was clear that I had a serious interest in the organization. Help of any sort is a precious resource for a volunteer organization so it made perfect sense for the executives to pull me into the BRC. It was valuable for them to get some assistance, and there was work that did not require music industry expertise for me to do.

The BRC faced a constant need to nurture current volunteers and also to recruit new ones. Commenting on the workings of the organization, Don Eversley, who had served as the BRC's executive director, told me, "The BRC has survived through the good graces of individuals who burn out." Depending on volunteers meant things did not always get done in the most organized way or get done quickly or, in some cases, get done at all. These stresses built camaraderie among those who did participate actively, although they also became frustrated because things did not run more smoothly and lost patience with members who did not help out. Indeed, members consistently criticized those who expected the BRC "to do for them," but who did not volunteer. Lack of broad support, many argued, hindered efforts to take the BRC "to the next level." For example, Gerard recalled:

We've had some stagnant times where it just was not growing, where we weren't getting enough of the energy from the membership and that was all the way back when there were only fifty or sixty members to even now when there are several hundred members. . . . There are times when you just feel like *nothing's* happening, no one's kicking it in, you're doing all the work. And I was one of those cats. When my performance series was going down, I was making the fliers, I was putting on the stamps, putting them in the mail.

Going to meetings, contributing to the newsletter, performing onstage, or coordinating a show—in short, "being active"—were ways of simultaneously contributing to and benefiting from the organization. These activities established who belonged, who was "down with the BRC." At every meeting, executive committee members urged people to volunteer to work on projects and events. "Please step to us," they would say. Anyone who attended meetings and shows regularly was a prospective member and volunteer. As individuals demonstrated their commitment to the BRC and its mission, they became insiders. They were the ones who could be called on at the last minute to monitor the door at a club; to stage manage an event; to hold the money from a weekend show until Monday when it could be deposited in the BRC's bank account; and to fold, label, and stamp newsletters in the wee hours so they could be mailed on time. They did these things strictly for the cause since, as so many members reminded me, there was no money to pay them.

New members and long-time members alike would express concern about the commitment of the general membership and the survival of the BRC.

NEW MEMBER: I have a question.

BEVERLY: Ask me.

NEW MEMBER: Okay, I was talking to some people I know about coming to the meeting today and they were all like, "Aw, the BRC is just a clique." So I want to know, is it really open? I mean are you really open to new people coming in?

BEVERLY: Yes. Yes. We are definitely open. This is not a clique. It is *definitely* not. I'm sorry to sound so strong, but when I first came on, I heard that complaint all the time and I've worked hard to address it. You know, "The BRC is just a clique. The BRC is just a Vernon Reid fan club or a Living Colour fan club." But it's more than that. I've worked hard, all of us on the executive board have worked hard, to de-clique it. Now the reason you see the same bands onstage or the same musicians onstage at our hits is because all the same people come out. You can depend on this person, this person, and this person all coming out. The same ten people. That's why we're talking about how you as members need to step up. I made Kelvyn have open auditions for one of his Orchestra shows. I told him he couldn't just pick his players and he had to have auditions. So we announced it in the newsletter, put it on the hotline, and I paid $53 for a room so there would be a place to hold the auditions. And do you know how many people came? [*She pauses.*] The same ten people.

[*laughter*]

BEVERLY: I'm not joking. Now, what am I going to do? Except encourage you to participate.

BILL TOLES: The thing to keep in mind is that people use the BRC in different ways. They see it in different ways and use it in different ways. I think the point is to use the organization because the organization doesn't do things for you.

JIMMY: Right, but you have to give something back.

BILL: Sure, but you know, when it started, the BRC was just supposed to be a time on the weekend when people could sit around and bitch. And then go have grits.

[*laughter*]

BILL: Seriously, the original idea was to get Vernon's band signed. Then all of that energy got channeled into an organization.

BEVERLY: We need to have a campfire meeting with you and Vernon and Tate so you can sit around and reminisce about the old days.

MONTE: What's the purpose of the general meeting now?

BEVERLY: It's a chance to let us see each other.

BILL: My question is why aren't people coming to the meetings? When we first started, there used to be fifty, sixty, seventy people coming every other week. Now we're meeting only once a month. But no one's showing up.

JIMMY: Well, some people come. I'm here. You're here. We're here.

BEVERLY: I think people came out because they liked to see each other and hang out.

BILL: Do you think it would make a difference if we held the meetings uptown? Or if we did it on a weekday night instead of Saturday afternoon?

ANITA: A lot of people rehearse on Saturday afternoon. It's the only time they can get together.

JIMMY: It's a double-edged sword. On one side, we want to have a membership that is busy and involved—touring, on the road, in the studio, rehearsing for gigs. But then we also want people at meetings.

ANITA: It's difficult to get people out to *anything*. Not just a meeting. I'm talking about shows. How much do you spend on stamps for the newsletters?

JIMMY: A lot.

ANITA: I spend a lot, too—on postcards and stamps plus the time it takes to address and mail them. Just trying to get people to come out to a show.

BEVERLY: I hear that.

ANITA: You should have a party. Let a band play then have a meeting. Or the other way around. Maybe "a meeting" sounds too heavy.

JIMMY: That's not a bad idea.

When discussing the organization with me, long-time members always stressed that the BRC has its ebbs and flows as member energy waxes and wanes. Sometimes, the membership was very active, producing lots of shows and panels. At other times, there was very little going on under the BRC banner. This unevenness is an inevitable problem for a volunteer organization. The spontaneous energy that fueled member involvement in the early years of the BRC is no longer a natural part of the coalition. Thus, maintaining member enthusiasm and involvement was a constant concern for the executive committee and also became an issue for those members who were themselves active.[3] Change in member interest in meetings may have been connected to changing member needs: people who had been members for four or eight or ten years had formed their networks, were involved in projects, and did not need to attend meetings to make and sustain these connections. There is also the influence of life cycle: when in their twenties and early thirties, BRC members were mostly unmarried and working flexible jobs that allowed them to pursue their interests in the arts; consequently, they could devote almost unlimited time and energy to the new organization. Many fondly recalled "living, sleeping, and eating the BRC" in the early years. Over time, their responsibilities grew; many have families and demanding careers that limit their ability to participate. As they have grown older, their concerns have shifted, but over the years, people would cycle back into the BRC, participating in meetings and events when they felt the urge. A sense of investment in the organization led many members to be protective of it, even if they were not consistently active and even when they would lament its flaws and failings when events or projects did not work out as planned. This love/hate relationship with the organization revealed their pride in what they had accomplished and their frustration with what was still not achieved. In a fairly representative comment, Gerard told me:

> People will say, "Ah, fuck the BRC" because they dealt with an individual at some point or another and they didn't get what they wanted out of them. Or [they say] "What is the BRC?" And I would answer with this thing that "I am the BRC." Not to take an ego credit for anything, but just that I feel like [the BRC] set up my earliest circle . . . of how to be a musician in this town. I've learned some heavy things from these cats . . . so I've always felt I can say that. And I think anybody else in the BRC who really tries to do what the BRC is all about can say, "I am the BRC."

Meetings always ended with members standing and making announcements about upcoming shows, inexpensive recording studios or rehearsal spaces, and performance opportunities. Following announcements, participants broke into small groups to continue talking. People introduced themselves to people they did not know and greeted acquaintances they had not seen in a while. The volume level would rise as layer upon layer of talk and laughter filled the room. During these exchanges, band members with performances to promote circulated among the groups handing out the four-by-six inch colored cardboard rectangles that provide the date, time, and location of their shows.[4] People moved from group to group, passing out cards, catching up with one another, inviting or cajoling people to work on a project, and continuing the conversations that had been such an integral part of producing the BRC.

TALKING THAT TALK

Meetings were the first step in creating the postliberated black community that would carve out a cultural space for and mark the artistic presence of black rock in New York. Describing the early meetings in New York, Greg Tate recalled:

> Early on, there weren't really so many musicians involved. There were a lot of professional musicians who kinda gave Vernon the vibe like, "You're rockin' the boat. You'll never eat lunch in this town again. It's definitely gonna affect your career to be involved in this militant music organization." But the people who came in

were people like Tracie Morris, Don Eversley, people who were lawyers, there were folks who worked on Wall Street, who definitely
had some of the fire and the idealism of the '60s. They knew Vernon and they really wanted to be part of a Black situation where you
talk about the cultural, political and social situation of Black folks
in the country. There were times in those early meetings when we
talked about music, but we talked about everything else that was
going on, too. (Tate quoted in BRC 2001a:9–10)

For many of the people I spoke with, the very idea of an organization for African Americans who were interested in rock was enough
to entice them to a BRC meeting or event. James, a New York member,
explained how he first got involved:

I remember I was walking down 7th Avenue one night and I saw
this really cool flier with a picture of Little Richard superimposed
over this Japanese flag, because it was Pearl Harbor Day. . . . And it
said something "Blah Blah Blah Black Rock Coalition" . . . I had to
see what it was about. So I went to the party and it was fun. It was
great. All these different people. . . . I had just finished [college] in
'84 so I was sort of disconnected from an artsy kind of community,
you know. . . . At that point, I was just excited about the idea of
black people and their place in the context of rock 'n' roll. I didn't
grow up necessarily listening to a whole lot of black rock stuff . . .
so it was just interesting to see what it would be like. . . . So I went
to the party, I really, really enjoyed it, found out about the meeting the upcoming week and I went and I thought, "I want to stick
around this thing and see what it's about."

Seeing the promotional flier for the Drop the Bomb party drew James
and a number of others into the BRC. Those who "stuck around" were
able to connect with other African Americans who were encountering club owners who were skeptical about booking black rock bands.
I asked another long-time New York member how these experiences
contributed to the development of the organization:

MAUREEN: How do you remember the early meetings? What kinds of
things were pulling people in and generating [the] energy?
GERARD: I think that the basic thing was everyone felt pretty much
the same way about the music industry. The room was filled with
mostly musicians and then a couple of writers and one or two
people who did graphic art and that was like the body for a good

couple of years. And the general feeling was the frustration, but everybody could relate to each other so there was energy about that. All the meetings would start with everyone introducing themselves and somebody would always have something witty to say . . . and that would start it up. Vernon would spearhead the meetings and things flowed. And that was the main energy: that everyone could really relate. It was like, "Yo, this is where I need to be. This is what I'm talking about." And when new people would come in and they'd be like, "Yeah, I'd heard about it, I'd heard about it," that would fire up the people who had already been there.

These occupational similarities connected members. A significant number were employed in jobs related to the media and entertainment industries, either as business people or performers. Members on the business side worked for independent and major record labels, advertising agencies, periodicals, and cable television programs. The musicians were striving to make all or most of their money from playing. They did studio work, toured as sidemen, and played local clubs. Others held "day jobs" in retail or offices to get by financially. During the time I conducted fieldwork, several members worked as performers and project coordinators for a New York City arts-in-education nonprofit that Bruce Mack had ties to. The BRC helped musicians develop networks that could lead to this kind of paid work. Among the things younger members learned from older, more experienced members was how to make a living as a musician in New York.

The alliances and relationships formed through the BRC have extended beyond the organization into professional and interpersonal relationships. One woman told me that the BRC was "like family" and, as an example, spoke warmly about several BRC members who had attended her brother's funeral, lending her needed emotional support at a difficult time. One member observed that the BRC was a place where his age and experience in the industry were recognized and appreciated; he enjoyed being an "older brother" figure and took pride in using his wisdom to help out fellow black rock musicians. Others extended the family metaphor to describe relationships that were contentious and not chosen, but that persisted because of connections based on ties—artistic rather than biological—beyond their control. A number of bands were formed or reconfigured as a result of connections made through the BRC. Similarly, the BRC has fostered business alliances between artists and lawyers, publicists, graphic designers, and artist managers who first met through their involvement in the organization.

Reflecting on the features that attracted him to the organization, Paul, who attended the BRC's first meeting in New York, stated that among other things, "the intellectual level was pretty fucking high. I mean I mean, there's not a whole lot of dummies hanging around the BRC." He continued:

PAUL: I mean, some strange people, some idiosyncratic people—

MAUREEN: [*laughs*]

PAUL: [*laughs*]—some irritable people and different things. . . . I think it's the kind of organization where it's the more thoughtful, more smart or intellectual or analytical type of person that's going to go out of their way to come down to meetings and maybe some performances that are going to stretch their minds a little bit. I think there's a connection between those two.

MAUREEN: How would you describe that mindset? How are people in the BRC "like-minded?"

PAUL: Yeah, it's interesting. Kind of like black bohemian, black intellectual types. And I think that's one of the things that's important about it. It's not just about the stated goals, you know, which is to support alternative black music. . . . I think for a lot of people, it's also just another black intellectual organization, black arts/intellectual organization. And it's a social thing as well as an intellectual process where it's just a scene people hang out with . . . and I think it's important to understand it in that kind of a cultural peer group kind of context. I'm sure you anthropologists have a more technical term for it. [*laughs*]

MAUREEN: That's about as technical as it gets.

PAUL: [*laughs*] Okay. It's a really interesting phenomenon because, you know, people in the early days . . . there was a real feeling of almost like an Alcoholics Anonymous kind of a vibe where you're in a room with all these people who had the same interests, but they had no way of meeting each other. Like all these closet rock 'n' rollers come crawling out of the woodwork, out of bizarre towns in Jersey, Queens, the Bronx—

MAUREEN: [*laughs*]

PAUL:—into a meeting somewhere [*laughs*] and it's like, wow. Because some of the people knew each other or would see each other because they'd go to the big rock clubs and they'd see this one other black person. Maybe there's twenty people going to rock clubs on a regular basis, but maybe on a given night, there's only one or two. And maybe there's a few playing, [and] after a while, you meet one or two. But here is someone with a whole roomful. . . . There's this . . . feeling of "Wow, all these people are people who I don't have to explain shit to." "People who have a haircut just as bizarre as mine." You know what I mean? That kind of stuff. So you have all these people that are maybe the hippie in their neighborhood or the rocker in their neighborhood; now everybody from all the neighborhoods . . . [is] in the room. You've got thirty people with common interests and it's very interesting to see how that developed. How that developed in terms of connecting with each other musically, connecting with each other with friendship, connecting with each other romantically. *That's* a deep concept.

In describing the BRC, Paul calls attention to the striking demographic aspect of the organization: Characterizing the BRC as an organization for "black bohemian, black intellectual types," Paul distinguishes it from more mainstream black middle-class organizations and informal groups. The BRC offered "something kind of different" to individuals who were kind of different—"the hippie in their neighborhood," say—and brought them together. Not all members gave as detailed a sociological reading as Paul, but almost everyone acknowledged the demographic similarities, the "cultural peer group," that comprised the BRC. Concluding his comments, Paul observed:

> I think, coming together around music or art, is something that everybody can talk about. Not everybody has read Wittgenstein or whatever to talk about that shit. Or even has read Manning Marable. But music or art, things like that, people can talk about it. So I think there's a lot of people who are just kind of hungry for . . . something different, not just turning on the latest black radio palaver.

In the early days, the meetings where these discussions took place always ended with a promise to meet again, and it became increasingly apparent that there was something that could be formalized: a network for African Americans who shared an interest in extending the possibilities of black cultural production. Paul described the BRC as a space for a kind of intellectual and creative exchange that provided an alternative to either the arcane intellectual discourse of the academy or the mundane representations of African Americans that circulated in the U.S. public sphere. Paul indicated that music can provide a common ground from which people can address issues of race, identity, and power while also enjoying the cultural productions as entertainment. Commenting on this kind of process, anthropologist Victor Turner observed that music and art often become "metalanguages" for discussing everyday languages and codes (Turner 1977:45). In their meetings, BRC members subjected the categories of black music and black authenticity to critical readings, providing alternative commentaries on the existing languages and giving taken-for-granted categories "new and unexpected valences" through their discourses and activities (45). The result was musical production and cultural critique that challenged commonsense assumptions about black identity and reflected the experiences and concerns of the postliberated generation.

That these processes occurred as a consequence of talking was noteworthy to many members. Cofounder Konda Mason, for example, pinpointed the central role speech and the production of new meanings played in creating the BRC community:

KONDA: It was like-minded people. It was like you could almost look at people who would be in the BRC—because they just looked like outcasts. [laughs]

MAUREEN: [laughs]

KONDA: It's still that way [laughing]. I know a BRC person when I see one. And it was like all these wonderful outcasts coming together and having the best time. I mean, meetings every Saturday would last the whole day. That I looked forward to. I mean, you never missed a meeting for years. . . . And we would just strategize. And the language. Black people and their language. Just from being a rhetoric major, I love language . . . so, I think I just sat in those meetings with my mouth dropped [listening to] the madness that came out of people's mouths. It was incredible. To me it was like the Harlem Renaissance all over again with a *twist*. With a major twist [laughs], you know. It was incredible, it was just incredible. And also the impact it had on the city. The real impact it had on people's lives in the city and black artists and getting into CBGB—you know, we hadn't been in there before. And then Living Colour just taking off and all that. It was a phenomenal time and just phenomenal people learning how to be together and to create something that's coming out of nothing with no pre-agenda. I mean, you don't go in saying, "Well, I think we should start the Black Rock Coalition. It's September 1985, aren't we supposed to start the Black Rock Coalition?" It didn't happen like that. It was just spontaneous and

Promotional flier for an early New York BRC Orchestra event
that blaxploitated the early seventies vibe. Courtesy Mia Friday.

as it started to happen, it was an incredible process. Learning how
to communicate with each other, learning how to respect people's
thoughts and feelings that were totally wack. [*laughs*]

MAUREEN: [*laughs*]

KONDA: And I'm telling you, we had some wack shit up in there
[*laughs*]. Just process, black people processing and talking. It was
amazing. It was really a true renaissance, I think.

Individuals gathered at these meetings and talked about who they
were and what they hoped to accomplish. Out of these conversations
came the strategies that enabled the BRC to have the impact on New
York City's cultural scene that Konda described. The networks that
grew among BRC members as a result of these meetings had a concrete
impact in New York and Los Angeles as members of the new organization brought their music and politics into local music communities.
Under the auspices of the BRC, black rock bands began to package concerts that displayed the musical breadth of the organization at rock

Vernon Reid at the Blaxploitation Songbook performance. Photo by Janine da Silva.

clubs like New York's CBGB and Club Lingerie in Los Angeles. The BRC also created forums for exploring issues relevant to African Americans in the music industry by sponsoring panel discussions, publishing monthly newsletters, and hosting radio and television shows on public airwaves.

Meetings were not solely about taking care of business or developing projects. These instances of "black people processing and talking" enabled BRC members to create, name, and sustain a black rock community. Indeed, the ways Konda and other members describe the impact of these conversations echoes Turner's definition of communitas, a powerful social bond marked by "unmediated communication" that "arises spontaneously" (Turner 1974:46). None of the people attending early BRC meetings could have been sure of what would come of the gatherings. The social bonds forged through conversations—the exchange of ideas and information, the talk about similar background and interests—galvanized a critical mass of individuals who wanted to use the organization as a space for celebrating and promoting their perspective. Although the commonalities among the group were striking, conversations did not always lead to consensus; there were and continue to be differences of opinion among members, but meetings allowed members to mediate these differences (Myers 1986:432). Through conversation, they defined and negotiated who they were as musicians, as activists, as BRC members, and as African Americans.

In characterizing this organization as the Harlem Renaissance "with a twist," Konda links the BRC to previous African American arts movements and locates its members in a long and illustrious history of African Americans who have used language to place themselves on the cultural and political map. From the nineteenth-century slave narratives to the tradition of African American autobiography, from Alain Locke's declaration of the arrival of a "New Negro" to Harlem's ensuing literary renaissance, from Martin Luther King Jr.'s eloquent challenges to the poetry of the Black Arts Movement, African Americans have creatively manipulated language, some of the only capital available, to establish themselves in the United States. Speech helped BRC members forge connections, and the pointed act of putting the words "black" and "rock" together laid the groundwork for the BRC to begin challenging commonsense categories. For some, the BRC risked settling for only talk. "You have people talking much shit and doing nothing," one member observed. The words had to be backed up by sustained and public actions. While BRC members may have talked about more projects than they actually undertook, they did act. I discuss this aspect of the BRC in the following chapters, describing how BRC members took their views from their meetings to the mainstream by developing a language for talking about the work they were producing and by creating an alternative arena in which to perform it.

FOUR

BLACK ROCK MANIFESTING

We need the equivalent of a Civil Rights Movement in music. . . . We have to
stand up like Rosa Parks and say, "Enough is enough." We have to develop our
own projects independently while maintaining some outreach with sympathetic
people in the industry. —VERNON REID, COFOUNDER OF THE BRC AND LIVING COLOUR
GUITARIST

The pleasure of playing music led BRC members to develop strategies to express their musical and political concerns. In this chapter, I
analyze their "cultural activism" (Ginsburg 1997) by focusing on the
Black Rock Coalition Manifesto, the document through which members articulated their ideals, and club performances, a set of practices
through which they carried out their mission. While meetings were
sites for informal, private discussions, the BRC Manifesto was a public
document informed by these conversations and intended to publicly
represent the BRC. In the first part of the chapter, I discuss the ways the
BRC Manifesto addresses the issues of music, race, and appropriation
and show how the manifesto both critiques and deploys discourses
of authenticity. I also consider the repercussions of advancing "black
rock" in terms of the attention the organization garnered from the
press and the limitations the category presented. In the second part
of the chapter, I focus on the ways New York members addressed the
manifesto's programmatic concerns by producing a visible black rock
scene that celebrated the pleasures of black rock. The public act of
black people playing rock defied commonsense notions about black
cultural production. Gaining access to local performance venues exposed black rock bands and conveyed the BRC's message. I describe

an evening in the New York black rock scene, demonstrating how BRC members created an alternative black social and cultural space that was a site for the production of aesthetic values, social relations, solidarity, and group representation. As distinct but related forms of cultural activism, the BRC Manifesto and the BRC presence in rock clubs enabled members to identify their cause and locate themselves in the public sphere.

Music production supports the assertion of identities that have both individual and social significance and is an arena for pleasurable involvement as well as a repository of social meanings. In detailing the black rock scene, I am especially concerned with marking the centrality of pleasure in the BRC enterprise. Often, in the rush to recognize the politics of cultural activism—the participants' dogged persistence in the face of limitations and their resistance to an oppressive status quo—scholars give short shrift to pleasure, a factor that is a crucial productive force of these endeavors. There are a few important exceptions to this rule. Gina Dent's collection of essays on black popular culture (1992b) emphasizes the link between politics and pleasure. In the introduction, Dent astutely observes that scholars have yet to elaborate a critical vocabulary for discussing what she calls "black pleasure, black joy," the personal and collective experiences that constitute black identities and black popular culture (Dent 1992a; cf. Kondo 1997:13).[1] Certainly, issues of race and power informed BRC members' involvement in the organization. It was, however, the members' love of making and listening to music and a desire to do so on terms that were meaningful to them that kept them interested. Their activism responded to limitations on their participation in music, and it was through their pleasurable engagement with music that they pursued their cultural activism. Focusing only on the activist discourses of the manifesto and leaving out the pleasure, frustration, and joy associated with participating in the black rock scene as a musician or audience member would result in an incomplete representation of black rock. For BRC members, politics and pleasure, activism and aesthetics, art and consciousness, leisure and career are intertwined.

THE BLACK ROCK MANIFESTO

The enthusiasm that sustained those fall 1985 meetings encouraged Greg Tate, in consultation with other members, to outline the purpose of the organization in writing. The BRC Manifesto lays claim to the black roots of rock music, counters the ahistorical assumptions about

The BRC logo integrated into a design celebrating the
coalition's fifth anniversary. Courtesy Mia Friday.

race and rock that plagued contemporary black rockers, and critiques
the music industry's racial politics. Tate commented on the impact
of the document: "A lot of people told us they came down because of
the BRC Manifesto. They really identified with what the manifesto was
talking about. They identified with the militancy of it, the Black identification of it. A lot of these were also music people. Not everybody
played, but everybody was a serious listener, serious consumer, and
listened to a broad range of things" (Tate quoted in BRC 2001a:10).

The full text of the manifesto reads as follows:

The Black Rock Coalition (BRC) represents a united front of musically and politically progressive Black artists and supporters.

The BRC was formed in the fall of 1985 with the purpose of independently producing, promoting and distributing Black alternative music. The BRC intends to counteract competition among musicians through networking and sharing resources. The BRC also

opposes those racist and reactionary forces within the American music industry which deny Black artists the expressive freedom and economic rewards that our caucasian [sic] counterparts enjoy as a matter of course.

For white artists, working under the rubric "rock" has long meant the freedom to expropriate any style of Black music—funk, reggae, blues, soul, jazz, gospel, salsa, ad infinitum—then sell it to the widest possible audience.

We too claim the right of creative freedom and total access to American and International airwaves, audiences and markets.

Rock and roll is Black music and we are its heirs. Like our fore-bears—Chuck Berry, Jimi Hendrix, Sly Stone, Funkadelic, and La-belle, to name but a few—the members of the BRC are neither novelty acts, nor carbon copies of the white bands who work America's Apartheid Oriented Rock circuit.

The BRC actively supports the total spectrum of Black music. The BRC rejects both the spurious demographics that claim our appeal is limited and the demand that Black musicians tailor their music to fit into the creative straitjackets the industry has designed. We are individuals and will accept no less than full respect for our right to be conceptually independent.

Some of our immediate objectives are as follows:

1. Performance outlets for progressive Black artists.
2. Recording opportunities for progressive Black artists.
3. Videotape recording opportunities for the archival documentation of cultural events.
4. Educational opportunities for people inside and outside the organization in the form of lectures, workshops, library resources, audio-visual resources and public forums/discussions.
5. Creative funding and fund location resources for individual artist projects.
6. Networking opportunities so that like-minded individuals can come together and share ideas and resources. (BRC 1985)

The BRC Manifesto is a text in the tradition of earlier position papers like Langston Hughes's "The Negro Artist and the Racial Mountain," published in 1926, and Larry Neal's "The Black Arts Movement," published in 1968. These documents detail the forces that have limited black creativity and set the terms for freeing black artists. In his essay, poet Langston Hughes characterizes "the racial mountain standing in the way of any true Negro art in America" as the "urge within the race toward whiteness, the desire to pour racial individuality into the mold of American standardization, and to be as little Negro and as much American as possible" (1971:117). Hughes attacks white editors, white audiences, and the "Nordicized Negro intelligentsia" for their refusal to support black artists who unashamedly embrace blackness. He celebrates the black artist who attempts "to change through the force of art that old whispering 'I want to be white,' hidden in the aspirations of his people, to 'Why should I want to be white? I am a Negro—and beautiful!'" (121). Speaking for such African American artists, Hughes declares:

> We younger Negro artists who create now intend to express our individual dark-skinned selves without fear or shame. If white people are pleased we are glad. If they are not, it doesn't matter. We know we are beautiful. And ugly too. The tom-tom cries and the tom-tom laughs. If colored people are pleased we are glad. If they are not, their displeasure doesn't matter either. We build our temples for tomorrow, strong as we know how, and we stand on top of the mountain, free within ourselves. (121–22)

Hughes envisioned black artists drawing inspiration from Negro life, what he called "the eternal tom-tom beating in the Negro soul—the tom-tom of revolt against weariness in a white world . . . the tom-tom of joy and laughter, and pain swallowed in a smile" (121). The tom-tom as an emblem for black identity may fall a bit flat years after the Harlem Renaissance, but in the 1920s it was quite bold for a black American to celebrate the African roots of black identity. In this and other writing, Hughes made the revolutionary argument that black culture was a source equal to American and Western European art traditions. A similar call to black artists to represent black subject matter emerged in the 1960s in poet Larry Neal's discussion of the Black Arts Movement. As the self-described artistic arm of the Black Power Movement, the Black Arts Movement sought to develop an aesthetic that resonated with the issues facing black Americans. Neal explained that the primary duty of the black artist "is to speak to the spiritual and cultural needs of Black people" (1968:29). The Black Arts Movement, with its emphasis on assertively black self-expression, would bring on "a cultural revolution in art and ideas" that would represent the interests and desires of black Americans in the Black Power era (29; cf. Baker 1988).

The essays by Hughes and Neal talk of freeing black artists to produce meaningful black art. The BRC Manifesto undertakes a similar project although from a different perspective, one that reflects the different social and political context in which BRC members lived. Hughes and Neal insist that black artists should eschew stifling, European and Euro-American aesthetics that created in black artists what Hughes characterized as the desire to be white. Both Hughes and Neal were responding to a prevailing view that art that was "too black" could not be serious art. By 1985, BRC members faced a new set of racially defined limits. While their predecessors fought for the artistic right to emphasize their blackness, members of the postliberated generation had to reinscribe blackness onto a black form that had been whitened. To accomplish this, the manifesto reframes rock as an authentically black cultural production and uses discourses of racial inheritance, history, and counterappropriation to reclaim rock for black performers and audiences.

BRC members recuperate rock as a black cultural form through the manifesto's unambiguous statement, "Rock music is black music and we are its heirs," and legitimate their involvement in rock by anchoring their practices in the history of American popular music. The manifesto draws attention to the long line of borrowings of black culture that led to profit and pleasure for whites and the erasure of black creators.[2] This type of appropriation is a central feature of musical development in the United States, and "the rights and means to claim musical ownership" are a not always recognized part of rock performance (Feld 1994:270). BRC members assert cultural ownership, stressing that African American innovators made central contributions to the development of rock. The manifesto also attacks institutional practices like racially segregated radio programming that perpetuate the marginalization of blacks from rock and buttress the assumption that rock "belongs" to whites.[3] These historical claims, which identify specific musicians either by naming them or by musically evoking their styles, root BRC members in a tradition of black musical production. The manifesto places black contributions to rock at the center of the discussion and insists that contemporary black rockers should no longer be pushed to the music's margins. This approach to history "uses the past as genealogy" in order to develop a feeling of belonging to a community and a tradition, and to promote a sense of continuity which boosts self-esteem and credibility (Hobsbawm 1972:13–14). Building on their shared genealogies as artistic descendants of Chuck Berry, Jimi Hendrix, and Sly Stone, BRC members demonstrate that their claims to rock are valid precisely because the music has deep roots in African American history and culture.

The chronic historical amnesia that plagues Americans necessitates this process. One consequence of the type of recovery the manifesto undertakes is the "mediation of ruptures of time and history" (Ginsburg 1991:104).[4] As people who reached adulthood some twenty-five years after rock 'n' roll first took hold and in an era when all the best-known rockers with the exception of Hendrix were white, BRC members excavated the African American roots of the music so their desire to play rock made sense to those accustomed only to white rockers. In contrast, their efforts to demonstrate the blackness of rock may seem nonsensical to older generations. My mother's response to my research on the BRC provides an example. When I explained that I was writing about blacks who were being denied the right to play rock, she was taken aback. "But Maureen," she said, "I thought rock 'n' roll *was* black. Isn't Chuck Berry rock 'n' roll?" For older African Americans—said with all due respect to Mom, a member of Berry's generation—who remember Berry, Little Richard, and Bo Diddley from the 1950s, the concept of rock 'n' roll as anything *but* black is absurd. Those of us in the postliberated generation, however, confronted a different reality, one in which African Americans were not seen as having a connection to the music. The BRC linked the terms black and rock to underscore the fading fact that rock started as a black form and to explain their participation in the genre.

In some ways, the BRC's recuperation of rock as historically black depends on an assertion of authenticity and makes strategic use of essentialist concepts of blackness and black art (Spivak 1996). In addition to revealing the limits the music industry places on black musicians, the manifesto argues that members should be able to play rock because it is an authentic black music form. While doing important work in reclaiming the African American ancestry of rock, the BRC locates its legitimacy in the kinds of authenticity arguments that created many of the problems the organization sought to address. The manifesto does not explain that blacks play rock because they like it, the position that white artists who draw on African American styles usually take. Instead, it attacks the racial determinism that confines black musicians to R&B and rap with a more expansive but still racially centered argument, explaining that they are black people playing black music. I suspect that this occurred because the act of playing rock called their identities as African Americans into question. To forego a discussion of race and rock, to say simply, "We play it because we like it," would have avoided a direct confrontation with one of the most common charges leveled against them: that blacks who play rock "want to be white." For BRC members it was important politically, aesthetically, and personally to assert a black identity and to locate themselves in African American cultural traditions. Their process of recuperation involved two vital steps. First, they had to explain that they were not playing "white boy music" and second, they had to explain that they did not think of themselves as white boys or white girls. They reiterated the black roots of rock music both to draw attention to the absurdity of being denied the right to play it and to insist on the cultural and racial appropriateness of their musical choices. In short, they wanted to communicate that they were proud to be racially and culturally black and they were also committed to playing rock.

The situation and the personalities involved mitigated against a "color blind" approach. As a racially defined organization formed to attack a racially centered problem, BRC members were aware of and invested in discourses that recognize certain practices as "authentically black." This may explain the stark contrast the manifesto creates between black and white musicians: white musicians exploit the innovations of black artists, while black musicians are limited in the kinds of music they can pursue. Left out of this characterization of the unequal fortunes of blacks and whites in rock are references to the creative role white musicians have played in influencing not only rock music, but also the practices of BRC members. In the conversations I had during fieldwork, BRC members named as musical forebears not only black musicians, but also white artists ranging from the Beatles to Led Zeppelin to Joni Mitchell to Cream. This aspect of appropriation—black musicians borrowing from white musicians—is not accentuated in the manifesto, perhaps because doing so would further embroil BRC members in accusations that they were playing white boy music. Still, there are antiessentialist sentiments in the manifesto: the support of "the total spectrum of black music" and the demand for freedom from "the creative straitjackets" that confine African Americans, for example. In these cases, the manifesto uses an antiracist discourse that can appeal to anyone supportive of African Americans' ongoing struggle for full citizenship. In contrasting the limits placed on black artists to the breadth of expression allowed white performers, the manifesto critiques the way the music industry, like so many U.S. institutions, treats African Americans as an undifferentiated monolith. The statement "We are individuals and we will accept no less than full respect for our right to be conceptually independent" lays claim to the kind of humanity that has historically been withheld from African Americans in all walks of life. Individuality, respect, independence, and recognition of voice are the extremely American ideals that undergirded previous African American cultural and political movements and are central to the BRC's cultural politics.

BRC members' ability to represent these views in the mainstream depended largely on media coverage, especially by journalists who took the BRC seriously and wrote about the organization. BRC members, some of whom were affiliated with local New York media, implored journalists to cover their new organization. Nurtured on radio, magazines, records, and television, BRC members understood the value of media attention and free publicity. They created opportunities by sending press releases and developing connections with journalists in order to keep the organization's name in the public eye. As a result, the BRC received coverage in a range of local and national periodicals. The BRC has been discussed in national music magazines like *Rolling Stone, Musician, Spin, Down Beat,* and *Creem*; in national consumer magazines like *Essence* and *Newsweek*; in music industry press like *Billboard, Variety,* and *Black Radio Exclusive*; in local newspapers including the *New York Times, New York Newsday,* the *New York Daily News,* the *Los Angeles Times,* the *Washington Post,* the *Boston Globe,* the *Detroit Free Press,* and the *Chicago Tribune*; and in local weekly and special interest press like New York's *Village Voice,* Boston's *Boston Phoenix,* Los Angeles's music papers *BAM* and *Rock City News,* and the now defunct New York black newspaper *The City Sun.*[5] The BRC was a new enough idea and produced vibrant enough music and discourses to capture the attention of a number of journalists including Jon Pareles and Robert Palmer of the *New York Times,* Dave Fricke of *Rolling Stone,* Nelson George of *Billboard,* and Gene Santoro, who published in the *Daily News* and the *Village Voice.* Typically, these articles discussed the activist grounding of the BRC—often quoting directly from the manifesto—and described the content of the music performed onstage.

In its early years, press coverage of BRC events brought the organization's agenda to the attention of potential supporters, giving national visibility to a local movement while creating a dialogue about blacks and rock. For example, responding to a *Billboard* article about the newly formed BRC, Dez Dickerson, lead guitarist in Prince's band, wrote a letter that Nelson George excerpted in his column, "The Rhythm and the Blues":

If American blacks were told tomorrow that they will only be allowed to eat in certain restaurants or wear certain clothing, the uproar would be immediate and undeniable. But year in and year out, blacks in the music business are told "play r&b, build your base and then we'll cross you over." Those of us with black skin and rock & roll hearts are denied the opportunity to make the kinds of records we want to make or, in most cases, denied the opportunity to make records at all. (Dickerson quoted in George 1986:56)

Coverage like this galvanized BRC members and legitimated their cause. Articles advanced the BRC mission by explaining the organization's critique and addressing the issues of racism, power, and access that BRC members had opened up for discussion. Peppered with quotes from BRC members that communicated the coalition's perspective, these articles created an image of BRC members as outspoken, racially conscious artists and activists. In a *New York Times* article, Don Eversley, then the BRC executive director, made an uncensored comment about black music industry professionals: "Most blacks in the record business are very conservative, narrow-minded or just plain scared. . . . Even if they personally go home and listen to Tackhead or Fishbone, they're signing Whitney Houston or Freddie Jackson clones. We're realistic enough to know that some of the blacks in the record business are our enemies" (Eversley quoted in Sinclair 1991:19). Speaking to a *City Sun* reporter, Greg Tate explained that the coalition coalesced to critique the racism blacks routinely encountered in the music industry:

If you tried to do music that draws on the full range of Black music, then [the industry claims] you aren't commercial enough. If you tried to pursue a vision like Bruce Springsteen or David Bowie do, then you're told you're not realistic; you're too far above the heads of the audience. The funny thing is . . . Sting, Byrne, Springsteen and Bowie are considered intellectuals in the music world and their music is played on Black radio stations. Yet, a Black artist who wants to address some of his or her intellectual, social or political concerns is told his or her music isn't "Black" enough. (Tate quoted in Johnson 1986:11)

In calling for the African American musician's right to be innovative without being characterized as inauthentic, Tate is demanding that people rethink their definitions of blackness. Like civil rights activists before them, BRC members sought to ensure their individual expressive freedom (or individual rights) in part through group organization.

While press coverage was usually supportive, it raised new concerns. Vernon Reid explained to me that the name black rock was intended to be a deliberate attack on the whitewashing of rock, but, he continued, "black rock" went beyond critique:

> Now, also, [black rock] was about a self-defining term. The problem, though, with it is that . . . terminology and buzzwords become like another category. . . . It's one thing to define yourself, but [another] if you don't define the means, the media. You see that's the thing, in terms of controlling who you are, what your image is. . . . You can say whatever you like about who you are and what you are, but if you don't own or control the means to disseminate the information, you're still at a disadvantage.

BRC members could define themselves, but this process occurred within media structures that were shaped by the kinds of racial ideologies and racializing practices that the BRC set out to challenge. Members began to recognize that the new category black rock, intended to open up space for black rockers, was in its own way confining. In many of the press representations of the BRC, race was in the mix and sometimes threatened to supersede the music. Without control of "the means to disseminate the information," BRC members could not modulate the way they were discussed in the press. As articles focused more and more on the political, social, and industry issues that were important to BRC members, the music itself took a backseat. Unlike white rockers whose race is rarely a subject, BRC members' race was foregrounded. This dilemma was partly a result of the novelty of black rockers and a consequence of journalists taking seriously member assertions of racial pride. In some ways this is a textbook example of the double-bind of identity politics. On the one hand, it made sense for black rockers to organize based on race because their race was important to their self-identification and it was problematic in the eyes of industry executives. On the other hand, once organized on a racial basis, race itself became hard to escape. To underplay race would not have made sense to people who were proud to be black, but in voicing this identity, organizing around it, and connecting it to their musical productions and professional aspirations, BRC members experienced new kinds of racialization and new kinds of limitations, a situation that exemplifies the intractability of race in the United States.

Part of the BRC's "Stalkin' the 90s" series, Bluesland performs at CBGB. From left, Michael Hill, Roger Byam, and Kevin Hill. Photo by Janine da Silva.

THE MEANINGS OF STYLE

The BRC's early performances indicated how members understood the connection between art and politics. The Apartheid Concert, held at the Kitchen in 1986, was the coalition's first live band performance. Upon entering the venue, each audience member received a black or white card and was ushered into color-coded, segregated sections of the theater. During the evening, the BRC Orchestra played music by Sly Stone, James Brown, and the Special AKA's antiapartheid anthem "Free Nelson Mandela." Tate recalled the concert as being

> our musical coming out. It was definitely saying, "Yeah, there are some young Black players out there who are a force to be reckoned with." And the next year we did the first of the Stalking Heads concerts, which was two nights at CBS [CBGB], about ten bands. There were jam sessions at the end with Ronnie Drayton, Vernon and Dr. Know from Bad Brains. I remember one of the things they did was "Lift Every Voice and Sing," a three-guitar version of that. (Tate quoted in BRC 2001a:10)

The Los Angeles chapter was inaugurated with an event called "All Is Not Quiet on the Western Front/Black Rock Coalition Invasion

On Valentine's Day in 1991 the BRC performed Motown's Love Songs at Wetlands. From left, Dean Bowman, Sekou Sundiata, and Wynette Hill. Photo by Janine da Silva.

Part II" at the Music Machine in July 1989; performers included Los Angeles bands Civil Rite and Hello Children and New York band Eye & I. The show was hosted by Vernon Reid and Nona Hendryx. Over the years, the BRC has produced an array of live performances to showcase black rock. Shows at clubs were a key aspect of the BRC's cultural activism, playing an important double role of externally publicizing the organization and internally solidifying a sense of common cause among the members. By 1993, when I began my research, these shows were a well-established part of life in the BRC and much of the energy of the coalition's most active members was devoted to producing events. With these performances, BRC members put black rock into local music scenes and into the consciousness of local audiences.

As they performed, listened to, and talked about music, BRC members created the social space I call the "black rock scene" that offered them a personal sense of belonging while also providing a public re-scripting of black popular culture images. An early concern of the BRC was to assert a musical identity and develop a scene that would locate the organization and its members on New York's music map. An integral part of any viable music community, a scene is a heady combination of musical practices, musical knowledge, hair styles, manners of dress, performance and dance styles, and aesthetic values that mark groups of musicians and music fans. The history of U.S. rock is one of vibrant local music scenes. Some of the most notable include Memphis in the 1950s, San Francisco in the 1960s, and New York in the 1970s. In his study of the Austin, Texas, alternative rock scene of the 1980s, Barry Shank defines a music scene as an "intensity of fan commitment and cultural production" and as "an overproductive signifying community; that is, far more semiotic information is produced than can be rationally parsed" (1994:122). Through aural, visual, and ideological codes, participants in a music scene interrogate, challenge, and transform the dominant tropes of meaning and identity, substituting a self-defined system that has more immediate resonance (122). For me, part of being in the field meant attending shows at New York City clubs like CBGB, Wetlands, the Cooler, the Mercury Lounge, and the Knitting Factory. Seeing and hearing the performances of BRC-affiliated bands like Screaming Headless Torsos, Faith, Women in Love, Me'Shell NdegéOcello, Vernon Reid's Masque, Kelvynator, D-Tripp, Sophia's Toy, Michael Hill's Blues Mob, and D-Xtreme allowed me to participate in some of the processes through which BRC members put themselves and their music forward. My "deep hanging out"[6] in the New York City black rock scene gave me extended exposure to the BRC member performances and interactions that constituted a public space for the display and affirmation of postliberated music, identities, and sensibilities.

Local rock clubs are the primary public spaces where these scenes develop. In New York these venues comprise what BRC member and P.B.R. Streetgang vocalist Amafujo Inniss referred to as "the Downtown Chitlin Circuit," a network of small rock clubs in lower Manhattan. Here, the rundown amenities are understood as authentic rock 'n' roll atmosphere, liquor sales rather than cover charges bring in most of the money, and musicians expect to receive little if any pay for performing. Amafujo's use of the term Chitlin Circuit indicates the lack of glamour of these clubs and marks the persistence of the unfair practices that cheated previous generations of black performers who played in segregated southern music venues in the pre–civil rights era. Musicians playing at these small New York clubs usually do not sign contracts and have no union-guaranteed rights to cash at the end of the evening. I heard stories about club owners who resorted to short-changing bands in order to avoid coming up short themselves in the precarious game of running a rock club. Bands don't get rich on the Downtown Chitlin Circuit, but playing in clubs gives them a chance to gain exposure, improve chops, try out new material, and build a fan base, necessary steps in developing a career. For most bands, BRC bands included, the "big time" is elusive, and these are the only clubs that they will ever play on a regular basis. Consequently, these local clubs provide an important outlet.[7]

A distinctive element of the black rock scene was its "vibe." This was a look, sound, and energy that shaped the public spaces where the events unfolded. On most BRC nights out, the predominantly African American crowd of men and women, ranging in age from late twenties to early forties, blended materials drawn from the African diaspora, downtown New York art scenes, and rock sensibilities. BRC members manifested the rainbow of skin tones common among African Americans in the United States. Hair, such an important part of one's looks and in black American contexts an often-charged political symbol, was frequently attention-getting.[8] Well over half of the men wore dreadlocks, the varying lengths of which indicating the number of years the individual had willfully departed from mainstream black hair protocol. Women wore dreadlocks, braids, twists, and close-cropped naturals. Some members—male and female—straightened their hair chemically in spite of a valuing of the natural and nappy among BRC members. Whether straightened or dreadlocked, some members achieved a long mane that they could flick or swing freely during performances. Clothing might include a mix of any of the following: black leather jackets and pants, leather boots, West African print fabric, T-shirts emblazoned with the image of a jazz great, vintage clothing, tight Lycra pants in bright colors, faded blue jeans, solid black ensembles, baseball caps, or Kangol hats. Men and women wore bracelets, rings, earrings, and necklaces made of copper, leather, cowrie shells, silver, and semiprecious stones—the types of gear available from West African street vendors on 125th Street or along Broadway in the Village. The cultural politics of style evident in these hair and clothing choices had an immediate visual impact and marked BRC members' distinctive postliberated approach to self-presentation.

The mixing that was so much a part of the members' look also emerged in a range of attitudes that included an interest in African diaspora culture. Roughly a quarter of New York members are children or grandchildren of Caribbean immigrants. The combination of their affiliation with rock and their being raised in the United States may have "Americanized" them, but they were conscious of their non-U.S. ethnicity and made references to it in conversations and in their music. In New York, many members expressed interest in the West Indies and in Puerto Rico even when they did not have a direct bloodline to the islands. Living in New York, they had contact with the Caribbean through the city's numerous immigrants: they lived in the same neighborhoods and attended the same schools. For many, African diaspora resources provided alternatives to mainstream U.S. practices. In terms of popular culture, for example, the rhythms and politics of Jamaican reggae and its best-known practitioner, Bob Marley, appealed to members, and as I mentioned above, many adopted the stylistic feature most immediately associated with Rastafarians, dreadlocks.

The people and places I am describing have many of the characteristics of the subcultures that British cultural studies scholars examined in the 1970s (Hall and Jefferson 1975; Hebdige 1979).[9] These studies of British youth emphasized the ways working-class teens used clothing, hair cuts, and music preferences to express their rejection of dominant British culture. British cultural studies scholars argued, very anthropologically, that oppositional stylistic practices of working-class adolescents were sites of cultural struggle and viewed these "subcultural styles" as strategies of negotiation through which young people responded to their experiences as a subordinated class (Clarke et al. 1975:47; Hall and Jefferson 1975; Hebdige 1979; Willis 1977). This research focused on people who did not articulate social critique or agitate for political change; rather they "resisted ritualistically" their ascribed racial and class status. British cultural studies scholars observed that working-class youth subcultures, the products of justifiable anger and alienation, were "fated to fail" since they only enabled youth to live through the problematic of class inequality, but not to resolve it (Clarke et al. 1975; Willis 1977). In contrast, much of the anthropological research on cultural politics focuses on people who have developed analyses and have deployed media and popular culture practices in order to advance their perspective in culturally powerful ways (Dornfeld 1998; Ginsburg 1997; Kondo 1997; Myers 1991; Turner 1990). It is important, then, to note the difference between the rejection of establishment rules that informs most subcultures and the efforts of BRC members to change existing practices and perspectives. The project expressed in the BRC Manifesto and through member activities in local clubs brought together a critical mass of musicians and supporters who sustained a black rock scene and made the case for the viability of black rock.

I want to stress that the very presence of black people in downtown rock clubs—onstage, wielding guitars, turning up amps, and rocking out—is a significant cultural and political statement. Their visibility onstage and in the crowd disrupts commonsense ideas of black music and black identity and inserts a black alternative voice into a largely white rock 'n' roll scene. These BRC shows link and celebrate the categories "black" and "rock," allowing self-affirmation among BRC members and self-assertion to the rock community. Recognizing the political dimension of this kind of cultural production, anthropologist Faye Ginsburg (1997) uses the term "cultural activism" to draw attention to the consciously politicized aspects of this kind of expressive culture. She argues that politically conscious cultural producers deploy the arts for creative expression and other purposes that may include mediating "historically produced social ruptures"; shifting the terms of debates circulating in the dominant public sphere; attacking stereotypes and perceived prejudices; and constructing, reconfiguring, and communicating meanings associated with their racial, ethnic, gender, sexual, and national identities (Ginsburg 1991:96; 1997). Linking these practices of representation to larger anthropological questions about social process and social relations, Ginsburg argues that "focusing on people who engage themselves with new possibilities for their own collective self-production allows us to ask more general questions about the political possibilities inherent in self-conscious shifts in cultural practice" (1997:122). In contrast to the vague discontent that characterizes subcultures, cultural activism is rooted in the relationships between articulated political and artistic agendas and the potential of the resulting productions to transform the social milieu. Cultural activists connect their concerns to institutional structures and ideologies. BRC members, for example, are keenly aware of the constraints that institutionalized racism creates; their practices address these limitations and seek to "expand discursive space" (Fraser 1992:124).

Music, the form at the center of the BRC's cultural activism, is a medium of expression that involves the formation of social relationships, the construction of identity, and the development of collective practices. As both a cultural product and a social process, music brings people together, articulates who they are, furthers their political goals, and gives meaning to their lives (Turino 1993:5). The process of making and taking meaning from the performance of black rock is important to the BRC members playing and listening in the clubs and to me, the anthropologist interpreting the significance of their activities. The conversations, concerts, clothing, and camaraderie that shaped the kinds of black rock evenings I describe below allowed BRC members to create, consolidate, and publicize an artistic and social identity. At these communal events, BRC members asserted themselves as black rockers and reveled in the pleasure of performing and listening to the music they loved. Black rock, then, is an aesthetic form, a music scene, a political statement, and a pleasurable diversion that undergirds a cultural politics of race and identity.

IN THE FIELD: BLACK ROCK NIGHTS

Being at the shows was about seeing the bands and hearing the music, but it was also about being in the scene. For BRC members, nights in the clubs were opportunities to catch up with old friends, talk about long-time competitors, and make plans for future activities. For me, going to shows was a way to learn about the music, keep in touch with folks, and observe the production of the scene. For all of us, hanging out in the clubs with their beer-splashed floors and ramshackle seats was a way of participating in the scene while also perpetuating it. I learned about the themes of this study while standing in dim corners, chatting between sets, listening to comments shouted over feedback, leaning in to hear a joke, or waiting transfixed with others in the crowd for a solo to finish its soar. My deep hanging out in the black rock scene included a Thursday night show in January 1995 that I discuss in some detail because it involved a particularly effervescent confluence of cooperation, music making, and group representation. Held at Wetlands in the Tribeca section of lower Manhattan, this evening of performances encapsulates the politics and pleasures that marked the black rock scene.

During the 1990s, Wetlands had a reputation in New York as a place where the peace, love, and protest values of the 1960s were recycled for a new generation. The result was an atmosphere in which music and politics could easily be linked. The first thing you met up with when walking into the club was a brightly painted van that served as a display case for independently produced recordings—including the BRC's compilations—and T-shirts advertising bands or progressive political causes. Deeper in the club were a few tables displaying leaflets that promoted environmental and other left political issues. Typically, there were petitions—one in support of African American death row inmate Mumia Abu-Jamal was available that night for signing. Wetlands boasted a large floor space with a bar and stage. Audience members could stand directly in front of the stage or sit to its side in a slightly elevated clutter of tables and chairs and still have a good view. There were also a few small rooms downstairs where people could escape the high volume of a live show. Chuck Brownley, who was the BRC's director of marketing, was Wetlands' night manager. The combination of his employment at the club, the owner's goodwill toward the organization, and the club's fair treatment of bands encouraged BRC members to schedule events at Wetlands. This evening's show was coordinated by two BRC members, Lace (who did not use a last name) and Gregory Amani. This was their second event at Wetlands and there were more to follow. It was not unusual for BRC members to produce events like this: Kregg Ajammo had been running his Visionary Roots series at the Lion's Den in the fall and David Fiuczynski had curated a weekly guitar performance series at the Cooler in November. I paid $7.00 at the ticket window and Chuck, who happened to be at the door when I arrived, jovially vouched for my being old enough to drink when his coworker asked me for proof of age. Just inside the door, Lace and Gregory polled the patrons on who they had come to see.

"The whole thing," was my answer.

"Cool," Gregory said, making a tic mark under the name of each band in his notebook: Miss Mary Mack, Prime Directive, Women in Love, and the headliners Screaming Headless Torsos. Tonight the bands would be paid according to the number of people they drew. The admission take would be divided among them after the promoters took their percentage of the door. Lace and Gregory told me they would be leaving before the sets were over and the money was divided. They had to get to Midtown in time to host the BRC's weekly radio show "Crosstown Traffic" on WBAI-FM.

Inside the club, a series of seventies funk tunes with the bass turned way up provided the soundtrack for the evening. My quick survey of the bar, the stage area, and the downstairs lounge confirmed that there was a heavy BRC turnout. Over the course of the night I saw many of the people I had been interviewing, talking with, attending meetings with, and watching shows with. Like everyone else at the gig, I spent the evening moving from circle to circle of constantly shifting groups of people, hanging out, and enjoying the music. The high level of BRC visibility at the club and the active involvement of BRC members in the production of the evening's proceedings transformed Wetlands into a postliberated space. Each of the four bands were BRC members, BRC members organized the show, a BRC member was the club's night manager, BRC members were in the audience, and downstairs, a series of single and multiframe pen-and-ink cartoons following the travails of a black musician drawn by BRC member Gene Williams was on display. Although competitiveness and "me-first" thinking are not absent from the BRC—a source of irritation for some members—there is a good measure of collaboration and mutual support. At this and other similar multiband events there was a palpable feeling of collaboration.

These nights out in New York, entertainment for the audience, were working situations for the musicians and music professionals I was writing about. Gigging was a job: money was exchanging hands and careers were being developed. For example, at Wetlands, the Screaming Headless Torsos's manager Bill Toles was coordinating a video recording of the band's set for use in promoting its upcoming compact disc. The material taped on Hi-8 video during the evening's performance would be intercut with band member interviews and edited into a promotional video. This electronic press kit would be sent to music writers, radio stations, and video outlets—both local and national—to publicize the band. The Torsos's contract with the independent label Discovery Records had included a small stipend—Bill measured out an inch with his fingers when he described its size to me—for this project. Even the members who were showing up "just to watch" a gig were working. During one show, Chuck had led me to the vantage point of his choice—right up at the edge of the stage—where he could watch what the musicians did. "From this angle," he explained, "you can see which pedals and effects they're using and everything. This is like a clinic for me." At Wetlands on the night in question, Vernon Reid and Gene Williams were talking about the possibility of working together on a project. In another corner of the club, Wayne Livingston, who organizes the BRC Jimi Hendrix tribute show each year, and Greg Tate were talking about the new CD that Tate's band, Women in Love, had recorded, produced, and pressed independently. Shock Council, Wayne's band, was in the process of recording tracks in his home studio and he was getting Tate's assessment of the company that handled the CD. The two of them were discussing different CD pressing options and strategies for distributing these do-it-yourself recordings. Inevitably, there were also those who showed up just to watch the gigs, but who claimed to be working in some capacity so they could avoid paying the cover charge.

The fact that work was taking place and business was being conducted did not prevent people from having a good time. Audience members, many of whom were musicians, got the most out of each performance. I think it is fair to say that I was not the only one involved in a kind of "deep hanging out." We were all participating in the ballet of passing time between sets—and in some cases during them.

Indeed, there was nearly always a conversation in some corner that continued all the way through a performance. Milling around, buying another drink, sharing news, interpreting the events of the day, reviewing the band that just left the stage, and waiting for the next thing to happen are the rhythms of the night out. Inside the club, the haze of smoke hanging over the room, the volume of the live and recorded music, and the energy of the crowd contributed to the ambiance. The activity and atmosphere combined to create the texture of a night out at the club and produced the black rock scene.

Queen Esther was on first with her band Miss Mary Mack. Elegantly attired in a cocktail dress, Queen Esther was impeccably made up, her expressive eyes and arched eyebrows punctuating her vocals. Queen Esther was in fine voice, but her set was interrupted by an equipment breakdown that her guitarist Jack Sprat had to address. Trying to help the time pass, the rhythm section laid down a groove and Queen Esther improvised a few lines:

> I don't have enough money to pay the rent
> and I don't have a job
> and my man left me
> and life is hard in New York City.

The crowd cheered its approval. Throughout her set, Queen Esther kept up her patter with the BRC component of the audience. She said "Hey" to Flip Barnes who was standing close to the stage and she also sent a shout out to Bill Toles. She turned her attention to the other side of the house and spotted Steve Williams.

"Steve, will you marry me?" she called, winsomely.

"Do you want to do it right now?" he shot back.

Queen Esther waved to people, winked, and mugged. She invited Tate to come to the center of the floor and demonstrate the Swamp Boogie for everyone when she announced the song of that title.

"Okay," said Tate without moving from his spot in the crowd.

"And," she laughed, "you have to call him on things because he'll do it. That's how black he is."

At the end of "Swamp Boogie," Lace signaled that it had to be the last song.

"Just one more?" Queen Esther asked.

Lace nodded.

"How 'bout two more?"

Lace shook her head.

Queen Esther shrugged and sighed. "All right, this is our last

Always elegant, Greg Tate's Women in Love. From left, Jason Di Matteo (bass), Marque Gilmore (drums), Mikel Banks (vocals), Greg Tate (guitar), Helga Davis (vocals), Lewis "Flip" Barnes (trumpet and vocals). Photo by Barron Claiborne.

tune—" then she interrupted the introduction. "Is Helga Davis here?" This was a reference to her friend and Women in Love vocalist. There was a delay and then a distant but clear "Yo!" from Helga in the dressing room at stage right where she was preparing for her own performance later in the evening. Her friend's presence confirmed, Queen Esther and the band grooved into their last number.

As Queen Esther's performance demonstrates, the boundaries between onstage and offstage, performer and audience, were permeable. Most of the band members scheduled to play that evening stood in the audience to watch the sets of other bands. Lending this kind of support and keeping an eye on the competition was one of the ways BRC members consolidated the scene. Further, there was a feeling of camaraderie as people meandered around the club to greet each other or to stand together listening to the sets. This situation was not surprising given that so many of the people who were in attendance had known each other for years, had worked together, and had argued and commiserated with each other on numerous occasions. Queen Esther's playful repartee kicked off the evening's series of performances with a clear affirmation of the BRC community.

More of Motown's Love Songs, this time by Michael Hill and D. K. Dyson. Photo by Janine da Silva.

The audience greeted the first three acts enthusiastically, evidence of the evening's good vibe. Following Miss Mary Mack was Prime Directive. Gene Williams's band laid down a jazz-inflected black rock stew of time changes, genre shifts, freaky themes, and out-of-the-box solos. After a short break, Women in Love came onstage. Tate's ensemble presented an arty onslaught of soundscapes that added Flip Barnes's Miles-influenced trumpet to Tate's psychedelic guitar, a funky-but-elegant rhythm section, and Tate's trippy lyrics presented through the vocal interplay of Helga's multi-octave voice and Mikel Banks's hipster tenor. An additional factor contributing to the energy of the evening was the videotaping for the Torsos. Led by David "Fuze" Fiuczynski, the Torsos were one of the bands that had been signed to a deal during my time in the field. By late 1994, the Torsos were in the studio putting down tracks for their release on Discovery Records. Many BRC members identified the Torsos as their favorite band, and they praised Fuze's guitar playing and Dean Bowman's vocals, so it was not surprising that a good number of people had stayed to hear their set. It was, after all, turning out to be a late night. By 1 AM, the show was running anywhere from a half hour to an hour behind schedule—depending on who you asked—and the Torsos still hadn't gone on.

"Same old thing," Edric Debose said to me dryly after consulting his watch.

This was a case of what some around the coalition called "BRC time," a play on "CP (colored people's) time." The audience had thinned out because of the lateness of the hour and the ensuing workday. Remaining in the nooks and crannies of the club were diehard fans and many BRC members. The always-slow process of readying a band's equipment was complicated by the logistics of the three-camera videotaping complete with industrial strength klieg lights to provide illumination. Eventually, the Torsos, who were completing their first studio album, took the stage. The evening before, I had been in the studio with some of the band members, watching while they did some late night overdubbing. I was surprised to see them looking so fresh and alert onstage and put it down to adrenaline. Screaming Headless Torsos, two black guys and three white guys, went to work checking their instruments, amps, and monitors. They plugged in, tuned up, placed water bottles and soda cans in convenient locations, took measure of the room, and conferred one last time about the set list. Finally, they were ready. Someone laid down a count to set the time and then, seemingly from nowhere, the sonic assault the crowd had been waiting for arrived. What never failed to amaze me during all those nights in the clubs was the startling pleasure and energy that was part of seeing and hearing the music being made right in front of you. The best live music performances—the improvisations, the inventions, the wild riffs, and even the flubs—have an electricity and on the best nights, standing in the crowd, you can fall under the spell of the melodies and rhythms.

At Wetlands that night, there was an immediate kinetic response as Fima Ephron thunked out a funky bass line and Fuze began his guitar inventions. The energy level and the noise level rose simultaneously and the crowd pressed closer to the stage, under the unforgiving brightness of the klieg lights (which contrasted sharply with the usual darkness of rock clubs). The band members launched into the usual set opener, "Vinnie," and the friendly audience dug in with them. Some hands flew up, waving with the beat; other hands rested casually in pockets as the related head nodded to the rhythm. Still other hands formed raised fists and pumped them to keep time. People spontaneously shouted out "Yes!" and applauded and whooped. Dreadlocks flew as heads banged the loose-necked nod to the beat and bodies thrashed to the music. Guys turned to guys and shared enthusiastic hand clasps—an exaggeratedly long raising of the arm coming down into a solid, slow-motion slap with its mirror image as friends confirmed their pleasure at the Screaming Headless Torsos and their scrawl of sound. Being at a rock show is about being into the music and everyone has a different way of arriving at that place. So maybe someone dances, maybe someone else stands still taking it all in, nodding slowly, leaning up against the bar or a wall. A few people absent-mindedly mime playing a guitar or a drum riff alongside the real thing. Someone may make a calm but appreciative comment like, "Oh, that was nice," after an especially inspired solo. Someone else may signal approval with an affirming nod shared with the friend standing nearby. Mixed into the crowd are those who stand still, arms folded, challenging the band to impress them. Others are demonstrative, swinging their bodies to the music. Standing shoulder to shoulder, people watch the band, watch each other, light a cigarette, take a drink. We are moving to the music, swaying, and rocking. The atmosphere crackles. Behind me I could hear Helga Davis cheeeeeeer as the band glided through their deconstruction of the jazz classic "Blue in Green."

"My favorite song!" Helga shouted to me and anyone else listening between head bangs. She even sang along at some points in the set.

"Blue in Green," a metal-fusion reworking of the cut from Miles Davis's 1959 album *Kind of Blue*, is a tour de force example of the ways so many brc bands toss a bunch of musical influences into a single song and blend them together without apology. With "Blue in Green" you can start out skanking to the mellow, reggae downbeats and the Afro-Latin percussion on the verse and then bang your head as the chorus flows into a churning metal crunch with Dean shifting his vocals from postbop cool to a throaty and abstracted death metal roar. At the bridge, they shift forms again. Dean scats as Fuze works out a fusion-esque run of notes, once again breaking down and building up Miles Davis's lines. There was a unified bounce in the crowd as people rocked to the reggae, to Fuze's chromatic guitar chords, and to Dean's warbles. On this early morning of January 1995, Dean introduced another song like this: "It's November 1996 and we've voted out all the Republicans and—" the music started and Dean sang the first lyric: "I'm a free man." The crowd let out an enthusiastic yell and bopped to the downbeats.

Throughout the set, Dean stood at center stage at the mic, head tilted to one side, his hand cupped around his ear so he could monitor his vocals, leaning sometimes from the waist, and rocking a bit to the beat. Fuze was the bandleader but was usually low-key throughout the set, focused on gliding from jazz chord progressions into punk rock riffs into unclassifiable, enrapturing solos. For an audience that has seen this band so many times, part of the pleasure was just that: familiarity with the players and the set, but still not knowing exactly what was going to happen next. There is always an element of surprise and the unexpected in a live performance. The twin pleasures of repetition of the old and anticipation of the new merged as we watched, sinking into the music as the night flowed on. In spite of the envy some may have felt at the Torsos's success—they had a recording contract, they seemed to be on their way—members also expressed enthusiasm about one of their own getting a much-deserved break. The show went on until 2:30 AM and the energy hardly waned. It took the usual long time to get people out of the club after the set ended. While the band members and the video crew packed up their respective equipment, people continued to hang out. After spending some time chatting and saying my goodbyes, I finally tore myself away. Outside, the January night air was frosty and refreshingly clear after the smoke-and-beer stink of the club interior. Danny Sadownick, the percussionist from the Torsos, waited with me outside of the club to make sure I got a cab without incident. In the relative silence of the night, my ears were ringing after more than five hours of live and recorded music played at high decibels, and my voice was hoarse from shouting over the music and inhaling the smoke. I stepped into the taxi Danny had hailed and the driver pulled into the flow of traffic, taking me out of the field.

The sets of music at Wetlands are just one example of the sound and sociability produced during the nights in the clubs. Central to the BRC project, they are a manifestation of the Black Rock Manifesto's effort to reclaim rock. BRC members chose not to underplay their race or change the music they played to fit the preferences of recording industry executives. Instead, they worked to create a context for expressing their interpretations of African American identity and music among a supportive community. The result was a black rock scene, a public, social space for a form of black cultural production that has not been supported by the mainstream. BRC members produced these performances and the black rock scene for their own collective enjoyment, but they were also a critical part of the organization's cultural activism. Gathering together in public to participate in the pleasures of music making helped sustain a sense of group solidarity while also countering the invisibility of black rock in the white rock public sphere. Marked by the production and enjoyment of music and presenting an audible and visible challenge to the persistent ignoring of black rock, these nights in the clubs were at once socially significant forms of activism and personally pleasurable pursuits.

FIVE

BLACK ROCK AESTHETICS

We're approaching what we do from our roots, and our roots are a mish-mosh of lots of different things—jazz, Latin, gospel—all stuff from the soul. That's the one common thread through it all, for all of us.—MUZZ SKILLINGS, FORMER LIVING COLOUR BASS PLAYER

The Screaming Headless Torsos were starting out their Saturday evening at the Fez, a performance space in the basement of Time Cafe, a downtown New York restaurant. After the 8 o'clock set, lead singer Dean Bowman told me, they were heading to Wetlands for another gig. I thought he looked a little weary with the anticipation of playing the same forty-minute set twice in one evening. Perhaps to put a lighter spin on it, he suggested that I follow them through lower Manhattan like a Deadhead. I declined, chuckling at his reference to Grateful Dead fans who traveled across the country attending concerts, sharing bootlegged recordings of Dead performances, and ingesting hallucinogens. Next, Dean offered a joke:

"What does a Deadhead say when the drugs run out?" he asked.

"I don't know," I said. "What?"

" 'This music sucks!' "

We both cracked up. Presumably, the joke would not be as amusing to a Dead fan since it depends on the assumption that only a person on drugs would enjoy the Dead's country blues jamming. Dean told me the joke to entertain me and to pass time before going on stage. I am sure the last thing he intended was that I put it in my book. But in highlighting the fact that different bands and their fans produce and appreciate particular musical sounds and performance styles, the joke provides a starting point for my discussion of black rock aesthetics and the ways BRC members have adapted and expanded earlier black aesthetic paradigms.

The question of what aesthetic systems should govern black cultural production has long been a subject of debate for African American artists and critics.[1] Efforts to develop an authentic black voice and black art informed the work of those associated with the Harlem Renaissance of the 1920s and the Black Arts Movement of the 1960s. Indeed, these issues have preoccupied most black cultural producers throughout the twentieth century. By the late 1960s and early 1970s, the dominant black aesthetic discourse, shaped by Black Arts Movement practitioners, assumed that the productions of black Americans should follow a pro-black, socially engaged aesthetic unhampered by Western European–centered aesthetics that treat art as a privileged realm of production separate from the vicissitudes of the workaday world.[2] The ongoing struggle for full African American citizenship in the United States and an awareness of the influence of social relations and political context on black cultural producers has informed most debates about black aesthetics. In talking about aesthetics and politics together, I am continuing these traditions and indicating that for BRC members artistic and activist practices are intertwined.

BRC members were involved with music, the art form with which black Americans have had the most decisive cultural impact in the United States and around the world. Blackness is registered through engagement with certain musical forms and notions of what black music should sound like have become so naturalized that it is disruptive when performers move beyond the established limits.[3] Commenting on this relationship, black British cultural critic Paul Gilroy observes that music is often "identified as being expressive of the absolute essence of the group that produced it" and "thought to be emblematic and constitutive of racial difference rather than just associated with it" (1991b:114; 1993). He also notes that "a discourse of authenticity has been a notable presence in the mass marketing of successive black folk cultural forms to white audiences" (1991b:124). Music is a quick and easy tool for ascribing authenticity to black Americans. Part of what BRC members grappled with was the relationship between their identity as black people and their engagement with a music form whose blackness seems negligible. The persistence of a belief in the inseparability of aesthetic style and racial substance gives black rock musicians a keen awareness of the politics of art. Their music incorporates a range of cultural influences and acknowledges racial and political concerns. They by no means conflate art and politics nor do they view their music as a substitute for political activism. They do, however, recognize that their decision to play rock is not simply a creative choice, but one that demands attention to the relationship between music and race, content and context, and art and politics. In this chapter, I attend to the details of BRC members' music—its sonic and lyrical qualities, its form and style, and its connections to other genres—and to the social climate in which their productions occur. I have linked a discussion of politics to a discussion of aesthetics partly because it is what BRC members do, partly to make sense of their choices, and partly to highlight the impact of racialization on the creative work of contemporary African Americans.

THE POLITICS OF POSTLIBERATED BLACK AESTHETICS

One way that I learned about black rock aesthetics was through the writings of Greg Tate. In addition to being a BRC cofounder, Tate is a cultural critic whose articles have appeared in the *Village Voice*, where he is a staff writer, and also in the *New York Times* and *Vibe* magazine. In 1986, he published "Cult-Nats Meet Freaky Deke" in *Artforum* magazine. This article describes how members of his generation have developed an aesthetic that draws on, critiques, and expands the work of black cultural nationalists (cult-nats) of the 1960s.[4] He situates these post–civil rights era cultural productions in terms of black aesthetics and acknowledges the sociological particulars that have led members of the postliberated generation to develop their aesthetic. Tate locates himself by explaining that he is "part of a generation of bohemian cult-nats who are mutating black culture into something the old interlocutors aren't ready for yet. Though nobody's sent out any announcements yet, the '80s are witnessing the maturation of a postnationalist black arts movement, one more Afrocentric and cosmopolitan than anything that's come before" (1992:220). Tate's mixing of genres is typical; he mentions Afrocentricity, an impulse to mine the cultural resources of the race, but also invokes cosmopolitanism, an approach that encourages looking beyond one's group. Tate's list of black and nonblack influences speaks to this dynamic. He mentions African American anthropologist and novelist Zora Neale Hurston and Japanese filmmaker Akira Kurosawa, Jamaican religious figure Jah Rastafari and British punk rocker Johnny Rotten, Sioux holy man Black Elk and African American jazz pianist Bud Powell. He continues:

I'm not just namedropping here. The point is that the present generation of black artists is cross-breeding aesthetic references like nobody is even talking about yet. And while they may be marginal to the black experience as it's expressed in rap, *Jet*, and on *The Cosby Show*, they're not all mixed up over who they are and where they come from.

These are artists for whom black consciousness and artistic freedom are not mutually exclusive but complementary, for whom "black culture" signifies a multicultural tradition of expressive practices; they feel secure enough about black culture to claim art produced by nonblacks as part of their inheritance. No anxiety of influence here—these folks believe the cultural gene pool is for skinny-dipping. (207)

During the late 1960s, a period of desegregation and anticipated assimilation, there *was* anxiety of influence and a discourse of black cultural nationalism was ascendant. The aesthetic principles advanced by the cult-nats influenced BRC members and contributed to the understandings of black identity and authenticity that we continue to use in the post–civil rights era. While many members of the Civil Rights Movement proclaimed that a shared humanity and belief in the tenets of the U.S. Constitution linked all Americans regardless of class or race, black cultural nationalists emphasized black difference from the white mainstream. Writers and artists associated with the Black Arts Movement argued that "the Western aesthetic had run its course" and that it was time to develop a black aesthetic rooted in African American cultural traditions and Third World culture (Neal 1968:29). In his 1968 manifesto "The Black Arts Movement," poet Larry Neal positioned this movement as "the aesthetic and spiritual sister of the Black Power concept" and as being "radically opposed to any concept of the artist that alienates him from his community" (29). Neal described an aesthetic that destroyed "white ways of looking at the world" and advanced an art "that speaks directly to the needs and aspirations of Black America" (28–29). Distinct from protest art that directed its appeals to whites or attempted to explain blacks to nonblacks, black art came from a black perspective and addressed black audiences. A preoccupation of these Black Arts writers was "to confront the contradictions arising out of the Black man's [sic] experience in the racist West" (Neal 1968:28).

The arts, especially drama and poetry, were political tools that would help form revolutionary black consciousness and lead to social change. Black cultural nationalists elevated black culture as the proper focal point for black artists and a legitimate creative resource. It was in this period that black, once a derogatory term, became "beautiful." Like Black Power, Black Arts insisted on the "necessity for Black people to define the world in their own terms" (Neal 1968:28). And, like Black Power Movement adherents, artists associated with the Black Arts Movement saw two Americas: one black and one white, the two irreconcilable. Accordingly, appropriately authentic black behaviors—working and writing toward black liberation, for example—were contrasted with assimilationist actions—like getting a "white" education or a "white" job. Here, cultural nationalists exploited intraracial differences and contrasted authentic "Blacks" to inauthentic "Negroes" in order to define allegiance to the cause (Harper 1995:225).[5] This process fixed the meaning of "black" and set the terms of post–civil rights era notions of black authenticity.

There were many reasons for this emphasis on recuperating blackness. As African Americans gained access to white institutions, the question of what would happen to black culture became more pressing. The cult-nats believed that black identity was at risk of being subsumed by dominant white culture or severely compromised as a result of prolonged contact. If the "American dilemma" described in 1944 by Gunnar Myrdal was the inability to reconcile the contradiction between the nation's image as a democratic society and the refusal of its institutions to fully admit African Americans into its mainstream, there was also an African American dilemma. The erosion of segregation and the potential for integration made it relevant for blacks to question embracing a culture whose values had historically denied their humanity and to ask what doing so would mean to their future (Blauner 1970:356). "Do we want to integrate into a burning house?" asked some. Although the deeply embedded history of racism in the United States made it unlikely that African Americans would ever fully dissolve into the American ethnic stew in the way of European immigrants, there were fears that integration would undermine racial self-preservation and cultural autonomy. In becoming more equally American we could somehow lose our blackness and lose our soul.

Informed by these concepts of race and identity, post–civil rights era discourse about black authenticity—encapsulated in the wry reminder that upwardly mobile African Americans need to "stay black" —voices anxiety over integration.[6] For members of the postliberated generation, blackness could be a choice. Here, the relationship between class and authenticity is significant. The inclusive rhetoric of black solidarity privileges race over class but then tends to conflate race and class, equating blackness with working-class status and forcing middle-class blacks to choose this authentic status or surrender their claim to blackness (Boyd 1997; Gates 1992). BRC members work both within and against these discourses of black authenticity. They legitimate their music as the recovery of an authentically black form, but also try to move beyond simplistic versions of authentic blackness. Thus Tate acknowledges the debt his generation owes the cultural nationalists of the late 1960s, but also comments on their limits: "The founding fathers [Amiri Baraka and Maulana Karenga] have long taken deserved lumps for the jiver parts of their program (like the sexist, anti-Semitic, black supremacist, pseudo-African mumbo-jumbo, paramilitary adventurist parts)" (Tate 1992:199). These concerns duly noted, he continues, "to their credit they took black liberation seriously enough to be theoretically ambitious about it. Perhaps their most grandiose scheme involved trying to transform a supremacist notion of black cultural *difference* into the basis for a racially bonding black American zeitgeist" (199).

Along with their politicized aesthetic, central contributions of the cult-nats were their then (and in some quarters still) revolutionary notion of the validity of black culture and their belief in the liberating capacity of consciously black art. In advancing these radical concepts, the cult-nats were, Tate suggests, "our dadaists:"

> While the dadaists tried to raise anarchy to an artform and bring Western civilization down with style, the cult-nats figured a "black is beautiful" campaign would be enough to raze Babylon, or at least get a revolution going. The cult-nats' black-übermensch campaign obviously didn't do much toward liberating the masses, but it did produce a postliberated black aesthetic, responsible for the degree to which contemporary black artists and intellectuals feel themselves heirs to a culture every bit as def as classical Western civilization. (200)

Writing three years later, Trey Ellis, an African American novelist and a participant in the early BRC meetings, contributed to the debate about postliberated black cultural production. Writing in a 1989 *Calalloo* article, "The New Black Aesthetic," Ellis outlines the theory and practice of a critical mass of young black writers, artists, filmmakers, and musicians who all grew up feeling misunderstood by both the black worlds and the white. Alienated (junior) intellectuals, we are the more and more young blacks getting back into jazz and the blues; the only ones you see at punk concerts; the ones in the bookstore wearing little, round glasses, and short, neat dreads; some of the only blacks who admit liking both Jim and Toni Morrison . . . My friends and I— a minority's minority mushrooming with the current black bourgeois boom—have inherited an open-ended New Black Aesthetic from a few Seventies pioneers that shamelessly borrows and reassembles across both race and class lines. (1989a:234)

"Educated by a multi-racial mix of culture" and currently practicing a New Black Aesthetic (N.B.A.) these "cultural mulattos," as Ellis calls himself and his contemporaries, "no longer need to deny or suppress any part of our complicated and sometimes contradictory cultural baggage to please either white people or black" (235). Ellis's characterization of "cultural mulattos" as middle-class, second-generation college-educated blacks raised in white neighborhoods (apparently an autobiographical statement) is more common to African Americans younger than most BRC members, but the attitudes Ellis describes reflect those of many BRC members. The term "cultural mulatto" plays on the biological mulatto, the child of a black parent and a white parent. His intention is to rewrite the "tragic mulatto" who in literature and film struggles with the burden of being biracial and must decide whether to pass into whiteness or maintain blackness. Ellis argues that cultural mulattos do not take their blackness for granted because they have had to fight to maintain it during their tenure in white institutions and to prove it to blacks who questioned their being in those spaces (1989b:251). He explains that cultural mulattos avoid the tragic mulatto's dilemma by deciding to "choose blackness" and by defining what that blackness means on their own terms (1989a:236).

Ellis's euphoric polemic has been validly criticized for being unsystematic in determining who qualifies as New Black Aestheticians, for failing to attend to class differences among blacks, and for managing to produce an almost exclusively male list of N.B.A.-ers (Hunter 1989; Lott 1989). Responding to his critics, Ellis explains that "it is important to remember that the New Black Aesthetic I try to define is really an anti-aesthetic that defies definition. The N.B.A. is an attitude of liberalism rather than a restrictive code. I was not trying to induce from my observations a few precepts that would grip future artists into yet another aesthetic lock step" (1989b:251). By the 1980s, pre-

Vernon Reid in the early days of the coalition. Photo by Lamar Thompson.

vailing "aesthetic lock step" held that black rock was not authentic. For Ellis, however, black rockers like Living Colour and Fishbone along with filmmakers Spike Lee and Reginald Hudlin, actor Eddie Murphy, and playwright George C. Wolfe were exemplary N.B.A.-ers. Their cultural productions confounded the racial and aesthetic categories dictated by dominant black and white cultural gatekeepers. A feeling of black pride engendered by the Black Arts and Black Power Movements and access to material, intellectual, and institutional resources informed the consciousness and actions of these postliberated artists. In the mid-1980s, they were beginning to meet, network, and create their own artistic sphere by forming institutions like the BRC and the Black Filmmakers Foundation (Ellis 1989a:236).[7] These postliberated artists were not interested in downplaying their blackness. Instead, they believed there was something special about being black and about blackness itself that was worth celebrating. This "something" is neither quantifiable nor easily defined; it is an elusive quality that one could recognize, but not necessarily articulate. It is the "something" that marks black identity, black aesthetics, and, possibly, black rock. For those who argue the nonsalience of race as a biological category and scrupulously avoid conflating biology and culture, this perspective may appear dangerously essentialist or biologically deterministic. The notion, however, that black Americans possess a special quality has long been present among black intellectuals, artists, and nationalists. Following Herder's notion of *volksgeist*, Du Bois (1989), for example, emphasized the spirit of black Americans and celebrated the ineffable quality, the soul, that emerged from the historical circumstances and creative genius of black people. Postliberated cultural producers follow in this tradition and "choose blackness," laying claim to the rich distinctiveness of black identity, black culture, and black style.

Tate and Ellis outline an aesthetic position that embraces work that affirms blackness and addresses black concerns but does not have to be exclusively black. This work may go beyond the boundaries that have been established for black art, while still addressing black issues and primarily black audiences. They applaud work informed by a commitment to black liberation whether that means freedom from political oppression or from ideological limitations. They acknowledge difference among African Americans, while taking seriously shared struggles and shared culture based on race. Tate, Ellis, and BRC members refuse to oversimplify what black art or black identity can mean. Straddling black cultural nationalism, intercultural inclusiveness, and expanded conceptualizations of blackness, their cultural productions reflect a consciousness that is neither assimilationist nor separatist. As these African Americans "choose blackness" they also redefine it, both critiquing and advancing the black cultural nationalism that influenced them (Lott 1989:245). The "mixing" of

Poet Tracie Morris, an exemplary practitioner of postliberated aesthetics, was a songwriter, playwright, essayist, and the Nuyorican Poets' Café 1993 Grand Slam Champion.

elements is not a rejection of blackness, but an acknowledgment of the breadth of their American experiences (cf. West 1990). Motivated by a similar set of concerns about discourses of essentialism in discussions about black cultural production, Gilroy acknowledges "the syncretic complexity of black expressive culture" and refuses ahistorical conceptions of black cultural productions that assume the existence of an unchanging, essential black core (1991b:126). Instead, he applies Amiri Baraka's concept of "the changing same," insisting that if there is anything approximating an essence in black music (and by extension black culture), it is the ability to change while also maintaining conceptual links to facets of its past (126) (cf. Baraka 1967). Writing about Living Colour, Lisa Jones, another member of the post-liberated generation, makes a similar observation: "Living Colour are not some bald-headed stepchild that the Black Rock Coalition left on the rock establishment's doorstep one glory day in 1988, but offspring born of many years of artistic activity and political struggle by African Americans—not a new black aesthetic, but part of a continuum old as the African presence here in America" (1990:49). Assumptions about the relationship between art and authenticity, the enduring significance of race, and the persistence of racism have long informed black cultural production. Postliberated generation artists respond to these challenges, incorporating new influences, rejecting outmoded assumptions, and preserving still-valued ideas.

BLACK ROCK SOUND AND STYLE

BRC members do not claim to have invented black rock. On the contrary, they recognize that the genre predates the BRC and view their decision to adopt the term "black rock" as a way to carry on a legacy. Commenting on the organization's name, Marque Gilmore, a drummer and a long-time member, told me, "Rock is the freedom to express yourself musically and black is who we are. . . . Just by saying 'black' and 'rock' together is to challenge someone else's notion." Members liked to point out that the name Black Rock Coalition contained both a redundancy and an oxymoron. Rock music was originated by black people so having to define the genre as black ought to have been unnecessary, but most listeners had lost sight of rock's black roots. When I asked Vernon Reid about the organization's name, he recalled:

> That was a trip. . . . I wanted people to think about black—what it
> means to be black—and think about rock 'n' roll music and why

is it that the two of them are not supposed to be together. . . . But "black rock" was all about being provocative. Because "rock" meant "white" and "black" meant, you know . . . whatever was playing in New York on [radio station] WBLS at that time. Which . . . actually speaks to that whole problem of identity anyway.

The category "black rock" makes an external claim, telling the outside world that black people do play rock. "Black rock" also refers to the type of musical production I discuss in this section.

Following contemporary rock tradition, the guitar is the central instrument within the BRC. Jimi Hendrix is the most obvious BRC forebear chiefly because of the intersection of his musical and racial identities. The individuality that characterized his guitar playing— inventive use of distortion, effects, and volume along with his creative songwriting and soloing—is an inspiration to BRC members. Led Zeppelin, the white English rockers who carried on Hendrix's blues-inflected psychedelia, are also a palpable influence. In addition to adapting the vocal and guitar stylings that mark Zeppelin and heavy metal—in particular the high volume and intensity of the playing —BRC bands built on Zeppelin's characteristic rhythmic structure. One BRC member pointed out to me that Zeppelin's John Bonham was "a funky drummer" and his thunderous (some would say plodding) style resonated in the sound of many BRC bands. George Clinton's space-age funk bands Parliament and Funkadelic, known for their hard-rocking, guitar-heavy jams and jubilant merging of post-Hendrix hard rock with James Brown funk, are also key musical and spiritual influences. In a *Vibe* magazine interview, George Clinton explained the genesis of P-Funk to Vernon Reid. "We saw Cream and Vanilla Fudge and all them take the music that my mother liked, flip it around and make it loud and it became cool. We realized that blues was the key to that music. We just speeded blues up and called it "funk" 'cause we knew it was a bad word to a lot of people" (Clinton quoted in Reid 1993:45–46). BRC bands also take inspiration from performers like Sly and the Family Stone, War, Santana, Labelle, the Isley Brothers, Sonny Sharrock, Muddy Waters, Miles Davis, Bob Marley, and Bad Brains, artists who are associated with funk, jazz, blues, reggae, and punk. BRC bands express their voice and vision by combining genres that exist side by side historically, but that have not always come together musically. Mining the rich history of black music while also tapping into nonblack popular music forms are important parts of the BRC aesthetic.

Songs by New York and Los Angeles bands covered a broad spectrum of lyrical content, providing commentaries on topics like consumerism, sexuality, identity, racism, and romance. Members often mentioned a desire to address social and political themes. This impulse is likely connected to an early concern that industry executives were discouraging black musicians from pursuing "serious" material in their lyrics. Tate noted, "When people in this organization take their tapes to record companies, all they hear is that people don't want to hear about apartheid or police brutality on the dance floor, that it's too intelligent for black people. And that's from black people in the business" (Tate quoted in Himes 1987:D8). BRC members followed the tradition of Stevie Wonder, James Brown, Sly Stone, and George Clinton, all of whom mixed social commentary with rhythmic proficiency. Guitarist Michael Hill, a longtime BRC member and leader of Michael Hill's Blues Mob, talked to me about his songwriting in a way that exemplified this awareness:

> The songs have come from a lot of different places and, ultimately, I make an effort to include things in addition to romance. . . . My parents were always cognizant of and made *us* cognizant of the Civil Rights Movement and Martin Luther King Jr. and we had a *Black Heritage Encyclopedia* and that kind of stuff so I think that's the foundation . . . and the music that I've loved in terms of music that's spoken to me—well, like Bob Marley or "What's Goin' On" and Marvin Gaye, Curtis Mayfield, "Superfly," a whole bunch of stuff he's written—really talks about different aspects of life. . . . I see it in terms of literature and poetry and theatre—and in none of those arts do people just talk about romance, so I don't see any reason for our music to just deal with romance either. I mean, romance is a universal thing because everybody has to deal with it . . . but at the same time . . . life is really rich and varied and colorful, so I think there's room.

The cultural critique BRC members value is evident in song titles, like "Don't Just Say Peace" by Eye & I; "Hard Blues for Hard Times" by Michael Hill's Blues Mob; "No Country" by Civil Rite; "American Hunger/Mother Is a Skinhead Lover" by Women In Love; "Plantation Radio" by the Family Stand; "Soul on Ice" by Me'Shell NdegéOcello; and "Fight the Fight" by Living Colour.

Style, image, and attitude are extremely important parts of the popular music package and BRC bands consequently expressed black rock aesthetics through the ways they performed. Among members, there is a general expectation that bands should exhibit deep music knowledge and acknowledge significant musical precursors through a kind of musical signifying. Players with serious "chops," that is, formidable technical ability, were especially appreciated. For the most part, band members could keep time, handle mid-song time signature changes, and play through song structures that are more complicated than the simple three-chord, 4/4 time rock 'n' roll standard. Typical for coalition bands was a mix between the sartorial nonchalance that led to jeans and T-shirts being a common onstage uniform and the performative intensity that characterized the ways musicians played their instruments. For example, a guitarist might lean into a solo with eyes closed, body rocking, head nodding, and mouth wrenching while squeezing out a lead. Here, the show was not in intricate choreography, matching outfits, or space age costumes, but in the bodily gestures — sometimes laid back, sometimes ecstatically frenetic — that accompanied musical production. Vocal styles included screams, scats, and melodic singing that projected emotional intensity or cool reserve. R&B inflections were by no means absent (and often were enthusiastically received), but there were also punk, folk, and heavy metal vocals that were not as "audibly black."

I now turn to a discussion of some of the BRC acts that were popular among members and local audiences at the time of my research in the mid-1990s, in order to bring into relief the musical qualities that defined black rock aesthetics. As a researcher, I paid attention when various members extolled the virtues of favorite musicians and when they dismissed genres or artists. Not every BRC band appealed to every BRC member, but member comments and presence at live performances indicated a consensus that certain bands were exemplary black rockers. I focus on three such acts: New York's Screaming Headless Torsos, the Los Angeles band Civil Rite, and Me'Shell NdegéOcello, who started in New York and developed a national following after the release of her first recording.

Screaming Headless Torsos
Now, back to the Saturday night at the Fez that I referred to at the beginning of the chapter. I listened to the Screaming Headless Torsos that evening with Pete and Roger, members of two long-lived BRC bands. Their comments exemplify some of the ways BRC members approach black rock aesthetics. Once the music got underway, it was clear that the Torsos were in top form. Dean was in excellent voice; the rhythm section of JoJo Meyer on drums, Fima Ephron on bass, and

Daniel Sadownick on percussion was tight; and David "Fuze" Fiuczynski's guitar improvisations were typically inventive. In the midst of a solo he tripped onto an old cartoon theme song. "Flintstones!" Pete exclaimed, rocking to Fuze's playful riffs. At the end of the song, Pete pronounced, "He's the Son of Sonny. Son of 'Rock." He slapped hands with Roger who nodded his approval of Pete's connection between Fuze and jazz guitarist Sonny Sharrock, a musician who was well respected among BRC members. Sharrock's sudden death in May 1994 occurred shortly before he was scheduled to appear as part of New York's Central Park Summerstage concert series. Following a brief sequence of negotiations with the program organizers, BRC members were able to take over the performance. They turned the show into a Sonny Sharrock memorial featuring Bernie Worrell on keyboards, Vernon Reid and Kelvyn Bell on guitars, T. M. Stevens on bass, Cynthia Blackman from Lenny Kravitz's band on drums, and Dean Bowman on vocals. By invoking Sharrock's name in relation to Fuze, Pete was indicating the aesthetic links between his cohort and an earlier generation of black musicians.

After the Torsos had packed up and left for their next gig, Roger and Pete expressed their respect for the band.

"Dean Bowman's my hero," Pete proclaimed.

"Amazing set," Roger observed.

"The worst mistake our band ever made," Pete recalled, "was going on after the Torsos. We had them open for us. Thought we were doing them a favor and it was like—The audience was so blown away by them that it took us four songs to get them into our show."

Roger told me he loved Fuze's guitar style: the virtuoso arpeggios, the fretted and fretless chord progressions, the wry jazz references, his ability to improvise, and his willingness to bring together punk, European art music, and free jazz in his compositions. But it was, he pointed out, an approach that differed from his own. This led us to speculate about how Fuze viewed the music their own bands played.

"Oh, he's a snob," Roger assured me. "He probably thinks of someone like me as a guitar owner."

I must have looked puzzled.

"You know," he clarified, "not a guitarist, just someone who has a guitar. There's this difference between being schooled and having chops like Fuze—he went to a music school—and being like me, just self-taught." Roger explained that his playing was not based in jazz the way Fuze's was. "Fuze wants to move toward rock, but his head is in jazz. I think it kind of annoys him that someone like me, some-

David "Fuze" Fiuczynski (left) and Dean Bowman of the Screaming Headless Torsos. Photo by Lian Amber.

one who's unschooled, can get to some of the avant-garde style that he does in his playing."

"You know," Pete interjected, "I don't even think Fuze would like what you play."

"Fuze hates everything," Roger said laughing.

"But it's okay for him and David Gilmore [a black jazz guitarist with tangential links to the BRC through his brother, Marque] to be snobs because they're so good," Pete noted.

"All that's cool," Roger said, "but I have this thing that sometimes all that technical perfection—it doesn't get to the emotions."

"Like it's kind of cold?" I asked.

"Yeah," Roger nodded. "You know, the guitarist in your band," he turned to Pete, "is great. He's not just a 'guitar owner.' But he's not trained."

"Thank you!" Pete leaned forward, his intensity growing. "Thank you. But you see, some are not willing to give him props for playing well."

"That's jealousy," Roger said sagely.

"And it makes him insecure," Pete added. "He won't turn up his amp."

"Well, it's true with all musicians," Roger said. "Your personality comes out in your approach. So if he's insecure, or shy, he's going to turn it down."

"Of course, as the singer," Pete said, "I don't want him to get too loud."

"No, he should really turn it up," Roger, the guitarist, insisted.

Negotiating rock, funk, and jazz influences on musical and vocal style and favoring sloppy emotion or precise technique are part of an ongoing conversation within the coalition, carried out in their musical productions and in their discussions. Some of the observations Pete and Roger made about the Torsos were prescient. The Torsos's eponymous album, released in May 1995, about seven months after the conversation, was in many ways a "musician's album," a brainy offering of technical prowess that mixed jazz, rock, punk, rap, heavy metal, and Caribbean rhythms. Dean, identified in the album credits as the "vox populi," exemplifies the band's fluidity. His singing recalls jazz vocalists like Nina Simone and Leon Thomas, but he is just as adept at sliding into a heavy metal growl. The band located itself in the black rock tradition of genre blending. This was always evident in the music they played and often clear in the words Dean sang. For example, Fuze's lyrics for "Smile in a Wave (Theme from Jack Johnson)" refer to other black rock bands, Dean sings:

Give me some 'Colour,
give me some 'Bone,
give me relief or leave me alone,
give me some Boots',
give me some 'Brains,
got nothing to lose and all to gain.

Here, in short order, is the naming and claiming of four black rock dynasties: Living Colour, the band that launched the BRC with Vernon Reid's jazz and metal infused guitar virtuosity; Fishbone, the long-lived Los Angeles-based mavericks who have provided a frenetic mix of ska, punk, and funk for more than twenty years; Bootsy Collins, the deeply funky bass player who worked briefly with James Brown before joining Parliament-Funkadelic and helping to release their cosmic slop; and Bad Brains, leaders of D.C.'s early 1980s hardcore punk movement who meshed punk thrash and reggae groove to produce a unique expression of Jah love and righteous anger. The song's celebration of black rock includes a reference to Jimi Hendrix—"Next thing to dark blue is a deep purple haze"—and features a refrain that proclaims a refusal to produce "a shackled down music that's nothing but hype." In many ways this is a quintessential black rock song, characterized by a verbally stated desire and musically enacted impulse to advance the form.

Fiuczynski had done studio work and toured with jazz artists like Ronald Shannon Jackson's Decoding Society (as had Vernon Reid), and in 1994 he recorded an instrumental album with keyboard player John Medeski under the name Lunar Crush. These were jazz-rooted projects. The Torsos was a way for him to delve into rock, punk, and funk complete with nods to the likes of German art rock diva Nina Hagen and the French composer Oliver Messiaen who taught Pierre Boulez and Karlheinz Stokhausen. In the Torsos's music, references to Miles Davis's late 1950s recordings and complicated time signature changes that indicated a connection to jazz came alongside the guitar pyrotechnics associated with Jimi Hendrix and vocals extending from traditional crooning to eccentric wails. Screaming Headless Torsos took pleasure in the densely layered musical references. There was also, I believe, a bit of showing off involved, as if to say, "Yeah, we know all of this shit, now listen to what we can do with it."

New York members supported the Torsos before the band released its CD and continued to do so in spite of the band's lack of stateside commercial success. Some music critics were also impressed. In June 1994 Fiuczynski had been singled out in a *Guitar Player* magazine survey of young guitarists to look out for. In February 1996, following the release of the Torsos's first album, *Musician* magazine named the Screaming Headless Torsos one of the "Ten Bands You Need To Hear"; Medeski, Martin, and Wood; Tricky; and Radiohead were also cited. The band did well overseas. VideoArtsMusic, a Japanese label, released the Torsos's second album, *Screaming Headless Torsos Live*, in response to the brisk sales of the band's first release in Japan. Fiuczynski and the Torsos have toured in Europe and Japan where musical boundaries are less rigid. Overseas and among the black rock cognoscenti, the kind of musical precocity and diversity that the Torsos embodied were valued.

Civil Rite

Los Angeles BRC member band Civil Rite had a dedicated following that turned out for the band's exhilarating live sets. These fans were the chief audience for the band's 1995 self-produced, self-distributed CD *Corporate Dick*. In the late 1980s and early 1990s, L.A. guitarist Torrell "Tori" Ruffin made his living as a studio musician and

Civil Rite as they were following a personnel change after the release of *Corporate Dick*. From left, Torrell Ruffin (guitar and vocals), Satnam S. Ramgortra (drums), Jai U. Dillon (bass and vocals).

sideman, and his work included backing up musical guests on the *Arsenio Hall Show*. During this period, he also focused on Civil Rite, his all-black rock band that featured Anthony Johnson on drums, Carl "Spooky" Young on bass, and J. J. Brown and Ruffin on guitars and vocals. Echoing the band name's dual invocation of the Civil Rights Movement and cultural ritual, the band's lyrics delved into social concerns while also celebrating life beyond the political. The mid-tempo rocker "No Country," for example, probes the question of black citizenship, asking how it is possible for a black man to feel he belongs in a country that has always excluded members of his race. "Billie Ann" is a loving, jazz-inflected tribute to Ruffin's mother. The band also delighted in diving headfirst into the ludic tendencies of 1970s funk forebears like the Ohio Players, the Gap Band, and Parliament-Funkadelic as well as the in-your-face attitude of punk. This is clear in the CD title, a slap at mainstream music industry professionals underscored by the cover art, an anthropomorphic cartoon penis wearing a tie and a frown. Like George Clinton before them, Civil Rite used the rude as an irreverent tool for cultural critique and social observation. P-Funk songs like "One Nation Under a Groove,"

"Free Your Mind (and Your Ass Will Follow"), and "Think, It Ain't Illegal Yet" mix public and personal politics. Playful and sometimes puerile, P-Funk tunes provided irresistible dance rhythms and clever lyrics that celebrated the body and the bawdy. Throughout their career, they have twisted the genre name funk into *almost* familiar phrases like "funk you up." P-Funk's music is accompanied by performance practices that include the band members' outrageous (especially for men), Vegas-gone-psychedelic costumes: wild patterns, glitter and sequins, feathered headdresses, long blond wigs, oversized hats, and Bootsy Collins's enormous, star-shaped sunglasses. Probably the most well-known element was the onstage landing of the P-Funk Mothership.[8]

Following in the tradition, Civil Rite's CD includes songs mixing social criticism and flippant fun. "Big Ol' Bitch," for example, seems to be a politically incorrect romp and a raucous crowd pleaser that delves into the dozens.[9] Trading verses, vocalists J. J. Brown and Ruffin try to top one another in their exaggerated depictions of the overweight woman each claims to love:

I went to McDonald's
And dropped to my knees
That bitch ordered everything
But "come back, please"

She weighs a lot
300 plus
and when she puts on yellow
you might think she's a bus

Tori told me, with some resignation, that some fans gave the band a lot of heat for the lyrics because of the unsporting use of the term "bitch" and the misogyny it represents. Aware of its potential for stirring controversy (as well as elation) at some live performances, the song includes a spoken word explanation. Near the end of the song, Ruffin interrupts his singing to state for the record who he has been talking about:

Now, this is not about your Aunt Hazel.
It's not about your big sister Bertha.
It's about America. Reaganomics, homelessness, AIDS . . .
It's about control . . . Control all the borders, border lines, Texas,
      Florida, California.
I'm going to stay here. This is my land, just like it's yours.

I was intrigued by Tori's concern about clarifying the song's meaning. Whether or not the original intention when writing the song was to attack the consumerist gluttony of the mainstream United States and the social policies that protect it, by the time Civil Rite committed the song to compact disc, they were framing it that way. Here, it is worth noting that there is pressure for a certain (but unspecified) degree of respectability in the BRC. In 1987, some New York members were concerned with member band 24–7 Spyz whose onstage antics included play with a blow-up sex doll. Irritated by questions about the act, the lyrics, and a feeling of being shut out of opportunities in the organization because their imagery crossed the bounds of what some influential members saw as propriety, 24–7 Spyz quit the organization. Reflecting on the question of image when talking to me about his band Women in Love, Greg Tate commented that within the BRC, sexuality remained a taboo subject. Indeed, an emphasis on a "politics of respectability" (Higginbotham 1993) that has shaped black middle-class social protest may have played a role in BRC member band choices about self-presentation.

In contrast, rudeness directed at the music industry required no justification or apology. In the song "Corporate Dick," Civil Rite revels in a foul-mouthed attack on music industry decision makers who determine the fate of musicians' careers:

Mr A&R publicity
You wanna fuck me?
But you can't find middle C
On the piano, on the piano

The words in the verses come fast and furious in the tradition of hard-core punk. The tone of voice coupled with the driving blast of the music ensure that the listener gets the point—rage—even if he or she cannot catch all of the rapidly delivered lyrics.[10] The chorus brings a slower tempo, but there is no relief from the attack; instead, the vocalists repeat the words "corporate dick" and the confrontational line "Why don't you suck my—?" The question is not completed, but by alternating the two phrases, it is easy for listeners to get an idea of exactly what the executive is being invited to suck. This venting of anger against the music industry is serious fun for the band and its audience. In terms of tone, content, and style, it is the polar opposite of the radio friendly, easily digestible music that "corporate dicks" seek.

Civil Rite also comments on its seemingly contradictory racial and musical identity. "Black Assid," a song about the music the band plays, encompasses many elements of black rock. The respelling of acid underscores the double meaning of the title: a self-naming of the musical genre black acid rock (after acid rock, a heavy metal offshoot of the 1970s) and an invocation of the colloquialism "kiss my black ass," presumably directed at anyone who objects to the band's musical proclivities. Civil Rite launches into the song with a fast guitar riff celebrating the musical individuality that confuses listeners who expect a certain sound from black musicians. All of the band members sing the refrain:

> I've done nothing wrong
> I put my heart into my song
> And hear what you say
> Just like Frank
> I'm gonna do it my way

Civil Rite's way had little do with Sinatra's cool vocal style and everything to do with the unapologetic individuality that Sinatra proclaims in his version of "My Way." This push for artistic freedom and the desire to escape the limits that monolithic notions of black identity and black music place on black artists are embedded in this song and, generally, in the black rock aesthetic. Civil Rite toggles between "sounding black" and "sounding white" in terms of their linguistic and musical style and demonstrates a facility with both racial modalities. Even if the sound of the music and the vocals are not "audibly black," the humorous lyrics erase any doubts about the band's identity. The song's opening lines are:

> I am big and black
> And I'm intimidating you
> That's okay
> I intimidate me, too
> I am loved and pretty
> And I'm bothering you
> That's okay
> I bother me, too

With two verses and two choruses sung, the song shifts time, dropping into a funk rhythm that puts a heavy accent on "the one," the first beat of the measure. This continues for a few bars and then the song switches back to speed metal, giving Ruffin an opening for a guitar solo replete with rapid fire, screaming notes. The guitar remains in the foreground and then is accompanied by the funkily swinging rhythm section. These shifts from punk to funk, from "white" to "black" are repeated a few times, leading the band to sing the musical question, "Should I dance, should I dance or bang my head?" This lyric describes the position Civil Rite and other black rock bands occupy between funk and rock, black and white, dancing and headbanging. The sound of the music indicates that they refuse to choose between the poles.

Me'Shell NdegéOcello

Civil Rite's Tori Ruffin and Screaming Headless Torsos's David Fiuczynski both played with the final BRC artist I discuss, vocalist and bass player Me'Shell NdegéOcello (the CD sticker on her first album, *Plantation Lullabies*, advised that the pronunciation is "n-DAY-gay-ochello). Articles hailing her ascent routinely mentioned her BRC roots: Me'Shell had joined the coalition and played bass with Tate's Women in Love before going solo. She worked with a management team of BRC members Bill Toles (a former BRC Orchestra director) and Beverly Jenkins (the BRC executive director) and a band that featured a number of BRC-connected musicians. With the release of *Plantation Lullabies* in 1993, Me'Shell received national exposure and achieved critical and popular success. A multi-instrumentalist, NdegéOcello wrote, arranged, and coproduced the album. She drew on the black pop of the late sixties and early seventies and fused it with the hip-hop and black rock of the early 1990s. Her albums and live performances evoked the musical and lyrical textures associated with Marvin Gaye, Stevie Wonder, and Curtis Mayfield. The title and lyrics of "Digging You (Like an Old Soul Record)," for example, made clear the commitment to a previous decade's musical riches. She slipped in the Four Tops lyric "Ain't no woman like the one I got" and built her song around the soul classic's melodic structure.

A post–civil rights revisiting of the Black Power era, the songs on *Plantation Lullabies* displayed a lyrical preoccupation with the state of black America and an aesthetic concern with embracing black music traditions and connecting them to contemporary soul and rap. Her compositions used R&B, funk, rock, and jazz instrumentation and the energetic musicality of her band recalled that of Sly and the Family Stone whose melding of R&B and rock reverberates in many BRC bands. Larry Graham, the Family Stone's bass player, put the rhythm instrument into the musical foreground, laying down the irrepressibly funky groove for which the band was known. Me'Shell invoked and expanded that sound, inflecting it with lush musical arrange-

Me'Shell NdegéOcello gets down. Flier for party celebrating the release of *Plantation Lullabies* at the Supper Club in Manhattan.

ments that built a layered soundscape characterized by the interplay of in-the-pocket grooves and inspired guitar leads. At a time when most black pop was performed by vocal groups with no musicians in evidence, Me'Shell fronted a tightly rehearsed live band. Through her onstage role as bass player, occasional keyboard player, and band-leader, she carved out a position as instrumentalist usually denied to women in contemporary popular music. Me'Shell is a distinctive black female performer because in her singing she does not adhere to soul or gospel-derived style, the modes of vocal expression, one BRC member complained to me, expected of black women, even within the BRC. Exploiting the warmth of her alto voice, Me'Shell perfected an evocative talk-singing style reminiscent of Hendrix's flow. Finally, she also diverged from the mainstream in terms of visual presenta-tion. In the early 1990s, the dominant pop types were scruffy white male grunge rockers, the last vestiges of heavy metal hair bands, black rappers—gangsta and otherwise—and slickly styled black vocal pop artists. She wore close-fitting tank tops and baggy pants and kept her hair closely cropped. Me'Shell stood outside both black and white dominant expectations for female beauty, playing up an androgynous image and conveying an onstage presence that projected sensuality and charismatic cool.

As an unconventional songwriter taking on "controversial" subjects and an openly bisexual black woman musician, Me'Shell provided both musical and identity alternatives for her audience. The lyrics of *Plantation Lullabies* dealt with black community, black masculinity, and gender relations. To the dismay of some fans and critics, her focus was on heterosexual relationships rather than explicitly women-centered lyrics (NdegéOcello 1994). "Dred Loc" celebrates the physical charms of black men in an ode to the black countercultural hairstyle. Cooing seductively, she implores,

> Let me run my fingers through your dread locs
> And run them all over your body
> Until you holler "Stop"

Me'Shell's come-on frames the man's black beauty—his non-European looks and locks—as the essence of male attractiveness, the very reason she is singing the song. Continuing her problack sentiments in "Soul on Ice," she addresses black men who pursue white women and criticizes the "illusions of her virginal white beauty dancing in your head." Confronting the race-crossing offender, she observes, "You let the sisters go by," and asks, "Does your white woman go better with your Brooks Brothers suit?" Some white music critics argued that this song was an example of "reverse racism" (NdegéOcello 1994), but from the perspective of NdegéOcello, the frequency with which black men chose to date and marry white women represented a crisis that was worthy of comment and critique. In a more lighthearted cut, "If That Was Your Boyfriend (He Wasn't Last Night)," NdegéOcello turns the song's title into a playful boast. Her recitation of lyrics shifts between singing and rapping as when she delivers the singsong taunt, "Boyfriend, boyfriend. Yes, I had your boyfriend" and then provides the spoken word gloat:

> Now late at night he calls me on my telephone
> That's why when you call him all you get
> Is a busy busy tone

It was inevitable that Me'Shell would have to carry the weight of representation. Fans revered her because of her sound and image, and some felt it was her responsibility to speak for and represent lesbians and especially black lesbians. A black woman who was a professional musician complained to me that Me'Shell was not playing her instrument enough in her live performances. "She should be *stomping* on the bass. Not just up there singing," she insisted in disgust. "Everyone knows black women sing." Whether she intended it or not, Me'Shell had certain responsibilities as a black queer-identified woman and musician. At some level, she met these demands. The genre-defying aspect of her music was matched by her concern with attacking stereotypes. Her band had a provocative name: The Watermelon Philosophy. Furthermore, its shifting personnel always featured both genders and at least two races, an unusual feature during the still-segregated 1990s. The liner notes of *Plantation Lullabies,* the concert tour T-shirts, and the tour's "All Access" passes featured an emblem of an encircled, minstrel-style cartoon of a black face with a red diagonal line across it. The "No Wogs" symbol made a forceful point—no black stereotypes tolerated here—while using a still-disturbing image. Me'Shell NdegéOcello's insistence on pushing musical, ideological, and image boundaries, the difference of her voice and of what she said—both verbally and musically—and her magnetic stage presence attracted a dedicated multiracial fan base.

THIS IS BLACK ROCK

So what exactly is black rock? There are similarities among the three black rock acts I've just described, but they are by no means alike. In fact, in spite of their shared identity as black rockers, no two bands in the organization approached the musical materials in exactly the same way. There was no single Black Rock Coalition musical style, a point that many reviews of early New York BRC events acknowledged and subsequent recordings confirmed. "Hybrid" and "eclectic" were the frequently invoked terms used to discuss BRC bands' music. Much as I have done in the preceding discussion, reviewers referred to the "sprawling diversity," the "hyperkinetic, polyglot style," and the practice of "weaving elements of jazz, rhythm-and-blues, and fusion into an eclectic tapestry" to characterize BRC bands (Kot 1991; Sinclair 1991:18). From band to band, even from song to song, it was difficult to pinpoint a dominant style. Members were conscious of the aesthetics that shaped their black rock productions, but putting these aesthetics into words was difficult. Some said they preferred to let the music speak for itself, invoking a typical musician's position: "Anyone who likes good music will like the music my band plays."

One of the most helpful definitions of black rock that I collected came from guitarist Kelvyn Bell, a New York member who played with jazz saxophonist Arthur Blythe and Joseph Bowie's Defunkt, and also led his own band, Kelvynator. He discussed black rock in terms of funk:

> Funk put even more emphasis . . . on heavy rhythms [than R&B]. . . . It's all based on the power of the electric guitar and the overdrive and the distortion. When you get like wah wah wah [*he imitates a screaming guitar*], you play one note and it's waaaah. . . . When you use that kind of sound to create rhythm, especially extremely syncopated rhythm, everything's exaggerated because of the volume. . . . You play that rhythm with all the distortion on an electric guitar [and] it's going to be a much bigger, more powerful rhythm.

> So black rock to me is funk because funk is an easier way of talking about the whole spectrum of our music. Which is what we mean when we say black rock. It means heavy rhythm, it means heavy volume, heavy physicality to the music. . . . Funk really means an emphasis on the rhythms that are African-based, heavily African-based. And funk is a better term than black rock—personally, I find it. . . . White artists were free to take jazz and blues and whatever and use it in their music and to exploit and make money off of it whereas we were not. But when we do, that music that we come up with is the black rock art form. Like George Clinton. [Or] Earth, Wind & Fire. . . . James Brown [led] the ultimate funk band, a lot of heavy rhythm and it's rock 'n' roll without being diluted by the white standards, so to speak. James Brown is black rock. [He] is the classic example of where rock 'n' roll went when it stayed all black. It turned into funk.

Interestingly, Kelvyn's description of black rock might not have won approval in Los Angeles. There were marked regional differences between East Coast and West Coast bands. In New York, the music scene in the mid-1980s embraced avant-garde jazz, funk, and punk, and BRC members overlaid these styles onto their metal, fusion, and hard rock impulses, producing "funkier" sounds. In contrast, heavy metal dominated Los Angeles in the mid-1980s, and its sound took precedence in most BRC member music. Elaborating on these regional variations, Los Angeles Executive Director Beverly Milner explained:

> The L.A. bands get closer to "pure" rock, you know, "white boy rock." We like to bang our heads. There are always a lot of debates

about this within the L.A. BRC and between me . . . and others from the New York chapter. Some say that to be "black rock" means you have to incorporate some of the more obvious elements of "black music"—something soulful, something funky. Others say that anything produced by a black person is de facto black rock and, since blacks invented the music in the first place, anywhere we take it is "black" regardless of whether it incorporates "black" elements. I remember once we got into this pretty heated debate . . . and people were arguing both sides. Finally, I just said the main issue is the apartheid music industry and the fact that there's so little chance for recognition of blacks unless we limit ourselves to the "black" genres. I figure, we can have the argument among ourselves forever, but the real issue is getting attention and recognition.

The different meanings associated with the term black rock reveal the complexities of the relationship between aesthetics and racial politics. The "white boy rock" prevalent among West Coast BRC members is music whose black roots seem submerged. This is music that could "pass" for white but is named black rock because of the identity of the performers. Regardless of whether the music seems or sounds white, Beverly argues, the form is black because black people perform it. In contrast, East Coast BRC members were committed to the notion that there is something musically distinctive about black rock. The music is "black" not simply because black people play it, but because of its audible debt to forms that are still recognizably (or easily argued to be) black—the "something soulful, something funky" that Beverly referred to. Here, there was more of a burden of representation with black rock drawing on black music traditions. One example of the differences within the organization is the fact that some West Coast members felt that the BRC compilation *Blacker Than That*, produced by New York BRC members, "didn't rock hard enough." The question of whether black rock had to "sound black" was one that many took seriously, but that the organization had not resolved. In the end, the redundant oxymoron black rock operated in contradictory ways, with "black" serving as an unambiguous adjective describing racial identity *and* as a complex signifier conveying cultural values. The different perspectives shift the focus from the aesthetic to the political and generate the members' agreement that they should concentrate on exercising the freedom to create using whatever musical vocabulary they liked.

BRC members are demanding the right to rock on their own terms, however unusual these may seem. Here, they are making a very American claim to individual expressive freedom, but doing so under the auspices of a united organization. This viewpoint creates the conditions for an elastic aesthetic and a wide-ranging variety of BRC sounds. When commenting to me about BRC bands, Tate observed that musically people are not coming from the same place. "It's just people doing their own bugged out shit and not really worrying about what everyone else is thinking," he explained. "It takes a lot of arrogance and a lot of humility to do this. On the one hand, you're playing music that doesn't seem to make any sense and claiming, 'yeah, it's black'— and on the other hand pleading, 'we hope you like it.'" BRC members are seeking the freedom that rock, purportedly a safe space for expressing maverick ideas and mentioning the unmentionable, is supposed to offer. With no easily definable black rock sound, the primary issue for the BRC is to support the projects of African American musicians working in any form that is an alternative to the narrowly defined "black music" of urban radio, MTV, and BET. This enables the support of both blacks playing "white boy rock" and "black rock," because the mainstream music industry discourages *both* practices. The breadth of aesthetic and political meanings associated with black rock demonstrates the ways concern about artistic content and awareness of social context influence musical production. Aesthetics can be political; politics and the social climate can shape artistic choices.

And black rock can be many different things—an updated blues aesthetic, the next, logical progression of seventies funk, Jimi Hendrix-y jazz, or Miles Davis-y rock. The arguments about what black rock is or should be and the attempts to define it through examples of favorite past records or favorite current bands have gone on since the organization formed, and a precise, aesthetically based definition is elusive. As a politicized cultural practice and as a concept meant to undermine commonsense racial ideologies, however, a definition of "black rock" is a bit easier. In a BRC newsletter column, East Coast Executive Director Beverly Jenkins explained the allegiance to the name "black rock" even though bands are tapping into so many other styles in their work. "'Rock' according to [the] BRC is the umbrella term for all the musical forms we have created, that we are continually being denied recognition and benefits. 'Rock' will continue to be used in the BRC's name as a reminder to all that we must protect our art, keep claims on it and never allow what happened to Blacks and rock 'n' roll to happen to any of our art again" (BRC 1993a:1).

Articulating the mission of the BRC in the same newsletter, National President Bruce Mack stated:

> We exist to assist Black musical artists of a free mind, and to broaden the minds of others with what "Black" music was, is, or could be. We are not asking to be told who we are, what we do, or where we're going. This is information that comes from within our "Black" souls whether we know it or not. By understanding this, one realizes that "Black Rock" is a state of mind. The state of mind is what creates the sound we produce individually. (BRC 1993a:1)

Blackness, here, is a slippery signifier. It can mark who we are—an unconscious state "from within our black souls whether we know it or not"—but it is also who BRC members create themselves to be: free-minded artists who go beyond the practices they are pressured to assume. In this regard, there is something special about blackness that cannot be relinquished and something valuable about black culture that must be addressed. These assumptions are rooted in black cultural nationalist concepts of art and identity, but expand in the post-civil rights era to proclaim the importance of supporting the total expressive freedom of black musicians. Less an aesthetic of a prescribed set of sounds, the black rock aesthetic is the freedom to create. The BRC's activities provided a public space for these explorations, brought together an audience to support the work, and enabled BRC members to articulate who they were as postliberated African Americans. Commenting on the contemporary conditions of black cultural production, Tate observed, "On the downlow, every creative black intellect derives pleasure from blackness as a realm of both burden and infinite possibility. Out of the pain comes the will to Black Power, an invitation to join a historic circle of creators, and a mechanism to confront the racist forces mounted from birth against your expansion and evolution as an individual" (1994b:113). As a researcher, dealing with this realm of burden and possibility has been crucial to approaching the Black Rock Coalition as an artistic and social phenomenon. To appreciate black rock in terms that make sense to most BRC members requires working at the provocative intersection of text and context, of aesthetic pleasure and cultural activism, and of culture and race.

SIX

LIVING COLORED IN THE MUSIC INDUSTRY

I got to see a little more of the inner workings of the record company and I learned a lot in terms of how things are done and I got a chance to see just the politics of the whole thing. Music is very political and that was the one thing I thought that wasn't that way, you know. Because I thought it was freedom. But it's just—it's a business. It's a business and it's political just like any other business. Politics that are really rough.—ANDRE, BRC BANDLEADER AND GUITARIST

IN THE FIELD: LIVING COLOUR LIVE

On Veteran's Day 1993 in New York City, the marquee of the Academy reads "Living Colour" on the first line, "Candlebox" on the second line, and "Sold Out" on the third line. Turning the corner onto 43rd Street, I start encountering scalpers making their offers: "Need Living Colour tickets?" I approach one, a youngish black guy stationed less than half a block from the venue. "How much?" I ask him. "Well, some guys are asking $75," he begins. He doesn't name a price right away but adds, "The guys asking seventy-five, well, some of them are smoking crack." He explains that he's just trying to unload before the show starts and offers me a chance to bid on the ticket. I tell him I already have one (face value $20) and explain that I was just curious. Before he loses interest, I ask him, "Are you going to the show?" He says, "No," and then does a double take. "Are you?" he asks. "Yeah," I say. "Do you *like* them?" he asks. His voice has a puzzled tone. "Yeah," I say again, and go up the street and into the club.

The Academy has hung onto the neoclassical ornamentation of

its ballroom past. The elegant columns and ornate balconies clash extravagantly with tonight's performances by Living Colour, decibel-shattering black rockers, and Candlebox, a white band inspired by the Seattle sound. There are a number of black folks in the crowd, mostly men but a considerable number of women, and more black people than I see at most rock shows I go to. Once the break following Candlebox's set ends, the house lights dim, and a jazz sax solo comes over the sound system. Crowd members start cheering with anticipation as wafting smoke and red and gold lights fill the stage. The band members take their places and the applause and cheers intensify in response to the guitar chords, drum beats, and bass reverberations that launch the set. The band plays older songs like "Funny Vibe" and "Love Rears Its Ugly Head" as well as "Ignorance Is Bliss" and "Bi" from the new album, *Stain*. I'd heard from a few folks around the BRC that Epic had insisted that Living Colour hit the road again that fall. *Stain*, which they had promoted in late spring on a national tour with Bad Brains, had not been selling the way the label executives wanted. They felt further touring would give the record a boost.

The overall spectacle is impressive considering three-quarters of the band members stay relatively still throughout the set. Vernon is stage right, wearing bi-colored locks and a black T-shirt bearing a neck-to-hem image of Bugs Bunny's Martian. He plays most of his riffs and rhythms stationary, but once or twice he takes flight, whizzing across the stage. Sometimes he spins his head and lets his locks fly, turning himself into a swirling dervish. At stage left Doug is on bass, dreadlocks pulled back into a ponytail, wearing leather pants and a sleeveless T-shirt. Doug leaves a cigarette dangling from his lips for the better part of the show, and it crosses my mind that this might be a gimmick he picked up from Keith Richards during the time he spent playing bass with the Rolling Stones. But he looks so cool, it doesn't matter if it's an act. He lays down solid bass lines, often breaking them into fluid, melodic phrases, especially when he is featured on a couple of numbers. Upstage, center, and high up is Will at the drums. His short locks stand at attention on his head. When the band leaves the stage at the end of the set, he takes his time ambling off, pausing at the edge of his kit. He is rewarded with tremendous shouts of approval. Drumsticks raised in gloved hands, a headset strapped on, and a triumphant expression, he milks it for a moment and then exits. He's the first one back on for the encore and he plays us a long, killing solo, reminding us that drummers hold a band together. Jazz

Vernon Reid (left) and Corey Glover live and in Living Colour. Courtesy Mia Friday.

trained at the Berklee College of Music, Will has the ability to open up the rhythm creatively, to improvise, to depart from the strictures of 4/4 time into freer and freakier time signatures—keeping it funky and rocking hard.

And then there's Corey. His cropped and dyed locks are reddish and his stocky body is compressed into black and white spandex gear. During the set, Corey romps all over the stage, even leaning over its edges to grab fans' hands and make contact. He complements the finesse of his co-members with spasmodic bursts of energy and sustained emotion. Most of his movements and attitude project power and strength. He gives the audience something to look at and something to listen to. Corey sings and screams, gets bluesy, rocks out, and even has a couple of introspective moments. Living Colour ends the set with "Cult of Personality," their first and biggest hit, and Corey does his thing. Nearing the song's end, he dives from the stage into the crowd where the fans catch him and support his outstretched body, handing him around so he can traverse the room, before returning him to his rightful place on stage. Two forbiddingly large bouncers keep an eye on him, making sure that the crowd doesn't get so carried away that they carry him away.

Living Colour worked hard to earn their reputation as a phenomenal live band and are acting like they intend to keep it. The tenor of the set changes about halfway through when the band plays "Memories Can't Wait," an old Talking Heads tune that appeared on Living Colour's first album. Corey takes a gospel turn into a more churchified spirit for the song and Vernon's guitar offers up an evanescent, spiraling noise. The energy behind this number—both of the band and the audience—brings everyone to a higher level and that's where the rest of the show stays. Following "Memories," they play the Clash's "Should I Stay or Should I Go?" They take it funky on the verse and then break into a hardcore thrash on the choruses with Corey repeating the title super fast numerous times. He also inserts a loaded hesitation into the English punk rockers' original lyrics: "One day it's fine and next it's—" he holds up his hand in a dismissive gesture, rolls his eyes during the pause, and spits out the final word: "Black!" The foursome ends their encore with "Crosstown Traffic," their contribution to the 1993 compilation *Stone Free: A Tribute to Jimi Hendrix.* Corey, Vernon, and Doug sing the familiar "doo do do do do doo doo" that starts the song and the audience joins them. By the end of the number, the crowd is euphoric and Corey caps it by intoning "Welcome to the Living Colour Experience" at the song's end. Then he adds the words that echo over the sound system as the audience flows out of the theater: "This is your world."

THE POLITICS OF RACE IN THE RECORDING INDUSTRY

The politics of race are central to the development, production, and consumption of popular music in the United States. Put simply, recording industry decision making feeds and is fed by assumptions about racial identity and musical taste. In 1993 when I attended this concert, linking blacks with rock was unusual as the ticket scalper's response to my interest in Living Colour and the predominantly white composition of the crowd indicate. In this chapter, I examine some of the structural limitations and ideological barriers that black rockers confronted when they came onto the professional scene in the late 1980s. My purpose here is not to provide a history of black performers in the popular music industry. Instead, I discuss the ways race and racialization have circumscribed the creative and economic lives of black musicians and music professionals. The industry that Living Colour and other black rock bands were struggling to succeed in is, above all, a profit-centered enterprise developed to sell an artistic product (Frith 1981; Negus 1992, 1999). As I conducted my research, BRC members frequently reminded me, "The music business is not about music, it's about business."[1] Following their lead, I focus on the ways the music industry's very businesslike emphasis on profit is exacerbated by its very American problem with race. I refer to this aspect of the contemporary music industry as its "racialized political economy."[2] This is the convergence of economic, racial, and artistic ideologies and practices that have produced a business and creative environment in which African Americans occupy a subordinate position even as African American cultural productions serve as a central creative resource. Music industry executives and musicians work within and struggle against these constraints, occasionally changing but more often reproducing the industry's structures as they go about the business of making and selling music (Dornfeld 1998:13).

While a discussion of any black rock artist would illuminate the role of race in the music industry, I foreground Living Colour because the band achieved widespread critical, financial, and popular success and because it was bandleader Vernon Reid's frustration at not being able to get a major label record deal that galvanized the formation of the BRC.[3] As Living Colour rose into the ranks of best-selling rock artists, the band's members continued their critiques of racism in interviews and in song lyrics, even as they eluded the worst racial barriers. Reid founded Living Colour in 1983 as a rock outlet for him to pursue when he wasn't playing in Ronald Shannon Jackson's avant-garde jazz ensemble, the Decoding Society. The band was always "Vernon's Thing," right down to the anglophilic spelling of color, which may have been a nod to Reid's London birthplace or just a way to be different.[4] Living Colour went through several personnel changes before settling into the foursome of Reid on guitar, Will Calhoun on drums, Corey Glover on vocals, and Muzz Skillings on bass that recorded the 1988 debut album *Vivid* on Epic Records. Doug Wimbish joined the band after Skillings left in 1992. Living Colour offered the right balance of politically conscious lyrical content and rock 'n' roll flair. The band mined the post-Woodstock hard rock of the late 1960s and 1970s, fusing the styles of Hendrix and Zeppelin with doses of funk, fusion, punk, and metal to create a meaningful musical expression in the 1980s and 1990s. Arguably, it was Reid's guitar virtuosity that launched Living Colour and earned them respect as a serious rock band. Masterfully operating in the heavy metal tradition, he provided the requisite complicated, quick-noted solos while melding technical sophistication with sonic invention.[5] Building on Hendrix's psychedelic era adaptation of the blues, Living Colour used feedback, distortion, effects, and high volume to produce layers of arresting sounds and textures. Living Colour was a hard rock band, but it also drew on audibly black sources ranging from the words of Malcolm X to the heavy funk of James Brown. The four black men were playing music perceived as holding little interest to the mainstream black music market, and their race raised doubts that they could attract rock's predominantly white audience. As such, Living Colour was a complicated act and one that brought into relief the workings of race in the U.S. music industry.

British music critic Charles Shaar Murray has observed that "the central thrust of twentieth century American popular music [is] the need to separate black music (which, by and large, white Americans love) from black people (who, by and large, they don't)" (1991:86). Historically, aesthetic shifts and economic success in the music industry have resulted from the exploitation of black American creativity and the marginalization of black American people. Indeed, much of what has taken place in the music industry can be construed as an effort to solve the "problem" that black people presented without abandoning their appealing and profitable music. Like so many American institutions, the recording industry creates a separate and unequal place for African Americans. Black artists and executives work within a restricted range of creative possibilities, control fewer economic resources, and have limited decision-making power. Certainly, white executives and musicians face limits, but racially motivated patterns of discrimination have shaped every aspect of the production and distribution of the music black Americans have created from the 1920s to the present.[6]

Rock 'n' roll was supposed to be about freedom, but by the 1980s black rockers confronted restrictions rooted in the contradictory ways the music industry has treated African American performers. Like most celebratory American myths, the tale of rock 'n' roll plays more smoothly if the presence of racism is pushed aside, but racism is part of the story. A prime example of the complexities of race, rock 'n' roll embodies the cultural richness of the Great American Melting Pot and reveals the ways black Americans are economically and socially marginalized from the U.S. mainstream in spite of being a defining influence on it. In the period after World War II, performers blended blues, hillbilly music, jazz, and gospel to produce rhythm and blues, rockabilly, and eventually rock 'n' roll. These forms were associated with poor blacks and poor whites, the bottom of the southern class and caste system. Black and white rock 'n' roll artists like Elvis Presley, Chuck Berry, Little Richard, Jerry Lee Lewis, and Bo Diddley made indelible contributions to the form. Still, as music industry historian

Reebee Garofalo cautions, this apparent integration should not override the fact that "most of the formative influences of rock 'n' roll as well as virtually all of its early innovators were African American" and that they "had to struggle for a less than proportionate market share of a musical form in which they predominated" (1993:229). Rock 'n' roll went a long way to knocking down social boundaries between black and white Americans. Still, alongside an extremely American process of miscegenation, the equally American practice of segregation was at work. A system of separate and unequal markets, music divisions, sales charts, and touring circuits sustained the music. Indeed, twenty years after the apex of the Civil Rights Movement, popular music production continued to occur in a racially segregated fashion, spurring the BRC into existence.

The dialectic of miscegenation and segregation surrounds the appropriation of black music by whites. Borrowing and mixing are normal aspects of musical development, but in the case of rock 'n' roll, white appropriation of black sound and style was devastating to many of the music's originators. Music producers and promoters recognized that it would be easier to sell white artists to a segregated, majority white nation. At the same time, bias against blacks encouraged and protected the use of unfair business practices that have always been a part of the American recording industry.[7] White and black were mixing at a significant cultural level, but racial hierarchy was still very much in effect. Overall, access and opportunities were better for white performers. Black performers struggled to get a fair chance and were confined to inferior contracts, resources, and opportunities. In the end, with their greater visibility and a growing white fan base, white artists took over rock 'n' roll. From ragtime to swing to rock 'n' roll, this cycle of black innovation and profitable white appropriation has been repeated in American musical history (Chapple and Garofalo 1977:246; cf. Baraka 1963). Black artists like Ike Turner, Fats Domino, Little Richard, Chuck Berry, and Bo Diddley developed rock 'n' roll in the 1950s, but by the late 1960s, only a handful of black rock artists—Sly Stone, Jimi Hendrix, and Arthur Lee of the band Love—were visible. By the time the BRC was founded in 1985, the white appropriation of rock was so complete that it was counterintuitive to imagine blacks playing rock at all. The interplay of miscegenation, segregation, and appropriation had so muted rock's blackness that black musicians had to insist that they had the right to rock.

In 1920, Mamie Smith became the first African American to make a commercial record. Her "Crazy Blues" on the Okeh label sold an astonishing 7,500 copies a week (Chapple and Garofalo 1977:2). Responding to the success of Smith and other black recording artists, record labels targeted the African American market with a product they called "race music." This category was "a separate and unequal counterpart to the white controlled major record labels" (231–33). After World War II, juke boxes, record stores, clubs, and *Billboard*'s sales charts remained segregated, but radio was undergoing a seismic shift. Newly specialized stations took greater risks, programming pop, hillbilly (later "country and western"), R&B, classical, and jazz shows according to their anticipated audience (Peterson and Berger 1990:148). Black R&B music, a staple of the nation's handful of stations with black-oriented programming since the mid-1940s, was beginning to get airplay on white stations and whites, especially white teenagers, were listening (George 1988:28).[8] Recordings on independent record labels supported by newly affluent black and white working-class consumers provided the soundtrack for the radio revolution. Indeed, urbanization and the war economy played a significant role in the emergence of rock 'n' roll. Rural southerners moved to cities to take advantage of high-paying defense production jobs; the result was a concentration of potential audiences with money to spend on music (Lipsitz 1990:116; cf. Gillett 1983). Memphis, Chicago, Detroit, New Orleans, and Los Angeles became critical crossroads for millions of blacks and whites from Texas, Mississippi, Louisiana, Tennessee, and Arkansas and for the music they preferred: southern forms like blues, rhythm and blues, and hillbilly music that major labels ignored.

Memphis-based Sam Phillips and his Sun Records label epitomize the new breed of white independent producers that recorded and distributed this music.[9] Phillips spent the early 1950s recording African American artists including B. B. King, Rufus Thomas, and Jackie Brenston and his Delta Cats (with chief Cat Ike Turner), whose 1951 song "Rocket 88" some consider the first rock 'n' roll record. Phillips recognized that the social climate was preventing talented black artists from breaking into the pop market. He surmised that the person capable of crossing over would have to be, as the now-legendary phrase goes, A White Man With the Negro Sound and the Negro Feel (Guralnick 1994:96). The story of the rise of Elvis Presley, the man

Publicity shot for *Time's Up*, the second Living Colour album. Photo by Michael Lavine.

most famously embodying this crucial combination, is well known: A poor white boy from Tupelo, Mississippi, migrates with his parents to the bustling musical metropolis of Memphis, Tennessee. He learns to sing and play guitar by imitating the spectrum of southern music he encounters on the radio and in the community. One day in 1954, Presley records a session that is uneventful except for his inspired rendition of "That's All Right, Mama," a song originally recorded by African American blues artist Arthur "Big Boy" Crudup. The rest is history. A tidy example of the simultaneity of miscegenation and segregation, Presley and the other Sun Records artists, by dint of their white skin, solved the problem of black people in black music.[10] They produced the appealing "Negro Sound and Negro Feel" while avoiding the baggage of actually being black.

Almost forty years after Presley's first recording, Living Colour weighed in with its take on the Elvis phenomenon. "Yo, Corey, man . . ." Vernon says, "I saw *Elvis* the other night." Thus begins "Elvis Is Dead," an irreverent read of Presley's position as the so-called King of Rock. Falling in the middle of *Time's Up*, the band's second album,

"Elvis Is Dead" swings on a funky James Brown beat, is punctuated by Glover's Brown-esque "give it to me's," features the saxophone of long-time Brown sideman Maceo Parker, and spotlights the glorious falsetto of Little Richard, the self-proclaimed Architect of Rock 'n' Roll. Together, these references allow Living Colour to acknowledge the black artists who shaped the evolution of rock 'n' roll, but who have not garnered the reverence that Presley does. Through lyrics like "Just imagine a rotting Elvis shopping for fresh fruit," the song assails the bizarre trend of Presley sightings that became common after the singer's death in 1977. The chorus is a single line sung repeatedly to drive home a simple point that irrational fans were ignoring: "Elvis is dead." In addition to asserting the fact of Presley's literal death, Living Colour was also concerned with undermining his position as king of rock and were engaging in musical regicide. A centerpiece of the song is Little Richard's spoken-word solo in which he states, "Presley was a good performer, on stage he was electrifying." Coming from one who was there, the line pays respect to Presley as an artist. The larger point, though, is that in an era that produced Ruth Brown, Etta James, Little Richard, LaVern Baker, Bo Diddley, and Chuck Berry— black pioneers with compelling onstage styles—Presley was not the only noteworthy rock 'n' roller; he simply had the advantage of whiteness. "A black man taught him how to sing," the lyrics observe, "and then he was crowned King." Many black Americans feel bitterness toward the white truck driver who benefited from the racist sleight of hand that made him king of a form created by African Americans. In the 1950s, black Americans could recognize that Presley borrowed his hip swivels and vocal delivery from black performers. In contrast, these styles were largely unknown to mainstream white audiences, and many took Presley to be their originator.

As Presley's stature rose, he eclipsed the blacks who preceded and influenced him. To add insult to injury, in 1957, a rumor circulating in black communities charged that Presley had said, "The only thing Negroes can do for me is buy my records and shine my shoes" (Guralnick 1994:426). Presley denied making the remark and *Jet*, the black news weekly, published an article assuring its readers that "to Elvis, people are people regardless of race, color or creed" (quoted in Guralnick 1994:426). Among many black Americans, however, the feeling remained that Presley was an ungrateful appropriator of black music. To represent the hype surrounding the rock 'n' roll star, Living Colour includes a litany of phrases spoken by male and female voices toward the end of the song. There's the "shine my shoes and buy my records" statement, exclamations like "Elvis is King" and "Elvis está muerto," and the sardonic announcement, "Elvis has left the building!" Living Colour's attack on Presley's iconic status is linked to the BRC's concern with centering the black American contribution to rock. In a related example of paying tribute to black rock forebears, in August 1987, on the ten-year anniversary of Presley's death, the BRC celebrated the music of Otis Blackwell in an event at Brooklyn's Prospect Park Bandshell. The show, "Otis Blackwell Meets the Black Rock Coalition Orchestra," featured BRC members and a performance by Blackwell, the African American who wrote Presley's hits "All Shook Up" and "Don't Be Cruel" as well as "Great Balls of Fire" and "Breathless" made famous by Jerry Lee Lewis. The BRC's tribute show and Living Colour's "Elvis Is Dead" respond to the prevalent appropriation of black music and marginalization of black artists, factors that motivated the formation of the BRC.

White appropriation of rock 'n' roll was possible in part because of the genre's murky definition. Some argue that rock 'n' roll is a distinct music form while others maintain that it is simply a marketing term for R&B. Originally, the term "rock 'n' roll" was black slang for sex. Cleveland disc jockey Alan Freed had applied the name, unfamiliar to his white listeners, to the rhythm and blues he played on his radio show. For many, this was not a benign change. Bo Diddley asserts, "R&B don't stand for nothing but rip-off and bullshit" (Diddley quoted in Murray 1991:86). Diddley observes that what he and Chuck Berry played was called rock 'n' roll until whites started playing it and then, suddenly, "*they* was rock 'n' roll and we were R&B" (Diddley quoted in Murray 1991:86). In the 1950s, claiming the name "rock 'n' roll" or being defined as R&B was more than a question of semantics. The black R&B market offered less money and fewer opportunities for exposure. Technology also shaped economic success. Music for the black market continued to be released on 78 rpm records as late as 1957. Meanwhile, rock 'n' roll singles were pressed on 45 rpm records. This new format required different playback equipment and, as radio stations and juke boxes changed over to the new apparatus, the music and musicians consigned to 78s were effectively left behind (Chapple and Garofalo 1977:241). In spite of segregation, there were black rock 'n' rollers who were successful on both the pop and R&B charts; they appeared on television, toured the United States, and were featured in the spate of rock 'n' roll movies like *The Girl Can't Help It* (1956) that were produced during the mid-1950s. Fats Domino blended country-style vocals with a boogie-woogie sound in a number of now-classic early rock 'n' roll hits. Little Richard attracted a black and white teenage audience using exuberant vocals and an irresistible high camp performance style. Bo Diddley's signature guitar rhythms have appeared in numerous rock songs and are such a genre staple that they are identified as "the Bo Diddley beat." Chuck Berry, renowned for songs featuring teen culture lyrics and what music critic Robert Palmer described as "country-and-western inflected light blues melodies" and "twangy electric guitar shuffle rhythms" (Palmer 1995:31), provided the backbone of a rock aesthetic for the next generation. Commenting on his career, Chapple and Garofalo assert that "Berry had only one problem: he was black. But for that he would have probably rivaled Elvis Presley as king of the fifties rock 'n' rollers" (1977:37). Generally speaking, artistic innovation could not override segregation. African American artists experienced racism in bookings, promotion, and salaries. Independent labels that released R&B recordings grossed over $15 million in 1952, but almost all of the money went to executives (Eliot 1989:41). Typically, the artists were paid between $5 and $10 (and, if they were lucky, a case or two of whiskey) for a recording. They did not receive royalties, nor did they own their publishing rights; these were potential revenue streams that would have ensured their economic success over many years (Eliot 1989:41).[11]

Rock 'n' roll's blackness and its growing popularity among white teens rankled white social conservatives who attacked the genre. The out-of-control onstage personae of Jerry Lee Lewis and Elvis Presley and images of white teenage girls kissing Little Richard's cheeks or swooning before Chuck Berry confirmed fears that rock 'n' roll promoted "race-mixing." The moral panic around rock 'n' roll—the threat of juvenile delinquency, unleashed sexuality, and the loss of good American values—stemmed from a fear of African American culture. The attack that had a longer-lasting effect on rock 'n' roll and the place of African Americans in the genre, however, came from within the recording industry itself. Initially, major label executives ignored rock 'n' roll, assuming it was just a passing fad, but black music's grip on consumer dollars persisted and the majors realized they had to find a way to capitalize on it to avoid losing ground in the marketplace. Rather than signing black artists, label executives had their contracted white pop artists record songs originated by black performers on independent labels (Chapple and Garofalo 1977:46). White pop covers were released at the same time as the original independent label versions, but by promoting these covers through their

superior national distribution networks, the majors were able to maxi-
mize sales and exposure (238). In these covers, what was viewed as
black—prominent rhythm, shouted vocals, risqué lyrics, and sexuality—was minimized. Covers excluded blacks from the most lucra-
tive aspects of the growing rock 'n' roll market and laid the groundwork for the redefinition of rock 'n' roll as a white cultural production.
At first, white teens purchased the covers, but they soon were able to
discern the difference between the originals and the remakes. In 1956,
for example, Little Richard's version of "Long Tall Sally" outsold Pat
Boone's (Shaw 1974:126). Denied success in the market by discrimi-
nating consumers, the majors took another approach. "Working in
tandem with radio station chains, [major labels] encouraged smaller
radio playlists (Top 40 radio) which had built-in advantages for the big
companies with their established connections to station managers. . . .
When Top 40 radio came in, much of the rougher, wilder, blacker,
and more working-class music disappeared from the radio" (Lipsitz
1990:124). Lipsitz characterizes this as the "white washing of rock"
through which the sexual repression, racial separation, and class divisions that rock 'n' roll had been exploding were retrenched (126).
By the end of the decade, rock 'n' roll's major innovators had been
silenced: Elvis Presley was in the army, Jerry Lee Lewis was ostracized
by the press for marrying his fourteen-year-old cousin, Little Richard
had left the raucous secular scene for the ministry, and Chuck Berry
had been arrested on charges that he had violated the Mann Act.[12]
Racialization, marketing decisions, and fate set in motion the processes that forced the majority of African Americans into the margins,
even as the music they had pioneered became mainstream.

BRITISH INVASION AND JAGGER'S PERSUASION

The disappearance of prominent American rock 'n' rollers facilitated
the "British Invasion." Beginning with the Beatles who arrived in the
United States in person and on record in 1964, and continuing with
Gerry and the Pacemakers, the Rolling Stones, and the Animals, British bands began to appear on the American pop charts. Having devoted themselves to the collection and study of black American blues
records by Muddy Waters, Willie Dixon, Screamin' Jay Hawkins, Robert Johnson, and John Lee Hooker, these performers brought the
blues to white American audiences for the first time. The British
bands played covers and developed their own songwriting, mixing

black American music, rock 'n' roll attitude, and a postwar British sensibility. The Rolling Stones, who took their name from a Muddy Waters tune, were formed by Brian Jones, Keith Richards, and Mick Jagger in London in 1962 and are the longest-lived of these bands. Although the Stones are notorious for appropriating black American music, the band members have always talked openly about their debt to black musicians and often invited blues artists like Howlin' Wolf and R&B pioneers like Etta James to join them on television appearances and on tours, exposing their audience to these influential performers. It is not altogether surprising, then, that Stones vocalist Mick Jagger would play a role in advancing black rock.

Discussions of Living Colour in the press and within the BRC addressed the ironic and, for some BRC members, problematic way the band got its record deal. In the mid-1980s, Living Colour had a reputation as one of New York's best unsigned bands. After years of shopping Living Colour demos to record labels and two years as BRC president and spokesman, Vernon Reid finally got a break. Mick Jagger hired him to play on his solo album *Primitive Cool* and offered to finance and produce some demos for Living Colour. With one of rock's leading personalities in its corner, Living Colour obtained a recording contract. The band signed to Epic Records and recorded and released *Vivid* in 1988. In 1989, Living Colour joined the Stones on their 36-city "Steel Wheels" tour of the United States. While on the tour, MTV put the Living Colour single "Cult of Personality" into heavy rotation, a move that generated airplay on rock radio. Sales of *Vivid* soared, and the album peaked at number six on the U.S. charts and went double platinum after selling two million copies. Living Colour earned Grammy Awards in 1989 and 1990 for Best Hard Rock Performance and in 1991 was one of the bands to headline the first Lollapalooza summer music tour. This is the way Living Colour "blew up" —insider parlance for breaking into the mainstream. Good timing, the right connections, talent, and luck made Living Colour the kind of success story that the press loves to hype. The rise of Living Colour brought even more media attention to the BRC, attracted non–New York members, and laid the groundwork for opening the Los Angeles chapter.

That Living Colour got its deal in part through the support of a white English rock star who symbolizes the white appropriation of black culture was troubling to some members. One recalled that tensions emerged within the organization as they debated the situation:

GERARD: In the early stages when Living Colour got that offer, the BRC was split down the middle. I mean really split down the middle philosophically . . . fifty percent of the people felt, "Yo, that was fucked up. How are you going to talk about the Rolling Stones as racists in a BRC meeting in the early days." I mean quote unquote.

MAUREEN: Right.

GERARD: "And then, when Mick Jagger sees you play and he pays for a demo deal and whatever, whatever, whatever. I mean yes, we want you to get a deal; yes, we want to see you signed. But that's not the way to do it, because that reflects [on] the BRC. You represent us and that was misrepresenting us . . . [The BRC was] doing things, trying to do things on the level of racism in the industry, which is definitely what the BRC is about. And then [you] turn around and do that."

Then there was another half of the BRC that was like, "Yo, it's your band. This is your decision. You've got to get out there somehow. We know who you are; we know who the Rolling Stones are. So we know how you played it . . . Even if you sold out consciously — we still know how you played it and we're down with that because you've got to do what you've got to do." I think some of the older people in the BRC who had been around for just a little minute were kind of like supporting that decision. And a lot of the younger people who were just gung-ho and very much fired up about the BRC concept . . . were like — no, that wasn't right.

MAUREEN: So where were you?

GERARD: I was on the nah, that wasn't right side. And I stepped off for a few minutes. You know, it was just what I felt I had to do at that point . . . It just seemed weird.

Whether one reads Living Colour's alliance with Jagger as the calling in of a debt, the ultimate sellout, or a savvy manipulation of resources, it exemplifies the race and power dynamics of the music industry. Most disturbing for BRC members was the fact that a white star had to validate a black band before it could gain recognition. They believed that Living Colour and other black rockers deserved deals because of their talent and originality. Another concern, as Gerard stressed, was that the action of the band reflected on the integrity of the entire organization. Living Colour seemed to be capitulating to the fact that black power could not supersede white bias in the recording industry. If this was the case, what was the purpose of the BRC? In addition to exploiting the forces that the BRC set out to change and using a white man to get a foot in the door, Living Colour's path to success called into question the viability of the BRC's cultural politics. The industry had responded to the black rock band, not because of the BRC's astute analyses or Living Colour's exciting performances, but because of Jagger's enthusiasm. Still, members point out that although it took Jagger's involvement to make Epic executives take notice—and there was hesitation among some executives even *with* his support—Living Colour would not have been signed if they had not been a great band. Furthermore, there had been interest among some executives before Jagger stepped in. Jagger used his economic and cultural capital to give a crucial push to the career of musicians he believed in. His intervention highlights the dynamics of race, power, and appropriation in popular music production. Like so many white pop and rock musicians, Jagger built a successful career by adapting black music forms into a unique mode of expression. As a person who has depended on the unruly genre of rock 'n' roll for the soundtrack of her life, I am hardly opposed to this kind of musical crossbreeding. The problem is these creative processes occur in an industry context that gives white musicians high degrees of power, access, mobility, and respect while limiting black musicians—until a generous white supporter speaks on their behalf. BRC trio the Family Stand outlines these racial politics in their 1991 song "Plantation Radio":[13]

> Christopher Columbus, please discover me discover me
> Mr. Jagger, Mr. Simon, Mr. Sting if you're busy
> Please tell them that I'm happening
> So that they will believe
> I need a Christopher Columbus
> So I'll win a Grammy

Assailing the informal requirement that black artists be validated by a white spokesperson, the lyrics refer to the rock stars with the respectful term "Mr." to indicate a hierarchy that keeps blacks in an inferior position. Interestingly, this attack came from within. The Family Stand was one of the BRC bands signed in the wake of Living Colour's success, and Vernon Reid is a featured soloist on several songs on *Moon in Scorpio*, the 1991 album on which "Plantation Radio" appears. Is he endorsing the Family Stand's view, critiquing his own path to stardom? Would the Family Stand have been signed if Living Colour, who took advantage of the type of "discovery" that "Plantation Radio" derides, had not been so successful? Finally, could the Family Stand have circulated this critique of music industry practices without the involvement of the music industry? "Plantation Radio" addresses some of these questions, underscoring the contradictory position black musicians in the industry occupy. The invocation of the plantation suggests that blacks who want to succeed in the music business are forced into a contemporary situation with parallels to slavery. The freedom of expression that rock promises was not possible within the racialized industry structures. Instead, African Americans had to play a subordinate role. A black artist's best bet for exposure, it seemed, was discovery by well-known white musicians like Mick Jagger, Paul Simon (who "discovered" South African band Ladysmith Black Mambazo), and Sting (who "discovered" African American saxophonist Branford Marsalis). Like Columbus, these white musicians have the power to make visible to other whites people of color who would otherwise be ignored. In short, the Family Stand is suggesting that the industry is unlikely to pay serious attention to nonwhite artists who don't have a white sponsor.[14] Like Jagger, Simon and Sting achieved professional success in part because of their appropriation of black music—Simon by rejuvenating his career in the 1980s with an infusion of South African music and Sting by using reggae rhythm and a Jamaican vocal inflection as front man of the 1980s new wave band the Police. The Family Stand's song suggests that in the music business, as in the antebellum south, black resources provide white wealth. The survival of black artists, like the survival of slaves, depends on adjusting oneself to the rules of a racist domain. The lyrics do not let black musicians—including Grammy-winning Living Colour and the Family Stand itself—off the hook. Are the fame, recognition, and the Grammy important enough to follow the demeaning racial rules of the plantation? Offered the chance to attain them, how many black artists would resist?

AUTHENTICITY AND CROSSOVER

In music, crossover is the process by which an artist initially targeted to one audience becomes popular with another. Many black artists and audiences see crossover as a choice that requires crossing out aspects of one's blackness to gain mainstream pop chart visibility. In this view, the black artist stands at a crossroads deciding whether to stay true to his or her black identity or to take the path toward "universality," which usually requires minimizing markers of racial difference. Embedded in this scenario are deeply held beliefs about racial authenticity and artistic integrity.[15] The possibility of crossover exists in part because of the entrenched tradition of segregation in the music industry that leads to racially delineated listening and purchasing preferences. Segregated music charts buttress these habits and are a product of them. Since 1942, music marketed to black audiences has been tracked in *Billboard* magazine. Over the years, the relevant single sales chart has been called "Harlem Hit Parade," "Race Records," "Rhythm and Blues," "Soul," "Black," and "Hip Hop" (Whitburn 2000:vii–viii). These racialized charts define what is "really black" black music. Meanwhile, the pop chart tracks the sales of music aimed at mainstream white middle-class listeners. Garofalo explains, "The pop charts are constructed on the basis of reports from mainstream radio and retail outlets; the rhythm and blues charts from outlets based in the black community. For a rhythm and blues release to become a pop hit, it must 'crossover' from the rhythm and blues charts to the pop charts . . . By and large, African American artists must first demonstrate success in the black market before gaining access to the mainstream" (1993:237). In this racialized context, Living Colour, a black band marketed chiefly to the white rock audience, was more vulnerable to suspicions about their authenticity than black artists who were initially marketed to black audiences before being "crossed over." This was the case even though Living Colour used their hard-won visibility to call attention to racism in the music industry and beyond. By the time Living Colour came onto the scene, the fact that the majority of the rock-buying audience and the musicians whose records they purchased were white made it almost impossible to represent rock as a legitimate black cultural pursuit. In a context with sharply demarcated visions of how black musicians should sound, it seemed fair to ask what it meant for a consciously black band like Living Colour to play for mostly white fans. Perhaps they were just "selling out."

Living Colour received a great deal of positive press early on. Writers for *Rolling Stone* and the *New York Times* covered the band and the BRC, often echoing their critiques of the music industry. (Admittedly, it is rarely difficult to encourage rock music critics to attack the recording industry.) These articles endorsed the view that it was wrong to deny black artists the right to rock, and they often praised Living Colour's music. Even critics with only tempered enthusiasm for the band as a musical entity often supported its sociopolitical critique. Similarly, negative reviews could attack the band's music, its politics, or both. Writing in 1988 for New York's *City Sun*, a black weekly newspaper, cultural critic Armond White panned Living Colour's *Vivid* and Vernon Reid for producing "seriously inauthentic" music (1995:88). White contends that Living Colour "narrows the definition of rock 'n' roll" by following "the strictest—whitest—ideas of what rock music should be" (87). Living Colour, he says, is too preoccupied with "the imitation of white rock idioms" and too self-conscious "about proving its awareness of white culture" (87–88). White does not acknowledge hearing the black musical influences that are also present in Living Colour's repertoire except where they are the most obvious—on the song "Funny Vibe," for example, which features black rappers Chuck D and Flavor Flav from Public Enemy. Psychologizing, White argues that "Reid has made a political fetish of white rock as a result of the guilty pleasure it's given him" (88). In White's view, the entire project is "an expression of the Black middle class's multiethnic ambivalence" (88).

When I have presented this research in public lectures, I sometimes have heard echoes of White's dismissive contention in audience comments: "These guys are just middle class and confused about who they are." In response I have struggled to demonstrate that BRC members are concerned with exploring a broader range of possibilities for black American identity so that stepping beyond the boundaries of what currently constitutes "acceptable" blackness is not interpreted as inauthentic, an identity crisis, or otherwise pathological. Even a politically progressive black critic like White ignores the significance of the social challenge the BRC position represented to the habit of American racism. Instead, he interprets these black rockers as being too much aligned with white concerns, white music, and white people. White's critique of Reid and his band is fair because it engages with the discourses Reid and the BRC introduced and because it addresses the band's music, which he does not like. His understanding, though, is incomplete. He charges that black rockers are caught up solely in "winning the acceptance and approval of the white rock establishment (who else would refuse Reid, or care?)" (88). While sarcastically disapproving of black artists concerning themselves with what white audiences think, White overlooks the fact that these black rockers were reclaiming the blackness of rock. He is also incapable of imagining that Living Colour and other black rockers were interested in what black people thought about them as musicians and community members. Apparently (if inadvertently) invested in the segregated model promulgated by the music industry, White assumes that black men playing "white boy" music are not interested in black people and black culture.

Some of the suspicions about authenticity that crossover arouses are rooted in a simplistic conflation of race and culture. In spite of American cultural anthropology's ongoing efforts to separate the closely linked categories, it is common for artists, their handlers, and critics to depend on racial or biological explanations for cultural proclivities, reflecting and producing intertwined beliefs about popular music and racial identity. The rhetoric around the careers of Prince and Lenny Kravitz, two of Living Colour's most successful black rock contemporaries, is instructive. As Prince crossed over from black music to pop, he took advantage of the light-brown skin, narrow nose, and curly perm that gave him a biracial look; in fact, for a brief period he claimed to be the product of an interracial union even though this was not the case. My point here is not to deny that Prince is mixed race; like many black Americans, he has non-African descent ancestors. Prince, however, conjured up a Euro-American parent. Arguably, he was trying to smooth his appeal to white audiences by diluting his potentially threatening blackness (especially considering his highly sexualized persona and lyrics) and to explain his use of musical styles associated with whites. Reid critiqued Prince's tactic of "play[ing] up the quasi-mulatto angle . . . 'I'm not black, I'm not white, that's why everyone can relate to me.' Why should you have to be that for people to relate to you? If you say something truthful, it'll connect anyway" (Reid quoted in Fricke 1987:66). Similarly, discussions in the white and black media of Lenny Kravitz devoted what always seemed to me disproportionate attention to his parentage. Virtually every article painstakingly explained that Roxie Roker, his mother, was a black woman familiar to many from her role on the 1970s situation comedy *The Jeffersons*; and that Sy Kravitz, his father, was a white Jewish television producer. Genealogy might have been intended to account for the young black guitarist's Jewish name or demonstrate his Hollywood connections. Still, I believe there was also at play an effort to make sense of his otherwise irrational involvement with "white" music. In the cases of both Prince and Kravitz, biology offered a more logical explanation than the simple possibility that a black person liked rock.

Racialized music genre separation perpetuates the idea that race and culture are coterminous and creates confusion about artists whose identity and music don't fit this model. Living Colour and other black rockers disturb racial common sense and occupy a tenuous position that led journalists to use phrases like "black rock in a hard place" (Smith 1989) to characterize them. Similarly, members often referred to the danger of "falling through the cracks" as a result of the perceived mismatch between race and genre embedded in black rock. Along with crossover, these spatial metaphors describe problematic movement and position, indicating the absence of a comfortable place for black rockers. The racial segregation of rock music runs deep in spite of the miscegenation that produced it. Whether or not biology is invoked, black rockers like Prince, Kravitz, and Living Colour as well as those of us who write about them must explain why black Americans are involved with "white boy" music. Skepticism about their identities, music, professional viability, and sanity comes from all sides. Black rockers are at once too black to be real rockers and not black enough because they rock. Indeed, they *are* in a "hard place."

IS THE ONLY COLOR GREEN?

The ways artists are marketed, the positions executives are assigned to, and the organization of radio and cable television stations are shaped by patterns and practices of racialization that have a deep and deleterious effect on black participants. Segregation already in place for reasons of social tradition was transferred to segregation for economic expediency. Following the recommendation of a Harvard Business School study it had commissioned, CBS started a black music division in 1972 in order to target black audiences, a market major labels had been neglecting (George 1988; Sanjek 2002). CBS went from having two black bands (Santana and Sly and the Family Stone) to having a roster of 125 (George 1988:134). Black music departments underwrote the 1970s black musical renaissance, but the formation of these racially specific divisions perpetuated segregation in the interest of sales. Ironically, at the historical moment when schools, workplaces, and housing were desegregating (however slowly), the music industry formalized the use of racial separation to sell music. Although African Americans were the primary audience for black music, labels would also "cross over" singles by black artists when they believed they could successfully market them to a white pop audience.[16] The crossover phenomenon demonstrated that the boundaries of black music could shift according to chart success. Commenting on this situation, Mark, who had worked for a major label, observed:

> Once you reach a certain level of sales and you're starting to crossover then—because there're more white pop stations than there are black stations—[pop] becomes your main thrust, to exploit the larger market first. So that those products that are geared to that

marketplace get taken over by that department. So Michael Jackson, Earth, Wind & Fire, all those things that come out of the black music department are immediately applied to the pop music department.

In the 1980s, Whitney Houston, Michael Jackson, Janet Jackson, and Prince were among the African American artists who crossed over. They are black, but their presence on pop stations and pop charts put them in a different category. Money they earned is moved, with the artists, to the pop division where they are promoted to the pop market (NAACP 1987:4). Rank and file black performers are handled by black music divisions with small budgets, promoted to black-oriented stations with smaller audiences, and usually enjoy smaller sales. Paul, a music industry professional with a decade of experience working with major labels, makes an important—and facetious—point about race and crossover. "Within the record companies because of the separation, you have the pop/rock department and . . . you have a black department," he explained. "It's not called the white department, black department. It's called 'rock and pop' and 'black.' Which is not the same type of category because there've been cases of black artists who sort of graduated to being pop, like Lionel Richie. Maybe he's not black anymore. I don't know." When black artists cross over into pop success they cease to be black in the music industry sense of the word. They get promoted from racialized black music to universal pop music in an economically driven process of racial transcendence.

Crossover is just one example of racialization's impact on black participation in the music industry. The NAACP's 1987 report on the position of African American artists and executives in the recording industry details the ways race and racism influenced the distribution of resources, the hiring of label staff, the marketing and promotion of artists, and the organization of departments.[17] In each instance, the report finds, African Americans were in subordinate positions:

The record industry is overwhelmingly segregated and discrimination is rampant. No other industry in America so openly classifies its operations on a racial basis. At every level of the industry, beginning with the separation of black artists into a special category, barriers exist that severely limit opportunities for blacks. The structure of the industry allows for total white control and domination. While the intent may not be to deliberately and consciously keep blacks out, the results are the same. (NAACP 1987:16–17)[18]

Although the NAACP conducted its research in the mid-1980s, the pattern of exclusion of blacks from decision-making positions that it documents continued well into the 1990s (Kelley 2002; Muhammad 1995; Negus 1999; Reynolds and Brown 1994). As a private concern, the music industry eluded and ignored federal government strategies for promoting the inclusion of people of color and white women in the business ranks (NAACP 1987:2). Reflecting on his encounters with the politics of race in the music industry, Mark recalled:

> My experience in record companies is that black people and women are marginalized as workers. The music business is the last legally segregated industry. . . . There's a black music division, there's a pop music division; there's a black music marketing team, a pop music marketing team. The budgets are different, the mindsets are different. They're all run by some white person at the top and the aesthetic parameters are different. All sorts of music gets done under the aegis of pop music and rock 'n' roll, but under black music, you know, it's like dance music—and that's it at major record companies. Blues is happening under blues labels, jazz happens on jazz labels. On a major label, you got to do dance music. And in the infrastructure, black people are shuttled off into black music marketing and promotion. Women are shuttled off into publicity. . . . Art means nothing. Which is no different from anything else, but . . . uhm, it's just particularly painful that there are separate rules for black music.

As he moved from an internship into a staff position, Mark learned that there was a separate but unequal place for black executives and black music. In adding that white women were similarly marginalized, he develops a description of the major label as a white male dominated institution with little interest in incorporating black men, black women, or white women. Later in our conversation, Mark described the environment at his label:

> I was in sales. There is no black and white in sales, just green. Make your quota or you don't make your quota. But black salesmen didn't get promoted generally because the people who are the district sales managers—it ends up just like a little white club, you know. And they can go on being a little white club. American business—now, you've been in school—American business is a white boy's club, period. It's damn near white boy's golf. They can tell nigger jokes when they get ready. They can do all that wild

shit. . . . There were no mentors for me. All my mentors were over in [promotion]—they tried to get me to come over to promotion. I don't want to be marginalized, you know. My experience—I listen to everything and I'm into everything. Why should I marginalize? Why should I squeeze my knowledge down to fit your preconceived notions of who I am when you don't even know who the fuck I am? No thank you. They didn't understand that.

Throughout its history, rock 'n' roll fans and detractors have emphasized its links to teenage rebellion and threats to the status quo. Music label executives have traded on this renegade image to build a multibillion dollar industry that, in the end, mirrors the nation's social inequalities. Both Mark's comments and the NAACP report reveal the extent to which the reproduction of dominant racial and gender hierarchies are part of the day-to-day workings of major labels. Some African American executives work outside of black music divisions, but few are involved in decision making about music, artists, budgets, and overall label policy or in jobs that traditionally lead to upper management positions (NAACP 1987:4). By the early 1990s, the NAACP had signed Fair Share Agreements with CBS in July 1990 and with MCA in February 1991 which committed the corporations to expanding opportunities for African Americans and other minority groups (Black Radio Exclusive 1991:10). Still, an analysis of the industry in a 1994 *Black Enterprise* article found that despite black music's sizable contribution to the industry's economic health, African Americans remained largely excluded from production, marketing, packaging, and distribution, the profit centers of the business (Reynolds and Brown 1994:84). Paul described the ways this persistent industry segregation affects the possibilities of black executives and of alternative black music acts:

> If you're black and you're in the record business, you're going to be in the black department which is really sad. Because I know black people who are totally qualified to be rock [Artist and Repertoire] men who just sign new wave groups or new age groups or punk groups or whatever. They lived that shit, they know that shit. Chances of that are very slim . . . And, you know, because of the segregation within these companies—aided and abetted by a lot of black executives who want to build an empire—that's the set-up.

Viewed as experts on "black music" and generally prevented from working in any other genre, it is in the interest of African American music industry executives to maintain racialized marketing categories because they allow them some semblance of power in the industry (Perry 1989:78; Zimmerman 1992:89).

By the 1990s, the explosion of R&B and rap as "crossover" music led to optimism as more black executives were hired and promoted. Most, however, remained in black music departments, and even as R&B and rap became mainstream, most black music executives did not gain power. Andre Harrell, who had briefly served as Motown's President and CEO, commented, "As soon as the black executive's artist reaches platinum, suddenly the artist and manager have to deal with the president of the corporation, because *he* controls the priorities at pop radio. The black executive becomes obsolete. As his music gets bigger, his power diminishes. He's more or less told, 'Go find the next act and establish it'" (Harrell quoted in Negus 1999:89). Some observers argued that black music executives were actually *losing* ground. Noting that the majors were not filling vacated positions in black music divisions, industry commentator Steven Ivory proclaimed the new reality of "The Incredible Shrinking Black Music Executive," describing "a situation in which the majors are deciding they can do the black music business thing without black folks. They can promote those records. Hell, they can simply do deals with black custom labels and production companies and not even need black divisions at all" (Ivory 1993:44; cf. Kelley 2002; Perry 1989; Reynolds and Brown 1994). Furthermore, in spite of the economic success of black music, black music departments continued to have "an unstable and uncertain existence" (Negus 1999:87). Writing at the end of the 1990s, Negus observed that a black music department

> can easily be cut back, closed down or restructured by the corporation (whether this is due to an assessment that the genre has changed or simply because cuts have to be made). . . . It is often the black music division that is subject to greater cutting than others. A notorious example of this occurred in February 1996 when Capitol Records closed its urban division, cancelling the contracts of most artists and sacking eighteen members of staff (most of them black). (Negus 1999:87–88)

Negus and the black industry professionals he consults stress that these are not strictly economic decisions—especially since rap and R&B represented 21 percent of the U.S. music market in 1995—but choices that reflect value judgments about black people, black culture, and black music (88).

Racial segregation and limits were also present in radio. Black radio stations did not include the full range of contemporary black musical production on their playlists. Commenting on this compromised state of affairs in 1992, black rockers Mother's Finest released an album called *Black Radio Won't Play This Record.* The title was a bitter and accurate prediction of the fate of their hard rocking funk. During the early stages of black-owned black-oriented radio in the 1970s, programmers experimented with varied music formats meant to encompass the "360-degree black experience" and played a fairly wide range of music by black artists (Alexander 1981:160–61). Over time, though, competition with white-owned stations that played black-oriented formats and changes in industry marketing and programming practices resulted in a narrowing of black radio playlists. A heightened sensitivity to marketing and demographics led to more sharply segmented radio programming across all commercial stations, as stations sought to attract and retain advertisers by delivering an easily identifiable audience. Black radio stations had to project an image of well-off black radio audiences to potential advertisers who continued to be wary of investing in advertising to blacks in spite of statistical data that demonstrated the commercial viability of the African American market (Alexander 1981:164; Billboard 1993:83, 1994:70; George 1988:160).[19] Programmers avoided music that did not fit the perceived preferences of the target audience. By the late 1980s, the records that black radio would not play included those by black rap, rock, blues, and jazz artists. Instead, black radio favored adult soul, arguing that they would lose advertisers if they were overly identified with rap, a genre perceived as music for the less affluent teen market (Nelson 1992:6). In this climate, black musicians operating outside of mainstream black music were left off black radio. Black radio could not afford the risk of playing the rock of Mother's Finest, Lenny Kravitz, or Living Colour. The financial stakes were too high and the competition was too keen. For the most part, black rock artists depended on rock stations, college stations, and public radio stations with music programming for their airplay.

At the time BRC members were beginning to work as professional musicians, MTV, cable television's twenty-four-hour music video station, was becoming the chief venue for promoting pop music.[20] Following radio programming trends, MTV targeted a demographically specific audience—middle-class, white, suburban, twelve to thirty-four year olds—with a rock-oriented format (Banks 1996:34). MTV focused on rock to the exclusion of R&B, funk, and disco, music associated with black performers (Sanjek 1988:640). The station's treatment of black music came under attack as music critics and black musicians publicly questioned the programmers' refusal to play black artists. Observers calculated that in the first eighteen months of MTV's existence, the station showed over 750 videos, fewer than twenty-four of which featured black artists (Harris 1995:75). Writing in the *New York Times* almost two years after MTV's debut, television critic John O'Connor remarked:

> The problem is that MTV seems curiously bent on returning the black musician to the status of "invisible man." The program can be watched for hours at a time without detecting the presence of a single black performer. Critics have wondered if this "oversight" is intentional, a demographic ploy for making MTV more palatable to the suburbs of middle-class white America. MTV executives, for their part, have insisted, not a little arrogantly, that their product is focused on rock-and-roll, an area of music that supposedly is not frequented by black performers. Roll over, Chuck Berry. (1983:23)

In 1983, Rick James, the keyboard player and guitarist whose singles "Super Freak" and "Give It To Me Baby" had propelled his 1981 album *Street Songs* to sell over three million copies, declared that MTV's rejection of videos by commercially successful black artists like himself, Earth, Wind & Fire, and Stevie Wonder was racist (Banks 1996:39). "We have great videos," James asserted. "Why doesn't MTV show them? It's like taking black people back 400 years" (James quoted in Banks 1996:39). Some commentators pointed out that MTV programmed videos by white artists like Hall and Oates, Madonna, and George Michael who drew heavily on R&B, funk, and dance music—in other words, black music (George 1989:20). Indeed, their high visibility raised questions: If MTV was a rock station, why include nonrock artists? And if it included nonrock artists, why not include African American R&B and funk musicians? Black artists and executives worried about the exclusion, not because of an idealistic desire for integration, but because of a pragmatic interest in the increased record sales that MTV exposure guaranteed. By late 1982, a *Billboard* survey of retail record stores found that "new acts who appeared on MTV saw an immediate 10 to 15 per cent increase in sales" (Sanjek 1988:640). Locked out of MTV, black artists depended on black-owned and black-oriented Black Entertainment Television (BET) which by 1983 was programming 15 hours of music a week on *Video Soul* (Sanjek and Sanjek

1991:251). MTV's de facto color bar came down in 1983 when MTV executives programmed "Billie Jean," the first single from Michael Jackson's CBS/Epic Records album, *Thriller* (Denisoff 1986:362). Most industry commentators claim that MTV's "choice" was forced when CBS threatened to deny MTV access to the videos of *any* CBS artists unless Jackson's video, which rumors suggested MTV was not going to air, went into rotation (Banks 1996:39–41; Denisoff 1986:362; Harris 1995:75).[21] Jackson's success opened the door for black artists like Eddy Grant, Lionel Richie, Prince, and Tina Turner to be played on MTV. Blacks were more visible on MTV through the 1980s, but MTV's critics remained skeptical about the new place for blacks on cable, charging that MTV only played black artists with large white constituencies. MTV increased its black music programming in August 1988 with the launch of *Yo! MTV Raps*, one of the network's highest-rated music programs (Harris 1995:75). The presence of rap on MTV increased the genre's sales to white teens, helping rap to begin crossing over.

As it became clear that videos with higher production values received more airplay and generated more album sales, videos became an essential and increasingly costly part of promoting an artist's recording (Banks 1996; Negus 1992). A mini-industry of music video directors, producers, and choreographers has developed, but in another example of racialized limitations, the number of African American video directors is small (Banks 1996:170–74). Furthermore, record labels were reluctant to produce videos for black artists not deemed to have crossover potential, reasoning that MTV would not give them "enough exposure to justify the expense of the production" (139). In a pattern that followed the allocation of funds to black music departments, black artists typically had smaller budgets for producing videos (139). Black artists faced a Catch-22: Without a video, they would have difficulty developing an audience and without the audience, they might not get the chance to produce a video. *Yo! MTV Raps* and the black music-oriented programming of BET became outlets for black rap and R&B artists, but these venues did not embrace black rock. Living Colour's hard rock sound and its label's backing helped get their video for "Cult of Personality" into rotation on MTV. This exposure boosted sales of *Vivid*, increased the band's radio airplay, and contributed to the visibility that helped Living Colour to break the rock color line, log impressive sales, and garner Grammy nominations. Living Colour's success marks one end of the spectrum.

Generally speaking, though, black rock bands could not depend on getting regular airplay on MTV or BET. They fell between the cracks of these race- and genre-defined outlets.

SELLING LIVING COLOUR

From a marketing and sales perspective, Living Colour's musical genre and racial identity represented a confusing challenge. On the one hand, Living Colour was a black band and should have appealed to African American listeners, but African Americans were not seen as a potential rock audience. On the other hand, Living Colour was a rock band and should have appealed to rock fans, but rock fans were white and might have been unwilling or unable to identify with black rockers enough to want to buy their records. Responding to this calculus of race and taste is an integral part of any music marketing plan and was a serious consideration. In the end, Living Colour, a black rock band, was promoted with the hope that rockers would embrace the band's music and accept their blackness; there was considerably less attention to the black market. Many BRC members believe recording executives view Living Colour's success as a fluke and have not seriously considered ways to repeat their success. To conclude this chapter, I present some BRC member comments about the marketing of black rock.

Most BRC members were critical of the ways the recording industry's racialized organizational structure affected black artists. Here, Paul describes how the label handled Living Colour:

> The problem is the black [music] department wasn't involved . . . in the marketing, probably because they weren't asked, and maybe they wouldn't have wanted to do it anyway, but the point is, I thought there should have been a strategy to sell [the group] to the black community. Because I'm convinced there's a certain segment that's going to dig it right away and another segment that's going to eventually dig it. And I think that the assumption that the people who listen to R. Kelly are automatically not going to listen to Living Colour is wrong, because I think myself and a whole bunch of other people are living proof. Look at my fucking record collection. You know, people have the ability to like more things, more things at once. Now, I don't doubt that things have changed and maybe I grew up with more musical influences and more diverse radio . . . but still, I think it's perfectly possible. I think it's com-

pletely against the way entertainment in general is sold now. . . . I think rock people that can understand the rock thing maybe can't understand black people. And black record guys who understand black people, maybe can't understand rock [*laughs*] and that's a big problem.

The lack of involvement from black music division executives could be explained as a practical decision since black music department executives are hired for their expertise in R&B and rap. Still, Andre, a BRC bandleader, told me that when he took his demo to a major label, the black women executives were impressed. "They loved it," he recalled. "They saw the video and they were like—and they were R&B people— and they were happy to see us doing some shit other than what they see and hear every day. They were so elated and that's why I think there's a big market in the black community for what we're doing." Liking a band and working to market a band, however, are two different things. BRC members and industry executives agree that black rock is a hard sell. And if selling black rock to white audiences is difficult, the perception among executives is that it would be nearly impossible to market rock—even black rock—to black audiences. Speaking along these lines, Andre continued:

> I think definitely that my band and the type of music we do, we're definitely geared to be great in the black community. And I think that's one of the markets everybody's been missing. When they marketed Fishbone, they skipped right over the black community. They didn't even try the black community, you know. They aimed at white audiences. I think the black community would embrace a new form of music. Not everybody, but there would be a definite market, a new bohemian sort of scene.

Bringing black rock to African American audiences, even if only targeting the "new bohemians," would require willingness to build an audience. Historically, major labels have depended on independent labels to produce and promote new music and develop audiences for it. Only when the market is clearly defined do majors step in. Rosalie Sandelbach, a white record executive whose independent label, Enemy Records, signed BRC band Kelvynator, said the following about marketing black rock acts:

> It can be very hard. Because of the versatility of the musicians and the many influences within black music, there can be such a range

of what can be included in the music. Unfortunately, because of our society, and the way the business is set up, we are forced to try and fit into formats and define music into categories. It's the only way to successfully market a record in the U.S., but at the same time, it's limiting and controlling. (Sandelbach quoted in Muggleton 1992:22)

The range of musical influences that give black rock its vitality conflict with the simplicity a format-focused environment demands. Even some label executives became frustrated by their limitations. Paul explained:

The problem [is] that you may have some record companies who say, "Hey, this band is pretty good, but . . . how am I going to sell it?" Or even if they get over that in the case of a group that's obviously outstanding like Fishbone, Living Colour, and they *are* signed, there are difficulties with getting it out there. And I think Living Colour got lucky with the Rolling Stones tour and landing on MTV at the right time—when they felt like playing [the video] . . . I think what's never really been done is to really put together a comprehensive strategy that markets the stuff in a multiplicity of ways, that markets it as the music that it is, rock, and also as the people they are, black. And I'm not saying it's going to be easy [or] it's going to happen the first time or it's going to strike a chord immediately. But I think it's a strategy that can be explored.

Without the kind of effort Paul describes, however, music marketing will continue to follow simplistic perceptions of how a black artist should sound. Sharon, a music industry professional, expressed her frustration with these narrow parameters:

It's just amazing . . . how someone of a different culture is always telling you that your music isn't black enough. You know? That kills me. And it happens on all levels. It's like, "Well, how do you know it's not black enough?" And how can I tell someone else, "Your music isn't Puerto Rican enough?" [*laughs*] You know what I mean? . . . That's the stuff that we as an organization have to fight against because that just creates . . . prejudices in your own head. . . . It's *music*. It's music. Why does it have to have a color? It killed me that for years in *Billboard* they had the pop charts and the black charts. What the hell is a "black chart?" *What's a black chart?* Because my skin is brown, I got to be on the black chart?

The black chart, black music, and sounding black enough have become commonsense music industry concepts that place black rock musicians in the intractable position encapsulated in a comment Kelvynator's Kelvyn Bell made to me when I first began my research. "Record companies automatically want to send black musicians to the black music department," he explained. " 'You don't rap, you don't sing like Luther Vandross—we can't use you,' [they say]. Or, if you sound like Guns 'n' Roses or Springsteen, they say, 'You're black; you won't sell to a white audience.' " Black and rock had become mutually exclusive and, as BRC members told me again and again, those artists who put the two together risked falling through the cracks. Paul described how the music industry infrastructure stymied black rock:

> If you deal with a Follow for Now or a Living Colour or Bad Brains or Fishbone, I mean, you put the record on, it's rock 'n' roll. So pretty much, if you accept the givens of the music industry, you got to work it through rock 'n' roll channels, rock 'n' roll radio in particular. . . . It needs to be in the rock section [of record stores]. . . . But, because rock has become synonymous with white people, there's kind of a disconnect there. And so you might have rock stations saying, "Well, we don't want to play a record by these black people." Seriously. Or they might say, "Well, no one's heard of these guys" or "No one wants to hear these guys" or whatever. Similarly, black music stations . . . play music by black people—supposedly. But they really play a relatively narrow range of music, of whatever is currently defined as contemporary R&B, which may include rap . . . but basically it boils down to a handful of songs in two or three current formulas. Which rock really doesn't fit in and blues doesn't fit in and jazz doesn't fit in . . . so that even though those groups are black and they're "black" stations, they're not going to play it. . . . You have a group that's black rock—by definition it sits in two different categories that are mutually exclusive so they can't really figure out how to sell it.

Too often, the efforts to unite blackness and rock are undermined by record industry executives who, upon seeing a black artist, *only* see black.

When I asked Sharon how she would advise record companies trying to market black artists, she told me they should take a simple approach. "I would suggest that they put their blinders on first and listen to the music and let that dictate what category they have to put it in," she said. "And if they can't put it in a category period, then they can't put it in a category, but if they believe in it, then you work those several markets . . . And be adventurous. People's jobs are on the line; that's why they don't want to be adventurous . . . But record companies are the first ones to steal from people who [are]." A few moments later, Sharon referred to the success of the Seattle-based band Nirvana that, in the early 1990s, launched industry interest in "grunge." The signing of "Seattle sound" bands marked the industry's response to Nirvana's high sales. This is a sore-spot for some BRC members who believe that the labels should have put this kind of energy into signing black rock bands in the wake of Living Colour's high sales, making Living Colour the first in a series of black rock triumphs. A long-time member described the atmosphere around the coalition at the time. "Living Colour had jumped off so big, it was a thing like, 'Well, who's next?' 'I'm going to be next.' . . . However, that wasn't the case," he explained. "What actually happened was after Living Colour, the industry really closed off to any other black bands . . . And it took us maybe a year or two to actually figure that out. And as we see now, [Living Colour has] come and gone, and that's kind of like it, in a sense."

After Living Colour "blew up," there were a few signings of BRC bands to major label deals. New York's Eye & I and Los Angeles's Total Eclipse got contracts, but they did not, according to many BRC members, receive the promotional and marketing support necessary to sell them to either white or black audiences. Instead, they suffered from the industry's chronic inability to figure out what to do with black rock. In the end, their recordings did not sell well enough to maintain industry support, especially in the face of a growing number of successful and comparatively easy to sell grunge bands. Meanwhile, Living Colour's highly praised second album, *Time's Up*, disappointed from a sales perspective, reaching gold but not platinum level sales. Determining how to sell black rock bands, all with reputations as stellar live acts and solid local followings, proved too difficult a challenge and the major labels backed away from black rock.

The shift in industry practice BRC members had idealistically hoped Living Colour's breakthrough would precipitate did not occur. The 1995 breakup of Living Colour, the one BRC band that had made it, was upsetting for many BRC members because it symbolized the end of the dream. Living Colour's career was marked by critical acclaim, widespread popularity, and financial success. The band succeeded in spite of the ways the industry approaches black artists. While Living Colour was in the limelight, they played a lot of great riffs and gave a lot of great performances. They also raised audience awareness about the impact of racialization on black performers and the industry's history of segregation and appropriation. Along with other postliberated generation black American artists like Prince, Lenny Kravitz, Fishbone, 24–7 Spyz, Terence Trent D'Arby, Me'Shell NdegéOcello, Follow for Now, Dionne Farris, Ben Harper, Tracy Chapman, Chocolate Genius, Toshi Reagon, and the Veldt, Living Colour demonstrated the commercial viability of styles that expanded the definitions of black music. By the end of the 1990s, African Americans had made progress both in the administrative and artistic realms of the recording industry and had taken on leadership roles that would have been difficult to attain in previous decades. With distressingly few exceptions, however, black performers and executives still operate in what is principally a separate and unequal segment of the industry under conditions shaped by racialized practices, economic interests, and aesthetic concerns. These conditions led black rockers to start and sustain the BRC and to argue for the more equal participation of African Americans in an industry we have so definitively shaped over the years.

SEVEN

MEDIA INTERVENTIONS

We go to MTV [with our video] and they try to explain to us in their best terms that "Where do we put it? It doesn't fit our format." What? It's rock, isn't it? Yeah, but there's something, something about it . . . So we go to BET which is black entertainment. . . . And they say, "Well, it's rock." Okay. And it's like, that's the Catch-22 that we're in.—BERNIE KAYE, LEAD SINGER OF TOTAL ECLIPSE

Long before BRC members had to grapple with the music industry's racialized dynamics as aspiring professionals, they had been influenced by the industry through its widely circulated forms. In many of our conversations and interviews, BRC members connected their exposure to music in the media to their decisions to begin playing musical instruments. In the following comment, Jesse describes his first guitar and his subsequent musical development:

JESSE: [It] was this little cardboard Roy Rogers guitar. It had a picture of Roy Rogers on it and a horse and I turned it around and Dale was on the back. What it was was a real cheap guitar and I was stoked . . . I beat on the guitar and banged on it. Didn't know how to tune it . . . but I had that guitar. Really didn't seriously consider playing the guitar until I saw the Beatles. When I saw the Beatles I was just amazed. It changed life, you know. I said, "These guys are cool. I mean they're cool." They've got this long hair—which I had no concept of what that was like. But they had Beatle wigs, then. You could buy a Beatle wig for two dollars. So my mother bought me a Beatle wig and I had my Roy Rogers guitar . . . and this was when I was approaching fat boy days, so you have to get this image of this little fat black kid with a Beatles wig on play-ing an orange Roy Rogers guitar. . . . I loved that guitar and my mother said, "You know, maybe we can get you an electric guitar." She found some pawn shop somewhere where you could buy the guitar, the amps, the stand, the case, you know, the whole boxful of picks, and a wah-wah pedal for $99. You just had everything. A big guitar with strings like fenceposts on them, you know, never stayed in tune [and it] was shaped like a . . . "V." . . . But I was stoked. I said, "Now I have arrived." Of course, when that happens, the neighborhood kids get involved so you always find another kid who has a drum set or wants to get a drum set. So we had the little neighborhood band.

MAUREEN: How old were you?

JESSE: I must have been about 12. And it was just the thing. I think at that period in time, you're just getting into music . . . and those people who were so intrigued by it they actually want to become musicians just kind of all gravitate to each other. I remember the first song I learned was "Light My Fire" [by the Doors]. . . . I re-member the first record I bought was Led Zeppelin's first album and then I discovered Jimi Hendrix and that just changed the whole situation. All of a sudden, a $99 guitar was not good enough.

Jesse's recounting of the impact of musicians like the Beatles and Jimi Hendrix on his interest in playing guitar is representative of how BRC members discussed the media encounters that informed their musical, professional, and personal development. Influenced by the images and debates they were exposed to through the media, they be-came increasingly interested in participating in media and making their own imprint on public culture. Media studies scholars describe the process of production, distribution, and reception of media as an ongoing circuit and analyze how various forms are produced, dissemi-nated, and consumed (e.g., Fiske 1989; Hall 1980). Media produc-tions that move through this circuit influence audiences and, over time, create new cohorts of producers. Jesse's comments remind us that reception is not simply the site of the creative audience interpre-tations and appropriations that media scholars emphasize, but also a crucial starting point for new productions. When conducting field-work with BRC members, I was constantly reminded that they are not only culture producers; they are also culture consumers whose productions are influenced by the media (cf. Dornfeld 1998). The countercultural scene that performers like Jimi Hendrix, the Doors, and Led Zeppelin represented were part of a broader set of social forces that together comprised the public culture that BRC members experienced as they came of age. The BRC communities formed in Los Angeles and New York were shaped in part by sounds and spectacles available in late 1960s and early 1970s media: FM radio, TV and magazine images of Black Panthers and antiwar protesters, Woodstock and Monterey Pop (the concerts and the films), *Soul Train, Midnight Special, Rolling Stone* magazine, the lunar landings of U.S. spaceships, and the arrival of the P-Funk Mothership. These media images encouraged BRC members to participate in music making, club performances, and local music scenes, activities that instilled a desire to participate in media production: to make records and to have their music played on the radio and music video programs.

When they found their access to mainstream outlets limited, many BRC members developed alternative means for producing and disseminating their music. In this chapter, I discuss two BRC projects: *Blacker Than That,* a BRC compact disc compilation produced by New York members, and *Network BRC,* the coalition's public access cable television show, produced by members of the Los Angeles BRC. Participation in these independent media productions enabled BRC members to distribute their work, although at a much more limited level than is available through mainstream outlets. In addition to these coalition-sponsored projects, individual members have worked on independent labels and also developed self-produced, self-distributed recordings and videos. Alternative music festivals, independent music distributors, noncommercial radio, public access cable television, and the Internet are components of the nonmainstream music production and distribution networks that sustain independent musicians. These venues warrant attention because they demonstrate that people can create alternatives when mainstream access is restricted. I outline the BRC's involvement in these arenas while also indicating some of the challenges associated with independent media production. Overall, the media's pervasive influence is noteworthy. It enabled BRC members to have access to music and ideas that contributed to the development of their artistic interests and activist practices. It was also the sustaining source of many of the stereotypes that, among other problematic repercussions, separated blacks from rock. Finally, it was both a target of and a channel for the BRC's cultural activism.

Consuming media forms is simple. It is easy to turn on a television, go to a movie, or buy a compact disc. Gaining sustained access to media as a producer, however, is quite a bit more difficult.[1]

Although scholars talk enthusiastically about "public" culture and the "public" sphere, most of the institutions that constitute these arenas of representation are privately owned with relatively little responsibility to the public.[2] Profit orients decision making at sites of media production like record labels, television networks, and movie studios and access to these venues is far from guaranteed. This is especially true of institutions that have the widest influence at the national level. Mainstream media companies, whether black- or white-owned, have large budgets, far-reaching distribution networks, easy access to audiences, and stringent restrictions on participation. As I explained in the previous chapter, it was difficult for BRC members to get airplay on black or white media outlets because their music and image did not fit the narrowly defined formats. Although black-owned, black-oriented outlets like cable's Black Entertainment Television (BET) and many black radio stations disseminated black culture, black rockers found that these networks were not interested in promoting their music. Like their white counterparts at mainstream companies, black media executives guaranteed a specific audience to advertisers and programmed certain types of music to deliver it. The economic realities of media outlets coupled with ideological assumptions about black cultural production curtailed BRC member access to the mainstream and encouraged some to turn to independent outlets like public radio, public access television, and independent record labels that make the inclusion of "alternative" voices their mission. The trade-off is that they have limited resources, making it necessary to work with shoestring production and distribution budgets. A number of BRC members accepted these constraints in order to participate at some level in production and distribution.

DO-IT-YOURSELF

The compilations *The History of Our Future* (Rykodisc 1991), *Blacker Than That* (BRC Records 1993), and *Bronze Buckeroo Rides Again* (BRC Records 2000) addressed one of the coalition's initial goals: to assist in the recording and distribution of its members' music. These compilations also challenged the limited ideas about black identity that circulated in the public sphere. In his liner notes for *The History of Our Future*, Greg Tate explains how the music industry created the need for both the BRC and an independent, BRC-produced recording. "The reason that the musicians on this record have sustained a Black Rock Coalition for six years," Tate wrote, "is because they're not interested in anyone's formulas or formats for pop success. They've got big ideas of their own, thank you, and if they've got to go around people short of vision to get them out, so be it" (Tate 1991). The BRC compilations allowed members to produce their work without repackaging themselves to fit dominant notions of black music. Indeed, one of the ways members articulated the value of the compilations was by stressing their difference from mainstream black pop.

In 1992, the BRC formed its own label, BRC Records. The promotion for its first project, *Blacker Than That*, was underway when I started my research. The shift to self-production involved the BRC in the do-it-yourself (D.I.Y.) ethic that emerged in the late 1970s when punk bands in the United States and Great Britain demonstrated that a major label deal was not the only way to spread a musical message. Like their precursors in the 1950s, these independent producers created and distributed new forms of music. Taking advantage of cheaper technology and a growing network of independent studios, labels, and distributors, musicians produced low-budget recordings, usually using personal savings and earnings from gigs to support the enterprise, instead of waiting to be discovered and financed by a major label. These recordings are unlikely to reach as large an audience as mainstream productions, but their producers can reasonably hope to receive attention in alternative music networks. These include independently owned "mom 'n' pop" record stores instead of major chains; fanzines, local press, and Web pages instead of in the mainstream music press; and small clubs and bars instead of large arenas and concert halls. In addition to challenging the mainstream, these recordings often influence it as major labels incorporate successful "outsider" styles. During the 1980s and 1990s, the majors increasingly depended on independents to identify shifts in consumer taste, locate creative energy in music, and develop the artists most able to sell the new product. Rap and grunge are two examples of independently produced music that major labels picked up and successfully sold during the 1990s. Independent labels depend on their difference from the majors and their connections to lesser-known artists for a veneer of underground credibility that sells to fans the idea that the music is authentic and uncompromised by the demands of the mainstream market. It is important, however, not to overstate the independence of independent labels. Although they have a stronger commitment to supporting untested artists and music than the majors, independent labels are frequently connected to major labels through investment, licensing, and distribution arrangements (Negus 1992, 1999).

Blacker Than That began in the spring of 1992 with a call from the Independent Music Producers Syndicate (IMPS), a New Hampshire–based publications firm that also ran a music distribution service for independent labels. IMPS president Wayne Green had read about the BRC in trade and popular press. As an advocate of independent music producers and a service provider to them, Green was interested in supporting the BRC's mission; further, since the organization was a nonprofit, working with the BRC would allow a tax write-off for his company. Ideological and business interests coincided and Green approached the BRC with an informal proposal to collaborate on a project. What followed was approximately eighteen months of planning, negotiation, and coordination. The production of the compilation was spearheaded by two longtime BRC members: Bruce Mack, the national president, whose band P.B.R. Streetgang was one of the first to join the coalition, and Jimmy Saal, director of communications, who had joined the BRC in 1987 when managing the black rock band the Good Guys. Jimmy told me that initially some of his fellow members "were kind of leery" about the project. He attributed this hesitancy to the BRC's experience with *The History of Our Future*. The BRC had anticipated a positive balance between freedom and backing from Rykodisc. Although the label financially supported the album's production, the BRC was at times frustrated with the label's promotion of the album. One of the things that made the IMPS deal attractive was the fact that the BRC would be in greater control of the marketing and distribution of its own product. "I always wanted to do a second compilation because I had been hearing so many demo tapes that sounded really good," Jimmy explained. Although members generally supported the project, Jimmy told me, "I don't think people believed that it was really going to happen and then when it did happen, people were like, 'Wow, it's here.'" Although the BRC exists to support musicians who want to challenge commonsense assumptions, they do not always escape them. Jimmy's comment indicates that the meager resources of the BRC, especially when compared to the pervasive power of mainstream labels, made it difficult for many members to imagine that the coalition would be able to produce its own record.

Bruce and Jimmy organized the production and financial arrangements to produce the compilation for a minimal amount of money. No new recording was necessary since the bands had submitted their own studio-recorded master tapes which, if selected, would be used directly. The only concern would be mastering tapes to achieve a consistent sound level across the recording. The twelve-song compilation

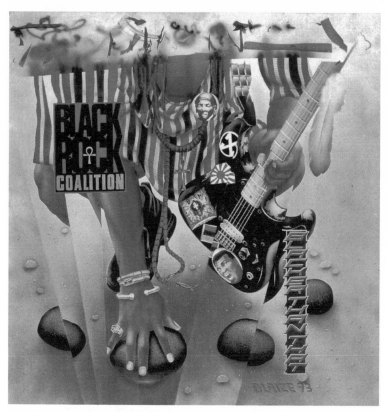

Cover art for the BRC's second compilation *Blacker Than That*. Original artwork by Sid Blaize, who also did the art for the first compilation, visible on the top left of the guitar body. Courtesy Jimmy Saal.

was released on only one format, compact disc, to further cut production costs. Under the contract that each band signed, artists allowed the BRC to use their recordings on the compilation, but the artists still held all rights, meaning they could use the song again on other compilations or on their own releases. The deal worked out well for the bands and the organization. "We felt like we put something together that offered something to the bands, which was a record . . . that would be commercially available with their music on it." Jimmy recalled, "It's something we thought would be of interest to the media. . . . So we said, look, this will get you some attention, it won't cost you anything, your tapes are sitting around anyway, so why don't you work with us?" Bruce and Jimmy selected nine East Coast bands and three West Coast bands for the disc. They tried a number of titles for the compilation and finally borrowed the contribution of Greg Tate's band, Women in Love. *Blacker Than That* plays on the phrase "blacker than thou," a colloquialism that critiques those who claim to be more authentically black than others. Both the compilation's title and the music it contained were about going beyond simplistic representations of blackness.

Cover art came from BRC member and graphic artist Sid Blaize, who had also designed the cover art for *The History of Our Future*. The image represents the membership at both philosophical and physical levels. The Afrocentric colors red, gold, and green are featured throughout. They appear in the BRC logo and on the striped pullover of the image's centerpiece: a crouching, brown-skinned figure holding a black guitar. The drawing is cropped so the face is not visible; thus, he becomes an everyman BRC member. The fact that a woman is not featured is indicative of the predominantly male composition of the organization and of rock generally. The figure's right hand balances on one of the scattered black rocks glowing blue, creating a visual pun about African American music genres. Also figuring prominently are dreadlocks, black combat boots, a gold ankh hanging from a chain, bracelets, and a button of Harriet Tubman. The guitar is decorated with a variety of stickers: a silver X for Malcolm X; the cover art of the first BRC compilation; a red, black, and green flag; and the face of Muhammad Ali. The placement of images of American heroes like Harriet Tubman who led enslaved blacks north to freedom, Malcolm X who exhorted blacks to free their minds, and Muhammad Ali who refused to go to war against other people of color alongside a prototypical black rocker visually links the BRC to the tradition of African American freedom fighters. The result is a visually arresting blend of African diaspora style and politics intercut with rock 'n' roll.

The BRC leadership believed that a compilation could represent the musical breadth of the organization and provide exposure for several member bands. The twelve songs collected on *Blacker Than That* epitomize the variety of approaches taken by BRC bands. D'Tripp's "Run From the World" uses vocal harmonies and a funky bass line that echo Sly and the Family Stone. Menace, a guitarist who has worked with George Clinton and Madonna, offers "Detroit (Old School Funk Remix)," a song that delves into the P-funk; in fact, Clinton sidemen Bootsy Collins (bass) and Bernie Worrell (keyboards) are featured on the cut along with James Brown's saxophone player Maceo Parker. In "Commercialized," Faith underpins its rock guitar solos with reggae bass lines played by leader Felice Rosser in a meditation about a man consumed by consumerism. Synaestisia's "Green Balloon" features an eerie soprano by Michelle Johnson and fusion-infused guitar by David "Fuze" Fiuczynski who, in the space allotted each act to print lyrics, liner notes, and acknowledgments, lists vocalist Nina Hagen, alto saxophonist Eric Dolphy, and German expressionist painting as musical inspirations. The song "Contradictions" by Drek DuBoyz mixes hip-hop beats and hard rock guitar in a song that explores the link between frequently articulated social concerns and rarely assumed social responsibility. "Home, Home on the Range" by Suburban Dog signifies on the traditional cowboy song and depicts the suburban postwar American dream home as a fortress against real world concerns. "Blacker Than That" by Women In Love uses witty lyrics shared between vocalists Mikel Banks and Helga Davis to comment on the simplistic way blackness is constructed in the United States.

A few songs are in the tradition of heavy metal and hardcore, genres that are associated with white musicians and audiences, but that claim important African American precursors including Mother's Finest, the Los Angeles heavy metal band, and Bad Brains, the black thrash-reggae band who were central figures in the 1980s hardcore punk scene in Washington, D.C. Guitar-made sirens lead into "N.Y.D.S. (New York Death Squad)" by D-Xtreme, the self-proclaimed "Original Slam Funk Posse." Their song uses high-speed, high-volume playing and singing to convey their anger about New York City Police Department activities in communities of color. The all-female Los Angeles band P.M.S. (who insist the initials stand for Play Me Seriously) in "Man With the Power" and Bozaque in "Shadow of Shadows" incorporate the vocal and instrumental approaches of hardcore punk and metal with lyrics that address freedom, empowerment, and black unity. Navigator, the band led by ex-Bus Boys bass player and Los Angeles BRC Orchestra Director Kevin O'Neal, contributes "Stolen Child," an elegantly arranged, mid-tempo groove featuring horns, strings, scats, and lyrics about the quest for freedom. Sophia's Toy contributes "Lifetime," the compilation's only clear-cut love song, a bright, slowly building number featuring Sophia Ramos's vocal finesse.

New York City radio personality Imhotep Gary Byrd, long associated with the black-owned radio station WLIB-AM (1190) and host of news and talk show *The Global Black Experience*, contributed the compilation's liner notes. He explains the paradox black rockers face and observes that the oxymoron "black rock" must be used because it is in keeping with the divisions made by the music industry. He adds that those who know music history recognize that in addition to the white rock groups that emerged in the 1960s and 1970s,

> the evolution of the music also produced Sly Stone, The Chambers Brothers, Richie Havens, Stevie Wonder, War, Earth, Wind and Fire, Isley Brothers, Mandrill, Commodores, Graham Central Station, Parliafunkadelicment [sic], Rufus, Kool and the Gang, Ohio Players, Edwin Birdsong, Jimmy Castor, Mother's Finest, and a host of others who were dedicated to a form which when compared to that so called "white rock" was definitely "Blacker Than That." (Byrd 1993)

After naming, claiming, and praising black rock precursors—a common practice among BRC members—Byrd turns to the question of selling black rock, "a music marketed primarily to white audiences projected in mass media as being 'originated' by white artists 'suddenly' being played by artists who were obviously 'Blacker Than That'" (Byrd 1993). He describes the formation of the Black Rock Coalition as a response to this dilemma and an effort to bring together the "children of Hendrix and Sly" in order to "unite their collective forces to somehow continue the legacy." In this capsule description, Byrd pays tribute to BRC members as defenders of and participants in an African American musical tradition. He concludes by describing the compilation as "an assault on the senses and the stereotypes related to what is being produced in Black music today. You will hear an extremely diversified mix of music and bands which touches Folk, Funk, Blues, R&B and Rap with messages that deal with where we are in the world today without having to call anybody Bitch/Ho/Nigger etc." (Byrd 1993). Collected in one recording, these twelve songs are sonic evidence of the musical talent in the BRC and also an example of the variety of ways members reclaimed their right to rock.

PROMOTING AND SELLING BLACKER THAN THAT

Having finally launched its own label, the BRC wanted to reach as many potential listeners as possible. Robert Fields, the New York director of publicity, sent copies of the compilation to magazines and newspapers that had been supportive of the BRC in the past. As a result, *Blacker Than That* was reviewed in the national publications *Musician*, *Vibe*, and *Billboard* (e.g., Gardner 1993). To publicize the record, East and West Coast chapters sponsored listening parties and record release parties at local clubs, and the New York BRC executive com-

P.B.R. Streetgang in a New Music Seminar showcase at Wetlands. From left, Anthony Peterson, Amafujo Inniss, Bruce Mack, and Mark Peterson. Photo by Janine da Silva.

mittee arranged for members of the coalition to participate in high-profile alternative music conferences. By putting together conference showcases featuring bands from the compilation, the BRC could expose member bands to a concentrated audience of music industry people. Alternative music conferences were founded to cater to the influx of independent labels and bands whose unconventional music marked them (usually to their delight) as industry outsiders during the 1980s. Developed to support less mainstream music and identify the rising stars of rock, rap, and electronica undergrounds, the most well-known of these conferences are New York's New Music Seminar/New Music Nights Festival (NMS), which operated from 1980 to 1994; New York's College Music Journal Music Marathon (CMJ), which started in 1980; and Austin's South By Southwest Music and Media Conference (SXSW), which has run since 1986. Like hundreds of independent artists and labels, the BRC and its members have been involved with each of these conferences. In addition to promoting music and networking, the conventions offer panel discussions about the labyrinthine workings of the music industry and topical issues of interest to music professionals. As mainstream taste began to embrace the more experimental sounds promoted in these conferences, major labels turned to NMS, CMJ, and SXSW to locate commercially viable new talent. What began as networks for the underground developed into major music industry events, the place for up-and-coming bands to be heard and seen by the right people.

These music conventions allowed fans, musicians, industry executives, and a researcher like myself to hear numerous unknown bands performing sets at dozens of rock venues around the host city. At the July 1993 NMS, the BRC presented a showcase at the Manhattan Center featuring New York bands Women in Love, Drek DuBoyz, and Sophia's Toy and Los Angeles band P.M.S., all of whom appear on *Blacker Than That*. Further raising the coalition's profile during the five-day conference, BRC member acts D'Tripp, Shock Council, the Ancestors, Faith, Me'Shell NdegéOcello, Tracie Morris, and D-Xtreme played in other venues during the week. A few months later at the November CMJ Seminar, the BRC executive committee arranged for Screaming Headless Torsos, Faith, and Sophia's Toy to appear in a BRC showcase with headliner Me'Shell NdegéOcello in a show hosted by poets Tracie Morris and Samantha Coerbell. A BRC showcase at the March 1994 SXSW featured Tracie Morris from New York, Monkey Meet from Los Angeles, Follow for Now from Atlanta, Sinister Dane from St. Louis, and Brothers From Another Planet from Detroit. BRC involvement in these conventions was important not only because it gave visibility to member bands and black rock. By connecting rock with African Americans, the BRC created at least one space that disrupted the genre-dictated separation that in turn produced the racial segregation of black and white convention-goers that marked most of the non-BRC NMS, CMJ, and SXSW sets that I attended during the years I conducted research. Furthermore, the BRC's involvement ensured the onstage presence of black instrumentalists who were typically absent in contexts where rappers and vocalists comprised the overwhelming majority of black performers. BRC participation in the conferences also boosted the black presence on industry panel discussions. For example, at the 1993 CMJ, Me'Shell NdegéOcello and Tracie Morris sat on a panel called "The 'F' Word: Being a Feminist in the Music Industry"; Bruce Mack spoke on the panel "Bitches Ain't Shit But Hos and Tricks," a session exploring men's perspectives on women in music; and Beverly Jenkins moderated a panel on the image of African Americans in popular culture. Chiefly, however, these conventions are scenes for business and self-promotion. "It's about schmoozing," Jimmy Saal told me during the coalition's NMS showcase. The BRC executives and band members were working that event, talking to industry professionals—journalists, publicists, record executives, and distributors. When I asked Robert Fields about his activities during the NMS, he told me, "I've been shaking a lot of hands." He also explained that he was making a special effort to connect with European and Japanese distributors, both for the BRC and for some of his own black rock clients.

To increase the impact of the NMS showcase and to further promote the compilation, Steve Williams broadcasted some of the proceedings on the BRC's radio show, "Strange Vibrations from the Hardcore," a few hours after the performances occurred. He recorded the bands' sets and then played highlights during the show. He interspersed these "live" cuts with tracks from *Blacker Than That* and brief, on-air interviews with band members who came by the studios. Greg Tate, Konda Mason, and Vernon Reid had started the radio program in 1986, securing a slot for it on New York's WBAI-FM. This Pacifica Radio station had a 50,000 watt signal that reached out from midtown Manhattan into the boroughs and beyond to New Jersey, Connecticut, and parts of Pennsylvania and Delaware. WBAI was a noncommercial, nonprofit, listener-supported station with news, arts, political, and cultural coverage in addition to music programming. By 1993, Steve Williams and Earl Douglas Jr. hosted and produced the show on alternate Fridays, from midnight to 3 AM, providing a regularly available radio venue for black rock.[3] In a BRC newsletter article published a few months before the showcase, Steve urged his fellow members to support the show during WBAI's pledge drive. Reiterating the service the program provided, he noted that "Strange Vibrations" had been a strong and consistent voice for alternative black,

> providing listeners with the opportunity to hear music that has been shut out of mainstream radio airwaves. I'm talking about such artists as Defunkt, Eric Gales, Eye & I, Follow for Now, the Family Stand, and Divine Styler—bands that have managed to obtain recording deals, but yet still don't enjoy the same access to commercial radio as bands like Nirvana or U2. It is through "Strange Vibrations" that we're able to play music by unsigned bands such as Miss Mary Mack, Shock Council and Drek Du Boyz, which helps strengthen their audience base for their live performances. In addition, we've also been able to bring to you music by artists like Ice-T and Bodycount, who has come under fire for his statements about police violence in the song "Cop Killer." (Williams 1993:1)

On the night of the NMS showcase and the WBAI post-showcase broadcast, Living Colour played on the *Tonight Show with Jay Leno* to promote its new album, *Stain*. Obviously, most bands—BRC or otherwise—could not reasonably hope for that kind of national exposure. Inclusion in a set of music spun by Steve Williams and Earl Douglas on WBAI offered another kind of opportunity. Member bands often sat in on "Strange Vibrations." Here, they could air newly produced recordings, promote upcoming events, play some of their favorite songs by other artists, and talk with Steve and Earl about music. This black rock presence on the radio was another way members publicized their musical vision and expanded the black public sphere.

As the BRC embarked on the *Blacker Than That* project, a member who had been involved with the first BRC compilation reminded the executive committee that "making a record is not the same as selling a record." The freedom that enabled the production and energized the launch of the CD was tempered by limited resources for distribution and promotion. The BRC could not saturate the market with their product in the fashion of major labels and, indeed, selling the compilation was an uphill battle. The modes of distribution were through IMPS's 800-number, purchase at band gigs and BRC events, and mail order directly through the BRC. Initially, *Blacker Than That* was on sale at Tower and HMV record stores in Manhattan and in two independent record stores in New Jersey. The BRC eventually had to sign a contract with a regional distributor when Tower changed its policy and stopped accepting product from independent producers, insisting instead on dealing with distributors. In a change that is typical in the independent side of the recording industry, Wayne Green sold IMPS, leaving the BRC with no contacts in the new management. This eliminated the BRC's access to a nationally distributed mail order catalogue as a sales outlet. Jimmy was philosophical when commenting to me in an e-mail message about the end of the IMPS association: "I think the whole deal was tricky to begin with," he wrote, "but with smoke and mirrors we got a CD out of the deal."

Generally speaking, compilations are easy to produce, but difficult to sell. Usually they are a way of repackaging hit songs by multiple artists that are already familiar and a "safe buy." Independent and major labels also use compilations as a tool for introducing new artists and upcoming releases; these compilations are sold cheaply or given away to targeted consumers. A compilation of unknown, unsigned bands priced at $12 was a much harder sell, especially since there was no easily identifiable single or hit to focus on. In promoting the CD, the BRC hoped that the general concept of black rock would inspire interest. One of the founding concerns of the BRC was to encourage networking, support, and collaboration among musicians. Choosing one band from among all the members and focusing the organization's limited energies on that artist's record would have meant giving one band unfair attention. Producing a compilation involved and invested a cross section of the membership, making it a BRC enterprise rather than a showcase for a single act. It was, therefore, something more members could feel comfortable supporting. The efforts to protect the interests of the BRC as an organization while also attempting to engage in the marketplace reflected a concern with internal relations, morale, and resources. The question remains whether it would have been better in the long-term to have recorded one group, followed by another (and another and another). Some members argued that there was really no point to the label if it did not release the work of individual bands. In the end, practical considerations also influenced the form the label took. Members of the BRC executive committee, already overburdened with the work of running the organization (and doing so on a voluntary basis), knew how much time and energy running a viable independent label would require.[4] The approach they chose may have limited sales, but it also protected personnel. They developed a project that could trade on the organization's reputation, gain attention in the media, and provide bands with exposure. The CD was just one instance in which the BRC had to confront the challenges of running a nonprofit organization in a profit-oriented arena, negotiating the tensions between competition and community in the process.

The length of time it took the BRC to start its label is another reflection of the competing value systems with which the organization operates. The coalition's role as an artists' organization with a mission to promote alternative black music has been fairly clear, but determining how best to offer this support has been less so. Most members agreed that the BRC should preserve and advance black popular music, using any means available—independent labels and the Internet, for example. BRC Records was a way of "taking it to the next level," as many members told me, but some felt it took the BRC too long to reach this stage. One member argued, "You've got to be independent: The BRC, independent, nonprofit, finally started a label. I mean, I feel that we should have started that *way* back—even when we just had cassettes from live gigs—from jump. And we didn't do that and I think that does reflect a lot of where the BRC is at now." I suspect that the slowness to move toward the D.I.Y. model is related to the members' early interest in pursuing the mainstream. This is a focus that resulted from the musicians' assumption that if they were talented enough, they could follow in the footsteps of artists like Jimi Hendrix, Sly Stone, and Led Zeppelin. Rock and funk acts of the late 1960s and 1970s typically had contracts with major labels which were, at that time, responsible for an outpouring of diverse music. Another member commented:

> I read an interview with Prince once where he was talking about how it used to be. [Black] music used to be artist-driven and then once it becomes a producer's medium, the stuff started getting really constricted. So in the seventies you could have a Parliament, Earth, Wind & Fire, War, Ohio Players, Isley Brothers—all these different bands, completely different sounds, and all being successful—played on the radio. Stevie Wonder, you know. And now, you listen to the radio and there are definite parameters on what you hear. So at that point, [in the mid-1980s] black musicians—at least the musicians I knew—were all trying to deal with the black music industry, you know, trying to write and get into that whole black pop thing. And getting in touch with the Black Rock Coalition was great—seeing the people dealing with original music and different stuff.

While the narrowing of mainstream channels may have convinced BRC members to develop their own distribution networks, the financial realities of undertaking such a project coupled with the time required to run a label apparently were deterrents. Instead, the BRC primarily produced shows intended to generate media interest, build a fan base for black rock, and attract the attention of deep-pocketed major labels. The signing of Living Colour and the band's success made the dream of getting a major label deal seem within reach and may have detracted from a focus on the independent route. Talking about his band's early years, Vernon Reid recalled, "At that time, the whole thing was to get a [major label] record deal. Times have really changed now. Even though a record deal is still considered to be something that's significant, its significance has changed" (Reid quoted in BRC 2001b:11). There may have been ideological factors at work, as well. Having framed its critique around issues of race and access in the mainstream music industry, it was important for the BRC to focus on entering the mainstream. Arguably, this is not an unusual perspective for beneficiaries of civil rights–era demands for equal opportunity for African Americans. Participating in the somewhat separate and unequal independent media network did not seem attractive when the coalition started. As time passed and major labels passed most black rockers up, however, going independent became a viable option. By producing *Blacker Than That*, the BRC represented the musical range and multifaceted nature of the organization. "We never expected a million seller," Jimmy told me. What they hoped for and developed was a product that would get the music of BRC bands into the marketplace while also providing a permanent document of the Black Rock Coalition in 1993.

PUTTING ON A SHOW

Producing recordings was one part of the battle; another was finding ways to disseminate them. The importance of video to music promotion and the difficulties of access to national cable music stations encouraged many musicians to seek alternative ways to show their videos. Public access cable television provided one outlet. In the 1970s when cable television was first being developed in the United States, the Federal Communications Commission established a requirement that cable systems in the nation's largest 100 television markets provide channels devoted to public, educational, and government services (Kellner 1990:188). This ruling created public access or community access programming.[5] Public access stations inject a local focus into otherwise national cable programming and serve groups that are excluded from mainstream cable offerings. Advocates of public access television believed that it could democratize the media by creating a space for public discussions of traditional political concerns like voting, legislation, and policy that received inadequate attention in commercial outlets (182). Arguably, the push for public access was rooted in an understanding that the media played a significant role in the public sphere and that privatization curtailed accessibility. Although initially geared toward informing viewers about politics, public access stations quickly became forums through which an array of local, nonmainstream interests were able to gain a voice. In Los Angeles, BRC members were among those involved in public access programming.

Members of the Los Angeles BRC produced their program, *Network BRC*, at the San Fernando Valley studios of community access cable station United Artists Cable–Channel 25, a station serving parts of northern and western Los Angeles County. Produced and written by the husband and wife team of Rod and Melva Miller, *Network BRC* featured interviews and performances with BRC musicians. Like all BRC members, Rod, Melva, and the show's host Todd Washington worked on a strictly volunteer basis. To put together an episode, the three would hold a production meeting with the guest several weeks before the shoot to determine what issues they would cover in the interview and preview the songs the artist would perform. Based on these conversations, Melva would develop a script, working closely with Rod to outline the precise timing of the show.[6] *Network BRC* guests had to provide a copy of the broadcast-quality videos they wanted to present. Guests without videos could lip synch to a broadcast-quality audiotape, miming a live performance in the station's studios. Because of financial, equipment, and time limitations, there were no live performances on the show, a necessary compromise that stemmed from the program's low budget. In March 1995, I attended a taping to see how the production operated and meet the producers. While setting up for the shoot, Rod explained that he had to take Channel 25's sixteen-week training course in order to earn the certification that all individuals involved in the production aspects of any program on the station had to have. The training was completely free—that was part of the station's contract with the city—but anyone interested in participating had to make the effort to get to the sessions.

"The certification itself isn't really worth much," he admitted. "It's not like any network TV station will hire you, but it does allow me to work on the show. Now, I'm the producer and all the techs on the show—the guys on the cameras and the sound board—are interns. Only the director, the one who calls the show, is on the station's staff. He was also in my training group, but he was the best in the class, so they hired him."[7] Rod described the training program as "totally hands on." He recalled, "The first night I came to class, they told me I was on Camera 2. I'd never run a camera before, but they let me fool around with it for a little bit and I learned my way. While we were shooting."

Rod's description of United Artists Cable Television–Channel 25 delineates practices that are typical of public access stations nationwide. Their original objective was to make television production equipment and airtime available to any member of a given community. Individuals received access to the training and technology needed to produce programs on which they could say or do anything as long as they avoided obscene or libelous material (Kellner 1990:207). Training sessions, equipment, and time slots were available on a first-come, first-served basis and were usually free of charge. Through the kind of internship Rod described, community members could get working knowledge of the studio equipment, station rules, and production practices; ideally they would be prepared to produce a program on a small budget. At Channel 25, for example, the BRC's only expenditures were for the three-quarter-inch videotapes onto which each episode was recorded. Based on their resources and energy, cable access producers can program weekly, bimonthly, or monthly series as well as occasional shows; their main constraint is the number of programs already in rotation at the station (213). The titles of programs scheduled to air on Channel 25 in March 1995 reveal the mix of shows typical of public access: *Assyrian Weekly Magazine, Tinsel Town's Queer, Astrology and You, Tele Romania, Senior Scene, Chick TV, Your Democratic Party* and, of course, *Network BRC* (Cablecast 25 News 1995:2–3).

"It's funny," Rod recalled while we waited for the taping to begin. "When I was planning the show, I kept putting off actually starting it. I kept coming up with reasons why I wasn't ready or the show wasn't ready. This woman I work with noticed what I was doing because she'd hear me on the phone, plus I was talking to her about it. Finally, she said, 'Look, Rod. Just schedule the time and do it. You'll probably never be completely ready.' So I took her advice."

"So it worked out," I said.

"Yeah . . . I mean, the first show was rough. Really rough. But there was a First Show."

Network BRC was taped on two simple sets. Bands prerecorded "live" lip-synched performances on a bare soundstage using their own equipment as props. Todd interviewed guests on a talk show style set: a carpeted platform with straight-backed chairs arranged around a small table and a large, leafy plant off to the side. Each episode of the program fits in a half-hour time slot and is structured similarly. The show opens with Todd's welcome to the viewers, a short description of the BRC, and an introduction of the guest. There is an immediate cut to a public service announcement and then a return to Todd and his guest. A brief conversation ensues and is followed by the first video or performance. The show returns to the host and guest who chat again before introducing the second song. After the second video or performance, Todd and his guest make a few final comments and then Todd wraps up the show with a reiteration of the guest's name, information about any recordings available in stores or through mail order, and a pitch for the BRC. In order to give each show a longer shelf life, there is no mention of time-sensitive information like upcoming club dates. The BRC's Los Angeles address and hotline numbers are displayed, followed by production credits.

At this point, I turn to a specific *Network BRC* episode in order to illustrate how the program provides a forum for black rock and black rock musicians. It was not unusual for the host and the guests to draw attention to this aspect of the show as the following transcription of a segment demonstrates. This episode, shot in 1993, featured Bernie "BK" Kaye, lead singer of Los Angeles BRC band Total Eclipse, in an interview with Todd. I had heard about Total Eclipse soon after I arrived in Los Angeles for my three months of fieldwork. Their story was a textbook example of the difficulties black rock bands faced. Signed to a major label deal on A&M Records and able to release an album and produce a video, Total Eclipse was stymied when MTV refused to put their video into rotation. Introducing the video, Bernie described "Fire in the Rain" as "probably the most commercial song" on Total Eclipse's first album. The video is typical of MTV rock fare of the early 1990s: a slick compendium of the requisite cryptic images—a shadowy boy playing outdoors, bricks being laid, a fire burning—intercut with footage of the four band members performing amid a moodily lit studio arrangement of fog-swathed, leafless trees. The difference is that the rockers are black. After screening the video, Bernie and Todd discussed its fate on music television. The following is my transcription of a portion of their interview (BRC 1993b). I have bracketed and italicized descriptions of camera movements and speaker actions.

TODD: [*midshot of Todd smiling and nodding*] Nice video. I like that. "Fire in the Rain." That was Total Eclipse here on *Network* BRC. And this is the album [*holds up CD case*] if you can find it anywhere.

BERNIE: [*laughs*]

TODD: I would definitely try to find it [*puts CD case on table*]. Now let's talk about that video. Who directed that video?

BERNIE: [*close-up of Bernie*] That's Josh Taft out of Seattle.

TODD: Josh Taft. Okay.

BERNIE: Yeah, yeah. He's part of that Seattle scene, Pearl Jam and Alice in Chains. A real nice cat. We shot that in Seattle.

TODD: Great. Liked those images [*cut to close-up of Todd*]. I have never seen that video before—

BERNIE: [*cut to Bernie*] No one has! [*Bernie leans forward in his seat, twists as if about to stand up, grabs vest and sits back in the seat*] [*cut to midshot of Todd and Bernie seated*]

TODD: [*laughs*] Okay. Why don't we talk a little about that?

BERNIE: Oh, man [*pause*]. Okay, I'll try.

TODD: Okay, try to dig up a little of that information.

BERNIE: [*close-up of Bernie*] Here's the thing about it, as far as the BRC, people out there know this is the BRC and that stands for Black

Rock Coalition and that initially started with a lot of black rockers, right. So this leads me into this video. We did this video and being black [*punctuates by hitting the side of his right hand against his open left palm*] and playing rock [*the same gesture, now with a sarcastic laugh*] are like, you know, shit (did I say that?), two evils. So here's the deal—

TODD: It hasn't always been.

BERNIE: [*camera still on Bernie*] So here's the deal. We go to MTV and they try to explain to us in their best terms that "Where do we put it? It doesn't fit our format." What? It's rock, isn't it? "Yeah, but there's something, something about it."

TODD: [*cut to reaction shot of Todd*] Something about that video . . .

BK: [*close-up of Bernie*] So we go to BET which is black entertainment and I'm not downing anybody here, okay, but I'm just—this is the bottom line. And they say, "Well, it's rock." Okay. And it's like, that's the Catch-22 that we're in, because I think each one should have played it on its own merits.

TODD: Right.

BERNIE: Period. But there it is, as they say.

TODD: [*cut to close-up of Todd who speaks directly to camera*] Ladies and gentlemen, here you have a quality video, quality band, no airplay. We need you, you need the BRC, we need to come together. Call up the stations, call up these networks, talk to them, write letters, say, "Look, I saw this band Total Eclipse, I've never seen them on your program." Let's get the people together, let's put this stuff on the air. It's going to take some letters, it's going to take some people coming down to support these bands so people can see that these bands have something to say that needs to be heard. [*Todd turns to Bernie*] I personally would like to see an alternative to MTV so we don't have to depend—

BERNIE: True.

TODD:—on MTV.

BERNIE: That's so true.

TODD: Or BET. The beginnings of what we have here may generate some of what we need in the future, but unfortunately MTV provides a service but they don't really have any competition as far as what I can see. So when they say this is the number one video, who's going to argue with them? You know what I'm saying?

BERNIE: [*cut to Bernie*] Everyone jumps on the train.

TODD: MTV is a radio [*sic*] station that basically has no competition, so bands like you come along, put their heart and soul in the music, and they say, "Well, sorry." [*camera has been on Bernie during this statement. He smiles slightly and affirms Todd's observations with emphatic nods*]

BERNIE: True.

TODD: So where do we go [*cut to Todd*] from here? I mean —

BERNIE: We go to Europe.

TODD: [*laughs*] Let's talk about that. You guys been over there?

BERNIE: [*midshot of both of them*] No, but we sell a lot of records, a lot of records over there.

Although the existence of *Network* BRC is an implicit critique of MTV and BET, in this clip, Bernie and Todd are direct in their attack, a result of Total Eclipse's bitter encounter with the two national cable networks. Their comments about the band's experiences trying to get included on MTV and BET playlists underscore the ways race informs executive decision making and influences the production, distribution, and reception circuit. For Los Angeles BRC members, the fact that video director Josh Taft, whose videos for white rock bands Alice in Chains and Pearl Jam were put into rotation on MTV, was unable to produce an equally acceptable video for a black rock band was an indication of MTV's continued racism. While the station featured black rappers on its popular *Yo! MTV Raps*, it abandoned black rockers, even a band with a major label deal and a quality video. A&M Records had the familiar difficulties marketing Total Eclipse, and these were probably exacerbated rather than relieved by the presence of other black rock bands on the scene. Many BRC members told me that the industry seemed reluctant to sponsor more than a handful of black rock bands. Lenny Kravitz, Living Colour, Fishbone, Bad Brains, and 24–7 Spyz were already out there. The logical question for the industry was whether there was a need or market for Total Eclipse, another black rock act. Any differences in sound, style, and ethos were trumped by their most notable similarity to existing nationally known black rock bands: their blackness. In the end, A&M dropped Total Eclipse from its roster because of the failure of the record to sell — or, as BRC members saw it, after the failure of the label to sell the record.

Bernie's invocation of Europe as a viable alternative to the U.S. mainstream is a revealing response. At one level, it indicates the range of approaches musicians can take when seeking outlets for their work. At another level, it points out that the problems black rock bands encounter have been constructed in a U.S. context that constrains African American cultural production. American media outlets are

Cover of the program for the 1991 BRC organized Black Rock Festival in Bari, Italy. The tour, comanaged by Beverly Jenkins and Janine da Silva, included Jean-Paul Bourelly, P.B.R. Streetgang, Michael Hill's Bluesland, J. J. Jumpers, D-Xtreme, Kelvynator, the Good Guys, and the BRC Orchestra featuring Bernie Worrell. Courtesy Bill Toles.

BLACK ROCK COALITION ORCHESTRA

Missä AACM-yhteisö Chicagossa ja sen St. Louisissa sijainnut vastine BAG-liike vetivät 60-luvun puolivälin tienoilla puoleensa sekä taiteellisesti että poliittisesti valveutuneita nuoria mustia jazz-muusikoita siinä M-Base ja Black Rock Coalition järjestöt pyrkivät New Yorkissa kerimään kokoon afro-amerikkalaisen musiikin tämän päivän diasporan.

Black Rock Coalition (BRC) perustettiin syksyllä 1985 vaihtoehtoliikkeeksi heijastamaan koko mustan musiikin kirjoa. Yhdistyksen alkuunpanevina voimina toimivat mm. Living Colour-kitaristi Vernon Reid ja pianisti Geri Allen.

BRC-orkesteri (BRCO) lähti liikkeelle puoli vuotta myöhemmin. Sen ohjelmisto ulottuu afrikkalaisista juurista ja lähteistä rockin ja R&B:n kautta jazzlin ja funkiin.

Where AACM community in Chicago and its St. Louis equivalent, the BAG movement, attracted in the middle 60's both artistically and politically conscious young black jazz musicians there M-Base and Black Rock Coalition in New York attempt to gather together today's diaspora of Afro-American music.

Black Rock Coalition (BRC) was founded in the fall of 1985 as an alternative movement to project the whole kaleidoscope of black music. The primus motors of the movement were, among others, Living Colour guitarist Vernon Reid and pianist Geri Allen. The BRC Orchestra (BRCO) started out half a year later. Its repertoire covers black music from African roots and sources through rock and R&B to jazz and funk.

Page from the 1992 Pori, Finland Jazz Festival program. From left, Muzz Skillings, Bill Toles, Eric Person, Marque Gilmore, Jerome Harris, Beverly Jenkins, Graham Haynes, Myrna Colley-Lee, Jared Nickerson, Michael Hill, and Wayne Livingston. Original photo by Sikay Tang. Courtesy Bill Toles.

structured by economic imperatives and racialized assumptions that limit the ways both producers and consumers can engage with music. As Bernie noted later in the *Network* BRC interview, Europe is an appealing alternative "because the people there, they don't need MTV to convince them." Historically, European outlets and audiences have been more willing to embrace music "on its own merits" rather than based on the image of the performers, leading a long line of African American musicians to turn to overseas markets. Black rockers found that in Europe their creativity was not stifled by U.S. racial politics. Furthermore, to the extent that image is important, black Americanness is often a positive selling point for many Europeans—at least in the realm of music. Not surprisingly, many black rock musicians— including BRC members Gene Williams, Michael Hill's Blues Mob, Screaming Headless Torsos, and Kelvyn Bell—have focused touring and distribution efforts on Europe and also in Japan. The comparative openness of European audiences also led the BRC to produce a BRC Orchestra tribute to Jimi Hendrix in Bari, Italy, in 1991 and a black rock set at the 1992 International Pori Jazz Festival in Finland.

Although offering alternatives to the music available on MTV and

BET, *Network BRC* was constrained by the conditions of its production: the limited reach of its show, its low budget, and its modest production values. Still, by providing a forum where black rockers could perform and discuss their music, *Network BRC* expanded mainstream media representations of black music and black people. Other cable access programs share this mission and have featured BRC artists. In New York, Fikisha Combo dedicated several episodes of her program, CACE *International TV*, to coverage of the BRC's 1993 Jimi Hendrix Birthday Tribute. Her program was in rotation on four Manhattan and Brooklyn cable stations. In 1995, *New York New Rock*, a local music program airing on Manhattan Cable, covered the 1995 Hendrix Tribute Show and in 1994 it featured a group interview with BRC executive committee members Bruce Mack, Jimmy Saal, and Chuck Brownley. In Los Angeles, *Video Nouveau*, produced by Clarise Wilkins and Erica Bristol, dedicated an episode to screening videos by BRC artists from New York and Los Angeles in 1995. The Los Angeles-based cable program *City TV*, produced and hosted by Terry Cross, devoted a 1992 program to documenting the Los Angeles BRC's weekly Black Rock Cafe band showcase at the Gaslight in Hollywood. Both programs were played several times on Los Angeles cable access stations.

During the 1990s, cheaper and more accessible technology made it easier for artists to produce their videos and CDs independently. BRC bands like D-Xtreme, Civil Rite, and Drek DuBoyz made their own videos that could be screened on these outlets when the opportunity arose. They also used these videos when seeking performance opportunities internationally or nationally. Through networks of friends and acquaintances, bands usually had a connection to someone with inexpensive but professional video production equipment and the ability to use it effectively. D-Xtreme made its video for "N.Y.D.S." when a fan volunteered his equipment and services. A number of BRC members have home studios where they record their own work and make a little cash on the side by renting the space to other musicians. Others took advantage of special deals offered by independent studios in Los Angeles and Manhattan where, for around $50 an hour, they could get the services of an engineer and the use of a professional studio and equipment for a recording. Bands also found creative ways to subsidize professional quality recordings. Suburban Dog cut a session in January 1993 at a New York technical school where the band had volunteered to play so the class could be trained on studio recording equipment.

In spite of the high prices charged for them at stores, compact discs

Michael Hill's Blues Mob captured the contemporary urban
blues experience. From left, Bill McClellan (drums), Michael
Hill (guitar and vocals), and Pete Cummings (bass and vocals).

are relatively inexpensive to produce. In the mid-1990s, it cost less
than $2,000 to press and package 1,000 discs. By going to a CD produc-
tion company, bands could turn their studio recordings into compact
discs in jewel boxes with artwork. Among the BRC bands who released
and distributed recordings independently were Suburban Dog, Civil
Rite, Gene Williams, Women in Love, and Faith. Los Angeles band
Rainbows End sold cassettes of its self-produced recording *No Far Out*
to underwrite the cost of compact disc production; those who supported the band by purchasing a cassette received a copy of the compact disc once it was available. Bands sold these recordings at shows
and also sent them to radio stations, independent record distributors,
booking agencies, and alternative music press with the hope of getting
some attention. Other BRC bands signed contracts with independent
labels. The greater open-mindedness, flexibility, and autonomy of the
independent labels compensated for their more limited production,
promotion, and distribution resources. BRC members who have re-

leased recordings on independent labels include Screaming Headless Torsos on Discovery, Queen Esther and Elliot Sharp's Hoosegow on Homestead Records, and Michael Hill's Blues Mob on Alligator. The Blues Mob, incidentally, exemplifies the ways BRC members use the organization's network to support projects. Hill started the band with his siblings, but over the years, the personnel changed, and Hill called in fellow BRC members to play in the band. In its 2003 incarnation, the Blues Mob featured Hill on guitar and vocals; Pete Cummings, formerly with Shock Council, on bass; and Bill McClellan, formerly with P.B.R. Streetgang, on drums. The 1994 album *Bloodlines* features liner notes by Greg Tate and cover art by Sid Blaize who contributed the artwork for BRC compilations. Soon after the record's release, the band opened for Me'Shell NdegéOcello's 1994 performance at Irving Plaza in New York.

Since the mid-1990s, the Internet has expanded the possibilities of independent production by giving performers access to an inexpensive and wide-reaching marketing tool that offers some professional autonomy. After being disappointed by a lack of support from his independent record label, David Fiuczynski, with the help of his wife Lian Amber, regained the rights to the first Screaming Headless Torsos album. He released it on his own Fuzelicious Morsels label and distributes it, along with his other projects, through his Web site. Like Fiuczynski, a number of BRC members set up Web pages that provide information about their bands, club dates, and merchandise as well as links to other sites of interest—these can be for other bands, online publications, and favorite rock venues. Many BRC bands also included a link to the BRC Web site, a clearinghouse for black rock information. The coalition's Web site features the BRC Manifesto, an events calendar, band names, links to the Web sites of black rock and BRC artists, information about the radio show, photographs of events, articles about and interviews with BRC members, and frequently asked questions about black rock and the BRC.[8] These independent outlets provide a space for audiences who are willing to go to the trouble of seeking nonmainstream fare through the World Wide Web, alternative publications, e-mail lists, and word of mouth.

In their struggle over representations of blackness, BRC members engage the very media that have influenced the music and identities they produce and the images they critique. Using alternative circuits to disseminate their message, they push the boundaries of race and genre that shape the U.S. popular music industry and circumscribe African Americans—in the media and beyond. This kind of cultural activism produces *Network* BRC, *Blacker Than That*, the BRC's radio show—which by 2002 was being streamed online—black rock-oriented Web sites, and independent videos and recordings. Together these independent productions address the exclusionary nature of the music industry and challenge the ways racism has shaped music industry practices, audience expectations, patterns of consumption, and the erasure of African Americans from the history of rock. A refusal or inability to fit the demands of mainstream media led many BRC members to turn to more accessible independent outlets. Of course, a local public access cable TV program affords different audience access and career cachet than mainstream national channels like MTV or BET. Similarly, the BRC record label is not the same as a major label or even a large independent label. Still, these grassroots outlets allow bands to have their music commercially available—if on a smaller scale. By working in independent media, BRC members develop alternatives to the mainstream. At one level, this is a compromise—members lose out on large audiences and the accompanying recognition that most artists desire. At another level, however, this is a critique of the mainstream media. Many members view independent production as a way to avoid compromising one's musical and individual integrity. Konda Mason, commenting about the importance of taking an independent approach, observed:

> We have to break outside of the box. We have to be in charge of our own destinies creatively. It won't happen inside the industry. There have been little gains. But if you're in the middle of the industry, they are going to control what you do in order to meet their bottom line. And they aren't going to touch those things that are outside the box. The Internet has changed everything. We need to redirect our focus not on how to get a record deal, but how to set up our own companies and how to make good music. Like I said, I have a love/hate relationship with the industry, but it's mostly hate. I have seen this business kill too many great artists' spirits. (Mason quoted in BRC 2000/2001:10–11)

Media, the context that led to the emergence of the BRC, became a context into which BRC members intervened as they sought to do the primary thing musicians desire: produce and share music while keeping their spirits intact.

EIGHT

PLAYING ROCK, PLAYING ROLES

Not only is Faith out here, not really playing reggae and not really playing rock,
but we don't look the part. Not just Felice and Diana as women, but me as a guy.
I'm not blond. I don't look like Slash or Lenny Kravitz either. I'm a dark-skinned
man. How are they gonna package me as a guitar god? — FORMER FAITH GUITARIST
RENE AKAN

Like all rockers, black rock musicians contend with the fantasies of
race, gender, and sexuality that are an integral part of the form. Rock
'n' roll is rooted in black music traditions, drawing heavily on the
musical and vocal inflections, linguistic choices, and body movements
that characterize African American performance. Over the years, this
blackness has been recoded and naturalized as white rock 'n' roll attitude, a blend of the rebelliousness, sexuality, and cool that black
Americans often represent. Arguably, this is one of the ways black-
identified "rock 'n' roll" of the 1950s became white-identified "rock"
in the 1960s. The vocals and onstage personae of performers like Elvis
Presley, Mick Jagger, and Janis Joplin demonstrate this indebtedness
to black performance tropes and indicate the ways rock has served as a
site for the reformulation of white masculinity and femininity. While
these white rockers embody the white attraction to blackness, others
verbalize it. In "Rock 'n' Roll Nigger," Patti Smith lets off a laudatory
wail in honor of the outsiders whom she admires and dubs "niggers."
She and her band mates apparently relish repeating the taboo epithet
and align themselves with the integrity and rebellion they imagine
"niggers" to personify. Lou Reed satirizes this stereotype of blackness

in the song "I Wanna Be Black." Describing a desire to have "natural rhythm," "a big prick," and "a stable of foxy whores," Reed's narrator dreams of escaping his boring life as "a fucked up white middle-class college student" and joining what he imagines to be the more enticing black world. Smith and Reed are both responding to the oppositional valences embedded in rock 'n' roll and other black popular culture forms. From Harlem's white jazz fans of the 1920s to the Beats and rock 'n' rollers of the 1950s to the blues revivalists of the 1960s to the rap fans of the 1990s, white Americans have immersed themselves in black culture, finding in this exotic arena an exhilarating way to elude the stodgy status quo (Jefferson 1973). These appropriations involved a certain amount of mythologizing and stereotyping of the emotions, sexuality, and spirituality of black people whom many whites believe embody the freedom, naturalness, and joy for life that whites had lost. Rock 'n' roll parallels these traits; it symbolizes freedom of expression, the rejection of mainstream white American society, and the pursuit of pleasure—especially illicit pleasures derived from sex and drugs.

Rock has enabled experimentation with categories of race and sexuality, but rock is also a sharply racialized and gendered terrain. The expression of rebellion against mainstream social constraints has been articulated from white heterosexual male perspectives. For white men, rock is a platform for defining and performing masculinity, usually in the form of a cool persona that, as one BRC member explained to me, "guys want to be like and girls want to be with."[1] BRC members had to deal with the notion that a white man was the proper embodiment of a rock musician and the fact that those who are not white and male have a difficult time winning acceptance as rockers, especially at the industry level. In this chapter, I examine the ways race and gender shaped the ways BRC members participated in rock. Following a brief discussion of women in rock, I focus on Faith and Sophia's Toy, BRC bands led by women, in order to explain the ways the racism that limits the participation of blacks in rock and the sexism that marginalizes women from the genre had particular and devastating effects on BRC women. The intersection of race and gender also informed relations among BRC members. In the second section, I consider the gender dynamics within the organization and their impact on the ways men and women negotiated working together. In the final section, I discuss the impact of race and gender on BRC men, focusing on the performance of black rock and the question of black masculinity.

Over the years, I have learned that being a female fan of rock requires a willingness to deal with a lot of egregious male posturing. Songs are often adversarial (Frith and McRobbie 1990:374). For example, Mick Jagger brags about keeping his girlfriend under his thumb and, more notoriously from my perspective, his knowledge that "black girls just want to get fucked all night"; meanwhile, Robert Plant relentlessly insists on giving the woman in question what he thinks she needs: every inch of his love.[2] A preoccupation with the penis is indexed by symbolic gestures accompanying guitar playing (Bayton 1998; Frith 1981) and also in the names of rock bands that focus on the phallus—the Sex Pistols, the Dickies—and its sexual excretions—10cc (purportedly the amount of semen in an average ejaculation) and Pearl Jam. These onstage versions of masculinity are supplemented by related offstage performances. Probably the most widespread commonsense notion associated with a young man's decision to become a rock musician is that playing in a band means easy access to women. No-strings-attached sex is one of the appeals of being in a band and, I heard and heard, of going on tour. "Bring condoms," was the cheerful, brotherly advice one veteran player gave his black rock compatriots when he returned from a long time out on the road. Another member confided to me that since he had committed to a monogamous relationship, touring was less fun because he could no longer seduce women.

Rock is a male-dominated space and women's participation in the form has been limited by fairly conventional constructions of masculinity and femininity.[3] In rock men are supposed to take the stage, play instruments, write music, and sing songs; women, often the objects of desire or resentment in rock lyrics, are supposed to watch and revere them. Throughout rock 'n' roll history, there have been women performers—Tina Turner, Grace Slick of the Jefferson Airplane, Janis Joplin, Patti Smith, and Chrissie Hynde of the Pretenders—but they are relatively rare and are usually confined to being vocalists.[4] Bo Diddley, Sly and the Family Stone, the Velvet Underground, Talking Heads, and Sonic Youth are among the handful of bands that included women musicians. Generally, when women play instruments in mixed-gender bands, they play bass or keyboards, honoring a universally understood prohibition against women playing the guitar. Female guitarists like Bonnie Raitt, Joan Armatrading, Tracy Chapman, and Toshi Reagon, for example, are usually placed outside the official canon of rock, a realm whose borders are obsessively policed. Only in all-female or female-dominated bands is one likely to find a female guitarist. Pop music history includes many successful all-female groups, but these have been, almost exclusively, vocal ensembles—"girl groups" like the Supremes and the Ronettes in the 1960s and En Vogue, TLC, and Destiny's Child in the 1990s—whose members did not play instruments. In rock, where the value is placed on writing and playing one's own songs, all-female bands have been rare. In 1982, almost thirty years into the existence of the genre, the Go-Gos became the first all-female band to have a number one album in the United States with their debut *Beauty and the Beat* (Gaar 1992:271). In the mid-1970s, the emergence of punk and its democratizing ideology that anyone could form a band helped increase the participation of women in rock through bands like X-Ray Specs, the Raincoats, the Patti Smith Group, Blondie, and the Pretenders. In the early 1990s, a critical mass of all or predominantly female bands and their female supporters known as "Riot Grrrls" offered rock a much-needed infusion of female energy. Notable for their refusal to squeeze into stereotypical female images as either cute girls or sexy vixens, women in bands like L7, Bikini Kill, and Hole played their own instruments, wrote their own songs, and played fast and loud music (Gottlieb and Wald 1994). Women who played rock were breaking into male terrain and flouting established gender roles. Frequently, they attacked men with the same verve that male rockers used to disparage women. Often they were up front about their desire for sex or their anger, stances that are still taboo for women.

I was familiar with both the persistent strain of conservatism that coexists with rock's more rebellious impulses and the marginal position of women in the genre when I started this project. Still, once in the field, I was surprised to see how deeply naturalized the stereotypical male and female rock roles were. The people I met in studios and clubs usually asked if I was a vocalist or, much more frequently, a girlfriend of one of the men I was talking with. Only a handful of people asked if I played an instrument. Time in the field was time in a male milieu. BRC members were primarily men; the clubs and studios they worked in were staffed almost entirely by men; and the stores where they shopped for instruments, recording equipment, and CDS were populated almost exclusively by men. When visiting these locations, I amused myself by speculating on the reasons that magazine writers didn't advise single women wanting to meet eligible bachelors to frequent these places. Was the stereotype of the financially insolvent, resolutely nonmonogamous musician the deterrent?

Like women who become construction workers, fire fighters, or surgeons, white women rockers are interlopers in a jealously guarded male arena. For black women rockers, the challenges increase exponentially. Their gender and race mark them as doubly outside of rock 'n' roll's white male club. Like white women they are intruding in male space and like black men they are treading on white territory. As black women, they have to fight for recognition and respect as legitimate rock performers. Reflecting on her experiences managing the all-black, all-female band Ibis, BRC cofounder Konda Mason recalled the climate they confronted in the mid-1980s:

> There were really problems in terms of race and gender, yes. If you were a woman, you had to be in what was called a "girl group." You had to have a certain "look," show a lot of T&A, be "sexy." Ibis wasn't down with that. All of the record companies I took Ibis to couldn't get where we were coming from. Here were these sisters who could play their asses off and were doing sold-out shows everywhere they went, opened some shows for groups like Fishbone and Living Colour. But they couldn't get a deal. Not one label executive got it. All they saw were these strong sisters with an Afrocentric flair, with some Eastern influences, who were rocking out and kicking ass. There's no reason why Nona Hendryx shouldn't be much larger than she is. It's pathetic the way the industry looks at Black women, given the talent that's out there. (Mason quoted in BRC 2000/2001:10–11)

As this example indicates, music industry executives were inclined to view the race, gender, and genre of Ibis and other black, female rockers as problems. Mason sought to address the resulting resistance to black women and men in rock by helping to organize the meetings that led to the founding of the BRC.

The BRC has always included women performers in its ranks. Along with Ibis, the New York BRC counted among its founding female members pianist Geri Allen, vocalist Cassandra Wilson, vocalist and songwriter Sandra St. Victor of the Family Stand, and vocalist D. K. Dyson of Eye & I. The first BRC show I attended—long before I started this research—featured guitarist and songwriter Toshi Reagon and her very special guest Nona Hendryx, the black rock diva who had contributed her funky flair and effervescent sex appeal to the seventies black rock group Labelle. Hendryx became a BRC board member and has hosted and performed at a number of BRC events. By the early 1990s, the East and West Coast chapters featured several women performers. They included Los Angeles groups P.M.S., an all-female heavy metal quartet, and Strange Fruit, a seven-piece all-female jazz funk ensemble led by saxophone player Goz Inyama. In New York, Helga Davis was one of the lead vocalists in Greg Tate's Women in Love and Queen Esther fronted the band Miss Mary Mack. Tracie Morris, a poet who sometimes performed with her musical ensemble Words and Muse-ic, was a long-time BRC member and a key figure in New York's spoken word poetry scene of the early 1990s. With the 1993 release of *Plantation Lullabies*, Me'Shell NdegéOcello, one of the first artists to be signed to Madonna's Maverick Records, became one of the most nationally visible BRC members. She has released five albums over a critically celebrated career and her success, although marked by an ongoing battle for airplay and acceptance on black radio, was inspiring—and unusual. I now turn to two artists, Felice Rosser of Faith and Sophia Ramos of Sophia's Toy, in order to discuss some of the challenges nonwhite women who play rock face. Faith and Sophia's Toy had strong local fan bases and serious industry interest, but ultimately they were undermined by industry executive concern that a nonwhite woman rocker would present an insurmountable sales challenge.

Faith

Faith was an all-black quartet made up of two men and two women that played psychedelic soundscapes and reggae-inspired grooves. Rene Akan provided the seductively spacey guitar riffs, Diana Baker played keyboards and sang, Gary Sullivan played drums, and Felice Rosser, the bandleader, played bass and sang lead vocals with a quaking, sincere resonance. The very features that I found compelling—Faith's sound, personnel, and image—were the same ones that put the band in a complicated professional position. As a black rock band led by a woman and with a defiantly nonmainstream sound, Faith faced resistance that reveals how strongly race and gender shape participation in rock. In a *Village Voice* feature about Faith, cultural critic Lisa Jones quotes long-time Faith supporter Greg Tate to describe the aesthetic complexity of the band. "Faith doesn't fit any of the clichés of what it means to be a rock band," he said. "It's fronted by a big sister with dreadlocks who plays bass. The music is very soothing vocally, then they rupture that. They're about as comfortable with being benignly psychedelic as they are with being straight-forward dubwise. Basically, they shatter all conventions of what genre is" (Tate quoted in Jones 1992:10). Jones labeled the whole package "tribal grunge" and by 1997, Faith was using "soul-core" to define itself (Faith 1997;

Faith, a miracle of black bohemian style and rock substance. From left, Diana Baker (keyboards and vocals), Felice Rosser (bass and vocals), Gary Sullivan (drums), and Rene Akan (guitar). Photo by Giselle May.

Jones 1992). Whatever you called it, Faith honed its eclectic sound while playing sets with artists like Living Colour, Youssou N'Dour, Stevie Ray Vaughan, and John Cougar Mellencamp (Jones 1992:10). The band built a fan base and began to attract the attention of the music industry. An actual recording deal, however, remained elusive. The absence of the usual R&B sound and the presence of black women created a serious challenge. The assumption was that it would be a struggle to convince the white rock audience—Faith's presumed target based on its sound—to embrace a female-led black rock band. Jones explains:

> [Faith held out] for major-label deals that hobbled along, then never happened. Word came back from the sniffers: this band's not ready (though how to be "ready" was never outlined.) Or the songs weren't there yet. (An odd one: You go to a Faith gig and what you get *is* songs. "Felice has that campfire ability," says a BRC-member. "Anyone can sit down with an acoustic guitar and sing along to her music.") Or, the most frustrating: We don't know how to market this band. This is usually a code for "weird, unclassifiable black folks don't sell; there's no audience for them," which American artists have had to prove wrong time and again. The question

was fast becoming not whether Faith was ready for the industry, but whether the industry was ready for them. (Jones 1992:10)

Felice Rosser is a statuesque, brown-skinned woman with a beatific smile and long dreadlocks that she swirls at opportune moments during a set. Onstage she is free of the conventional trappings of black female media star sexiness: straightened hair and body-skimming outfits. She and Diana Baker assumed a black bohemian style—dreadlocks, Afrocentric jewelry, and clothing that might be vintage cocktail dresses one night and jeans on another—that demanded a revisioning of what constitutes sex appeal. One of Faith's "almost deals," which involved black filmmaker Spike Lee who wanted to sign the band to his 40 Acres and a Mule Musicworks label, brings the race and gender issues into relief. In summer 1991, Lee and his label director Lisa Jackson were unable to get approval to sign the band from executives at Columbia Records, which would be distributing the recording. Jones reports that:

> Faith, in Lee's opinion, "deserved to be signed." Apparently word came from as far up as Columbia president Don Ienner's office that the band had, among other things, an image problem. Says Lee,

Felice Rosser on bass and Diana Baker on keyboards during Faith's 1992 CBGB showcase for Spike Lee. Photo by Giselle May.

"They just didn't like the way the band looked." Lisa Jackson, who has a mane of locks herself and has been in the record business for a decade, agrees: "I think Columbia's biggest objection to Faith was the fact that this was a rock band led by a black female. And not only is it led by a black female, but not your typical petite rocker. They weren't prepared to promote it. I can't say I got this verbatim from Columbia, but this was my feeling." (Jones 1992:22)

Jones observed that Faith's onstage interactions revealed black love absent from media representations that typically showed black men and women "going at each other like cannibal pit-bulls" (11). Considering the perceived "problem" of their image, she mused, "Why is it easier to sell Ice Cube's letter bombs to white America these days than a band like Faith, who grew up in the college boys' backyards, went to school with them, and speak their language?" (22).

The processes of industry decision-making and shifts in musical fashion prevented Faith from securing a major label deal. Instead, they took the do-it-yourself route and released a seven-inch single, "Springtime," in 1994. By this time, personnel shifts had occurred and the band had been reconstituted with Felice Rosser on bass and vocals, Patrick Seacor on drums, and Naotaka Hakamada on guitar. With a white male drummer and Japanese male guitarist, Rosser had created a multicultural downtown ensemble. In 1997, Faith released *Time to Fall in Love Again*, a full-length CD, with production help from Andy Cox of British new wave ska bands the English Beat and Fine Young Cannibals and Fred Smith of New York punk band Television. The obstacles that Faith encountered had much to do with the dynamics of race, gender, and genre, but rather than be stopped by these forces, the band kept working, kept gigging, and kept the faith.

Sophia's Toy

Sophia's Toy was a more traditional rock 'n' roll band than Faith—albeit a black and Latino version. The four members were Michael Ciro on guitar, Eddie Martin on bass, Leslie Ming on drums, and Sophia Ramos on vocals. Their music maintained a connection to R&B and their cover of "Tell Me Something Good" by Rufus and Chaka Khan was a concert staple that emerged organically from their set of original tunes. The band was also indebted to Hendrix's hard rock. The result was an energetic melding of heavy metal, funk, and R&B. Sophia was a great singer who could effortlessly shift her vocals from coy and girlish to an open-throated roar. An effervescent entertainer,

Sophia Ramos, a rocking voice from the
Bronx. Photo by Per Gustafsson.

Sophia was also an attractive woman with plenty of dark, curly rock
'n' roll hair and a curvaceous figure that she outfitted strategically.
Arguably, Sophia Ramos was a front woman who could have won
over a white male rock audience. In the end, though, Sophia's Toy, a
black and Puerto Rican rock 'n' roll band led by a self-described dark-
skinned, Afrocentric Latina (Tate 1995a:44), presented a confusing
combination of race, ethnicity, and genre. Notably, the BRC Manifesto
had considered Puerto Ricans part of the organization's constituency.
The founding members recognized that as nonwhites, they were also
prevented from entering the rock mainstream. The experiences of
Sophia's Toy bear out the logic of this inclusion. In the early 1990s
Latino/a artists who did not perform Latin music or sing in Spanish
were a puzzle.

In 1994, Epic signed the band, enabling Sophia's Toy to get over the
hurdle that most bands of any gender and racial configuration have
difficulty traversing. The band recorded tracks for their debut record,
completing them ahead of time and under budget. Within a year of
the initial signing and before the record could be released, however,
BRC members' positive buzz about Sophia's Toy shifted to distressed
comments about the label's treatment of them. After changes at the
top of the label's hierarchy and a review of their roster, Sony executives
dropped the untested band. In a *Vibe* interview with Greg Tate, Ramos
explained that her band was dropped before their album was released

because "the president of the company had decided there was no market for female rock 'n' roll. The next week [rock singer/songwriter] Liz Phair made the cover of *Rolling Stone*" (Ramos quoted in Tate 1995:44). The story of Sophia's Toy's contract also received coverage in *Ravers*, the BRC's occasional arts magazine. Ramos described the situation to Earl Douglas:

> The Bad Brains record didn't do well and they were dropped. Living Colour's last record did well by most standards, but didn't meet Epic's expectations, industry cutbacks were coming, and [Epic A&R executive Michael] Kaplan got afraid and decided to drop us. 1994 was also the year that the Best Rock Performance Female was dropped from the Grammy's so there was a lot of misogyny and sexism in the music industry at the time. (Ramos quoted in Douglas 1995:33)

Douglas added: "The official reason for the dismissal was that there was simply no market for female rock bands" (33). Echoing Sophia's observation about Liz Phair, Douglas noted that 1994 "was a watershed year for female rockers—Me'Shell NdegéOcello, Melissa Etheridge, the Breeders, Bonnie Raitt, and Dionne Farris all enjoyed commercial and critical success" (33). Even so, Sony/Epic erred on the side of the rock 'n' roll tradition that excluded women and nonwhites. Tate's article elaborates on the "problem" that Sophia's Toy presented:

> In Ramos's and Ciro's minds, their deal went awry when a promotion honcho from the company came down and witnessed their legion of nonwhite fans. "The guy had this look of absolute terror and fear in his eyes," says Ramos. "I know that look. I'm trying to be cool and make him feel comfortable, but he says, 'You know, I was surprised there were so many black people in your audience.' That was it, end of story."
>
> Ciro adds, "There's a serious color barrier I've seen come up when we start playing. Mostly it's black and Latino people who are our supporters. If we play a mixed club, soon as we come on-stage, there's this separatism that occurs, like people feel it's not their music, like they shouldn't be able to understand it." (Tate 1995a:44)

The "color barrier" that Ciro and Ramos refer to is a persistent problem for black rockers: on the one hand, industry executives worry that a nonwhite band will be viewed as "too other" for whites, the primary rock audience. On the other hand, they are concerned that a nonwhite fan base will not be broad enough to sustain the band or that it will alienate whites.

In the case of Sophia's Toy, already difficult questions of race and rock are exacerbated by issues of gender and sexuality. One BRC member bitterly assured me that the executives did not want ethnic Sophia Ramos; rather, "they wanted a white girl." The notion that audience members must identify with or desire the people on stage became complicated—even in the multicultural nineties—when the anticipated audience was white and the people on stage were not. And, to be frank, with Sophia as front woman, sex was definitely in the air—too much so for some observers. The writer of a *New Yorker* magazine feature about Ramos stated, "A man who sees Sophia onstage, strutting in a leather bustier and tiny shorts, one hand gripping her crotch, her head bobbing back and forth, and her tongue making snaky movements through her lips, is likely to conclude that she is more serious and strenuous fun than he feels comfortable with" (Wilkinson 1996:145). This passage describes the image she projected when touring with the band Psychotica, but it was also what I recalled from seeing her with Sophia's Toy. In my experience, however, there were plenty of men who were comfortable with Sophia's show. In fact, after attending a number of Sophia's Toy sets, it dawned on me that only rarely did I see the band. A crush of men—mostly black and Latino but some white, too—always packed solidly in the front of the audience trying to keep Sophia in view. I often didn't feel up to squeezing myself in among them. Apparently, the guys appreciated the energy of the music and what one plain-speaking fan approvingly referred to as "Sophia shaking her booty." Rock 'n' roll is theatre and sex appeal is part of the package. Sophia worked it on a couple of levels. She played the sexy girl to the hilt, lending a sexual undertone to the band's name as if to ask, "Would you, man in the audience, like to be Sophia's toy?" Sophia also gently mocked the image. She would come onstage in high heels, but it was unusual for her to get through more than a couple of songs before kicking them off, singing the rest of the set in barefooted comfort. Often there was a sense of irony to her act. At set's end one evening, Mike finished introducing his fellow band members and then asked for "a round of applause for the outfit," indicating Sophia's apparel: a cleavage-revealing blouse tied at her waist and hip hugging slacks. Sophia stood preening for a minute, stroking the sides of her breasts before saying, "I'm wearing a serious push-up bra. You know my titties ain't this firm. Actually," she continued, "it's to draw attention away from my—" and pinched a layer of skin at her midriff and raised an eyebrow.

Sometimes the sexism of rock 'n' roll seems too deeply entrenched for even the most radical women to effectively undermine it. Ramos's play with traditional female sexiness is markedly different from the more stripped-down sincerity and sensuality that Me'Shell Ndegé-Ocello and Felice Rosser project. Still, whether they opt for high-voltage sexuality, low-key sensuality, or something in between, black women rockers have to pursue their vision in a white male-dominated arena where their race and gender upset the balance. Selling rock, especially the rock of female performers, is often about selling sexuality, and a black woman's sexuality can be problematic. Mainstream American media representations construct black women as inadequately feminine—either oversexed or not sexually attractive at all (Combahee 1995; hooks 1981; Morton 1991). Generally, black women's complexions, facial features, hair, and body types diverge too much from European-centered beauty standards, and only a handful manage to win acceptance. Industry experts assumed that white male rock fans would not identify with these black women rockers in any of the required ways: they would not want to be them or be with them. That Faith and Sophia's Toy were viewed as unwise gambles in the wake of the multiplatinum success of Living Colour, Lenny Kravitz, and Tracy Chapman, a brown-skinned, dreadlocked, female guitarist, reveals the depth of industry resistance to black people and especially to black women. Like anyone seeking a career in pop music, Me'Shell NdegéOcello, Felice Rosser, and Sophia Ramos had to deal with image and sexuality. What is notable is how restricted the possibilities are for black women. The challenges they encounter are linked to but not wholly identical to those faced by black men and are worth noting because they deepen an understanding of the ingrained race and gender rules and roles that circumscribe participation in rock.

BLACK ROCK SISTERS

Black feminists have observed that "women's" organizing for rights has been dominated by the interests of white women and "black" organizing for rights has been dominated by the interests of black men. They also note that when working in these struggles, black women typically had to contend with the racism of white women and the sexism of black men.[5] Black women rockers faced race and gender bias in the mainstream rock scene and also confronted conflicts over the involvement of women in the BRC. The coalition's primary mission was to rearticulate the racial meanings associated with rock, but this process was inflected with gendered race issues, some of which I discuss in this section.

The invisibility of black women in rock was a concern for many BRC women and in the early 1990s, Beverly Jenkins was one of the members working to address it. Beverly had been tapped to serve as the New York BRC's executive director because of her background in arts administration, her experience with black arts organizations, and her commitment to activism in the arts. She was also selected because men in leadership positions had begun to take seriously complaints about the organization's insensitivity to women. Bringing in a skilled female administrator was an important step toward making changes, but Beverly and other members still had to push for the inclusion of women in BRC events. Beverly especially wanted to involve more black women instrumentalists. The small number of women musicians in the BRC was an extension of the small number of women musicians in rock 'n' roll generally. Finding black women rock musicians was a challenge, so while she pressed those who were organizing BRC events to include a spectrum of women, she also had to be politic in making her demands. She knew from experience that harsh criticism and difficult requests could lead a volunteer to quit. Beverly had initiated a series of shows in March, Women's History Month, that put women in the spotlight. Called Sister Ax, these performances featured black women musicians, vocalists, poets, writers, and comedians. Beverly told me she was surprised to find that some of the women contacted to participate refused the invitation because they did not want to be marginalized in a "women's show." Still, she and several BRC women remained committed to producing the March Women's History Month events, and they developed into a successful, money-making series.

Beverly was not the only BRC member concerned about the male focus of the BRC. A number of the women I spoke with referred to the challenges of participating in a male-centered organization, not only at the level of performance, but in the day-to-day operations of the BRC. Considering the gender dynamics of the BRC, one woman told me:

> I think they're working on it now and I think in certain ways it's improved, but there was a macho strain that was very strong in the eighties. It was really very conservatively sexist in certain ways. Under the guise of being open, but it's a way that men can be sexist

without even trying. [*laughs*] . . . They just assumed leadership or just assumed that they knew things or just dismissed the ideas of women. Whereas if a man would say the exact same thing I said, it would not have been dismissed.

BRC members faced internal as well as external battles, but confrontations with other BRC members might have been more unsettling because the rhetoric of "like-minded people" downplayed the very real differences of opinion and the varying levels of power and influence that people held within the organization. The views of musicians tended to take precedence over those of nonmusicians and, as is always the case in organizations, some people commanded more respect and wielded more influence through sheer force of personality. Gender introduced another element of difference. Men expected women to go along with their decisions. The difficulties of addressing this assumption were exacerbated by the unwillingness of some of the women to challenge men for fear of being labeled "difficult," "angry," or "antimale." This situation was inevitable, one woman assured me, in light of the sexual politics that emerged as BRC members found not only working partnerships and friendships, but romantic relationships through their involvement in the organization. It was as if women had to make a choice between discussing the sexism with men and maintaining connections with them. Paul commented on the relationships that developed through the BRC:

PAUL: Because a lot of the musicians [who joined the BRC] didn't know a lot of other black musicians, a lot of the bands that would come in originally were integrated . . . maybe there would be a black person . . . and he'd have white musicians. But now he's starting to meet all these black rock musicians. Some of those bands turned out to be all-black because now he knew killing black guitarists or what have you. . . . And the funny part is—just like on the romantic tip: a lot of people were dating white people [*laughs*] when they came in. Because they're rock 'n' rollers . . . but quite a few people— and that includes a couple of women that were dating white guys because they were hardcore rock 'n' rollers—all of sudden there were all these black rock 'n' rollers so I saw a number of romantic reformulations—[*laughs*]
MAUREEN: [*laughs*]
PAUL: . . . All of a sudden, it was like, "wow, there's someone else I can relate to on a number of levels." So cats were switching up their

musicians, switching up girlfriends, and all kind of things through the BRC. [*laughs*] It's been like a mad little networking situation.

The dynamics of the BRC—the ways power was distributed and who was supporting whom—made it difficult for women to change the structures of the organization. Black feminist critics have assessed the challenges black women face when confronting black men about sexism. In organizations, black men typically have foregrounded racism as the problem to concentrate on and tended to overlook or refuse to address their own sexism (Combahee 1995:237; cf. Davis 1983; Giddings 1984; Wallace 1979). As bell hooks notes, "This 'not seeing' can be, and often is, a process of denial that helps maintain patriarchal structures" (hooks 1990:74). Continuing, hooks points out that in many cases black women are equally "unwilling to confront sexism," reflecting upbringings that have taught "that black men have borne the brunt of racist oppression" and "that racism is harder on males than females" (74–75). The marginalization of gender issues during the early years of the BRC reflects the tendency to rank forms of oppression, placing racism above sexism, rather than viewing racism and sexism as "interlocking systems of domination which uphold and sustain one another" (59) (cf. Combahee 1995:239). Along with a number of black feminists, hooks argues that black men and black women must come to terms with "the complexity of our experience in a racist sexist society," acknowledging that it is both possible and necessary to be "concerned about the brutal effect of racist domination on black men and also denounce black male sexism" (hooks 1990:62).

Certainly, there is no monolithic view that I can isolate as the BRC male perspective. James, for example, was a man who spoke out against the marginalization of women in the organization. He told me:

> The men have been woefully negligent in their regard for the input of women within the organization. And I think it's also a reflection of rock 'n' roll music, too, and the role of women in the context of the music. I think that's been a big problem and when the women decided to address it, I supported that and was verbal about it, too . . . I wasn't comfortable with being "the man speaking out," although I recognized the importance of men informing other men about that kind of shit.

Other men told me that there were too few women involved in the BRC, but stressed that those who were members played important roles as artists and administrators. Few men were prepared to discuss in detail the marginalization of women's views. Indeed, some usually talkative and opinionated men gave uncharacteristically succinct descriptions of women's participation and suggested women I should speak with about the issue. In spite of being years younger than Civil Rights and Black Power Movement activists, members of the BRC reproduced some of the same practices for which these earlier movements have been criticized. Black women, although always key organizers and workers, have rarely been allowed to move to the forefront of black activist organizations in which men were present. Black feminists have observed that all too often "black" organizations reframe the gender specific interests of black men as those of black people. In the early days, the BRC did not fully escape this tendency.

A major part of the BRC was the promotion of black male alliances against the racism black men encountered in the music industry. These connections fostered close bonds among men that sometimes excluded women. Some men in the organization who talked to me about the BRC would comment on "brothers who want to play rock" and "cats who I got to know through the BRC," overlooking the female presence. Frith has characterized the rock world as a place for male friendship in a restive, unregulated life-style where women represented unwelcome demands for "routine living" (1981:85–87). In certain ways, the BRC fits this profile. The majority of BRC men were single; if they were unmarried and had children (a few did), they usually were not the primary caregivers. Demands on time, distractions from creative work, and limitations on movement are problems that some BRC men associated with marriage and women. Significantly, BRC men whose long-term relationships and marriages have been successful took care to note that the supportiveness of their wives or partners allowed them to pursue their craft. One woman who was a long-time member told me she had been surprised that so many single, heterosexual black men paid so little attention to the women in the organization; in her view, the men "just wanted to talk to each other about music, music, music" and were not dealing with women substantially on any level—professional or personal. The BRC was, she resignedly told me, "a boy's club." In contrast, another woman echoed Paul's comments and recalled that in the early days, the BRC "was like Peyton Place with everybody dating everybody." She felt that some women who were not serious about music and the politics of the organization had joined because "they saw men, plenty of single, talented, black men." Her interpretation may be a reflection of the way women are viewed in rock—not as truly committed to music but opportunistically interested in musicians—and BRC men may have shared her analysis. It is true that extramusical forces had motivated some women to join the organization. Several women in New York told me that they were "not really into rock" and had joined the organization to support its progressive artistic agenda and the black musicians who were its members. As supporters of the BRC's mission and as friends of BRC musicians, women played an integral role in producing and promoting the shows. The majority of women were vocalists, not instrumentalists, and others were not performers at all. Although the outcomes were not fair, at a certain level it made sense for the men to treat the women differently, not only because of their gender, but because of the different paths they took into the organization and the possibility of their having different investments in the issues.

Here, it's worth noting that it would have been impossible for me to be a "gender neutral" fieldworker. Clearly, my gender shaped my experience in the field. My interest in black rock, representation, identity, access to the media, and racism dovetailed with the way men framed their own issues. Given these similarities, BRC men were predisposed to think I was conducting a worthwhile study, and many of them became enthusiastic and invaluable guides. The fact that I did not frame my research in terms of gender in the BRC helped; had I done so, some of the men might have felt that I was looking for ways to accuse them of sexism and avoided participation. At the same time, being one of a small number of women around the organization enabled me to collect important information from women about gender. Sometimes it was disclosed out of a sense of solidarity and a feeling that these were issues I needed to know about as much for self-preservation as for research purposes. Women's input coupled with my observations about women's roles in the BRC and my experiences in the field encouraged me to pay attention to the intersection of gender, race, and rock both in terms of the experiences of black women and the interactions between men and women that I have discussed so far. Attention to the impact of gender and race in the context of rock also led me to attend to the concerns and experiences of black men to which I now turn.

BLACK ROCK BROTHERS

Gender in terms of the construction of black male identities and black masculinity was a concern of BRC men even if they did not directly articulate it as such. Typically, rock performance highlights hetero-sexual male virility and power, but rock's association with whiteness raised a thorny problem of racial authenticity for black male rockers. Rock music and black identity are two fields of cultural production in which participants pay obsessive attention to authenticity and worry constantly about compromise and pollution by sellouts. In rock, a musician who deviates from what are understood to be his or her true roots risks being maligned. Similarly, a black person who en-gages in activities not deemed authentically black is suspect. Black male rockers negotiated these two discourses of authenticity, work-ing to disrupt the notion that rock is a "white boy" thing and to convey their legitimacy in spite of the "disconnect" that their race and music represented. Their presence challenged the notion that an authentic rocker was a white man or that true black music was R&B or rap. Sig-nificantly for black men, the accusation of "acting white" carries a denotation not only of racial inauthenticity, but also the connotation of not being fully male.[6] Black Arts and Black Power rhetoric drew a parallel between "inadequate manhood and inadequate black con-sciousness" (Harper 1996:51). Much of the ideological labor of these nationalist activists was invested in recuperating black heterosexual masculinity from a debased condition that centuries of white oppres-sion had created.[7] They envisioned black manhood as resolutely force-ful and heterosexual in contrast to what they saw as the weakness and effeminacy of white and black middle-class men. By the mid-1980s, the "whitened" black man who had lost his true black self in the course of integrating into the American mainstream became a stock film character (Boyd 1997; Gates 1992). This type, the black upwardly mo-bile professional or "buppie," speaks standard English, is middle class, well educated, a bit fussy, and usually ill at ease with his physical self; in short, he represents a dramatic loss of black masculinity and of black culture. Unlike the ideal male rocker, men did not want to be like him and women did not want to be with him. In view of these race and gender dynamics, it is ironic that "punk," the term for one form of rock that many BRC members embraced, is also a derogatory black English colloquialism for a homosexual male. Black male rockers had their work cut out for them.

Producing a masculine gender identity is a part of rock perfor-mance. In his study of heavy metal, musicologist Robert Walser points out that this process often involves negotiating the contradictions of Western masculinity in which a demand for assertive, spectacular display competes with a demand for rigid self-control (1993:108) (cf. Frith and McRobbie 1990). Black male rockers had to address these mainstream rock notions of masculinity as well as African American ones. For BRC men to be true to the music and true to themselves, they needed to defend their interest in rock through a rearticulation of what constituted acceptable black cultural production. The black masculinity they projected from the stage usually avoided the exaggerated sexuality of Hendrix, Little Richard, or Prince. Also absent for the most part was the inspired goofiness that led George Clinton to take the stage in a long blonde wig and madcap costumes. They were neither the semicriminal toughs emergent in rap nor R&B-style lovermen or preachers. Generally speaking, male BRC musicians were studiously cool. There was plenty of energetic, flashy guitar playing and emotive vocals, but these usually communicated power and dominance while performers put forward a veneer of control. The hair and haberdashery that I came to take for granted among BRC men—dreadlocks or closely shorn hair; pierced ears, bangles, and rings; T-shirts and leather jackets worn with beat-up jeans—were key visual signifiers. This bohemian image, their engagement with an atypical musical form, and their refusal to follow a standard middle-class path produced a kind of black masculinity that suggested an adamantly black and progressive consciousness, one that departed from mainstream black working- and middle-class expectations and from the images available from Hollywood and the music industry. They were black and different and proud.

On a number of occasions, BRC men discussed their perceptions of the different ways black men and black women experienced racism in the United States. Some BRC men used Me'Shell NdegéOcello's success and the prominence of black women like talk show host Oprah Winfrey, Nobel Prize–winning novelist Toni Morrison, and music industry executive Sylvia Rhone to substantiate their claims that American racism was tougher on black men than on black women. I inadvertently elicited one such rumination when I asked a member about his audience:

MAUREEN: Do you think about audience for stuff that you're working on? Do you have an audience in mind when you're doing your projects?
RALPH: Uh. . . . Yeah. Anybody but America.
MAUREEN: [laughs]
RALPH: Not by choice, but only because America's just so closed off.

Especially when it comes to progressive black music. They don't want to hear about it. Anywhere else in the world is more open to what I'm doing than here. So whenever I'm putting something together, I'm always thinking about Europe, Japan, South America . . . because they'll accept what I do. The American market is just so—this whole anti–black male thing is just really incredible here. You know, going through it, you don't want to live your life in paranoia, but there's definitely something anti–black male in America. Especially the last couple of weeks. I look at Darryl Strawberry going down. O. J. is—O. J. is gone. Then this guy who just shot all those people in Long Island, he's totally nuts. He don't represent—I mean, what does he represent? He don't represent any of the black people I know, because he's gone. And you know it's just such a trip. Like I look at Jimi Hendrix and I look at Prince and you think there'd be so many more black rock guitarists, so many more black rock groups led by black men. And it's just not the case. After Living Colour jumped off, we were thinking, "Okay. Cool." . . . [But] it just ain't going to happen, it just ain't about that. It just ain't about that. Then I look at black women really getting a lot of respect and it's the whole thing about, where they know, dealing from [the perspective of] the powers that be, they know they can get this sister to work because they know she's going to take care of her kids. And by her being a woman, she's not going to be this aggressive revolutionary; she's just going to do her job because all she wants to do is take care of her kids. I'm trying to think of [the name of the] black woman who just got a big, high-powered position somewhere. They made her head of something because she represented women and blacks and she was talking about the difficulties, about how that was a challenge, and how that's a much more popular thing to do—

MAUREEN: Not as threatening?

RALPH: Yeah. And also the whole thing about the white man's desire to have a black woman. So empowering a black woman is like, "I hooked her up so I [can] really demand—" But I try not to live my life dealing with that, but it is a real thing.

When we spoke in 1994, Ralph detected what he calls an "anti–black male" atmosphere in the national fascination with retired football player O. J. Simpson, accused of murdering his ex-wife; baseball player Darryl Strawberry, in trouble for drug and alcohol abuse; and Colin Ferguson, who killed six people on a Long Island Railroad commuter train. Each of these black men fit stereotypes of black masculinity as depraved and violent. Ralph reads the media's obsession with these images as attacks on all black American men and was frustrated that they had come to represent black manhood. Positive or neutral images of black men are not reinforced with the same kind of fervor, and Ralph interprets the lack of support for black male rockers, even after the success of Hendrix, Prince, and Living Colour, as further evidence of a pathological refusal to deal with black men in anything but a derogatory way. This problem extends from the general experiences of black male rockers to his personal experiences as a black man in the United States. Later in our conversation, he described the fallout of what Living Colour called the "funny vibe" that leads whites to fear and distrust black men. He gave the example of being denied entrance into clubs because of his race and gender in spite of the official end of Jim Crow. He contrasts this to the position black women occupy: they are the "safe" black people and white Americans are more willing to deal with them. Further, he suggests, as have many black male commentators, that white men's long-standing sexual interest in black women—from the days of slavery to the present—gives black women an advantage. Conversely, the fact that black men and white men are in competition with each other for power and for women makes it impossible for them to negotiate, a situation that fans the flames of the anti–black male feeling that Ralph describes. Ralph persuasively outlines the ways race and gender confine black men, but overlooks the combination of sexism and racism that black women routinely encounter, creating an idealized image of black women's experiences in the United States. Ralph's commentary and my responses to it are examples of the different ways black men and black women experience and analyze intertwined racial and gender ideologies.

IN THE FIELD: BLACK MASCULINITY

The challenges of gender relations, concepts of black masculinity, the persistence of American racism, and critiques of the "anti–black male" bias that Ralph identified were a part of the consciousness of male BRC members and were sometimes articulated with great clarity. At a rehearsal for the annual Jimi Hendrix Tribute in 1994, I witnessed a conversation in which the participants, all black men, addressed the position they occupied in the United States. As the group went into the rehearsal studio to work out their set of songs, Carlton launched into a black verbal performance. Playing "Who Knows," he sang a more R-rated version of Hendrix's "I just want to talk to you" lyric: "I've had your mama and your aunt from around the way/Even had your sister and your cousin, too, and they weren't no good anyway."

William looked at me and said, "Maureen is noting the rampant sexism that goes unchecked in the organization."

"You think so?" I asked, and left it at that.

It was a laid back rehearsal and the musicians relaxed into a quick and efficient session. After flubbing some lyrics, Marcus predicted, "Kelvyn's going to fire my ass from the BRC if I don't learn the words to that song." Next, they played the official version of "Who Knows." Someone sang the melody for those who didn't know it well. "I never learned the song because I was always too busy rolling a joint while it played," one said to explain the gap in his Hendrix knowledge. After the songs were worked to everyone's satisfaction, they ended the rehearsal. There was a pause and some murmured conversations. Carlton began improvising a new song. "A black man did it," he sang. "A black man did it." This was partly a reference to the case of Susan Smith, the white South Carolina woman who a few weeks before had admitted that she had killed her children; she had first claimed that she had been carjacked by a black man who kidnapped her two sons. It was mid-November 1994; a Republican majority Congress had just been elected and the O. J. Simpson murder trial was starting. Reflecting on current events, William predicted: "These are going to be some harsh and ugly times—for black folks and for everybody—with this new New Order we've just elected. What else can you expect from a man named Newt Gingrich?" The conversation flowed as they packed up their equipment and walked to the elevator.

CARLTON: Now, what was a black man going to do with some white kids in South Carolina?

WILLIAM: That was an absurd story that everyone believed because she said a black man did it.

RALPH: It's like what happened in Boston with that man—

WILLIAM: Right. Killed his wife then said a black man did it. And the cops went out to find the brother.

MARCUS: They were *arresting* brothers.

WILLIAM: But then on the other hand, you have the whole O. J. Simpson thing where white people don't want to believe a black man did it. I think the most interesting thing about all of this O. J. stuff is the way white people are losing their shit over this because he was the one black man who white male sports fans really identified with. They loved him.

CARLTON: Yes, they did.

MARCUS: But I think the whole O. J. thing—it's not just about race. It's more about celebrity. There's this "Black Celebrity Class" and they're just on a different plane than regular black folks.

CARLTON: I don't even know if black people are even that interested in O. J. I mean really concerned. He was never down.

TJ: Jim Brown was down and he tried to get O. J. to get with him, but he just wouldn't do it.

WILLIAM: O. J. got over though.

RALPH: He thought he did.

WILLIAM: Oh, no, O. J. ain't going to jail. O. J. is not going to jail. He can't. Because it would disrupt the whole crossover myth: that if you're good you can crossover. You can efface your blackness.

CARLTON: Yeah, I don't think he's going to do any time.

MARCUS: You think he did it?

WILLIAM: Oh, he did it, all right.

CARLTON: When I first heard about the murders, I thought, if they were doing coke then he probably really killed her. Then, that night when I saw him driving down the highway with the gun pointing to his head, I said to myself, "Now that's some crackhead shit." You know, "Oh, I'm going to kill myself." Yeah, he did it.

WILLIAM: Well, I'll say this—and I'll only say it once—you have to have been married to understand that you could get to the point where you want to kill her.

[Some gasps of surprise]

WILLIAM: I'm not saying that you would kill. Just that you get so close and there's so much feeling—Sometimes, the anger, you just don't know where to go with it.

RALPH: Doesn't mean you need to try to cut off her head.

WILLIAM: I'm just saying, I can understand getting to that point.

MARCUS: Now, three of y'all been married and three of y'all are divorced.

TJ: Women are that hard to get along with?

CARLTON: My wife was.

[laughter]

RALPH: Marriage is work.

WILLIAM: I hate it when people say that.

RALPH: It's true, though.

WILLIAM: The day I was served my divorce papers, this guy knocks on the door and gives me the papers and says, "Have a nice day." Have a nice day.

RALPH: But it's funny, I've had some nice conversations with my ex-wife.

CARLTON: Yeah, you can have a nice conversation for an hour. But whenever I talk to my ex, in the last minute, she'll say, "Oh, by the way, did I remind you again that you still ain't shit?"

[*laughter*]

CARLTON: Do you want to say anything to defend your sex?

MAUREEN: What could I say?

If the rock world is an emphatically male arena, then the BRC provided a distinctively black male space in which black men could bond, talk, and work together. Of course, I was not one of the guys. It was not just Carlton's blues vernacular lyrics that underlined my gender difference. Nor was it the fact that some of the men whom I had met for the first time during the three or four days of Hendrix rehearsals had replaced my name with "Hon" or opted for flirting as a time passer during the hours of waiting around. These were sometimes amusing, sometimes tedious, but hardly unexpected forms of behavior. In fact, as the rehearsals wore on, I started to believe that the cause of these assertions of masculinity was the looming spirit of Hendrix, the super stud—more about him in the next chapter. Carlton's invitation for me to speak on behalf of women was as much a polite attempt at inclusion as it was a reminder that I had not managed to disappear into the background. I was welcome to hang around the rehearsals, but there was no "honorary male" status for this female anthropologist.

Still, the conversation was illuminating. Part of what they were responding to—as Ralph was in the exchange I described earlier—is what film critic Ed Guerrero calls the "schizophrenic way of representing black males as concentrated at the poles of celebrity and pathology" (1994:183). The BRC members holding forth in the conversation above are, of course, real black men and not the media-generated abstractions that anthropologist Helán Page has called "unembraceable black male imagery" (1997). Embedded in the BRC men's discussion is a critique of the ways media images have demonized black masculinity and of the distance between these simplified images and black men's reality (Golden 1994a:19). All of the speakers were keenly conscious of the impact of these stereotypes on their self-image, professional opportunities, and everyday interactions. Here is a simple example of the problem: One night, when Ralph and I were parting in midtown, he offered to hail me a cab. He was only in the street with his arm raised for an instant before a middle-aged white man, intending to be helpful, rushed out into the street with him. He explained that he knew how hard it would be for him, Ralph, to get a taxi, and therefore was offering his assistance. The sensitivity that made him take seriously the much-documented refusal of New York cab drivers to pick up black men did not extend to an understanding that a black man might feel patronized by this kind of "help," especially when a black woman was present. It is the daily accumulation of these kinds of slights that weary and anger black men, making the assertion of their masculinity all the more important. Between the media's representations of black men as either positive model citizens or evil scourges of society, there is what Guerrero calls "a vast *empty space in representation*" (1994:185). Although this space between the extremes is a void at the level of media images, it is the complex and rich terrain in which most black men live their lives. Part of what the BRC offered was a context for experiencing and representing black identity, black music, and black interests in ways that affirmed the realities and dreams of these contemporary black men.

BRC men and women contended with the same dominant assumptions that proper rockers were white men. As BRC members attacked the racial ideologies that marginalized blacks from rock, ideologies about gender shaped the ways in which they carried out the organization's agenda. BRC men and women had to deal with the intersection of race, gender, and rock although from different perspectives and emphasizing different concerns. At the level of their battles with the music industry, there was a notable amount of unity among members as they rallied to support colleagues in their efforts to break through. At the level of internal relations, however, gender difference presented an obstacle that not all members were willing to confront. Some men and women argued for greater inclusion and influence of women in the organization's administration and performances but other men and women supported (either actively or passively) the maintenance of a male-dominant status quo. As an ethnographer, researching and describing the external battles was the easy part. The cause, the enemy, and the desired result seemed clear. Contending with the internal race and gender issues was considerably more difficult and recalled the challenging position black women have faced historically. As the writers of one black feminist statement put it, "We struggle together with black men against racism, while we also struggle with black men about sexism" (Combahee 1995: 235). My purpose in identifying the layered race and gender conditions that BRC members confronted has not been to recklessly air dirty laundry in public—although some will take it as just that—but to talk analytically about the ways the intersection of race and gender shapes our art, struggles, and lives.

NINE

JIMI HENDRIX EXPERIENCES

MAUREEN: So, I'm thinking about getting a guitar.

TATE: Oh, yeah? What kind of guitar're you going to get?

MAUREEN: I don't know exactly. That's what I wanted to ask you—

I mean, I want an acoustic—

TATE: Aw, you just want to be a sensitive poet.

MAUREEN: Ha!

TATE: You should get an electric guitar, an amp, and some effects—

MAUREEN: But I thought an acoustic guitar—

TATE: Well, we all started with acoustic guitars. But then we

wanted to sound like Jimi.

—AN EXCHANGE IN THE FIELD

Guitar wizard, early dying genius child, and quintessential black rocker, Jimi Hendrix was an irrepressible, undeniable force animating this study. As I carried out my fieldwork, BRC members led me to Hendrix through their frequent comments about him. These references convinced me that I had to pay careful attention to a person who had died before most BRC members had graduated from high school. Hendrix is one of the most iconic rockers ever—both a brilliant musician and a brilliant rock star (which are not the same thing). His music, musicianship, and onstage persona departed from the existing standards, enabling him to push sonic and social boundaries with idiosyncratic style. For BRC members, the racial and musical identities Jimi Hendrix embodied intensified the impact of the expressive and spiritual freedom he represented. Hendrix is, in addition to everything else, a complex figure who takes on different meanings according to context and audience. For BRC members, he is a key symbol of their quest for artistic and social freedom.

I begin this exploration of race and rock with a biographical sketch of Hendrix and an outline of his career and then turn to an examination of the ways BRC members and others have interpreted Hendrix's music and career.[1] I conclude with a brief discussion of the BRC's Jimi Hendrix birthday tributes that New York and Los Angeles chapters produce. This public reclaiming of Hendrix as a black rocker is another example of the processes through which BRC members assert the usually ignored black rock experience. Rather than accepting the naturalized view that Hendrix's racial identity did not matter to him or his fans, I discuss the racial ideologies embedded in discourses about his music, image, and significance. I draw on the remarks of BRC members to indicate Hendrix's impact on them and to document their analysis, much of which informed my own thinking about Jimi Hendrix. In claiming Hendrix as a key musical influence through conversation, musical practice, and Jimi Hendrix tributes, BRC members countered constructions of rock and Hendrix as "white boy" pursuits. This consideration of Hendrix and his significance to BRC members allows me to explore what it means to be a black rocker, crystallizing the challenges entailed in expanding limited constructions of black music and black authenticity in the post–civil rights United States.

JAMES MARSHALL HENDRIX

In the 1990s, Jimi Hendrix, although dead for twenty years, became big business. The Ambassador Gallery, located in SoHo, New York City's downtown gallery district, hosted an exhibit of art inspired by Hendrix, photographs of Hendrix, and Hendrix miscellany like lyrics scribbled on scrap paper, handwritten letters to his father, and a photo of preteen Jimi posing with his guitar. Taking the bizarre to the sublime, Hendrix, who died in 1970, went on tour in 1994–95. The "On The Road Again" traveling exhibition visited college campuses across the United States, bringing the gospel of Hendrix to a new generation of consumers. The tour's red trailer truck, embossed with a purple-tinted Hendrix photo from the *Are You Experienced* album, doubled as an exhibition space for Hendrix paraphernalia similar to that displayed at the Ambassador Gallery.[2] These shows coincided with the 1993 reissue of Hendrix's first three studio albums—*Are You Experi-*

enced (1967), *Axis: Bold As Love* (1967), and *Electric Ladyland* (1968) —
and *The Ultimate Experience* (1993), a greatest hits and singles compilation. This sumptuous CD box set, *The Experience Collection*, featured
glossy photos, biographical information, and sheets of Hendrix collector stamps with reproductions of album cover art. There was also
the release of *Stone Free: A Tribute to Jimi Hendrix* (1993), featuring
Eric Clapton, Living Colour, and the Cure among others performing
Hendrix's best-known tunes.

Hendrix was big business when he was alive, too. By the late 1960s,
he was consistently the highest paid act on the rock concert circuit.
In 1969 he earned $125,000 to perform at the Newport Jazz Festi-
val; at the time, this was the largest sum ever paid to a rock act for a
single appearance (Henderson 1983:257; Murray 1991:51). His journey to superstardom began in Seattle, Washington, where he was born
John Allen Hendrix on November 27, 1942, to Al and Lucille Hendrix. His parents separated soon after he was born and divorced by the
time he was eight years old. He spent his earliest years raised by various relatives and family friends before settling down with his father
who legally changed his name to James Marshall Hendrix. When he
was thirteen, Al gave Jimmy his first guitar. He taught himself to
play, restringing the guitar to accommodate his left-handedness. As
a teenager, Jimmy played in a few bands with friends and school-
mates. Never much of a student, he dropped out of high school in
1959 and enlisted in the 101st Airborne Division of the army. He was
stationed at Fort Campbell, Kentucky, where he soaked up the music
of nearby Nashville, developed a base-wide reputation as an eccentric,
and formed a band with a black bass player named Billy Cox.

By 1962, Hendrix, having injured his back on his 26th jump from
the skies, had been honorably discharged from the army and began
to seek work as a sideman. Little Richard is the most famous of the
musicians who hired young Jimmy Hendrix to tour with him on
the southern Chitlin Circuit. None of these gigs lasted very long because Jimmy's employers would tire of his showy playing and dis-
tracting stage presence. He was supposed to be a sideman, but he
too often overwhelmed the main attraction. In 1964, Hendrix moved
from Nashville to New York City where he continued working as a
sideman and also began to play on the Greenwich Village music scene.
He performed regularly at the Cafe Wha? and the Cafe Au Go Go.
Hendrix began to make a name for himself among the downtown
glitteratti and in 1966 Chas Chandler, formerly of the British Invasion
band the Animals, offered to manage him. During their trans-Atlantic

flight to London, Hendrix and Chandler decided that Jimmy would become "Jimi." They arrived in London in September 1966 and quickly hired two white Englishmen, Mitch Mitchell on drums and Noel Redding on bass, to form Hendrix's band, the Jimi Hendrix Experience. Jimi Hendrix began to hang out with and perform before London's musical royalty: Eric Clapton, the Rolling Stones, Cream, and Pete Townshend. These young Brits were confirmed worshippers and appropriators of black American music and were keen to hear what their black American contemporary had to offer. Hendrix began to record material for his first album including the songs "Hey Joe," "Stone Free," and "Purple Haze" which did well on the British charts. A critical year for Hendrix, 1967 saw the release of *Are You Experienced*, its follow-up *Axis: Bold As Love*, and the performance at the Monterey International Pop Festival in San Francisco that introduced him to the U.S. audience both live and via the film *Monterey Pop*. Hendrix's innovative approach to the guitar—his use of distortion, effects, feedback, and volume—created a shockingly and seductively different sound that attracted the American rock audience. His onstage antics, rooted in an unrestrained physicality and sexuality, only heightened the attention—sometimes positive, sometimes negative—that he received. Hendrix offered a delicious mix of rock 'n' roll style and substance.

From 1967 to 1970, the Jimi Hendrix Experience toured exhaustively in the United States, United Kingdom, and Western Europe. Hendrix's star rose quickly and he became known, revered, and criticized for his extravagantly loud, psychedelic playing, for the showy stage histrionics that caused him so much trouble on the Chitlin Circuit, and for his reputation as an avid druggie and sexually insatiable rock 'n' roller. The other side of the rock star high life was the financial disarray that plagued his career. Even though Hendrix was earning an extraordinary amount of money, he had signed a highly exploitative contract early in his career and consequently banked only a marginal amount of what he earned. He also began to feel that his management team was stifling his creativity. By 1968 when he released *Electric Ladyland*, Hendrix wanted to go beyond what he perceived as the limited confines of the rock vernacular and to experiment with the comparative freedom of jazz. He even came close to recording with Miles Davis whose music he greatly admired. In addition to these concerns, Hendrix's relations with sidemen Mitchell and Redding had deteriorated considerably. In order to have a satisfying creative outlet, he formed an all-black group, the Band of Gypsys, with his army buddy Billy Cox and drummer Buddy Miles. Under pressure of management and the bills from the Electric Lady Studios he had built in New York, Hendrix continued touring with Mitchell and Cox, making his last recorded appearance at the August 1970 Isle of Wight Pop Festival in the United Kingdom. In September, Jimi went to London for a respite, staying in his girlfriend Monika Dannemann's apartment. On the morning of September 18, 1970, Dannemann was unable to rouse Jimi from his sleeping pill-induced slumber. He died later that morning without regaining consciousness. The infamous, unfortunate cause of death was suffocation caused by his vomit. He was twenty-seven years old. R.I.P.

HENDRIX AND THE BLACK ROCK COALITION

Throughout his career, Hendrix was simultaneously locked into and locked out of certain images and practices because of the uneasy relationship between his racial and musical identities. These limitations, a consequence of the music industry's political economy and assumptions about black authenticity, shaped the ways black and white audiences and critics responded to him. They also inform the ways BRC members relate to Jimi Hendrix. BRC members have appropriated Jimi Hendrix for their own agendas certainly because of a passionate appreciation of his music. Beyond this, though, Hendrix is important to them because of the freedom he signifies as a black rocker. In his valuable book on Hendrix, music critic Charles Shaar Murray identifies as a central problem the decontextualization of Hendrix from black culture, community, and musical history (Murray 1991). His study historicizes Hendrix as an African American artist with creative and philosophical connections to previous generations of black musicians and as a formative influence on African Americans who came after him.[3] Given his interests, it is fitting that Murray dedicates his book to Vernon Reid and the Black Rock Coalition. Murray observes that although Hendrix drew on musical styles and performance tropes with clear black cultural roots, he is treated as an anomalous phenomenon, a wild thing unto himself. Many white fans, musicians, and critics approached Hendrix from a perspective that can be paraphrased as "not black, not white, just Jimi." By taking him out of a black context and downplaying his race, whites were able to solve the problem of blackness that Hendrix's undeniable ethnicity and racial background posed: they figured him as something other than, better than, and less problematic than black. In making his case about the whitening of Hendrix, Murray includes a quotation from Vernon Reid describing his shock at hearing Hendrix's blackness erased so he could be accorded status as a rocker:

> The first thing that made me aware of race in music and the role it plays . . . was when I was in high school. There was a local rock radio station I used to listen to all the time, and late at night on the anniversary of Hendrix's death they were playing some Hendrix music and the deejay said that Hendrix was black, but that the music didn't sound very black to him. Yeah, it was a white deejay . . . and I flipped out. At the time I was very culturally aware of the race issues because of Martin Luther King and Malcolm X and all the ferment that was happening in the Black Power movement. I didn't really connect it all so much to *music*, but that really threw it in my face. . . . It was not only an insult to his music, but I took it as an affront to me personally. Because if what the deejay said was true, what is he saying about me as a listener who loves Hendrix *as a black artist*? That started my awareness of these things in music. (Reid quoted in Murray 1991:3)

The erasure of Hendrix's blackness was especially painful because Reid, like so many of the BRC members I spoke with, identified with Hendrix *because* he was black and a particular kind of black man. His sound, image, and attitude resonated with these postliberated African Americans who were also rock fans and who wanted to play rock. David, a guitarist and bandleader, described his first encounter with Hendrix:

> I had always been into the Beatles and the Rolling Stones, the whole British Invasion. I realized later on it was primarily because they played guitar . . . because in black popular music, it was about singers, you know. The band was always hidden somewhere. In Motown the musicians didn't get credit . . . but these guys were up there playing and I realized later on that was the attraction. . . . I was reading a magazine called *Hullabaloo* which talked about all these rock 'n' roll bands, and it had a picture of a black guy and two white guys and it says "The Jimi Hendrix Experience is this, that, and the other and their album will be coming out." And I was fascinated. I couldn't believe it. I didn't understand how you could have a band with three guys, first of all, only three guys. And then, I mean, it was like this *black* guy. So I went and got the album at Hearn's. I was with a couple of friends who said, "You buying that weird music?" And I went home . . . I had this record player in my

room, sat on the end of my bed right by the window, put that album on, and changed my life. I heard that, I was like, "Whoa."

For David, Hendrix expanded the possibilities of what a black musician could be. By breaking out of the vocal-centered R&B and soul modes, Hendrix charted new territory for black guitarists, picking up where Chuck Berry and Bo Diddley left off and moving into psychedelic space. Immersed in the British Invasion's self-contained bands, David was excited to see a black man stepping into this burgeoning musical arena and so assertively claiming it as his own. Jimi Hendrix was a revelation for David, making concrete the until-then vague possibility that he could be a rock guitarist.

Hendrix's sound, style, and image inspired BRC members, opening them up to the performative and expressive possibilities of rock. Commenting on Hendrix's influence on him during his teen years in the early 1970s, Mark, a guitarist, explained:

MARK: My father bought me an acoustic guitar. And then, when I did get an electric guitar, I got the Strat that I [still] own . . . but at the time, it was just an old, beat-up looking guitar. Now, it's a collector's item. . . . It's a dope guitar. We didn't even know how good it was. It cost me $150. But my father just made sure that if I was going to get an instrument, it was going to be a decent instrument. And I said, "I want a Stratocaster." 'Cause I saw Jimi Hendrix play a Stratocaster. So, the first time I got it, I plugged it in, turned it up, and I was waiting for it to do all those sounds I saw in *Woodstock*. And it didn't and I said, "Mommy, I'll take it back. It's broke."

MAUREEN: [*laughs*]

MARK: I sat and fiddled with that thing for a week trying to make it do all those things. "It was broke." . . . Slowly but surely, I figured out that, "Okay. It ain't the guitar, it's the player." . . . And it ain't just the player, you got to turn this sucker *up*.

The amazing sounds Hendrix made with his guitar were impressive to BRC members, but David was careful to draw attention to the artistry of Hendrix's compositions:

The thing about Hendrix is he was as great a songwriter as he was a guitar player and a lot of times people overlook that. But to me the greatest guitar players in terms of rock 'n' roll—maybe any music, but especially rock—are guitar players who are able to write music that is almost like a canvas for their playing and creates an environment. . . . Hendrix's writing is what enabled that guitar playing to jump out the way it did. He could play with anybody else, and he would stand out. But the combination of his writing and guitar playing created a whole other thing. . . . So, yeah, Hendrix.

The fact that Hendrix drew on black music forms like blues and R&B and reworked them to fit his own eclectic vision inspired Vernon, David, Mark, and other BRC members. Hendrix's musical excavation and refashioning drew on African American cultural roots while integrating them with the cultural material of the moment: British Invasion rock (itself an idiosyncratic adaptation of black American blues), the rising youth counterculture, Black Power concerns, antiwar demonstrations, civil rights agitation and legislation, and calls for sexual and gender freedom.

Hendrix is also known for being a black artist with a predominantly white audience, an uncomfortable position that Living Colour similarly occupied. BRC members were acutely aware of the general absence of interest in rock, even when performed by a black rocker, among many of the African Americans they grew up with. As I have discussed in previous chapters and as David's story reminds us, friends accused them of listening to "that weird music." BRC members and other young African Americans who were dealing with the trials of school integration may have recognized a parallel between the "only black" syndrome that Hendrix faced in the white rock world and their own experiences in predominantly white schools.[4] One member's description of his efforts to explain to black friends that the so-called white boy music he was listening to had African American antecedents developed into a critique of what he viewed as a lack of interest in the history of black music among African Americans:

CALVIN: If you look at the history of black music in America, we create and throw it away. And what happens is white people take it over because it's such a good form of music and then they claim it was theirs. . . . Like Kenny G. That's a perfect example of what I'm talking about. When I talk about jazz with a regular black person in America, they say, "Oh, man. Put on some Kenny G." That's their idea of jazz. They don't think of who John Coltrane was. Or Branford Marsalis or Wynton Marsalis. . . . I try to check brothers, I say, "Man, check *this* out." [They say], "I don't want hear that shit. Put on some Kenny G." I mean, when they think of rock 'n' roll, they want to hear Led Zeppelin. . . . If you listen back to old R&B, a lot of black people don't even like that, because . . . we're always looking for something new. We want to see the next thing. . . . Their idea of rock 'n' roll is you're playing some white boy's music. . . . "Man, stop playing that white boy stuff." And I would show them, and they weren't interested.

MAUREEN: Who are these people? Like relatives?

CALVIN: Just regular people [in my hometown], they just didn't want to hear it. They'd go, "Man, there you go with that teaching stuff again. Maybe you should have been a teacher."

Music critic Nelson George makes a similar observation in his study of post–World War II African American music. "The black audience's consumerism and restlessness," he argues, "burns out and abandons musical styles, whereas white Americans, in the European tradition of supporting forms and styles for the sake of tradition, seem to hold styles dear long after they have ceased to evolve" (1988:108). Unlike Calvin, George uncritically accepts that the "authentic black approach" is to constantly press forward without looking back and that the inclination to support old styles is a "white thing," a practice he understands as a predilection for reflexively holding onto the past. George embraces a black and white dichotomy that ultimately characterizes efforts like those of the BRC to reclaim rock or of African American jazz trumpet player Wynton Marsalis to preserve and institutionalize jazz as "not black."[5]

Limited as George's view is, it accurately describes the rapid changes in black music while also demonstrating the common practice of defining what is black in terms of music and behavior through an opposition to what is understood to be white. George observes that Hendrix and Sly Stone, another African American artist who achieved success in the rock mainstream, each drew on black music traditions with Hendrix using R&B and blues and Stone tapping gospel and soul. George explains that in contrast to Stone who had a considerable black fan base, Hendrix

drew from a style blacks had already disposed of. . . . Unfortunately, Hendrix fatally damaged his connection with black audiences because of his innovative brilliance on the electric guitar, an instrument that, with the declining black interest in blues, fell into disfavor. . . . In essence, Hendrix was the revenge of the R&B sideman, one with the ability to turn the voices inside his head into music— problem was, you just couldn't dance to it. . . . In a weird symmetry, Hendrix, with his young white-teen audience, was a sixties equivalent of Chuck Berry. Like Berry, his success with guitar-based music made him an outcast on Black Main Street. (George 1988:108–109)

George also notes that Hendrix and Stone grew up on the West Coast and flourished in San Francisco (Stone) and London (Hendrix), areas not as steeped in black American culture and limiting racial rules as the U.S. south and the East Coast (108). While Stone combined hippie sensibilities with enough black popular culture references to appeal to both black and white audiences, Hendrix, in George's view, ended up "dissolving into white rock culture" (194). Although his music had black roots, Hendrix was too heavily identified with the white rock community to be accepted as authentically black by mainstream African American audiences (and, apparently, by George). Along with identifying the logic African American audiences use to deem African American musicians authentic, George uses that logic to sustain an argument that ultimately reinforces stereotypes of blackness (e.g., black people like to dance, black people don't like guitars).

To sustain my own argument, I must point out that as an "Outcast on Black Main Street," Hendrix did have some black company. In the years I have worked on this project, I have met a number of non-BRC member African Americans who are Jimi Hendrix fans. Some avidly followed Hendrix's career as it unfolded, others discovered him after his death. Among the things that appealed to them, I suspect, is the spirit of cultural and creative independence that Hendrix embodied. This attitude is present in nearly all of his music, but is most clearly articulated in the lyrics of the song "If 6 Was 9" where in his signature cool style, he asserts his difference from the dull mainstream and insists on the sanctity of his individuality with the proclamation, "I'm going to wave my freak flag high." He concludes the song with the sober observation, "I'm the one that has to die when it's time for me to die. So let me live my life the way I want to." All the more poignant because of his early demise, this declaration is followed by a characteristic onslaught of inspired, eccentric guitar playing. "If 6 Was 9" is emblematic of Hendrix's commitment to going his own way in spite of the external pressures to conform, a position that his listeners, future BRC members among them, valued.

BRC members' appreciation of Hendrix's image as a freaky rebel outsider was always accompanied by a deeply felt regard for his musicianship. When I asked David to elaborate on Jimi's impact on him as a teenager, he told me the following:

Well, if I think about it . . . the guitar playing—the tones just sounded amazing to me. Just the whole sound of his guitar playing. The notes and the sound . . . and I guess also—he sounded cool. He sounded like a cool guy. He looked like a cool guy . . . his vocals, you know, that sort of singing/talking kind of vibe. And I liked the tone of his voice. I related to him completely. I mean, I let my hair grow long, I was wearing bell bottoms, they used to call me "hippie" in my neighborhood because nobody else was doing that uptown, you know [laughs]. And I used to wear headbands. I was like a real stand-out character in my neighborhood. . . . Then I saw Monterey Pop, I saw that about three, four, five times in the movies; it was just amazing. An amazing performer. So I really related to him really strongly. . . .

I guess part of it is a spiritual thing because you can see a lot of people and you'll see somebody that you relate to on a level that you can't explain, necessarily, verbally. But I guess I can say in the context of most black performers at that time, he really stood out . . . I mean compared to anybody else who was popular at that time, there was this thing about being different and the freedom of that and I was [into it]. I guess I still am. I mean I'm not inclined to really think in terms of what everybody else is doing. [laughs] . . . And then seeing him live, I mean it was—I met him one time and he was signing autographs outside the Fillmore East after a Band of Gypsys show. And he just seemed like a gentle person, really nice and easy.

Jimi Hendrix was undeniably cool. The clothes, the hair, the attitude were all part of the scene David was connecting with and Hendrix, who easily fit the newly minted rock ethic of the musician-as-rugged-individualist, offered a black image to emulate. Hendrix was not a neatly attired Temptation or Top with a sleek process and choreographed dance steps. He was emphatically not an icon of the kind of black middle-class propriety that many BRC members were questioning. Nor was Hendrix the traditional black bluesman, a Muddy Waters or a Howlin' Wolf who were, in spite of all their musical richness, a little too old and a little too removed from the contemporary currents to resonate immediately with many young blacks. Hendrix was a musician they could relate to because he was young, black, clearly freaky, and brilliant. As a rule, you cannot ask for more from a rock star.

The dynamics of race and Hendrix's blackness played a role in the ways BRC members responded to Hendrix and influenced the treatment he received from the music industry, critics, and fans. In spite of his international success, Hendrix never achieved what music industry professionals viewed as substantial popularity among black audiences; his music was not and is not played on black radio. His biographers have addressed the question of his black fan base in order to dismantle myths about Hendrix as a for-whites-only performer. David Henderson, writing in fluid posthippie style, reports:

> One night at TTG Studios on Hollywood Boulevard, Jimi completed one of the countless guitar overdubs on "1983." There were several brothers in the studios doing work, also, who were really gassed to see him there. Jimi voiced his concern over the lack of black support for his music. But the brothers told him differently. There were a lot of black people who dug his music and bought his records. They saw him perform when they could, but they were outnumbered by the simple fact of his overwhelming popularity. This was the first time Jimi had heard this point of view. It was heartening. He opened up to the brothers and told them stories about his most recent tour. He had gone through the South and found a very nice vibe there—it had surprised him. In a way it related to what the brothers were telling him about his black support. The newspapers said one thing, but once you checked it out for yourself, you discovered something closer to the truth. (1983:226)

Charles Shaar Murray stresses that the racialized and unscientific system of recording record sales contributed considerably to the perception that Hendrix had no black fans (1991:83). Although blacks did buy his records, Hendrix's sales were reported on the pop charts and did not register on the R&B lists; consequently, all of his sales were interpreted as "pop," which translated to "white." The R&B charts tracked "black" sales and were based on black radio station airplay and black record store sales. With virtually no black radio airplay and with no appearances on the R&B charts, Hendrix was cornered into aligning more fully with the white audience his management was convinced he should target (83).

Henderson and Murray also comment on Hendrix's attempts to reach out to black audiences, to incorporate more ostensibly black roots in his music, and to speak about black issues—making remarks supporting the Black Panthers to the press, for example.[6] Henderson quotes Hendrix discussing race and rock:

> Almost anyone who has the power to keep their minds open listens to your music. Black kids think the music is white now, which it isn't. The argument is not between black and white now. That's just another game the establishment set up to turn us against one another. But the black kids don't have a chance too much to listen—they're too busy trying to get their own selves together. We want them to realize that our music is just as spiritual as going to church. (Hendrix quoted in Henderson 1983:215)

Murray suggests that Hendrix's long-term stay in the United States during 1968 made it impossible for him to duck racial and political issues the way he could while in England and that his decisions were not simply the product of a callous decision to try to appear "more black." Some BRC members interpret his Band of Gypsys project as an effort to make a public and personal connection to his blackness. Their eponymous album, a recording of a New Year's Eve performance at the Fillmore East, was released in 1970. The album featured an anthem called "Machine Gun" that Hendrix introduces by saying, "I'd like to dedicate this to all the, all the soldiers fighting in Chicago and Milwaukee and New York. Oh, yes, and all the soldiers fighting and dying in Vietnam." Here, he pointedly connects the "race riots" and daily struggles of black people in the nation's Chocolate Cities to the war in Vietnam where a disproportionate number of black Americans were fighting.[7] This move is a more politically and racially conscious one than typically associated with Hendrix and for many BRC members, it was all the more meaningful because he made it while fronting an all-black band.

All accounts of Hendrix's career indicate that he grew bored with the rock 'n' roll madman image he had cultivated, was tired of playing songs from his first album to screaming audiences, and became interested in experimenting with new forms of music. He had started to listen to jazz, to jam with black musicians schooled in jazz and West African forms, and to seek an opportunity to record with jazz trumpeter Miles Davis. I received a lesson on this aspect of his biography late one night while talking with two BRC members, Calvin and Angela, about pop music careers. Calvin described the importance of image to a musician's success, drawing on Hendrix as an example:

CALVIN: Hendrix had the whole hippie look—the wild hair, the head-band, the paisley clothes. All of that. It's interesting, though, if you look at him at the end of his life. He was trying to change, trying to go in a different direction. Like, if you look at him at Woodstock—that's one of his last performances—he has short hair, like a Pan-ther kind of vibe, and the shirt he's wearing is kind of a dashiki. He's leaving that hippie thing.

MAUREEN: Yeah. I know he was trying to play with Miles Davis then.

CALVIN: That's right. But his managers didn't want to let him because they had such a sure thing. He was making so much money for them. And he was making money for himself. He was the highest-paid performer back then—he made more than the Beatles and Stones per show. Like $100,000 per show.

ANGELA: Wow. But it's weird. I never think of him with the short hair. You always just see the hippie images.

CALVIN: Yeah. Well, he was definitely trying to change and go in a dif-ferent direction. You can hear it in the Band of Gypsys. . . . You can even hear it starting in *Electric Ladyland*. That he was starting to move. . . . It's amazing how much he changed during his career. You know, it's just a three-year period from 1967 and *Are You Ex-perienced* to 1970 when he died, but by 1970 he had changed. He was starting to identify with Black Power. But his management did not want to lose that money.

Here, Calvin enumerates the tensions surrounding commercial interests, musical sound, and racial identity that are central to Hen-drix's career and legacy. The white mainstream rock view of Hendrix as "not really black" is ironic not simply because of the significance of his blackness to African American fans, but because the white per-ception of Hendrix as something other than black was accompanied by a clear understanding that Hendrix was unquestionably something other than white. The otherness that was part of what made Hendrix so appealing to white audiences had much to do with his blackness. We can certainly hold Hendrix responsible for his over-the-top play-ing style and his decision to exaggerate his Chitlin Circuit moves for the rock 'n' roll stage. A 1967 film of his performance at a London venue shows him with the Experience decked out in Haight-Ashbury meets Carnaby Street couture, an updated version of his ex-boss Little Richard's eccentric approach to fashion. He wears black leather boots; narrow, checked pants; a wild-patterned shirt with flared sleeves; and a brocade vest.[8] He delivers the verses and choruses of "Purple Haze" with an easy, cool grace, first playing runs of notes with his right hand on the neck and then slashing out chords with his left hand. Next, he dramatically slides his left hand away from the instrument, smiling and nodding as we marvel at the reverb. When he solos, he holds the guitar body to his face so he can play it with his teeth, swings the guitar behind his back, and slips the fret board between his legs, sliding it along his thigh until his hands near his crotch. He holds the neck while thrusting his pelvis to the beat, before waggling his tongue and—something *interruptus*—lifting the guitar and playing it upside-down behind his head. Wow! The bottom line has always been "Jimi was a brilliant player," but it may be the case that no one would have been listening to this black guitarist if he had not also been a brilliant showman, one who cultivated a wild man image. For some audiences, this was the authentic black man in the first place: a highly sexualized, super-endowed stud. Hendrix could serve as an icon of the sex and drug freedom that the exponents of flower power, LSD, and free love supported while also playing a role that did not depart significantly from the ways black masculinity was (and all too often still is) represented in U.S. popular culture.

Murray observes that Hendrix shared the "tastes and obsessions" of white bohemians on both sides of the Atlantic and worked this commonality to his advantage:

> For a while at least, he was perfectly happy to give them exactly what they wanted, to play the part of—to quote *Rolling Stone's* John Morthland—"the flower generation's electric nigger dandy, its king stud and golden calf, its maker of mighty dope music, its most outrageously visible force." It was precisely this kind of role-playing which may have hindered acceptance by black audiences: he was enacting—in Summer of Love terms, admittedly—exactly the kind of stereotypes which many black Americans were so anxious to shake off . . . Hendrix was indeed flamboyant, exhibitionistic, obviously on drugs, fond of being photographed surrounded by blondes and almost totally lacking in the kind of dignity, discipline and restraint which black America had come to demand from its entertainers. It was the white critic Robert Christgau who saw Hendrix at Monterey and called him "a psychedelic Uncle Tom." (1991:81–82)

Hendrix's sexually suggestive showmanship was intended to attract attention and it succeeded. Once he had everyone's attention, however, he was not able to dispense with the gimmicks without sorely disappointing his audiences. In fact, what many of his fans wanted and what Hendrix might have meant to them—beyond all that great music—is connected to the racial obsessions that have shaped U.S. society and culture. Throughout the history of the United States, black people have played all kinds of metaphorical and mythical roles, but have rarely been able to carve out space as people with individual identities, idiosyncrasies, and concerns. African American playwright Lorraine Hansberry observed that "America long ago fell in love with an image. It is a sacred image, fashioned over centuries of time: This image of the unharried, unconcerned, glandulatory, simple, rhythmical, amoral dark creature, who was, above all else, a *miracle of sensuality*. It was created, and it persists, to provide a personified pressure valve for fanciful longings in American dreams, literature, and life" (1970:209). Hendrix ended his first major U.S. performance with a sloppy, sexy version of "Wild Thing." As the song came to its close, Hendrix sensually stroked his guitar and then symbolically ejaculated on it with a can of lighter fluid (at least this is how some choose to interpret his pyrotechnics), set it on fire, encouraged the flames with wiggling fingers and a goofy smile, and then bashed the burning instrument against a convenient amp.[9] By the end of the set, Hendrix had emerged as quite a wild thing himself, the latest "rhythmical, amoral dark creature" and "miracle of sensuality" on a countercultural scene deeply immersed in the pursuit of freedom.

In many ways, Hendrix's timing could not have been better. He had arrived in England at a moment when the country's leading pop musicians were living out a fascination with black American blues and roots music, trying their best to imitate the instrumental, vocal, and lyrical inflections of black southerners. Hendrix gave them a peer, a *young* black American who, unlike the older Chicago and Mississippi Delta bluesmen, was hip like them. Hendrix was not a southerner or a pure bluesman, but he was clearly a black guitar virtuoso and far closer to the genuine article than any of the Brits could ever hope to be. For Hendrix, going to England was crucial both for social and artistic reasons. Not only did his journey take him away from the American racial mire that might have squelched him, it also placed him at the center of a vibrant artistic community that appreciated what he was doing musically and gave him a supportive space in which to hone his craft. Upon his glorious return to the United States, it turned out that he also spoke to a generation of young whites who were reacting against mainstream American culture. What these audiences might have read as his primitivism—his embodiment of freedom, spirituality, and emotion—served as an opposition to the overly rational modern or "straight" culture that they prided themselves on rejecting. The specific ways people manipulate this primitive/modern dichotomy depends on the social, political, and cultural currents of their historical moment. In all cases, however, "the primitive does what we ask it to do. Voiceless, it lets us speak for it" (Torgovnick 1990:9).[10] The primitive stands for the richness of tradition and morality while the modern represents their loss. Literary critic Mariana Torgovnick notes that "the creation of specific versions of the primitive often depends on and is conditioned by a sense of disgust or frustration with Western values. The primitive becomes a convenient locale for the exploration of Western dullness or degeneracy, and of ways to transcend it (153). Implicit in this use of the primitive is a critique of life in the industrialized West. It was no accident that at the same time hippies were rejecting Western mores and belief systems, they were embracing Native American medicine, adopting Eastern philosophy, and lionizing a spacey black guitarist named Jimi Hendrix. Moderns who need release from the strictures of their daily existence can turn to the life-affirming Primitive to tap into the freedom and sensuality it represents. Torgovnick's useful outline of Primitives and Moderns fails to account for the experiences of nonwhite Westerners who simultaneously embody the Primitive and the Modern. Murray suggests that it is this duality that caused many African Americans to condemn Hendrix's wild man image. He was too close to the stereotypes that they, as Black Moderns, wanted to escape and replace with more flattering representations of respectable contemporary blackness. For many BRC members, however, Hendrix stood for the rejection of the mainstream white world that they were being trained to enter and that the Civil Rights Movement had started to open up. Much as he provided for white middle-class youth a preferable primitive other, Hendrix's freaky, futuristic persona offered middle-class black youth an alternative to the black middle-class propriety that they, as promising and well-educated African Americans, were expected to enact.

White Americans' long-standing fascination with the Negro-as-primitive is intertwined with the enduring practice of white appropriation of African American music and style that has been a driving force of American popular culture. In terms of U.S. theatrical history, the starting date is usually marked as 1829, when Thomas "Daddy" Rice used burnt cork to paint on "blackface" and launched the minstrel show. Some of the white minstrels who borrowed from black culture may have done so with respect for their sources, but direct acknowledgment of the black originators was rare and financial recompense unheard of. This complex relationship of appropriation and erasure, of "love and theft" (Lott 1993), raises the specter of the White Negro, an archetype that white American writer Norman Mailer introduced in a 1957 essay to describe the outsider status of white hipsters and the blacks they (and Mailer) stereotyped and admired (Mailer 1968). In the uncertainty of the post–World War II era, Mailer argues, Beats and others developed an existential consciousness that mirrored that of the Negro who lived in the racist United States with no real certainty and under the constant threat of danger.[11] While Mailer accentuates the marginality of the White Negro, African American cultural critic Margo Jefferson observes that this figure is a wayward, privileged descendent of the white minstrel. "You can't lose playing the White Negro," she notes, "because you are in the unique position of retaining the material benefits of being white while sampling the mythological ones of being black" (1973:40). The history of rock 'n' roll (not to mention U.S. popular music more generally) is populated with white performers whose success was a result of their ability to mine African American traditions in a way that appealed to white audiences. Elvis Presley, Jerry Lee Lewis, the Rolling Stones, the Animals, and Janis Joplin are all types of White Negroes, borrowing the black mystique, language, music, and attitude and "identifying with archetypal misfits" (1973:44). Their more easily acceptable versions of black music and their ability to solve the problem of black people in black music do not undercut their talent, but are a very real part of their success. White Negroes wear a mask that allows them to experience the excitement of being the dark other, but it is a mask that they can remove if need be. This flexibility is, of course, a luxury no African American can enjoy.

Minstrels and White Negroes were involved in complex and contradictory racial performances. So was Jimi Hendrix. Notably, he was not a white man striking poses associated with black men, but the Real Black Thing. Breaking out of the bonds of black respectability, he reveled in the ludic freedom of the moment. Or was he pandering to whites and exploiting the myths and stereotypes of black masculinity? What is fascinating here is that at the same time Hendrix performed a persona that heightened his black otherness, his race was also being erased. Hendrix was whitened as his popularity with white audiences increased. They related to him because of his music, his performance style, and his cool sexiness. His fit with the white rock scene became more important than his blackness, which was of such an idiosyncratic nature that it was easy for many white fans to dismiss. Crucial here is the fact that racial identity (distinct from racial categorization) in the United States is not simply about descent and phenotype. If that were the case, Hendrix's blackness would never have come into question: any photo shows that he is what most of us raised in the United States would unhesitatingly identify as a black man. As I have demonstrated throughout this study, however, a combination of behavior, belief, and context define the contours of racial identities. In the late 1960s, blackness was a confrontational identification that stood in clear opposition to whiteness. Most visibly represented by advocates of Black Power, the Black Arts Movement, and the Black Panthers, it rejected engagements with white forms as signs of diminished black consciousness and black identity. Hendrix, a peace-loving, tripped out, hippie rock star did not demonstrate this kind of politicized blackness nor did he match any of the other widely circulated black images—for example, a respectably dressed civil rights activist, an athlete, or one of Hollywood's degraded comic coons. Indeed, for many onlookers, black and white, he did not quite embody blackness at all. His white fans could comfortably assert that he "wasn't really black" because he fit so seamlessly into the predominantly white rock milieu. Demonstrating the success of his client's racial disappearing act, Hendrix's road manager Gerry Stickells observed: "To me Jimi wasn't a black man—he was a white man. He didn't think like a coloured guy and he certainly didn't appeal to a coloured audience at all" (Stickells quoted in Murray 1991:84). Nonblack Americans whose understandings of blacks are often negative frequently interpret positive experiences with African Americans in ways that render the black person or persons in question "not (really) black." Jimi was "not black" to his road manager or his white fans because being black, in spite of symbolizing the life-affirming primitive qualities noted above, also embodied debased meanings that were irreconcilable with the positive things that Jimi Hendrix symbolized. Hendrix could not be both black *and* a fabulously innovative guitarist with whom so many identified. The problem of his blackness had to be dealt with and it was summarily eradicated by a discourse that characterized Hendrix as a wild and wonderful thing unto himself: not black, not white, just Jimi.

RECLAIMING HENDRIX

Over the years, the BRC has produced tribute performances to honor the contributions of African American musicians whose music

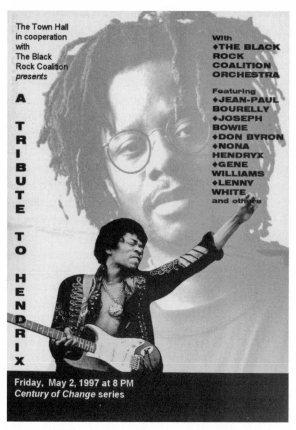

The Town Hall
in cooperation
with
The Black
Rock Coalition
presents

With
◆THE BLACK
ROCK
COALITION
ORCHESTRA

Featuring
◆JEAN-PAUL
BOURELLY
◆JOSEPH
BOWIE
◆DON BYRON
◆NONA
HENDRYX
◆GENE
WILLIAMS
◆LENNY
WHITE
and others

A
T
R
I
B
U
T
E

T
O

H
E
N
D
R
I
X

Friday, May 2, 1997 at 8 PM
Century of Change series

Promotional flier for the New York BRC's Town Hall Hendrix
tribute. Clarinet player Don Byron, whose image is superimposed in the background, was a featured artist.

shaped rock: Muddy Waters, Howlin' Wolf, Curtis Mayfield, Sly Stone,
Tina Turner, songwriter Otis Blackwell, and guitarist Sonny Sharrock
are some of the artists who have received this attention. While these
shows were produced on a one-time only basis, the Hendrix Tribute
Show was an annual event in both Los Angeles and New York, reflecting the significance of Hendrix to BRC members and his popularity
with their audience. In New York, Wayne Livingston produced and directed the first Hendrix tribute in June 1990. The financial success of
the show coupled with the members' enthusiasm about it contributed
to the BRC's willingness to organize the event on an annual basis. The
tribute shows recontextualized Hendrix as BRC members publicly embraced one of the most widely recognized rock musicians. In contrast

to color-blind characterizations of Hendrix that dissociate him from black culture and his own blackness, the BRC's tribute performances, sustained by an almost exclusively African American contingent of instrumentalists and vocalists, placed Hendrix in a black context and emphatically connected him to black Americans.

In New York, BRC members have demonstrated their respectful appreciation and artistic debt to Hendrix in various venues usually near his November birth date. In 1993 and 1994, performers crowded onto the gold lamé curtained stage of the Fez in downtown Manhattan to pay tribute. In 1995 and 1996, they launched their guitar-heavy onslaught in the gritty, basement-level concrete rooms of the Cooler in New York's meat-packing district. In 1997, an opportunity to play at the far more elegant Town Hall in midtown Manhattan led to a May performance. Town Hall's willingness to host the show as part of its Century of Change series speaks to the mainstreaming of Hendrix's image, the constantly growing economic and cultural power of the show's presumed audience of baby boomers, and the BRC's own cachet as a cultural organization. At all of these shows, BRC members and collaborators performed Hendrix's music, presenting crazy reworkings, respectful covers, and everything in between. Organized as BRC Orchestra events, the tributes featured performers from BRC bands, mixing and matching players as the instrumentalists and vocalists took turns on different numbers. The tribute producers also tapped black rock performers who did not have a formal affiliation with the coalition, but who were "down with the BRC mission" just the same. Some of the nationally known participants in the New York shows that took place during the mid-1990s include guitarists Eric Gales, Jean-Paul Bourelly, Hiram Bullock, Gary Poulson, and Vernon Reid; drummer Rashied Ali; keyboard player Bernie Worrell; trombonist Joseph Bowie; clarinet player Don Byron; vocalist Nona Hendryx; and former Band of Gypsys drummer Buddy Miles. In Los Angeles, the BRC has organized its tributes around band performances by two or three invited acts that play short sets of music by Hendrix as well as their own songs. In 1995, they turned the tribute into a musicianship contest judged by a panel that included Louis Johnson of the funk band the Brothers Johnson, Brian O'Neal and Kevin O'Neal of the Bus Boys, and Jimmy Hazel of 24–7 Spyz.

In addition to honoring Hendrix and claiming him as a black rock predecessor, tribute performances allowed members to play together outside of their usual band configurations and to collaborate on the Hendrix repertoire for their own pleasure and that of the audience.

Over the years I learned that performers took a couple of different approaches. I could expect to hear "straight" versions of classics like "Foxey Lady," "Angel," or "Spanish Castle Magic." For example, Wayne Livingston took advantage of his position as organizer to commandeer for himself "The Star Spangled Banner," getting as close to a note for note rendition as he could. Guitarist Karen Ashton, reproducing Hendrix's gum-popping cool and playing the guitar behind her head and with her teeth, had the audience wondering whether she was channeling Jimi during her solo on "Hey Joe." Members also played with the form of songs, bending the rock classics to connect with other black genres. Vocalist Gordon Chambers did gospel-inflected versions of "Wind Cries Mary" and "Little Wing." Guitarist Michael Hill, whose band Michael Hill's Blues Mob plays the blues with a contemporary urban sensibility, introduced his take on "Red House" and "Voodoo Chile" by explaining that he wanted to tap into Hendrix's roots as a bluesman. Coati Mundi, formerly a vocalist with Kid Creole and the Coconuts, offered an inspired goof on "Manic Depression." In his version, he represented the mania referenced in the song's title through shifts in New World black music genres, leading the band in changes from rock to reggae to calypso and back to rock while he alternated between sung and spoken performance of the lyrics. Above all, the Hendrix show is a love-in for the guitarist and the guitar; it's about jamming and evoking those long guitar solos for which Hendrix is (in)famous.

During these performances, there were the de rigueur remarks from the stage in support of the BRC or to celebrate Hendrix and black rock. At the Cooler in 1995, T. M. Stevens, a bass player who has worked with the Pretenders and Joe Cocker, said a few words before launching into his version of "Purple Haze" with guitarists Larry Mitchell and Ronnie Drayton. His comments were representative of the BRC's spirited reclaiming of Hendrix. Looking every bit the rocker with crimped, shoulder length, blonde-flecked brown hair, broad black aviator glasses, a military inspired jacket, and boldly patterned pants, Stevens reached for the microphone to make the following statement:

> I just had the pleasure last month of playing for Al Hendrix, Jimi's father. He just finally won back his son's music from the producer. [*applause*] . . . I had a chance to sing "Purple Haze" with Noel Redding and Mitch Mitchell. [*cheers*] However! These brothers up here is nasty! [*louder cheers*] And, uh, I just wanted to say to you—and

I'm not here to push anything—but I've been doing this for a long time and it's a war in this country to try to play some music. We've basically been cut from our roots. And they tell us we can't play rock 'n' roll and what have you, but that's bullshit. We *are* rock 'n' roll [*extended cheers*]. And now you put motherfucking Kenny G up there when you've got Coltrane. [*He shakes his head as the audience continues to cheer.*] Tonight I'd like to dedicate this to James Marshall Hendrix and also, with all the performers, I'd like to dedicate this to our roots, our music.[12]

The annual Hendrix Tribute is a way for BRC members to reconnect to their musical roots while creating an arena for the public performance and affirmation of black rock. It is another site of cultural activism through which BRC members and their supporters challenge the boundaries placed around black music and black identity. Because it is dedicated to Jimi Hendrix, this show is, I believe, a bit different from other BRC activities. While still about rock 'n' roll, it is also about laying claim to the black rocker who went the farthest, who wrote so many great songs, played so many brilliant leads, and who gave so much inspiration. Hendrix really made it, but of course in another sense, he did not make it at all. By the time they were playing these sets in the mid-1990s, the BRC members I was getting to know had already lived beyond Hendrix's twenty-seven years. For BRC members, these long, loud rock 'n' roll nights were a time to solidify musical and personal bonds and an opportunity to put Hendrix in the spotlight, keeping his music alive while paying respectful tribute. These were crucial gestures. They were acts as bold as love.

THE USES OF HENDRIX

As a highly mythologized public figure and a rock icon, Hendrix's image is open to appropriation, redefinition, and general use by everyone from music fans to guitarists to anthropologists. Part of Hendrix's success was a consequence of his ability to appeal to the "tastes and obsessions" of his era's rock audience. I should admit that I have focused on him because he speaks so directly to my own musical tastes and scholarly obsessions as one trying to get a handle on the vicissitudes of race and rock. When thinking about his life and work, I usually experience a sense of wonder at all he accomplished musically and a feeling of profound sadness at how he flamed out. Centering race and blackness in a discussion of Hendrix is common sense to me given my subject matter even though it goes against his raceless image. Indeed, as I have explained in this chapter, the complexities of Hendrix's race and music genre are emblematic of the vexed position that black rockers occupy because they do not fit neatly into existing ideological categories. That Hendrix could not convincingly assert a black identity *and* a counterculture persona parallels the difficulties BRC members had simultaneously claiming blackness and playing rock. Intense appreciation of Hendrix and involvement with rock coupled with the resistance they encountered because their tastes were not "really black" led BRC members to develop an organization whose mission is not only to reclaim rock, but to redefine blackness in ways that more fully encompass the experiences and concerns of postliberated blacks. Their private appreciation and public reclaiming of Jimi Hendrix as a black rocker respond to the powerful ways racial ideologies police us and demonstrate how disruptive it can be to refuse to go along with them.

A great deal of progress has been made since Hendrix had his honorary white status conferred upon him to account for his divergence from recognizable blackness, but African Americans continue to be locked into essentialized identities in the media, in business, in the academy, and in everyday life. The persistence of black stereotypes are partly responsible for the frequent references to the validity of difference in the discourses of black intellectuals and BRC members as they acknowledge the complexity of black identity that is so often denied. Hendrix's career and the BRC's "uses of Hendrix" bring the issues of black music and black authenticity to the fore. We will probably never know exactly how the black/white caste system and the role he played in it affected Hendrix, but, possibly reading from their own experiences in integrated and predominantly white settings, BRC members freely speculate. More than one BRC member interpreted Hendrix's turn to jazz, to Miles Davis, to the Band of Gypsys, and to even tentative public gestures for black causes as evidence that he was seeking a way to assert his blackness. Hendrix exploded the rules as he went about redefining how rock music could sound and how a rock star could look. A revolutionary artist, the one set of principles his flamboyant genius was unable to budge is the solidified assumption that black people don't play rock.

BRC members were enthusiastic about Hendrix from the beginning because he was a black musician. He was a figure they could identify with and, indeed, the ways Hendrix managed his racial identity and musical choices were also objects of hypothesizing, empathy, and critique. The BRC fostered a sense of belonging and kept people connected to others with shared interests. Calvin suggested to me that it was a lack of this kind of black community that ultimately undid Hendrix:

CALVIN: [This] was part of Jimi's problem. That's why he was . . . moving towards the more funky aspect. Because he was tired of being alone. That's a very lonely thing, being the only brother everywhere you go, everything you do. I mean *everything*. Everything he did—it was crazy, there was no black people anywhere. Why do you think he went back and got his old army buddy Billy Cox? Because he had nobody. He went back and got the only cat he knew that played music.

MAUREEN: That's right.

CALVIN: See, people don't think of that; they just think, "Wow, lucky that he hooked up with Billy Cox." No. He went looking for that motherfucker. He said, "I got to get somebody I know that's cool. I went through the army . . . with this dude, I know he's cool. That's who I'm going to hang with." But it was almost too late then. He was by himself.

In a sense, one price of his freedom was isolation. Hendrix died before he was able to shift his music to the new terrain he wanted to explore. Up to that point he had an extraordinarily successful career and was the "fluke" that proved that blacks could sell rock to white audiences if given the chance.

Remembering Hendrix's contribution is important to many BRC members because he was the one who went before and who encouraged their own dreams. To BRC members, Hendrix's music is an inspiration, but his demise is a cautionary tale, a warning about the price of fame, particularly for blacks in white contexts. His life story teaches a lesson about the value of the black rock communities that Los Angeles and New York BRC members formed. By naming themselves black rockers, they claimed and defined blackness in their own terms, something Jimi seemed unable or unwilling to do. Hendrix is a black rock forefather whose brilliant sounds paved the way for future generations and his struggles, especially his struggle for freedom in his career, are ones that BRC members identify with strongly. In a column in the New York chapter's November 1996 newsletter, Earl Douglas made the following observations in an unsigned piece that commemorated Hendrix's birthday:

As the 60s drew to a close, Jimi found himself facing a problem that still plagues Black rockers today: trying to embrace both white and Black listeners. Whites couldn't look past his rock 'n' roll wildman image and still insisted on hearing "Purple Haze" and "Foxey Lady." Blacks, who were leaning more toward the sounds of Motown and Stax, also couldn't deal with the rock 'n' roll image—and the fact that his band mates were white. Jimi wanted people to look beyond his outrageous clothes and stage show and judge him on his musical merits. . . . the battle for acceptance on one's own musical terms is something that the BRC is still fighting for today. Jimi Hendrix's imprint on the Black Rock Coalition cannot be removed. Whether as a songwriter, arranger, producer, and of course, guitarist, Hendrix embodies everything the BRC stands for: Our right to rock, our right to create. The opportunity to let our freak flag fly. (BRC 1996)

TEN

UNITL THE LEVEE BREAKS

The main thing that really solidified things for us was the first event, "Drop The Bomb." It was earth shattering. . . . It was like the new movement had landed. There were no limits. Here was this place of being completely expressive and not giving a shit about being in the little box that the industry tries to put us in. It was exciting and threatening to the industry. It was like watching a wild horse run.
—BLACK ROCK COALITION COFOUNDER KONDA MASON

I definitely think that Living Colour would not have happened without a BRC. And it doesn't take anything away from the musicianship of those cats, but in terms of making a noise around the band, there was definitely more noise around Vernon as head of the BRC than there was around Vernon as leader of Living Colour. . . . The early audience for Living Colour was definitely a Black BRC audience. And it really kept that band's name alive and afloat until things really started to happen for them. . . . On that basis alone, the organization had considerable impact.
—BLACK ROCK COALITION COFOUNDER GREG TATE

Well, we're just pretty much a gadfly kind of organization. We actually sparked the debate, the question of what is and what is not Black music. And what is and what is not rock 'n' roll. We started people thinking about—whether people dug it or not—we sparked discussion. And whenever you spark discussion, you cause things to happen. . . . You really have to wonder about taking direct credit for this or that. But I do know that once a discussion that's been in the closet is out of the closet, it's not going back in that closet. Once the genie's out the bottle, the genie's not going back in. — BLACK ROCK COALITION COFOUNDER VERNON REID

Given the speed with which rock movements come and go, it is notable that nearly twenty years after its start, the BRC still exists. The organization still counts many founding members among its numbers, still carries out events, still produces CDs, still issues newsletters (New York's version is distributed by e-mail), still sponsors a radio show (now online), and still gets its live shows reviewed in the local press. By 2003, with the changes in member energy and focus, BRC-sponsored live performances were fewer and farther between than in the early days. In New York, the emphasis shifted to having a smaller number of higher profile events at prestigious venues like the Brooklyn Academy of Music and Symphony Space in Manhattan. Many of the original members told me, with a mix of pleasure and pride, that they were surprised that the organization had survived for so many years. "I guess there's still a need for it," they would say. The BRC remains an independent, autonomous nonprofit. "The reason we still own it," one member quipped, "is because it doesn't make any money. It's not going to be appropriated by anybody." The BRC developed as a response to the pain, frustration, and anger that black musicians felt when others told them what their music should be and allowed members to form connections with like-minded people. BRC members organized to address the problems they were encountering, but how successful were they? What did they really accomplish, and did their organization really matter? To conclude, I suggest some answers to these questions.

Involvement in the BRC had a resounding impact on individuals in terms of their social networks, their musical development, and their identity formation. By participating in the organization, members created a black community that supported and publicized their right to rock. In claiming this right, the BRC also had a significant social impact. Prior to the BRC, there was no critical mass of black rock bands playing in New York rock clubs. There was also no public discussion of this absence and little public criticism of the problematically configured category "black music." Their persistent critique of the marginalization of blacks from rock helped pave the way for Living Colour's remarkable national and international success. But because only a small number of performers associated with the BRC have achieved that kind of widespread recognition and because there is still a pervasive assumption that African Americans are not interested in rock, one might assume that the organization failed in its mission. I want to suggest a different point of view. BRC members have succeeded because they have sustained their organization and their scene—with fluctuating levels of visibility and popularity, to be sure—for almost two decades. Although they do not have the celebrity of superstars, BRC members have made a consistent impact on the arts at a local and national level.

In any given month in Manhattan, BRC members were putting their stamp on the public sphere. I include a few examples of work from some of the BRC's more visible members to indicate the variety and reach of their activities: Greg Tate filed columns for the *Village Voice*, New York's alternative weekly newspaper, and for *Vibe*, a national black music magazine. In 1992, he published *Flyboy in the Buttermilk*, a collection of his magazine and newspaper essays. Tate's play, *My Darling Gremlin: A Tale of the Old West*, featuring music by Butch Morris, was performed in 1993 as part of Aaron Davis Hall's "New Faces, New Voices, New Visions Series." In 2003, he edited *Everything But the Burden*, a collection of essays by black writers, musicians, and artists about white appropriation of black culture (2003b). During the 1990s, he has performed and recorded with his bands Women in Love, Mack Diva, and most recently Burnt Sugar, an ensemble featuring longtime BRC members Rene Akan, Lewis "Flip" Barnes, Bruce Mack, and Jared Nickerson. In 1994, Vernon Reid wrote and performed music for the Bill T. Jones/Arnie Zane Dance Company's full-length dance production *Still/Here* which toured nationally, and in 1996 he released the solo CD *Mistaken Identity*. In 2001, he received a Grammy nomination for his production of guitarist James "Blood" Ulmer's *Memphis Blood: The Sun Sessions*, and in 2002, he released the CD *Front End Lifter* under the name Yohimbe Brothers, a collaboration with DJ Logic. During the 1990s, Konda Mason began working in the film industry, producing independent films as well as music for film and television. In 1995, she was executive producer of the short film *Tuesday Morning Ride* starring Ruby Dee and Bill Cobbs. The film's director, Dianne Houston, became the first African American female director to be nominated for an Academy Award and was the only African American nominated for any Oscar that year. Continuing her activism, Mason served for seven years on the board of directors of Outfest, an annual gay and lesbian media festival that by 1998 had become the largest film festival in Southern

California. In 1995, lawyer and former New York BRC executive director Don Eversley stepped down from the BRC board of directors to avoid a conflict of interest when he became General Counsel for the City of New York Department of Cultural Affairs. Poet Sekou Sundiata had his work anthologized in collections documenting the Nuyorican poetry scene (Algarín and Holman 1994; Blum, Holman and Pellington 1996). In 1995, he was featured in Bill Moyers's *The Language of Life*, an eight-part PBS series that focused on poetry in the United States. In 1994, his play *The Circle Unbroken Is a Hard Bop* was staged at the Nuyorican Poets' Cafe. In 2000, his album *Longstoryshort* was released on Righteous Babe Records, the label owned by singer-songwriter Ani DiFranco with whom he toured nationally in summer 2001. Poet Tracie Morris toured as part of the Lollapalooza music festival's 1994 spoken word series. In 1998, she wrote the text for *Geography: Art, Race, Exile*, a performance piece by choreographer Ralph Lemon (Lemon 2000). She has published a collection of her poetry (Morris 1998) and has been included in anthologies (Algarín and Holman 1994; Blum, Holman and Pellington 1996). In 2002, she was part of the Biennial sponsored by New York's Whitney Museum of American Art. In 1995, vocalist Queen Esther performed her one-woman play, *The Moxy Show*, at Dixon Place and P.S. 122, two of New York's experimental performance spaces, and in 2002 she had a featured role in George C. Wolfe's musical *Harlem Song*, which played in Harlem's Apollo Theater. Guitarist Michael Hill has recorded five albums with his Blues Mob and in October 2001, *Blues Revue* magazine featured him on the cover, naming him one of the "Best of the New Breed" of blues artists. Since the mid-1990s, drummer Marque Gilmore has been a key player in the British drum and bass scene, lending his rhythmic inventiveness to this emergent genre. In 1999, he received the New Music Commissions Grant from the Arts Council of England for a multimedia performance with Mailian musician Cheick Tidane Seck and in 2001, he and his brother, guitarist David Gilmore, performed with the Art Ensemble of Chicago at London's Barbican Centre. A number of BRC members were affiliated with WBAI-FM, a listener-supported radio station, producing programming and working as on-air hosts. And, as always, members were touring and working in the studio with other musicians, continuing their own projects, and promoting postliberated aesthetics.

An artist's work and his or her identity are intertwined and failing to be true to one's voice, vision, and experience can be devastating. "Just play you," Bernie Kaye, lead singer of Total Eclipse urged his fellow musicians. "The whole thing of being an artist is to play you and that's your job . . . to get as close to that as you can and let it flow" (Kaye quoted in BRC 1993b). In demanding that they work within the confines of "black music," the industry was asking BRC members to play and be something other than who they were. To accede to this request would have meant denying the places they had been, the things they had experienced, and the music they loved. It was not a viable option. This determination to pursue one's creative goals and professional dreams—regardless of how unusual they were—was a theme in member life story interviews and free-flowing conversations; it was also a theme that I seized on. In analyzing the reasons behind their choices, discussing their significance, and considering the limitations and possibilities of their activism, I have stressed BRC members' difference and outsiderness. I did not realize how much I had naturalized this image of the BRC until I sent an early draft of an article (Mahon 2000a) to Bill Toles, a member with whom I consulted frequently. He responded with some feedback via e-mail. "Can we discuss what it feels like to be defined as a marginal group?" he wrote. "Boy, it sure reads funny. You know, you strive so hard to be different, ground breaking, true to yourself and only end up marginal. Oh well. :) Other than that I really enjoyed your sketch and can't wait for the mini-series. Are we really that important? (I already know the answer to that). It's a good read. But seeing your adherence to obscurity validated in print is a little scary."[1] My purpose was not to consign BRC members to marginality, but it is true that I was moved to study and document their work because of their resistance to following the standard path. Their choices represented alternative ways of thinking, playing, and being and were notable challenges to dominant ideas about black identity and black music.

RECLAIMING THE RIGHT TO ROCK (SLIGHT RETURN)

By the twenty-first century, there were the beginnings, some claimed, of a black rock revival. Like the reports on black rock in the mid-1980s, articles about the new generation of African American performers like Cody ChesnuTT and Res described the "disconnect" between blacks and rock, traced the black roots of rock 'n' roll, and noted the emergence of African American performers who viewed rock as a vibrant form of musical expression (Caramanica 2002; Pareles 2001; Touré 2002). Prominent among these artists was Mos Def, a rapper whose critically acclaimed CD *Black on Both Sides* (1999) included

"Rock 'n' Roll," a song that linked rap to rock with the refrain "I am hip hop, I am rock 'n' roll," and identified Nina Simone, Jimi Hendrix, John Lee Hooker, and Fishbone as brilliant rockers who were far superior to Elvis Presley and the Rolling Stones. The song concludes with a noisy swirl of thrashing, hardcore guitar flourishes that predicts his next project, Black Jack Johnson. Here, Mos Def fronted a band featuring leading black rockers Bernie Worrell of P-Funk on keyboards, Dr. Know of Bad Brains on guitar, and Doug Wimbish and Will Calhoun of Living Colour on bass and drums, respectively. Other performers associated with rap like the Roots and spoken word artist Saul Williams also incorporated live instrumentation, much of it rock inflected, into their music.

Publishers were also paying attention to documenting the connection between African Americans and rock. African American rock critic Kandia Crazy Horse edited a collection of essays on foundational figures like Ike and Tina Turner, BRC members like the Family Stand, and contemporary rockers like Lenny Kravitz in order to mark and analyze the black experience in rock 'n' roll (Crazy Horse 2004). In 2003, Tate published *Midnight Lightning*, a book analyzing Jimi Hendrix's connection to and influence on black culture from a black perspective (2003a). There was, for a cross section of African American performers and fans, something valuable about rock that they didn't want to relinquish. "Rock represents creative freedom, the democratic ideal," Tate noted in a *Vibe* column celebrating the tenth anniversary of the BRC. He continued:

> Given that, it's no wonder independent-minded black artists, from Chuck Berry and Big Mama Thornton to Sly Stone and Grace Jones, have been drawn to its promise of power, rage, and eroticism. No wonder those forces in society opposed to black people freely expressing ourselves are concerned with the liberties we take in the influential and inspirational arena of popular music. Ten years since its formation, the BRC intends to keep on battling in the name of black rock 'n' rollers until hell freezes over—or until the levee breaks (1995b:52).

This is the spirit that motivated the music, pleasures, and politics I have discussed in this study. BRC members addressed the historical omissions that excluded rock from the canon of "black music," critiquing racism and racialization. They produced concerts, CDs, tapes, cable television shows, public radio programs, and Web sites. This cultural activism supported their efforts to reclaim the right to rock and expanded the possibilities of black art and black identity by representing the depth and breadth of their experiences as African Americans who came of age in the post–civil rights era. It was not the easiest path to take, but it was, for reasons I have described in the foregoing chapters, the path they chose. Partly because they didn't have a choice. They knew they wanted to rock.

Even the BRC band that had started it all had decided to keep rocking. Living Colour had disbanded in 1995, but by 2001 the members had reformed and returned to the touring circuit. I catch them in August 2001 on a hot and humid day in New York's Central Park. Their set, part of the free Summerstage series, is typically loud and energetic and the crowd receives them enthusiastically. During "Time's Up," a mosh pit gets underway; guys hurl themselves strategically against one another, their bodies angling and arching to the music. Vernon lets fly with an all-over-the-landscape solo while the moshers slam and dance to the curving melody lines and dissonant chords. Corey leads into "Elvis Is Dead" by singing the first verse and chorus of "Poppa Was a Rolling Stone" by the Temptations then slides into a rendition of Presley's "I Can't Help Falling in Love With You" mid-song. The crowd chants "Elvis is dead" on cue when the opportunity arises. The band plays a little bit of the reggae classic "Police and Thieves" with Vernon (!) singing a line or two. Later, the guys fill a segue between two songs with the opening riff from Foghat's "Slow Ride." The audience sings along to these songs and to Living Colour's compositions: the chorus of "Love Rears Its Ugly Head" ("Oh, no! Not again.") and "I am the cult of, I am the cult of, I am the cult of personality" at the end of the band's biggest hit. During "Cult," the moshers welcome Corey to their pit and jubilantly carry him on their shoulders. When I look away from the mosh pit and back into the throng behind me, I see a rainbow of hard rocking, head bopping folks, among them loads of black men and women in their twenties, thirties, forties, who seem to know the words and the rhythms of Living Colour's set by heart. Many of them, presumably, had been inspired by Living Colour's insistence that rock was for everybody. With the heat, I feel the press of the crowd more intensely. Later, I learn that the playing field was so packed that the Summerstage authorities had to turn away people at the gates. New York gave Living Colour a warm welcome back.

Way down in front, my ears bear the brunt of the decibels. I'm reminded of the physicality of live rock; it fills your body, reverberates inside you, and entrances you. Living Colour lays down its beautiful, crashing, organized cacophony and mad time signature changes,

Living Colour in the new millennium. From left,
Corey Glover, Doug Wimbish, Vernon Reid,
William Calhoun. Photo by Angie Gray.

weaving in and out of in-the-pocket grooves. Here, to paraphrase BRC
band Civil Rite, you can dance *and* bang your head. During the band's
rendition of Hendrix's "Power to Love," Corey sings, "With the power
of soul, anything is possible." This is sort of like the attitude that
brought the BRC into existence: if you believe and you work, who
knows what might happen. The last song in the encore is "American Skin," Bruce Springsteen's response to the New York City Police
Street-Crime Unit shooting of Amadou Diallo, a black West African
immigrant. Searching for a crime suspect, the policemen saw Diallo
as he was about to enter the front door of his apartment building.
When he tried to show them his wallet to verify his identity, they responded by shooting him. Adding to the outrage over the rash slaying
of an innocent man was the fact that the officers were found not guilty
of murder. At Summerstage, the festive spirit gives way to a somber
mood as Corey stands between Vernon and Doug singing the stark
lyrics that include the repeated phrase "forty-one shots," a reference
to the number of bullets the officers fired at Diallo. Will replicates the
gunshots on his drum kit and Corey delivers the lines: "Is it a gun? Is
it a knife? Is it a wallet? This is your life. . . . You can get killed just
for living in your American skin."

Living in an African American skin has been a challenge genera-tions of black Americans have confronted. In the far from color blind, post–civil rights era United States, BRC members responded to the discourses and practices of race in terms of race because these were the forces that were shaping their experiences. Consequently, the BRC served *black* musicians and *black* bands, called itself the *Black* Rock Coalition, and promoted the genre *black* rock. Through the BRC, mem-bers addressed the fact that they were institutionalized as blacks and excluded from certain possibilities because of their race. But being black was not simply a burden. Blackness was a positive force that they valued and drew strength from. Many held the notion that there was indeed "something" about blackness that could never be fully ap-propriated by nonblacks or completely taken away from blacks. These attitudes were brought home to me on many occasions in comments, jokes, and critiques that assumed particular qualities, abilities, and concerns were attached to and inseparable from being black. This ten-dency represents an investment in the concepts of soul and spirit that African American intellectuals from W. E. B. Du Bois to Langston Hughes to Zora Neale Hurston to Amiri Baraka have used to describe the core of black identity. Although the racial category black has been used against African Americans, it is the basis for a positive identity that grows out of a culture and a history of struggle and survival. Con-sequently, most African Americans are unwilling to "give up" black-ness. The point, as Du Bois argued one hundred years ago, is to rec-ognize the validity of black cultural productions and black people and to create a context in which blackness is no longer oversimplified, downplayed, or reviled. During our interview, Mark described African American identity and culture in terms that I believe would resonate with all BRC members and many black Americans:

> Nobody has it easy anywhere and I come from a culture of people who succeeded in spite of all that stuff. I mean, we're the grandchil-dren of slaves. I'm the great-grandchild of a slave. And I've been around the world, and continue to go and do whatever the fuck I want to do. As long as I imagine it. A lot of it is really about what you imagine, what you decide for yourself. So the possibilities are there for everybody. And it's such a rich culture, and it's as valid—regardless of what somebody else feels about it—it's as valid and beautiful and rich and inspiring as anything else on the earth. And the highest example of contemporary art, a lot of it comes out of our culture. We put the spin on what happens in this world. Black

Americans. Not Africans, not Central Europeans, not British, not French—*us*. Of all people. That's some deep shit. If you're going to be a musician, you've got to speak jazz sooner or later. You got to come to that . . . You can stop at Bach and be a great musician. But eventually, if you're going to move into the twentieth century, you're going to have to address our expanded forms. Ours . . . so, that's cool. I'm with that.

Our spin on culture and aesthetics and kinesthetics is a very deep thing. Everything that we do has a spin on it that nobody else in the world can match. When we do athletics, nobody else does it the way we do. . . . Basketball was one thing before we got to it. Now it's played in the air. With verve, you know . . . with flair. There's this line in *Henry V* when he's talking to Kate, Katherine, the princess of France. He says, "We're the makers of manners, we should not be confined by the weak list of a country's fashion." And that's us. We've been confined. Supposedly. You would think that the people who would be the most confined would be us. But we are the makers of manners. We're the people who decide, who create the spin that the rest of the world moves to.[2]

African Americans, the people who create Mark's spin, are in the middle and on the margins of U.S. culture, a driving force that is often denied or erased. We are, as anthropologist John Gwaltney observed, separate and inseparable from the cultural, historical, and social fabric of the United States (1980:xxviii). We are at once *a part of* and *apart from* the U.S. mainstream. At the same time, the cultural productions of African Americans have created "the spin that the rest of the world moves to." No matter how marginalized from the center, African Americans have produced and imagined in ways that rock the world and it is vital for us to mark and claim this cultural inheritance. The Black Rock Coalition is one example of this process. BRC members push the boundaries of blackness, rewriting accepted scripts in their life stories, in their music, and in their activism. They shape their cultural productions to express their generational, racial, and class experiences, their concerns, and their dreams. They put their spin on things, making their lives meaningful in conditions not of their own making.

DISCOGRAPHY

This is a selected list of recordings by many of the artists who have been affiliated with the Black Rock Coalition over the years. It was compiled by Maureen Mahon and Antero Garcia. For a more complete discography of black rock and funk bands, see Vincent 1996. Many of the artists on the list maintain Web pages.

BLACK ROCK COALITION
1991: *The History of Our Future*. Rykodisc.
1993: *Blacker Than That*. BRC Records.
2000: *The Bronze Buckeroo Rides Again*. BRC Records.

JEAN-PAUL BOURELLY
1988: *Jungle Cowboy*. Winter and Winter.
1992: *Trippin'*. Enemy.
1994: *Saints and Sinners*. DIW.
1994: *Blackadelic-Blu*. DIW.
1995: *Tribute to Jimi*. Koch International.
1997: *Fade to Cacophony: Live*. Evidence.
1998: *Rock the Cathartic Spirits: Vibe Music and Blues*. Koch International.
2001: *Boom Bop*. Jazz Magnet.
2002: *Trance Atlantic (Boom Bop II)*. Challenge.

BURNT SUGAR, THE ARKESTRA CHAMBER
2000: *Blood on the Leaf*. Trugroid.
2001: *That Depends on What You Know: The Crepescularium*. Trugroid.
2001: *That Depends on What You Know: Fubractive Since*. Trugroid.
2001: *That Depends on What You Know: The Sirens Return*. Trugroid.
2003: *The Rites: Conductions Inspired by Stravinsky's Le Sacre du Printemps*. Trugroid/Avantgroid.

THE BUS BOYS

1980: *Minimum Wage Rock and Roll*. Arista.

1982: *American Worker*. Arista.

1988: *Money Don't Make No Man*. Voss.

DON BYRON

1990: *Tuskegee Experiments*. Nonesuch.

1993: *Don Byron Plays the Music of Mickey Katz*. Nonesuch.

1995: *Music for Six Musicians*. Nonesuch.

1996: *Bug Music: Music of The Raymond Scott Quintette, John Kirby and His Orchestra, and the Duke Ellington Orchestra*. Nonesuch.

1996: *No Vibe Zone: Live at the Knitting Factory*. Knitting Factory.

1998: *Nu Blaxploitation*. Blue Note.

1999: *Romance With the Unseen*. Blue Note.

2000: *A Fine Line: Arias and Lieder*. Blue Note.

2001: *You Are #6: More Music for Six Musicians*. Blue Note.

WILLIAM CALHOUN

1994: *Housework*. WC Records.

1997: *Drumwave*. WC Records.

2000: *Live at the Blue Note*. Half Note Records.

CEPHAS, FEATURING REGGIE KOMET

1994: *Deviating From the Norm*. Tunnel Vision Records.

CIVIL RITE

1995: *Corporate Dick*. Rite House Entertainment.

STEVE COLEMAN AND FIVE ELEMENTS

1986: *On the Edge of Tomorrow*. JMT.

1986: *World Expansion*. JMT.

1987: *Sine Die*. Pangaea.

1990: *Rhythm People (The Resurrection of Creative Black Civilization)*. Novus.

1991: *Black Science*. Novus.

1992: *Dropkick*. Novus.

1993: *The Tao of Mad Phat: Fringe Zones*. Novus.

1994: *Def Trance Beat (Modalities of Rhythm)*. Novus.

D-XTREME

1990: *The Truth Shall Be Told*. Silenz.

EYE & I

1992: *Eye & I*. Epic.

THE FAMILY STAND
1988: *Chapters: A Novel by Evan Geffries and The Stand*. Atlantic.
1990: *Chain*. Atlantic.
1991: *Moon in Scorpio*. EastWest Records.
1998: *Connected*. EastWest Records.

DAVID FIUCZYNSKI
2000: *Jazzpunk*. Fuzelicious Morsels Records.
2001: *Amandala*. Fuzelicious Morsels Records.
2002: *Black Cherry Acid Lab*. Fuzelicious Morsels Records.

DAVID FIUCZYNSKI AND JOHN MEDESKI
1994: *Lunar Crush*. Gramavision.

FOLLOW FOR NOW
1991: *Follow for Now*. Chrysalis.

FREAK JUICE [TORRELL RUFFIN]
1999: *Juicemaker*. Rite House Entertainment.

MARQUE GILMORE/DRUM FM
2002: *Creation Step*. Tribal Broadcast.
2002: *Vortex Extension*. Tribal Broadcast.

COREY GLOVER
1997: *Live at CBGB's*. LaFace Records.
1998: *Hymns*. LaFace Records.

NONA HENDRYX
1977: *Nona Hendryx*. Epic.
1983: *Nona*. RCA.
1984: *The Art of Defence*. RCA.
1985: *The Heat*. RCA.
1987: *Female Trouble*. EMI.
1989: *Skin Diver*. Private Music.
1992: *You Have to Cry Sometime*. Shanachie.

JUNGLE FUNK [DOUG WIMBISH AND WILLIAM CALHOUN]
1999: *Jungle Funk*. Zebra Records.

KELVYNATOR
1987: *Funk It Up*. Blue Heron.
1993: *Refunkanation*. Enemy Records.

LIVING COLOUR
1988: *Vivid*. Epic.
1990: *Time's Up*. Epic.
1991: *Biscuits*. Epic.
1993: *Stain*. Epic.
1995: *Pride*. Epic.
1998: *Super Hits*. Epic.
2003: *Collideoscope*. Sanctuary.

MICHAEL HILL'S BLUES MOB
1994: *Bloodlines*. Alligator Records.
1996: *Have Mercy*. Alligator Records.
1998: *New York State Of Blues*. Alligator Records.
2001: *Suite: Larger Than Life*. Singular Records.
2003: *Electric Storyland Live*. Ruf Records.

ME'SHELL NDEGÉOCELLO
1993: *Plantation Lullabies*. Maverick.
1996: *Peace Beyond Passion*. Maverick.
1999: *Bitter*. Maverick.
2002: *Cookie: The Anthropological Mixtape*. Maverick.
2003: *Comfort Woman*. Maverick.

RAINBOWS END
1995: *No Far Out*. Eternity Records.

VERNON REID
1996: *Mistaken Identity*. 550 Music/Epic.

SCREAMING HEADLESS TORSOS
1995: *Screaming Headless Torsos*. Discovery Records/Fuzelicious Morsels Records.
2001: *Live!!* Fuzelicious Morsels Records.

SUBURBAN DOG
1996: *Suburban Dog*. Suburban Dog Music.

SEKOU SUNDIATA
1997: *The Blue Oneness of Dreams*. Mercury Records.
2000: *Longstoryshort*. Righteous Babe Records.

TOTAL ECLIPSE
1992: *Total Eclipse*. Tabu/A&M.

24-7 SPYZ
1988: *Harder Than You*. Combat.
1990: *Gumbo Millennium*. Combat.
1996: *Heavy Metal Soul by the Pound*. What Are Records?

GENE WILLIAMS
1996: *Welcome 2 My World*. World Alert Records.

DOUG WIMBISH
1999: *Trippy Notes for Bass*. On-U Sound.

WOMEN IN LOVE
1994: *Sound of Falling Bodies at Rest*. Madrina Records.

YOHIMBE BROTHERS [VERNON REID AND DJ LOGIC]
2002: *Front End Lifter*. RopeADope Records.

NOTES

CHAPTER 1: RECLAIMING THE RIGHT TO ROCK

In honor of the BRC's fifteenth anniversary, the newsletter editors published interviews with each of the three cofounders in 2000–2001 in which they reflected on the history of the organization and its accomplishments; the epigraphs for chapters 1 and 10 come from this series.

1   I talk about Faith in more detail in chapter 8. See Jones 1992 for an extensive discussion of Faith.

2   French sociologist Pierre Bourdieu has persuasively demonstrated that seemingly objective categories of taste and aesthetics depend on and constitute relations between different social classes (Bourdieu 1984).

3   Rosaldo is critiquing a classic norm of anthropology that says "to pursue a culture is to seek out its difference, and then show how it makes sense, as they say, on its own terms" (1993:201).

4   Challenging black stereotypes has been a part of anthropological explanations of the distinctiveness of African American cultures and communities and their relationship to the U.S. mainstream (e.g., Aschenbrenner 1975; Dollard 1937; Herskovits 1941; Liebow 1967; Powdermaker 1939; Stack 1974; Whitten and Szwed 1970). In some cases these representations contributed to the stereotyping and mythologizing of blackness (Szwed 1972). African American anthropologists have used their research to deconstruct distorted images of African Americans, to explain the internal logic of African American culture, and to demonstrate the impact of institutional racism on African Americans (Baker 1998; Bell 1983; Davis et al. 1941; Drake and Cayton [1945] 1993; Du Bois [1899] 1996; Gregory 1998; Gwaltney 1980; Hurston [1935] 1978; McClaurin 2001; Mitchell-Kernan 1972; Mullings 1997; Valentine 1978). For discussions of this tradition among African American anthropologists, see Harrison 1988; Harrison and Harrison 1998.

5   Hall notes that a more static understanding of black identity, one that emphasizes "'one true self'. . . which people with a shared history and ancestry hold in common," can be a productive force in the political and cultural struggles of marginalized and oppressed peoples (1992:221). As evidenced by the Négritude movement of black Francophone colonies and the Black Arts Movement of the

United States, a unified identity can "restore an imaginary fullness or plenitude, to set against the broken rubric of our past" (223). This "essentializing moment," however, does not take into account change over time, the existence of "differences and discontinuities" among blacks (223), or the "extraordinary diversity of subjective positions, social experiences, and cultural identities which compose the category 'black'" (Hall 1988:28).

6 While African Americans share a political and cultural history, differences related to region, gender, sexuality, color, class, education, and generation shape experience and perspective. For examples of the ways African American studies scholars have described and analyzed these differences, see Carby 1998; Davis 1983; Domínguez 1986; Giddings 1984; Gilroy 1991a, 1993; Gregory 1998; Hall 1992; Harper 1996; hooks 1981, 1990; Kelley 1994; Lorde 1984; McClaurin 2001; Mullings 1997; Rahier 1999; Smith 1998; Sutton and Chaney 1987; West 1990.

7 African American writers like Ralph Ellison (1986) and Albert Murray (1983) have explored this critical but underrecognized relationship; cf. Holloway 1990.

8 In using the term "cultural critique" I am drawing from George Marcus and Michael M. J. Fischer (1986). They suggested to anthropologists that a productive way to revitalize the discipline was to deploy "anthropology as cultural critique" by bringing "the insights gained on the periphery back to the center to raise havoc with our settled ways of thinking and conceptualization" (138). Working within U.S. borders, African American intellectuals have long been involved in this kind of project. Indeed, the black intellectual tradition has developed in part through an analysis and critique of U.S. economic, political, and social relations, advancing an argument for the full inclusion of black citizens.

9 During the time I conducted my fieldwork, BRC leaders estimated the combined membership of New York and Los Angeles BRC chapters to be 400. The majority of the members lived in the New York and Los Angeles metropolitan areas, although the coalition claims members in Atlanta, Philadelphia, Chicago, and San Francisco.

10 Ortner has characterized work with this focus on the relationship between agency (or human action) and structure (or "the system") as practice theory (Ortner 1984; cf. Bourdieu 1990; Giddens 1979; Sahlins 1985).

11 In his study of African American community organizing in Queens, New York, Gregory examines the ways in which people "contest and rearticulate racial ideologies and meanings and in the process construct new, potentially empowering political subjectivities and alignments" (1993:24). For other examples of scholarship on the cultural politics of race, see Brodkin 1998; Gilroy 1991a; Gregory 1998; Gregory and Sanjek 1994; Hall 1992; Harrison 1995; Hartigan 1999; Lipsitz 1998; Omi and Winant 1994; Williams 1989.

12 Omi and Winant note that "Reagan had opposed every major civil rights measure considered by Congress. He opposed the Civil Rights Act of 1964, denouncing it as a 'bad piece of legislation,' and the Voting Rights Act of 1965, opining that 'The Constitution very specifically reserves control of voting to local governments. Additional legislation is unnecessary'" (1994:133).

13   In recent years, a critical mass of humanities and social science scholars has made "cultural politics" a research focus. These researchers have extended their interpretation of politics beyond formal government institutions and worked from a broad, anthropological definition of culture to examine "the processes through which relations of power are asserted, accepted, contested, or subverted by means of ideas, values, symbols and daily practices" (Glick Schiller 1997:2; cf. Ginsburg 1989; Glick Schiller and Fournon 2001; Gregory 1998; Kondo 1990; Myers 1994; Williams 1991). British cultural studies developed a similar approach, using Gramsci's concept of hegemony and viewing power as a contestable and unstable force that social actors produce and struggle over (Gilroy 1991a; Hall and Jefferson 1975; Hebdige 1979; Willis 1977). Under the rubric of cultural politics, scholars examine the practices through which people respond to power and in some cases transform existing social relations and social structures.

14   Scholars have observed that representation as it occurs in film, music, and literature is a historically situated, discursive practice through which people contest and construct meanings. Stuart Hall has noted that representation is "a formative, not merely an expressive place" (1988:27). Commenting on Asian American cultural politics, cultural critic Lisa Lowe observes that through practices of representation, "subject, community, and struggle are signified and mediated" (1996:157).

15   Media, popular culture, and the arts—the realms in which BRC members were involved—enable the maintenance of alternative histories, the promotion of oppositional cultures, identity formation, entertainment, and profit making. They can also facilitate social critique, mobilize interest groups, and break social boundaries. Anthropologists concerned with the social and aesthetic role of popular culture have emphasized the ways these representations construct and disseminate ideologies about identity, community, difference, nation, and politics (Abu-Lughod 1993; Bright and Bakewell 1995; Dávila 1997; Dornfeld 1998; Fox and Starn 1997; Ginsburg 1997; Kondo 1997; MacClancy 1997; Marcus and Myers 1995; McLagan 1996; Myers 1994). For reviews of this literature and discussions of the relationship between art and politics, see Mahon 2000b; Spitulnik 1993; and Traube 1996.

16   In light of the public and political roles of these cultural productions, contemporary scholars have characterized the arena in which social actors produce and circulate their work as the "public sphere" (Calhoun 1992; Fraser 1992; Robbins 1993; Sreberny-Mohammadi and Mohammadi 1994). This is political philosopher Jürgen Habermas's (1989) term for the social space that is separate from the state and the market economy in which citizens can debate political ideas. Some scholars have replaced Habermas's white- and male-centered public sphere with a concept of multiple public spheres that reflect the wide-ranging sociopolitical concerns of the heterogeneous populations present in contemporary nations. This focus draws attention to the coexistence of distinct and occasionally intersecting spheres that are an inevitable part of stratified societies. Feminist political theorist Nancy Fraser calls these emergent alternative zones "subaltern counterpublics"

and describes them as "parallel discursive arenas where members of subordinated social groups invent and circulate counterdiscourses to formulate oppositional interpretations of their identities, interests, and needs" (1992:123). Scholars recognize that these privatized zones of profit-centered consumer popular culture and media have become locations of important social and political debates (Appadurai et al. 1994; Dornfeld 1998; Robbins 1993).

17 A number of studies of musicians use interdisciplinary approaches to examine the relationship between music productions, identity, aesthetics, institutional structures, and history (Cohen 1991; Born 1995; Feld 1988, 1994; Finnegan 1989; Gray 1988; Keil 1966; Keil and Feld 1994; Lipsitz 1994; Meintjes 2003; Monson 1996; Rose 1994; Shank 1994; Turino 1993; Waterman 1990).

18 For discussions of this type of African American community organization, see Drake and Cayton [1945] 1993; Gaines 1996; Giddings 1984; Gregory 1998; Higginbotham 1993.

CHAPTER 2: THE "POSTLIBERATED GENERATION"

1 Sociologist Karl Mannheim argues that the constant arrival of new generations produces social movements and leads to social change (1952:294; cf. Ginsburg 1989). Central to this process is "fresh contact" in which individuals and generations come "into contact anew with the accumulated heritage" (Mannheim 1952:293). Typically, this encounter results in "a novel approach in assimilating, using, and developing the proffered material" (293) as each new participant takes part in the culture while bringing new, generation-specific attitudes "towards the heritage handed down by his predecessors" (294). In the case of BRC members, the meanings of black culture and black identity, questions that previous generations of African Americans have confronted, are subjects of this reevaluation.

2 Gaines notes that "occupations within the black community widely perceived by historians as middle-class, including that of teacher, minister, federal office-holder, businessman, and professional, cannot be regarded as equivalent with the business, managerial, and craft labor occupations among whites from which blacks were largely excluded" (1996:14). Further, he observes that we must avoid using "a false universal standard for class formation that ignores the extent to which the very notion of the black middle class—indeed, of class itself—is built on shifting ideological sands" (14).

3 Bourdieu articulates this relationship in his research on France by observing that schools, with their "value-inculcating and value-imposing operations," train citizens not only in academics, but also in the cultural preferences and practices associated with the dominant group; as a result, they are essential to the accumulation of cultural competence and cultural capital (1984:23).

4 Even as she critiques the motivations of the integrationists, Ravitch acknowledges that although New York state law prohibited racial discrimination, "There were subtle administrative practices which were as racist in their effect as legal segregation: school-zoning lines drawn to keep minority group children out of white

schools; districts gerrymandered into odd shapes to preserve the racial status quo in certain schools; junior high schools kept white by the arrangement of their elementary school feeders" (1974:246).

5 Desegregation of housing was not officially mandated until 1968 at which point most BRC members' families were firmly established in black or predominantly black communities.

6 Post–civil rights coming-of-age novels frequently detail the complexities related to being one of a handful of blacks in predominantly white contexts. See, for example, Beatty 1995; Ellis 1988; Pinckney 1992. The postliberated experience is also documented in memoirs including Cary 1992; Lamar 1991; McDonald 2000. In these fictional and autobiographical texts, narrators struggle to maintain a balance between the middle-class ideals of upward mobility and loyalties to black identity and roots.

CHAPTER 3: SATURDAY GO TO MEETING

1 BRC meetings were much like the secular rituals described by Victor Turner (1977). The concept of secular ritual accounts for the ways ceremony and ritual are used in nonreligious contexts to legitimate certain views of social reality and inform the ways people think about social life (Moore and Myerhoff 1977:4).

2 The presence of women, never particularly welcome in rock, adds an additional layer of complexity to the scenario. See chapter 8 for more on black women in rock.

3 The executive committee and active members struggled to maintain and create enthusiasm through what Turner calls "normative communitas," a system of precepts and rules that capture and preserve the essence of spontaneous communitas (1974:46). The primary precepts are the continuation of the meetings, the development of performances and panels that promote and explore black rock, and calls for mutual support.

4 The information is printed on one side of the card and usually arranged around a graphic with the band's name. The reverse side is left blank so the cards can be addressed and mailed as postcards.

CHAPTER 4: BLACK ROCK MANIFESTING

1 Gina Dent (1992a) and Dorinne Kondo (1997) have drawn attention to the importance of addressing the significance and complexity of pleasure in scholarly accounts of popular culture. Kondo suggests that we take pleasure seriously "as a site of political contestation that might engage, and at times be coextensive with, the critical impulse" (1997:13) and also offer a critical appraisal in order to recognize our complicity with the dominant and "the effectiveness of our interventions" (14). Keil and Feld's (1994) collection of essays and dialogues about music highlight the pleasures of listening to and participating in music making as well as the politics associated with these practices.

2　Steven Feld stresses the importance of attending to both musical practice and economic structures in order to appreciate the complexity of musical borrowing and exchange in contexts dominated by unequal power relations (Feld 1988, 1994; cf. Meintjes 1990). See Jefferson 1973; Baraka 1963; Lott 1993; and Torgovnick 1990 for discussions of white appropriation of nonwhite cultures.

3　In the manifesto, Tate signifies on Album Oriented Rock (AOR), the industry term used to describe hard rock radio programming, with the term "Apartheid Oriented Radio" to characterize programmers' preference for white heavy metal and exclusion of black rock guitarists (Johnson 1986:11).

4　Ginsburg argues that cultural work produced by indigenous and minority producers can "heal disruptions in cultural knowledge, historical memory, and identity between generations" (1991:104).

5　For examples, see Fricke 1987; Gardner 1993; Gonzalez 1990; Himes 1987; Johnson 1986; Kot 1991; Sinclair 1991; Smith 1989.

6　I thank Betsy Traube for inventing this playful and fortuitous phrase to describe aspects of my fieldwork.

7　For studies of amateur and budding professional musicians and the important role performing plays in their lives, see Bayton 1998; Cohen 1991; Finnegan 1989; Shank 1994.

8　See Mercer 1994 and Rooks 1996 for discussions of the politics of black hair.

9　Deeply influenced by the writings of Italian Marxist Antonio Gramsci, British cultural studies scholars focused on culture, ideology, language, and the symbolic, emphasizing the role of popular culture both as a site of ideological domination from above and as a potential location of resistance from below.

CHAPTER 5: BLACK ROCK AESTHETICS

1　See, for example, Locke [1925] 1969; Du Bois [1899] 1996; Hughes [1926] 1971; Hurston [1934] 1981; Wright [1937] 1997; Neal 1968; Murray 1983; and Baker 1988.

2　Sociologists who have developed socially grounded frameworks for understanding artistic production include Becker (1982), who has talked about "art worlds," and Bourdieu (1993), who coined the term "the field of cultural production." These studies connect artistic production to the economic, social, and political context in which it occurs.

3　Amiri Baraka's *Blues People* (1963) is an eloquent example of the tendency to use black American music as an index and reflection of the black social and political experience as well as black identity. A number of artists and intellectuals, including Langston Hughes, Albert Murray, and Houston Baker, have identified black music, particularly the blues, as the source of a black aesthetic.

4　This article is collected with Tate's writings from 1981 to 1991 in *Flyboy in the Buttermilk* (Tate 1992), itself an effort to advance black cultural criticism and to create an infrastructure for appreciating these productions. Tate is concerned with supporting and sustaining what we might call, adapting Bourdieu (1993), "a black field of cultural production."

5   In spite of a discourse of solidarity based on common race and common condition, black nationalism in the 1960s depended on a rhetoric that underlined the social divisions within black communities (Harper 1995). The articulation of an authentic black consciousness required a black other; indeed, whites were only marginally important to the project.

6   Discussing the centrality of discourses of authenticity in nationalist movements, anthropologist Richard Handler observes, "The existence of a national collectivity depends on the 'possession' of an authentic culture . . . an authentic culture is one original to its possessors, one which exists only with them: in other words, an independently existent entity, asserting itself . . . against all other cultures" (1986:4).

7   Film producer Warrington Hudlin founded the Black Filmmakers Foundation in 1978. This New York-based nonprofit organization supports and develops the work of young black film directors, writers, and actors.

8   Members of Parliament and Funkadelic elaborated a funky science fiction fantasy linking space travel and references to the African motherland, and involving what P-Funk leader George Clinton called "the Mothership Connection." Music critic John Corbett connects Clinton's interest in outer space to that of black musicians Sun Ra and Lee Scratch Perry, observing that all three "take space iconography seriously and turn it into a platform for playful subversion, imagining a productive zone largely exterior to dominant ideology" (1994:8). For more on Clinton see Reid 1993 and Vincent 1996.

9   Part of the extensive repertoire of African American verbal art, this genre of ritual insult, also called "snaps," usually includes attacks on an opponent's family members, especially his or her mother. The phrase, "Your mama's so . . ." often introduces the comments. See Mitchell-Kernan 1972 for discussion and analysis of African American English and speech acts.

10 Like nearly all of the BRC members whose CDs I collected, Civil Rite's included a lyric sheet.

CHAPTER 6: LIVING COLORED IN THE MUSIC INDUSTRY

1   Norman Kelley (2002) accurately observes that the political economy of black music production has received scant scholarly attention. Still, there are some useful sources: Cashmore 1997; Chapple and Garofalo 1977:231–67; George 1988; Kelley 2002. For a discussion of independent black music production, see Gray 1988.

2   Here, I am building on what media studies scholars Peter Golding and Graham Murdock call a "critical political economy" perspective that illuminates "how the making and taking of meaning is shaped at every level by the structured asymmetries in social relations" (Golding and Murdock 1991:18).

3 For more on Living Colour, see Blush 1990 and Jones 1990.

4 Reid was born in London in 1958, but grew up in New York City.

5 See Walser 1993 for discussion of heavy metal aesthetics. In addition to coverage of Living Colour in general rock music magazines like *Rolling Stone* and *Spin*, the band's instrumentalists were featured in cover stories in specialized publications for musicians, for example, Calhoun in *Drums and Drummers* (November 1990), Reid in *Guitar* (January 1991), Skillings in *Bass Player* (May/June 1991), and Wimbish in *Bass Player* (June 1993).

6 For discussions of race and racism in the U.S. popular music industry, see Kelley 2002; Chapple and Garofalo 1977; George 1988; Baraka 1963; Murray 1981.

7 For discussions of the industry's business dealings see Chapple and Garofalo 1977; Dannen 1991; Eliot 1989; Sanjek 1988; Sanjek and Sanjek 1991.

8 This shift was a result of mainstream recognition of the black consumer market and the potential of black audiences to boost shrinking radio ratings as television increased in importance (Alexander 1981:104). In 1943, only four stations carried black-oriented programming; by 1956, 400 (15 percent) of all U.S. stations gave at least 10 percent of their air time to black-oriented programs (Alexander 1981:112).

9 Chapple and Garofalo estimate that more than 400 new labels started in the 1940s and about 100 of them survived until 1952 (1977:29). With few exceptions, these independent R&B labels were white owned (George 1988:26–28). Black-owned labels included Peacock started in 1949 by Don Robey, Red Robin started in 1951 by Bobby Robinson, and Vee-Jay started in 1952 by Vivian Bracken and Calvin Carter (George 1988:26–28). Vee-Jay was the first American label to distribute the music of the Beatles.

10 The white southerners associated with Sun Records had grown up enthralled by white pop crooners like Bing Crosby, Grand Ole Opry performers like Bill Monroe, and the blues and R&B they heard in nearby black communities. Jerry Lee Lewis and his cousin Jimmy Swaggart used to sneak into Haney's Big House, a black juke joint owned by his uncle, near Ferriday, Louisiana (Escott 1991:190). Carl Perkins, the son of Tennessee sharecroppers, learned to play guitar from John Westbrook, a black sharecropper (126).

11 There are scores of examples of these unfair practices. One involving Chuck Berry's first single, "Maybelline," illustrates the shady climate: "Disc jockeys Alan Freed and Russ Fratto were 'motivated' to play the record regularly—by being credited as part-authors" (Gillett 1983:31).

12 Berry had taken a fourteen-year-old girl whom he believed to be eighteen from Texas to St. Louis, Missouri. Chapple and Garofalo are among the commentators who see his arrest and two-year imprisonment in the early 1960s as an effort to silence the prominent black rock 'n' roller (1977:39–40).

13 "Plantation Radio," written by P. Lord, V. J. Smith, S. St. Victor, G. Routte, copyright 1991 by Leosun Music. In 1991, the Family Stand succeeded in getting its music on the airwaves by writing and producing several songs for R&B artist Paula Abdul's multiplatinum album *Spellbound*.

14   See Feld 1988, 1994; Keil and Feld 1994; Meintjes 1990 for discussions of Paul Simon and the complexities of this type of appropriation and "discovery."

15   For discussions of the conundrums of crossover see Garofalo 1993; George 1988; and Perry 1989.

16   CBS was known for introducing a single on black radio, building sales through airplay and promotion to the gold record range (500,000 units sold) before beginning to market it to mainstream pop audiences (George 1988:150). The pop market was and is the primary industry moneymaker, an important fact in the context of crossover (Garofalo 1993:237).

17   The NAACP Report is reprinted in Kelley 2002.

18   Echoing the NAACP report, the National Association of Black Owned Broadcasters, a trade organization representing radio, television, and broadcast company owners, and African American industry press like *Black Enterprise* and *Black Radio Exclusive* voiced concerns about music industry racism (Warren 1992:19).

19   Over the years, research on radio audiences has shown that black Americans consistently report higher radio usage at home than whites and exhibit greater consumer spending in proportion to their numbers in the population (Glasser and Metzger 1981).

20   MTV began its broadcast on August 1, 1981, showing as many as three hundred videos a day (Sanjek 1988:639). For discussions of MTV see Banks 1996; Kaplan 1987; McGrath 1996.

21   Executives at CBS and MTV deny that there was an ultimatum (Banks 1996:40). Instead, MTV executives say that their initial hesitation about programming a song that did not fit their station's format was undercut by their desire to show an extremely innovative and compelling video (McGrath 1996:100). Coming at a time when CBS artists dominated the charts and when MTV depended on free clips from labels for its programming, refusing CBS could have put the station at risk of losing access to a significant number of popular videos (Denisoff 1986:362). Within two weeks of the video's airing on MTV, *Thriller* sold one million units and went on to become the best-selling album in history (Denisoff 1986:362; Sanjek and Sanjek 1991:254).

CHAPTER 7: MEDIA INTERVENTIONS

1   By extension, it is relatively easy to identify and get access to potential research subjects who are media consumers. Indeed, most media studies by anthropologists focus on audiences and consumption rather than production. For discussion of the challenges associated with conducting fieldwork with producers, see Dornfeld 1998 and Kondo 1997.

2   For discussions of media and the public sphere, see Appadurai et al., 1994; Calhoun 1992; Dornfeld 1998; Neal 1999; Robbins 1993; Sreberny-Mohammadi and Mohammadi 1994.

3   In April 1994, Williams and Douglas stepped down from the show. After a tran-

sition period, Gregory Amani and Lace began broadcasting the BRC's "Crosstown Traffic" in January 1995 in a Friday early morning time slot. By 2002, the coalition presented *Radio BRC* online at www.soul-patrol.com/funk/blk_rock.htm. The show's hosts were LaRonda Davis, Earl Douglas, and Darrell McNeill, and occasional guest host Vernon Reid.

4   See Gray 1988 for a discussion of black independent record production.

5   During the 1980s, over 1,000 cable systems were launched across the United States (Kellner 1990:188). The high level of competition between different cable operators for local franchises gave cities and municipalities the leverage to demand that cable carriers provide services like public access in order to be awarded a contract.

6   To format the show for its thirty-minute time slot, Rod and Melva had to carefully schedule the minute and second point at which a public service announcement would be placed, how much time would be spent on a given segment of an interview, and how much time would be devoted to camera effects like fades and dissolves.

7   To "call the show" means to direct camera movement, supervise the composition of the shots, and select which shots from the two cameras are used in the broadcast.

8   The BRC Web site address at time of publication was http://www.blackrock coalition.org.

CHAPTER 8: PLAYING ROCK, PLAYING ROLES

1   The sexual ambiguity associated with glam rock or Little Richard undermines dominant behavior codes from another direction. For discussion of gender roles and sexuality in rock, see Frith and McRobbie 1990; Reynolds and Press 1995; Walser 1993.

2   In order, the songs are "Under My Thumb" and "Some Girls" by the Rolling Stones and "Whole Lotta Love" by Led Zeppelin.

3   Studies about the contributions women have made to rock offer an important rewriting and expansion of rock history. For examples, see Bayton 1998; Chapple and Garofalo 1977; Frith and McRobbie 1990; Gaar 1992; Gottlieb and Wald 1994; Hirshey 2001; O'Brien 1995; Reynolds and Press 1995.

4   These gender rules also operate in jazz where the most successful women performers have been, almost exclusively, vocalists. Instrumentalists Mary Lou Williams, Carla Bley, Alice Coltrane, the Uptown String Quartet, Terri Lynne Carrington, Regina Carter, and BRC founding member Geri Allen are exceptions.

5   This problem is pointedly stated in the title of the black feminist reader *All The Women Are White, All the Blacks Are Men, But Some of Us Are Brave: Black Women's Studies* (Hull, Bell Scott, and Smith 1982). Black feminist scholarship addresses black women's simultaneous experience of racism and sexism; some of these texts also interrogate the category of "black women," describing the impact of differences in class, ethnicity, and sexuality among black women (Collins 1991;

Davis 1983; hooks 1981; McClaurin 2001; Mullings 1997; Smith 1983; Smith 1998; Wallace 1979). For a historical overview of African American women in U.S. women's rights and civil rights movements, see Giddings 1984. Guy-Sheftall 1995 is a comprehensive overview of the black feminist intellectual tradition.

6 Although black women rockers also encountered the charge of "acting white," it is usually more acceptable for black women to traverse perceived racial boundaries (Fordham 1996).

7 For perspectives on black masculinity, see Boyd 1997; Golden 1994b; Harper 1996; Staples 1982.

CHAPTER 9: JIMI HENDRIX EXPERIENCES

1 My focus here is deliberately narrow. I leave it to others to detail the settlement of his estate, exactly who he slept with, which drugs he took, and the process of repackaging him in recent years in order to sell him to new generations of fans. For biographical information on Hendrix, I have depended on Henderson (1983) and Murray (1991).

2 In addition to its nostalgic resurrection of Hendrix, the "On the Road Again" exhibit was notable for its cutting-edge multimedia displays. The Jimi Hendrix Video Wall was an eight foot by six foot arrangement of television monitors that showed Hendrix concert footage. There were also interactive exhibits. The Jimi Hendrix Electric Church used infrared light beams and recordings of Hendrix's guitar riffs to enable the participants to "play the guitar like Jimi," as one explanation put it. The Jimi Hendrix Kaleidosphere was a touch-sensitive television screen and laser disc that allowed the participant to touch images of Hendrix and activate film and audio clips of his performances.

3 My analysis of race and identity as they relate to Hendrix draws on Murray's (1991) discussion of these issues. Murray takes race seriously in his analysis of Hendrix and attends to the particular problems Hendrix experienced as a black artist with a predominantly white audience.

4 This is not a connection that BRC members made when we spoke, but one suggested by audience members when I have presented this material in lectures. Although most BRC members experienced integration at school, almost all of them lived in black neighborhoods and thus did not encounter the same round-the-clock immersion in all-white arenas as their guitar hero did in his professional life. In fact, because they were in frequent contact with black peers, they had to defend their engagement with rock and their appreciation of Hendrix.

5 Although they share with Wynton Marsalis an interest in black music history, some BRC members criticize his adherence to a definition of jazz that refuses to embrace contemporary innovations of the form.

6 In 1970, Hendrix expressed interest in playing a benefit performance for the New York Panther 21, but his manager, Mike Jeffrey, refused to let him participate, fearing association with the Black Panthers would tarnish his client's image (Henderson 1983:309).

7 Murray notes, "Hendrix knew the score as far as the position of the black GI was concerned: in 'Nam they represented 2 per cent of the officers and were assigned 28 per cent of the combat missions. . . . Hendrix knew *exactly* who was paying the price of the politicians' games" (1991:23).

8 This performance is captured in the 1992 video *Jimi Hendrix Experience*, directed by Peter Neal.

9 I am referring to his performance of "Wild Thing" at the Monterey Pop festival. Footage of his performance appears in D. A. Pennebaker's 1968 film *Monterey Pop*.

10 Torgovnick (1990) asserts that this use of the primitive is deeply embedded in Western habits of thinking and persists today even as people become more attuned to the problems of the ethnocentric and racist biases attached to most conceptions of the primitive.

11 Mailer explains that these white hipsters "drifted out at night looking for action with a black man's code to fit their facts" (1968:341). Mailer is notable not only for naming this type of postwar racial interaction, but also for doing so with such racist overtones. He depicts black men as hypersexed, hypervirile, and forever in pursuit of orgasm—be it sexually or jazz-induced.

12 A highly condensed videotape of the fifth annual tribute was presented on the Manhattan Neighborhood Network cable access program *New York New Rock*. I transcribed Stevens's comments from this program.

CHAPTER 10: UNTIL THE LEVEE BREAKS

1 Personal communication received March 11, 1996.

2 Here, Mark invokes Shakespeare, an icon of the Western European canon, to affirm his pride in being black and to celebrate black American culture. Mark is paraphrasing Henry's attempt to woo Katherine: "O Kate, nice customs curtsy to great kings. Dear Kate, you and I cannot be confined within the weak list of a country's fashion: we are the makers of manners, Kate; and the liberty that follows our places stops the mouth of all find-faults." *Henry V*, Act V, sc. ii., lines 293–95.

BIBLIOGRAPHY

Abu-Lughod, Lila. 1993. Finding a Place for Islam: Egyptian Television Serials and the National Interest. *Public Culture* 5(3): 493–513.

Alexander, Kathryn L. 1981. The Status of Contemporary Black-Oriented Radio in the United States. Ph.D. dissertation, New York University.

Algarín, Miguel, and Bob Holman, eds. 1994. *Aloud: Voices from the Nuyorican Poets Cafe*. New York: Holt.

Appadurai, Arjun, Lauren Berlant, Carol A. Breckenridge, and Manthia Diawara. 1994. Special issue on the Black Public Sphere. *Public Culture* 7(1).

Aschenbrenner, Joyce. 1975. *Lifelines: Black Families in Chicago*. New York: Holt, Rinehart and Winston.

Baker, Houston A. 1988. *Afro-American Poetics: Revisions of Harlem and the Black Aesthetic*. Madison: University of Wisconsin Press.

Baker, Lee D. 1998. *From Savage to Negro: Anthropology and the Construction of Race, 1896–1954*. Berkeley: University of California Press.

Banks, Jack. 1996. *Monopoly Television: MTV's Quest to Control the Music*. Boulder, Colo.: Westview Press.

Banner-Haley, Charles T. 1994. *The Fruits of Integration: Black Middle-Class Ideology and Culture, 1960–1990*. Jackson: University Press of Mississippi.

Baraka, Amiri [Jones, LeRoi]. 1963. *Blues People: Negro Music in White America*. New York: Morrow Quill.

———. 1967. The Changing Same (R&B and New Black Music). In *Black Music*. New York: Quill.

Bayton, Mavis. 1998. *Frock Rock: Women Performing Popular Music*. Oxford: Oxford University Press.

Beatty, Paul. 1995. *The White Boy Shuffle*. New York: Houghton Mifflin.

Becker, Howard S. 1982. *Art Worlds*. Berkeley: University of California Press.

Bell, Michael J. 1983. *The World from Brown's Lounge: An Ethnography of Black Middle-Class Play*. Urbana: University of Illinois Press.

Billboard. 1993. Black Radio Listeners Spend More Time Tuned In. *Billboard*, June 26, p. 83.

———. 1994. Black Listeners Gaining Prominence. *Billboard*, May 28, p. 70.

Black Radio Exclusive. 1991. MCA Records Pact with NAACP. *Black Radio Exclusive,* February 8, p. 10.

Black Rock Coalition (BRC). 1985. The Black Rock Coalition Manifesto [flier].

———. 1993a. *LA Blurb* [BRC Los Angeles newsletter]. September.

———. 1993b. *Network* BRC featuring Total Eclipse [cable television program].

———. 1996. BRC *Newsletter* (New York), November.

———. 2000/2001. Progressive Forum: Konda Mason. BRC *Newsletter* (New York), December/January, pp. 10–12.

———. 2001a. Progressive Forum: Greg Tate. BRC *Newsletter* (New York), February, pp. 8–11.

———. 2001b. Progressive Forum: Vernon Reid. BRC *Newsletter* (New York), March, pp. 10–13.

Blauner, Robert. 1970. Black Culture: Myth or Reality. In *Afro-American Anthropology: Contemporary Perspectives on Theory and Research,* N. E. Whitten and J. Szwed, eds., pp. 347–66. New York: Free Press.

Blum, Joshua, Bob Holman, and Mark Pellington, eds. 1996. *The United States of Poetry.* New York: H. N. Abrams.

Blush, Steven. 1990. Living Colour: Black Diamonds in the Rough. *Seconds,* issue 12, pp. 2–21.

Born, Georgina. 1995. *Rationalizing Culture: IRCAM, Boulez, and the Institutionalization of the Musical Avant-Garde.* Berkeley: University of California Press.

Bourdieu, Pierre. 1984. *Distinction: A Social Critique of the Judgement of Taste.* Trans. Richard Nice. Cambridge, Mass.: Harvard University Press.

———. 1990. *The Logic of Practice.* Trans. Richard Nice. Stanford, Calif.: Stanford University Press.

———. 1993. *The Field of Cultural Production: Essays on Art and Literature.* New York: Columbia University Press.

Boyd, Todd. 1997. *Am I Black Enough for You? Popular Culture from the 'Hood and Beyond.* Bloomington: Indiana University Press.

Briggs, Charles L. 1986. *Learning How to Ask: A Sociolinguistic Appraisal of the Role of the Interview in Social Science Research.* Cambridge: Cambridge University Press.

Bright, Brenda, and Liza Bakewell, eds. 1995. *Looking High and Low: Art and Cultural Identity.* Tucson: University of Arizona Press.

Brodkin, Karen. 1998. *How Jews Became White Folks and What That Says About Race in America.* New Brunswick, N.J.: Rutgers University Press.

Byrd, Imhotep Gary. 1993. Liner Notes. *Blacker Than That* [BRC compilation]. BRC Records.

Cablecast 25 News. 1995. *Cablecast 25 News: United Artists Cable Community Access Newsletter.* March.

Calhoun, Craig, ed. 1992. *Habermas and the Public Sphere.* Cambridge, Mass.: MIT Press.

Caramanica, Jon. 2002. Electric Warriors. *Vibe,* February, pp. 85–90.

Carby, Hazel. 1998. *Race Men.* Cambridge, Mass.: Harvard University Press.

Cary, Lorene. 1992. *Black Ice*. New York: Knopf.

Cashmore, Ellis. 1997. *The Black Culture Industry*. London: Routledge.

Chapple, Steve, and Reebee Garofalo. 1977. *Rock 'n' Roll Is Here to Pay: The History and Politics of the Music Industry*. Chicago: Nelson-Hall.

Clarke, John, Stuart Hall, Tony Jefferson, and Brian Roberts. 1975. Subcultures, Cultures, and Class: A Theoretical Overview. In *Resistance Through Rituals: Youth Subcultures in Post-War Britain*, S. Hall and T. Jefferson, eds., pp. 9–74. London: Hutchinson.

Clifford, James, and George E. Marcus, eds. 1986. *Writing Culture: The Poetics and Politics of Ethnography*. Berkeley: University of California Press.

Cohen, Sara. 1991. *Rock Culture in Liverpool: Popular Music in the Making*. Oxford: Clarendon Press.

Collins, Patricia Hill. 1991. *Black Feminist Thought: Knowledge, Consciousness, and the Politics of Empowerment*. New York: Routledge.

Combahee River Collective. 1995. A Black Feminist Statement. In *Words of Fire: An Anthology of African-American Feminist Thought*, B. Guy-Sheftall, ed., pp. 232–40. New York: New Press.

Corbett, John. 1994. *Extended Play: Sounding Off from John Cage to Dr. Funkenstein*. Durham, N.C.: Duke University Press.

Cose, Ellis. 1993. *The Rage of a Privileged Class*. New York: HarperCollins.

Crazy Horse, Kandia. 2004. *Rip It Up: The Black Experience in Rock'n'Roll*. New York: Palgrave Macmillan.

Dannen, Fredric. 1991. *Hit Men*. New York: Vintage Books.

Dávila, Arlene. 1997. *Sponsored Identities: Cultural Politics in Puerto Rico*. Philadelphia, Pa.: Temple University Press.

Davis, Allison, Burleigh G. Gardner, and Mary R. Gardner. 1941. *Deep South: A Social Anthropological Study of Caste and Class*. Chicago: University of Chicago Press.

Davis, Angela Y. 1983. *Women, Race, and Class*. New York: Vintage Books.

Denisoff, R. Serge. 1986. *Tarnished Gold: The Rock Industry Revisited*. With the assistance of William L. Schurk. New Brunswick, N.J.: Transaction Books.

Dent, Gina. 1992a. Black Pleasure, Black Joy: An Introduction. In *Black Popular Culture*. G. Dent, ed., pp. 1–19. Seattle: Bay Press.

——, ed. 1992b. *Black Popular Culture*. Seattle: Bay Press.

Dollard, John. 1937. *Caste and Class in a Southern Town*. New Haven, Conn.: Yale University Press.

Domínguez, Virginia R. 1986. *White by Definition: Social Classification in Creole Louisiana*. New Brunswick, N.J.: Rutgers University Press.

Dornfeld, Barry. 1998. *Producing Public Television, Producing Public Culture*. Princeton, N.J.: Princeton University Press.

Douglas, Earl. 1995. Sophia's Toy: Alive and Kicking. *Ravers* [BRC Arts Magazine], Fall 1995, p. 33.

Drake, St. Clair, and Horace R. Cayton. [1945] 1993. *Black Metropolis: A Study of Negro Life in a Northern City*. Chicago: University of Chicago Press.

Du Bois, W. E. B. [1899] 1996. *The Philadelphia Negro: A Social Study*. Philadelphia: University of Pennsylvania Press.

———. [1903] 1989. *The Souls of Black Folk*. New York: Bantam.

———. [1926] 1996. Criteria of Negro Art. In *The Oxford W. E. B. Du Bois Reader*, E. J. Sundquist, ed., pp. 324–28. New York: Oxford University Press.

Eliot, Marc. 1989. *Rockonomics: The Money Behind the Music*. New York: Citadel Press.

Ellis, Trey. 1988. *Platitudes*. New York: Vintage Books.

———. 1989a. The New Black Aesthetic. *Callaloo* 12(1): 233–43.

———. 1989b. Response to NBA Critiques. *Callaloo* 12(1): 250–51.

Ellison, Ralph. 1986. What America Would Be Like Without Blacks. In *Going to the Territory*, pp. 104–12. New York: Vintage International.

Escott, Colin, with Martin Hawkins. 1991. *Good Rockin' Tonight: Sun Records and the Birth of Rock 'n' Roll*. New York: St. Martin's.

Faith. 1997. Faith Press Kit. New York: Boom Boom Records.

Feld, Steven. 1988. Notes on World Beat. *Public Culture Bulletin* 1(1): 31–37.

———. 1994. From Schizophonia to Schismogenesis: On the Discourses and Commodification Practices of "World Music" and "World Beat." In *Music Grooves*, C. Keil and S. Feld, eds., pp. 257–89. Chicago: University of Chicago Press.

Finnegan, Ruth. 1989. *The Hidden Musicians: Music-Making in an English Town*. Cambridge: Cambridge University Press.

Fiske, John. 1989. *Understanding Popular Culture*. London: Routledge.

Fordham, Signithia. 1996. *Blacked Out: Dilemmas of Race, Identity, and Success at Capital High*. Chicago: University of Chicago Press.

Fox, Richard G., and Orin Starn, eds. 1997. *Between Resistance and Revolution: Cultural Politics and Social Protest*. New Brunswick, N.J.: Rutgers University Press.

Fraser, Nancy. 1992. Rethinking the Public Sphere: A Contribution to the Critique of Actually Existing Democracy. In *Habermas and the Public Sphere*, C. Calhoun, ed., pp. 109–42. Cambridge, Mass.: MIT Press.

Frazier, E. Franklin. 1957. *Black Bourgeoisie*. Glencoe, Ill.: Free Press.

Fricke, David. 1987. Back in Black. *Rolling Stone*, September 24, pp. 64–66, 149–50.

Frith, Simon. 1981. *Sound Effects: Youth, Leisure, and the Politics of Rock 'n' Roll*. New York: Pantheon.

Frith, Simon, and Andrew Goodwin, eds. 1990. *On Record: Rock, Pop and the Written Word*. New York: Pantheon.

Frith, Simon, and Angela McRobbie. 1990. Rock and Sexuality. In *On Record: Rock, Pop and the Written Word*, S. Frith and A. Goodwin, eds., pp. 371–89. New York: Pantheon.

Gaar, Gillian G. 1992. *She's A Rebel: The History of Women in Rock & Roll*. Seattle: Seal Press.

Gaines, Kevin. 1996. *Uplifting the Race: Black Leadership, Politics, and Culture in the Twentieth Century*. Chapel Hill: University of North Carolina Press.

Gardner, Elysa. 1993. The Black Rock Coalition Mission. *Musician*. November, pp. 22–24.

Garofalo, Reebee. 1993. Black Popular Music: Crossing Over or Going Under. In *Rock and Popular Music: Politics, Policies, Institutions*, T. Bennett, S. Frith, L. Grossberg, J. Shepherd, and G. Turner, eds., pp. 231–48. London: Routledge.

Gates, Henry Louis, Jr. 1992. Must Buppiehood Cost Homeboy His Soul? *New York Times*, March 1, sec. 2, pp. 11–13.

George, Nelson. 1986. The Rhythm and the Blues. *Billboard*, February 15, p. 56.

———. 1988. *The Death of Rhythm and Blues*. New York: Plume.

———. 1989. At Last, Black Acts Making MTV Inroads. *Billboard*, 8 April, p. 20.

Giddens, Anthony. 1990. *Central Problems in Social Theory: Action, Structure and Contradiction in Social Analysis*. Berkeley: University of California Press.

Giddings, Paula. 1984. *When and Where I Enter: The Impact of Black Women on Race and Sex in America*. New York: Morrow.

Gillett, Charlie. 1983. *The Sound of the City: The Rise of Rock and Roll*. New York: Pantheon.

Gilroy, Paul. 1991a. *There Ain't No Black in the Union Jack: The Cultural Politics of Race and Nation*. Chicago: University of Chicago Press.

———. 1991b. Sounds Authentic: Black Music, Ethnicity and the Challenge of a Changing Same. *Black Music Research Journal* 11(2):111–36.

———. 1993. *The Black Atlantic: Modernity and Double Consciousness*. Cambridge, Mass.: Harvard University Press.

Ginsburg, Faye. 1989. *Contested Lives: The Abortion Debate in an American Community*. Berkeley: University of California Press.

———. 1991. Indigenous Media: Faustian Contract or Global Village. *Cultural Anthropology* 6(1):92–112.

———. 1997. "From Little Things, Big Things Grow": Indigenous Media and Cultural Activism. In *Between Resistance and Revolution: Cultural Politics and Social Protest*, R. Fox and O. Starn, eds., pp. 118–44. New Brunswick, N.J.: Rutgers University Press.

Glasser, Gerald J., and Gale D. Metzger. 1981. Radio Usage by Blacks: An Update. *Journal of Advertising Research* 21(2): 47–50.

Glick Schiller, Nina. 1997. Cultural Politics and the Politics of Culture. *Identities* 4:1–7.

Glick Schiller, Nina, and Georges Eugene Fouron. 2001. *Georges Woke Up Laughing: Long-Distance Nationalism and the Search for Home*. Durham, N.C.: Duke University Press.

Golden, Thelma. 1994a. My Brother. In *Black Male: Representations of Masculinity in Contemporary American Art*, T. Golden, ed., pp. 19–43. New York: Whitney Museum of Art.

———, ed. 1994b. *Black Male: Representations of Masculinity in Contemporary American Art*. New York: Whitney Museum of Art.

Golding, Peter, and Graham Murdock. 1991. Culture, Communications, and Political Economy. In *Mass Media and Society*, J. Curran and M. Gurevitch, eds., pp. 15–32. New York: Routledge, Chapman and Hall.

Gonzalez, David L. 1990. Is There Life After Jimi? *Newsweek*, April 30, pp. 68–69.

Gottlieb, Joanne, and Gayle Wald. 1994. Smells Like Teen Spirit: Riot Grrrls, Revolution and Women in Independent Rock. In *Microphone Fiends: Youth Music and Youth Culture*, A. Ross and T. Rose, eds., pp. 250–74. New York: Routledge.

Gray, Herman. 1988. *Producing Jazz: The Experience of an Independent Record Company*. Philadelphia, Pa.: Temple University Press.

Gregory, Steven. 1992. The Changing Significance of Race and Class in an African-American Community. *American Ethnologist* 19(2): 255–74.

———. 1993. Race, Rubbish, and Resistance: Empowering Difference in Community Politics. *Cultural Anthropology* 8(1): 24–48.

———. 1994. We've Been Down This Road. In *Race*, S. Gregory and R. Sanjek, eds., pp. 18–38. New Brunswick, N.J.: Rutgers University Press.

———. 1998. *Black Corona: Race and the Politics of Place in an Urban Community*. Princeton, N.J.: Princeton University Press.

Gregory, Steven, and Roger Sanjek, eds. 1994. *Race*. New Brunswick, N.J.: Rutgers University Press.

Guerrero, Ed. 1994. The Black Man on Our Screens and the Empty Space in Representation. In *Black Male: Representations of Masculinity in Contemporary American Art*, T. Golden, ed., pp. 181–89. New York: Whitney Museum of Art.

Gupta, Akhil, and James Ferguson. 1992. Beyond 'Culture': Space, Identity and the Politics of Identity. *Cultural Anthropology* 7(1): 6–23.

Guralnick, Peter. 1994. *Last Train to Memphis: The Rise of Elvis Presley*. Boston: Little, Brown.

Guy-Sheftall, Beverly. 1995. *Words of Fire: An Anthology of African-American Feminist Thought*. New York: New Press.

Gwaltney, John L. 1980. *Drylongso: A Self-Portrait of Black America*. New York: Vintage Books.

———. 1981. Common Sense and Science: Urban Core Black Observations. In *Anthropologists at Home in North America: Methods and Issues in the Study of One's Own Society*, D. A. Messerschmidt, ed., pp. 46–61. Cambridge: Cambridge University Press.

Habermas, Jürgen. 1989. *The Structural Transformation of the Public Sphere: An Inquiry into a Category of Bourgeois Society*. Trans. T. Burger, with the assistance of Frederick Lawrence. Cambridge, Mass.: MIT Press.

Hall, Stuart. 1980. Encoding/Decoding. In *Culture, Media, Language*. S. Hall et al., eds., pp. 128–38. London: Hutchinson.

———. 1988. New Ethnicities. *ICA Documents* 7:27–31.

———. 1990. Cultural Identity and Diaspora. In *Identity, Community, Culture, Difference*, J. Rutherford, ed., pp. 222–37. London: Lawrence and Wishart.

———. 1992. Cultural Identity and Cinematic Representation. In *Ex-Iles: Essays on Caribbean Cinema*, M. Cham, ed., pp. 220–36. Trenton, N.J.: African World Press.

Hall, Stuart, and Tony Jefferson, eds. 1975. *Resistance Through Rituals: Youth Sub-cultures in Post-War Britain*. London: Hutchinson.

Handler, Richard. 1986. Authenticity. *Anthropology Today* 2(1): 2–4.

Hansberry, Lorraine. 1970. *To Be Young, Gifted, and Black*. New York: Signet Books.

Harris, Carter. 1995. Station Identification. *Vibe*, November, pp. 75–80.

Harper, Phillip Brian. 1995. Nationalism and Social Division in Black Arts Poetry of the 1960s. In *Identities*, K. A. Appiah and H. L. Gates Jr., eds., pp. 220–41. Chicago: University of Chicago Press.

———. 1996. *Are We Not Men? Masculine Anxiety and the Problem of African-American Identity*. New York: Oxford University Press.

Harrison, Faye V. 1988. Introduction: An African Diaspora Perspective on Urban Anthropology. *Urban Anthropology* 17(2–3): 111–42.

———. 1995. The Persistent Power of "Race" in the Cultural and Political Economy of Racism. *Annual Review of Anthropology* 24:47–74.

Harrison, Ira E., and Faye V. Harrison, eds. 1998. *African-American Pioneers in Anthropology*. Urbana: University of Illinois Press.

Hartigan, John, Jr. 1999. *Racial Situations: Class Predicaments of Whiteness in Detroit*. Princeton, N.J.: Princeton University Press.

Hebdige, Dick. 1979. *Subculture: The Meaning of Style*. London: Routledge and Kegan Paul.

Henderson, David. 1983. *'Scuse Me While I Kiss the Sky: The Life of Jimi Hendrix*. New York: Bantam Books.

Herskovits, Melville J. [1941] 1990. *The Myth of the Negro Past*. Boston: Beacon Press.

Higginbotham, Evelyn Brooks. 1993. *Righteous Discontent: The Women's Movement in the Black Baptist Church, 1880–1920*. Cambridge, Mass.: Harvard University Press.

Himes, Geoffrey. 1987. A New Look for Black Rock. *Washington Post*, October 30, pp. D1, D8.

Hirshey, Gerri. 2001. *We Gotta Get Out of This Place: The True, Tough Story of Women in Rock*. New York: Atlantic Monthly Press.

Hobsbawm, Eric. 1972. The Social Function of the Past. *Past and Present* 55:1–17.

Holloway, Joseph E., ed. 1990. *Africanisms in American Culture*. Bloomington: Indiana University Press.

hooks, bell. 1981. *Ain't I a Woman: Black Women and Feminism*. Boston: South End Press.

———. 1990. *Yearning: Race, Gender, and Cultural Politics*. Boston: South End Press.

Hughes, Langston. [1926] 1971. The Negro Artist and the Racial Mountain. In *The Black Man and the American Dream: Negro Aspirations in America, 1900–1930*, J. Sochen, ed., pp. 117–23. Chicago: Quadrangle Books.

Hull, Gloria, Patricia Bell Scott, and Barbara Smith, eds. 1982. *All the Women Are White, All the Blacks Are Men, But Some of Us Are Brave: Black Women's Studies*. Old Westbury, N.Y.: Feminist Press.

Hunter, Tera. 1989. "It's A Man's Man's Man's World:" Specters of the Old Re-
Newed in Afro-American Culture and Criticism. *Calalloo* 12(1): 247–49.

Hurston, Zora Neale. [1934] 1981. Characteristics of Negro Expression. In *The Sanctified Church*, pp. 49–68. New York: Marlowe and Co.

———. [1935] 1978. *Mules and Men.* With introduction by Robert Hemenway. New York: Perennial Library.

Ivory, Steven. 1993. Ivory's Notes: The Incredible Shrinking Black Music Executive. *Black Radio Exclusive*, October 22, p. 44.

Jefferson, Margo. 1973. Ripping Off Black Music. *Harper's*, January, pp. 40–45.

Johnson, Martin. 1986. Vernon Reid's Cultural Revolution. *The City Sun*, January 29–February 4, pp. 11, 14.

Jones, Lisa. 1990. Living Coloured and Proud. *Spin*, October, pp. 48–50, 94.

———. 1992. This Is Faith: Tribal Grunge Takes Manhattan. *Village Voice Rock and Roll Quarterly*, winter, pp. 7–8, 10–11, 15, 22.

Juhasz, Alexandra. 1995. *AIDS TV: Identity, Community, and Alternative Video.* Durham, N.C.: Duke University Press.

Kaplan, E. Ann. 1987. *Rocking Around the Clock: Music Television, Postmodernism and Consumer Culture.* New York: Routledge.

Keil, Charles. 1966. *Urban Blues.* Chicago: University of Chicago Press.

Keil, Charles, and Steven Feld. 1994. *Music Grooves: Essays and Dialogues.* Chicago: University of Chicago Press.

Kelley, Norman, ed. 2002. *Rhythm and Business: The Political Economy of Black Music.* New York: Akashic Books.

Kelley, Robin D. G. 1994. *Race Rebels: Culture, Politics and the Black Working Class.* New York: Free Press.

Kellner, Douglas. 1990. *Television and the Crisis of Democracy.* Boulder, Colo.: Westview Press.

Kondo, Dorinne. 1990. *Crafting Selves: Power, Gender, and Discourses of Identity in a Japanese Workplace.* Chicago: University of Chicago Press.

———. 1997. *About Face: Performing Race in Fashion and Theater.* New York: Routledge.

Kot, Greg. 1991. Musical Apartheid: Black Rockers Trying to Break Down Stereotypes. *Chicago Tribune*, October 27.

Lamar, Jake. 1991. *Bourgeois Blues: An American Memoir.* New York: Plume.

Landry, Bart. 1987. *The New Black Middle Class.* Berkeley: University of California Press.

Lemon, Ralph. 2000. *Geography: Art, Race, Exile.* Hanover, N.H.: Wesleyan University Press.

Levine, Lawrence. 1977. *Black Culture and Black Consciousness: Afro-American Folk Thought from Slavery to Freedom.* Oxford: Oxford University Press.

Liebow, Elliot. 1967. *Tally's Corner: A Study of Negro Streetcorner Men.* Boston: Little, Brown.

Lipsitz, George. 1990. Against the Wind: Dialogic Aspects of Rock and Roll. In

Time Passages: Collective Memory and American Popular Culture, pp. 99–132. Minneapolis: University of Minnesota Press.

———. 1994. *Dangerous Crossroads: Popular Music, Postmodernism and the Poetics of Place*. London: Verso.

———. 1998. *The Possessive Investment in Whiteness: How White People Profit from Identity Politics*. Philadelphia, Pa.: Temple University Press.

Locke, Alain, ed. [1925] 1969. *The New Negro*. New York: Atheneum.

Lorde, Audre. 1984. *Sister Outsider: Essays and Speeches*. Trumansburg, N.Y.: Crossing Press.

Lott, Eric. 1989. Response to Trey Ellis's "The New Black Aesthetic." *Calalloo* 12(1): 244–46.

———. 1993. *Love and Theft: Blackface Minstrelsy and the American Working Class*. New York: Oxford University Press.

Lowe, Lisa. 1996. *Immigrant Acts: On Asian American Cultural Politics*. Durham, N.C.: Duke University Press.

MacClancy, Jeremy, ed. 1997. *Contesting Art: Art, Politics and Identity in the Modern World*. New York: Berg.

Mahon, Maureen. 2000a. Black Like This: Race, Generation, and Rock in the Post-Civil Rights Era. *American Ethnologist* 27(2): 283–311.

———. 2000b. The Visible Evidence of Cultural Producers. *Annual Review of Anthropology* 29:467–92.

Mailer, Norman. 1968. The White Negro: Superficial Reflections on the Hipster. In *Advertisements for Myself*, pp. 337–58. New York: G. P. Putnam's Sons.

Mankekar, Purnima. 1999. *Screening Culture, Viewing Politics: An Ethnography of Television, Womanhood, and Nation in Postcolonial India*. Durham, N.C.: Duke University Press.

Mannheim, Karl. [1928] 1952. The Problem of Generations. In *Essays on the Sociology of Knowledge*, P. Kecskemeti, ed., pp. 276–320. London: Routledge and Kegan Paul.

Marcus, George. 1998. *Ethnography Through Thick and Thin*. Princeton, N.J.: Princeton University Press.

Marcus, George E., and Michael M. J. Fischer. 1986. *Anthropology as Cultural Critique: An Experimental Moment in the Human Sciences*. Chicago: University of Chicago Press.

Marcus, George E., and Fred R. Myers, eds. 1995. *The Traffic in Culture: Refiguring Art and Anthropology*. Berkeley: University of California Press.

McClaurin, Irma, ed. 2001. *Black Feminist Anthropology: Theory, Politics, Praxis, and Poetics*. New Brunswick, N.J.: Rutgers University Press.

McDonald, Janet. 2000. *Project Girl*. Berkeley: University of California Press.

McGrath, Tom. 1996. MTV: *The Making of a Revolution*. Philadelphia, Pa.: Running Press.

McLagan, Meg. 1996. Computing for Tibet: Virtual Politics in the Post-Cold War Era. In *Connected: Engagements with Media*, G. E. Marcus, ed., pp. 159–94. Chicago: University of Chicago Press.

McRobbie, Angela. 1990. Settling Accounts with Subcultures: A Feminist Critique. In *On Record: Rock, Pop and the Written Word*, S. Frith and A. Goodwin, eds., pp. 66–80. New York: Pantheon.

Meintjes, Louise. 1990. Paul Simon's *Graceland*, South Africa, and the Mediation of Musical Meaning. *Ethnomusicology* 34(1): 37–73.

———. 2003. *Sound of Africa! Making Music Zulu in a South African Studio*. Durham, N.C.: Duke University Press.

Mercer, Kobena. 1994. Black Hair/Style Politics. In *Welcome to the Jungle: New Positions in Black Cultural Studies*, pp. 97–128. New York: Routledge.

Messerschmidt, Donald A., ed. 1981. *Anthropologists at Home in North America: Methods and Issues in the Study of One's Own Society*. Cambridge: Cambridge University Press.

Mitchell-Kernan, Claudia. 1972. Signifying and Marking: Two Afro-American Speech Acts. In *Directions in Sociolinguistics: The Ethnography of Communication*, J. Gumperz and D. Hymes, eds., pp. 161–79. New York: Holt, Rinehart, and Winston.

Monson, Ingrid. 1996. *Saying Something: Jazz Improvisation and Interaction*. Chicago: University of Chicago Press.

Moore, Sally Falk, and Barbara G. Myerhoff. 1977. Introduction: Secular Ritual: Forms and Meanings. In *Secular Ritual*, S. F. Moore and B. G. Myerhoff, eds., pp. 3–24. Amsterdam: Van Gorcum and Company.

Morris, Tracie. 1998. *Intermission*. New York: Soft Skull Press.

Morton, Patricia. 1991. *Disfigured Images: The Historical Assault on Afro-American Women*. New York: Praeger Publishers.

Muggleton, Terry. 1992. Enemy Records: Rock Solid Ambitions. *Black Radio Exclusive*, September 18, p. 22.

Muhammad, Tariq K. 1995. The Real Lowdown on Labels. *Black Enterprise*, December, 74–78.

Mullings, Leith. 1997. *On Our Own Terms: Race, Class, and Gender in the Lives of African American Women*. New York: Routledge.

Murray, Albert. [1970] 1983. *The Omni-Americans: Some Alternatives to the Folklore of White Supremacy*. New York: Vintage Books.

Murray, Charles Shaar. 1991. *Crosstown Traffic: Jimi Hendrix and the Post-War Rock'n'Roll Revolution*. New York: St. Martin's Press.

Myers, Fred R. 1986. Reflections on a Meeting: Structure, Language, and the Polity in a Small-Scale Society. *American Ethnologist* 13(3): 430–47.

———. 1994. Culture-Making: Performing Aboriginality at the Asia Society Gallery. *American Ethnologist* 21(4): 679–99.

NAACP. 1987. *The Discordant Sound of Music (A Report on the Record Industry)*. Bethesda, Md.: NAACP Press.

Nader, Laura. 1972. Up the Anthropologist: Perspectives Gained from Studying Up. In *Reinventing Anthropology*, D. Hymes, ed., pp. 284–311. New York: Pantheon.

NdegéOcello, Me'Shell. 1994. *No Rest for the Funky* [artist's press clippings file].

Neal, Larry. 1968. The Black Arts Movement. *The Drama Review* 12(4): 29–39.

Neal, Mark Anthony. 1999. *What the Music Said: Black Music and Black Popular Culture*. New York: Routledge.

Negus, Keith. 1992. *Producing Pop: Culture and Conflict in the Popular Music Industry*. London: Edward Arnold.

————. 1999. *Music Genres and Corporate Cultures*. New York: Routledge.

Nelson, Havelock. 1992. Rap and Black Radio: The Art of Integration. *Billboard*, November 28, p. 6.

O'Brien, Lucy. 1995. *She Bop*. New York: Penguin.

O'Connor, John J. 1983. MTV—A Success Story with a Curious Short-Coming. *New York Times*, July 24, sec. 2, p. 23.

Omi, Michael, and Howard Winant. 1994. *Racial Formation in the United States: From the 1960s to the 1990s*. Second edition. New York: Routledge.

Orfield, Gary. 1993. School Desegregation after Two Generations: Race, Schools, and Opportunity in Urban Society. In *Race in America: The Struggle for Equality*, H. Hill and J. E. Jones Jr., eds., pp. 234–62. Madison: University of Wisconsin Press.

Ortner, Sherry. 1984. Theory in Anthropology Since the Sixties. *Comparative Studies in Society and History* 26:126–66.

Page, Helán E. 1997. "Black Male" Imagery and Media Containment of African American Men. *American Anthropologist* 99(1): 99–111.

Palmer, Robert. 1995. *Rock & Roll: An Unruly History*. New York: Harmony Books.

Pareles, Jon. 2001. Black Musicians Reclaim Hard Rock. *New York Times*, August 4, sec. A, p. 20.

Pattillo-McCoy, Mary. 1999. *Black Picket Fences: Privilege and Peril Among the Black Middle Class*. Chicago: University of Chicago Press.

Perry, Steve. 1989. Ain't No Mountain High Enough: The Politics of Crossover. In *Facing the Music*, S. Frith, ed., pp. 51–87. New York: Pantheon.

Peterson, Richard A., and David G. Berger. 1990. Cycles in Symbol Production: The Case of Popular Music. In *On Record: Rock, Pop and the Written Word*, S. Frith and A. Goodwin, eds., pp. 140–59. New York: Pantheon.

Pinckney, Darryl. 1992. *High Cotton*. New York: Farrar, Straus and Giroux.

Powdermaker, Hortense. 1939. *After Freedom: A Cultural Study of the Deep South*. New York: Viking Press.

Rahier, Jean Muteba, ed. 1999. *Representations of Blackness and the Performance of Identities*. Westport, Conn.: Bergin and Garvey.

Ravitch, Diane. 1974. *The Great School Wars: New York City, 1805–1973: A History of the Public Schools as Battlefields of Social Change*. New York: Basic Books.

Reid, Vernon. 1993. Brother from Another Planet. *Vibe*, November, pp. 44–49.

Reynolds, Rhonda, and Ann Brown. 1994. A New Rhythm Takes Hold. *Black Enterprise*, December, pp. 82–89.

Reynolds, Simon, and Joy Press. 1995. *The Sex Revolts: Gender, Rebellion, and Rock'n'Roll*. Cambridge, Mass.: Harvard University Press.

Robbins, Bruce, ed. 1993. *The Phantom Public Sphere*. Minneapolis: University of Minnesota Press.

Rooks, Noliwe M. 1996. *Hair Raising: Beauty, Culture, and African American Women*. New Brunswick, N.J.: Rutgers University Press.

Rosaldo, Renato. 1993. *Culture and Truth: The Remaking of Social Analysis*. Boston: Beacon Press.

Rose, Tricia. 1994. *Black Noise: Rap Music and Black Culture in Contemporary America*. Hanover, N.H.: Wesleyan University Press.

Sahlins, Marshall. 1985. *Islands of History*. Chicago: University of Chicago Press.

Sanjek, David. 2002. Tell Me Something I Don't Already Know: The Harvard Report on Soul Music Revisited. In *Rhythm and Business: The Political Economy of Black Music*, N. Kelley, ed., pp. 59–76. New York: Akashic Books.

Sanjek, Russell. 1988. *American Popular Music and Its Business: The First 400 Years, Vol. III. From 1900–1984*. New York: Oxford University Press.

Sanjek, Russell, and David Sanjek. 1991. *American Popular Music and Its Business in the Twentieth Century*. New York: Oxford University Press.

Schwartzman, Helen B. 1989. *The Meeting: Gatherings in Organizations and Communities*. New York: Plenum Press.

Shank, Barry. 1994. *Dissonant Identities: The Rock 'n' Roll Scene in Austin, Texas*. Hanover, N.H.: Wesleyan University Press.

Shaw, Arnold. 1974. *The Rockin' 50s*. New York: De Capo Press.

Sinclair, Tom. 1991. No Rap. No Jazz. They Want to Rock. *New York Times*, September 1, sec. 2, pp. 18–19.

Smith, Barbara, ed. 1983. *Home Girls: A Black Feminist Anthology*. New York: Kitchen Table/Women of Color Press.

Smith, R. J. 1989. Black Rock in a Hard Place. *Village Voice*, May 2, pp. 21–23.

Smith, Valerie. 1998. *Not Just Race, Not Just Gender: Black Feminist Readings*. New York: Routledge.

Spitulnik, Debra. 1993. Anthropology and Mass Media. *Annual Review of Anthropology* 22:293–315.

Spivak, Gayatri Chakravorty. 1996. Subaltern Studies: Deconstructing Historiography. In *The Spivak Reader: Selected Works of Gayatri Chakravorty Spivak*, D. Landry and G. MacLean, eds., pp. 203–35. New York: Routledge.

Sreberny-Mohammadi, Annabelle, and Ali Mohammadi. 1994. *Small Media, Big Revolution: Communication, Culture, and the Iranian Revolution*. Minneapolis: University of Minnesota Press.

Stack, Carol B. 1974. *All Our Kin: Strategies for Survival in a Black Community*. New York: Harper and Row.

Staples, Robert. 1982. *Black Masculinity: The Black Male's Role in American Society*. San Francisco: Black Scholar Press.

Sutton, Constance R., and Elsa M. Chaney, eds. 1987. *Caribbean Life in New York City: Sociocultural Dimensions*. New York: Center for Migration Studies of New York.

Szwed, John F. 1972. An American Anthropological Dilemma: The Politics of Afro-American Culture. In *Reinventing Anthropology*, D. Hymes, ed., pp. 153–81. New York: Pantheon.

Tate, Greg. 1991. Liner Notes. *The History of Our Future* [BRC compilation]. Rykodisc.

———. 1992. Cult-Nats Meet Freaky Deke. In *Flyboy in the Buttermilk: Essays on Contemporary America*, pp. 198–210. New York: Fireside.

———. 1994a. He Is Truly Free Who Is Free from the Need to Be Free: A Survey and Consideration of Black Male Genius. In *Black Male: Representations of Masculinity in Contemporary American Art*, T. Golden, ed., pp. 111–18. New York: Whitney Museum of Art.

———. 1994b. As of Now, It's On. *Village Voice*, November 8, p. 38.

———. 1995a. Bronx Banshee. *Vibe*, November, p. 44.

———. 1995b. Till the Levee Breaks. *Vibe*, October, p. 52.

———. 2003a. *Midnight Lightning: Jimi Hendrix and the Black Experience*. Chicago: Chicago Review Press.

———, ed. 2003b. *Everything But the Burden: What White People Are Taking from Black Culture*. New York: Broadway Books.

Tatum, Beverly Daniel. 1987. *Assimilation Blues: Black Families in a White Community*. Northhampton, Mass.: Greenwood Press.

Torgovnick, Mariana. 1990. *Gone Primitive: Savage Intellects, Modern Lives*. Chicago: University of Chicago Press.

Touré. 2002. The Hip-Hop Generation Grabs a Guitar. *New York Times*, August 11, sec. 2, pp. 1, 28.

Traube, Elizabeth G. 1996. "The Popular" in American Culture. *Annual Review of Anthropology* 25:127–51.

Turino, Thomas. 1993. *Moving Away from Silence: Music of the Peruvian Altiplano and the Experience of Urban Migration*. Chicago: University of Chicago Press.

Turner, Terence. 1990. Visual Media, Cultural Politics, and Anthropological Practice: Some Implications of Recent Uses of Film and Video Among the Kayapo of Brazil. *Commission on Visual Anthropology Review*, (spring): 8–13.

Turner, Victor. 1974. *Dramas, Fields, and Metaphors: Symbolic Action in Human Society*. Ithaca, N.Y.: Cornell University Press.

———. 1977. Variations on a Theme of Liminality. In *Secular Ritual*, S. F. Moore and B. G. Myerhoff, eds., pp. 36–52. Amsterdam: Van Gorcum and Company.

Valentine, Bettylou. 1978. *Hustling and Other Hard Work: Lifestyles in the Ghetto*. New York: Free Press.

Van Deburg, William L. 1992. *New Day in Babylon: The Black Power Movement and American Culture, 1965–1975*. Chicago: University of Chicago Press.

Vincent, Rickey. 1996. *Funk: The Music, the People, and the Rhythm of the One*. New York: St. Martin's Press.

Wallace, Michele. 1979. *Black Macho and the Myth of Superwoman*. New York: Dial Press.

————. 1990. *Invisibility Blues: From Pop to Theory*. London: Verso.

Walser, Robert. 1993. *Running with the Devil: Power, Gender, and Madness in Heavy Metal Music*. Hanover, N.H.: Wesleyan University Press.

Warren, Renee E. 1992. NABOB Wins Truce with Sony. *Black Enterprise*, April, p. 19.

Waterman, Christopher Alan. 1990. *Juju: A Social History and Ethnography of an African Popular Music*. Chicago: University of Chicago Press.

West, Cornel. 1990. The New Cultural Politics of Difference. In *Out There: Marginalization and Contemporary Cultures*, R. Ferguson et al., eds., pp. 19–36. Cambridge, Mass.: New Museum/MIT.

Whitburn, Joel. 2000. *Joel Whitburn Presents Top R&B Singles 1942–1999*. Menomonee Falls, Wis.: Record Research.

White, Armond. 1995. Vernon Reid's Fear of Music. In *The Resistance: Ten Years of Pop Culture That Shook the World*, pp. 87–89. Woodstock, N.Y.: Overlook Press.

Whitten, Norman E., and John F. Szwed, eds. 1970. *Afro-American Anthropology*. New York: Free Press.

Wilkinson, Alec. 1996. What Sophia Wants. *The New Yorker*, August 26 and September 2, pp. 144–48.

Willis, Paul. 1977. *Learning to Labour: How Working Class Kids Get Working Class Jobs*. New York: Columbia University Press.

Williams, Brackette F. 1989. A Class Act: Anthropology and the Race to Nation Across Ethnic Terrain. *Annual Review of Anthropology* 18:401–44.

————. 1991. *Stains on My Name, War in My Veins: Guyana and the Politics of Cultural Struggle*. Durham, N.C.: Duke University Press.

Williams, Steve. 1993. Support the BRC Radio Show! *BRC Newsletter* (New York), May, p. 1.

Wilson, William J. 1978. *The Declining Significance of Race*. Chicago: University of Chicago Press.

Wright, Richard. [1937] 1997. Blueprint for Negro Writing. In *Richard Wright Reader*, E. Wright and M. Fabre, eds., pp. 36–49. New York: Da Capo Press.

Zimmerman, Kevin. 1992. Is the Music Biz Colorblind? *Variety*, March 30, pp. 82, 89.

INDEX

than thou" paradigm, 11; in black rock music, 137–41; BRC focus on, 16–17, 61–77, 96, 265–66; in BRC Manifesto, 96; cultural politics and, 11–14, 35, 273n.5; diversity and difference in, 11, 274n.6; double-consciousness and, 12–14; gender issues in, 221–25; in Hendrix's work, 235–49, 253–56, 283nn.3–4; intraracial differences towards, 53–58; musical aesthetics and, 114–41, 278n.3; of postliberated black generation, 35–36. *See also* authenticity

Black Jack Johnson (band), 262

Blackman, Cynthia, 126

black masculinity, 221–30; Hendrix and, 248–49

black middle class: BRC members from, 33–38, 41–42, 49–53, 77–85; perspectives of, 10–14, 32–33, 273n.4; race and consciousness in, 38–42. *See also* class politics

black musicians: aesthetics of, 6, 114–41; authenticity and crossover issues for, 158–62; MTV's exclusion of, 167–68; origins of rock 'n' roll and, 7–8, 91–93, 147–54; racialized marketing strategies for, 163–70

black nationalism, black aesthetics and, 35–36, 116–22, 279n.5

Black on Both Sides (album), 261

Black Panthers, 35, 178, 249; Hendrix and, 243, 283n.6

Black Power Movement: black aesthetics and, 117, 120; black identity politics and, 249; black middle class and, 40–42; Black Rock Coalition and, 9; gender issues in, 220–22; masculinity issues in, 222

Black Radio Exclusive magazine, 94, 165, 281n.18

black rock: aesthetics of, 29–32, 113–22; audience for, 71–72, 170–75;

BRC's advocacy of, 16–17, 67–77; cultural politics of, 17–18, 26–32, 91–112; current revival of, 261–66; definitions of, 8–9, 137–41; diversity of styles in, 137–41; intraracial differences towards, 53–58; live performance of, 105–12; marginalization of, 6–7; media coverage of, 94–96, 169–70, 176–203; New York music scene and, 82, 86–87, 98–112; racialized marketing of, 170–75; racial politics and, 147–54; recording industry and, 6–7, 145–54, 170–75, 209–16; representation and, 18–21; style and image in, 122–37, 183, 223; terminology issues surrounding, 32, 138; white musicians' support and sponsorship of, 154–58

Black Rock (album), 28

Black Rock Cafe, 200

Black Rock Coalition (BRC): aesthetics of, 114–41; bands belonging to, 2, 29–32, 259–60; black authenticity and double-consciousness and, 9–14; *Blacker Than That* produced by, 179–92; black identity and, 12–14, 91–96, 265; CD compilations of, 4, 179–85; core members of, 7, 15, 63; cultural politics and, 14–21, 86–112; discography, 267; educational background of members in, 42–53; European concerts by, 194–201; evolution of, 1–2; field-work methodology for research on, 21–26; gender dynamics in, 205–30; Hendrix's influence on, 231–32, 235–56; Hendrix tributes by, 105, 199–200, 225, 249–53; independent productions by, 179–85, 200–203; Internet use by, 202–3; intraracial diversity in members of, 8–9, 53–58; legacy and impact of, 258–66; live performances

Grand Master Flash and the Furious
	Five (band), 30
Grant, Eddy, 169
Grateful Dead, 28, 113
"Great Balls of Fire," 152
"Green Balloon," 184
Green, Wayne, 181, 189
Gregory, Steven, 17, 20, 41–42,
	274n.11
grunge music, 174, 180
Guerrero, Ed, 228–29
Guitar Player magazine, 129
Guralnick, Peter, 149–51
Gwaltney, John L., 23, 25, 266

Habermas, Jürgen, 275n.16
Hagen, Nina, 129, 184
hairstyles, cultural politics of, 100
Hakamada, Naotaka, 212
Hall, Stuart, 11, 101, 273n.5, 275n.14
Hall and Oates (band), 168
Hammons, David, 61
Handler, Richard, 279n.6
Hansberry, Lorraine, 246
"Hard Blues for Hard Times," 124
Harlem Renaissance, 27, 82–85, 90,
	114
Harper, Ben, 175
Harper, Phillip Brian, 11, 279n.5
Harrell, Andre, 166
Harris, Carter, 168, 169
Harris, Jerome, 199
Harvard Business School, 162
Haynes, Graham, 199
Hazel, Jimmy, 251
heavy metal: aesthetics of, 222,
	280n.5; by black musicians, 184
Hebdige, Dick, 101
Hello Children (band), 98
Henderson, David, 233, 242–43
Hendrix, Jimi, 6, 18, 20; biography of,
	232–35, 283n.1; black masculinity
	and, 248–49; as black rock icon,
28–29, 91–92, 123, 128–29, 262;
	BRC tributes for, 105, 199–200,
	225, 249–53; cultural appropriation
	of, 253–56, 262; exhibitions about,
	232–33; influence on BRC, 231–56;
	Living Colour influenced by, 146,
	264; mainstream images of, 244–
	49, 251–53; recording industry and,
	135, 242; sexuality of, 31, 223–30;
	Sophia's Toy influenced by, 212;
	success of, 148, 177, 191, 225, 233–
	35; white audiences for, 235–56,
	262, 283n.4
Hendrix Tribute Shows, 105, 199–200,
	225, 249–53, 284n.12
Hendryx, Nona, 98, 208, 251; discog-
	raphy, 269
"Hey Joe," 234, 252
Higginbotham, Evelyn Brooks, 40–41,
	132
Hill, Kevin, 97
Hill, Michael, 30, 108, 124, 252, 260;
	Blues Mob and, 97, 99, 198–99,
	201–2; discography, 270; recording
	industry and, 67–68
Himes, Geoffrey, 123
history, cultural politics and role of,
	91–92, 278n.4
History of Our Future, The (album),
	179, 181, 183
Hobsbawm, Eric, 91
Hole (band), 307
Holman, Bob, 260
"Home, Home on the Range," 184
Homestead Records, 202
Hooker, John Lee, 154, 262
hooks, bell, 216, 219
Hoosegow (band), 202
"Hot Fun in the Summertime," 28
Houston, Dianne, 259
Houston, Whitney, 163
Howlin' Wolf, 155, 250
Hudlin, Reginald, 120

Hudlin, Warrington, 279n.7
Hughes, Langston, 89–91, 265, 278n.3
Hunter, Tera, 119
Hurston, Zora Neale, 115, 265
Hynde, Chrissie, 206

Ibis (band), 208
Ice Cube (musician), 212
"If 6 Was 9," 240–41
"If That Was Your Boyfriend (He Wasn't Last Night)," 136
"Ignorance Is Bliss," 143
Independent Music Producers Syndicate (IMPS), 181, 189
independent producers, black rock and efforts of, 179–85, 189–92, 200–203
"indigenous analysis" concept, 25–26
Inniss, Amafujo, 99, 186
integration. *See* desegregation
intellectuals, in BRC, 80–85
International Pori Jazz Festival, BRC at 199–200
Internet, BRC's use of, 202–3
intraracial differences: BRC recognition of, 8–9, 53–58. *See also* authenticity; black identity
Inyama, Goz, 209
Isle of Wight Pop Festival, 235
Isley Brothers (band), 28, 37, 123
Ivory, Steven, 166
"I Wanna Be Black," 205

Jackson, Janet, 163
Jackson, Lisa, 211
Jackson, Michael, 163, 169
Jackson, Ronald Shannon, 30, 129, 146
Jagger, Mick, 6, 155–58, 204, 206
James, Etta, 7, 151, 155
James, Rick, 168
Japan, black rock visibility in, 199
Jarvis, Rayford, 16
jazz: aesthetics of, 109, 123, 128–29, 151, 155, 158; BRC view of, 238–39,

283n.5; Hendrix and, 243–44, 254–55; rock 'n' roll and, 7–8; women performers in, 282n.4
Jefferson Airplane (band), 206
Jefferson, Margo, 205, 248
Jefferson, Tony, 101
Jeffrey, Mike, 283n.6
Jenkins, Beverly, 63–64, 134, 140, 187, 198–99, 217
Jet magazine, 151
Jimi Hendrix Experience (band), 234
Jimi Hendrix Experience (video), 284n.8
J. J. Jumpers (band), 30, 48, 198
Johnson, Anthony, 130
Johnson, Louis, 251
Johnson, Michelle, 184
Johnson, Robert, 154
Jones, Brian, 155
Jones, Lisa, 122, 209–12
Joplin, Janis, 28, 204, 206, 248
Jungle Funk (band), 269
Just Above Midtown (JAM) Gallery, 61

Kaye, Bernie "BK," 177, 195–99, 260–61
Keil, Charles, 277n.1
Kelley, Norman, 164, 166, 279n.1
Kelley, Robin D. G., 11
Kellner, Douglas, 192–93
Kelvynator (band), 72, 99, 134, 171–73, 198; discography, 269
Kennedy, John F., 5
Khan, Chaka, 212
Kid Creole and the Coconuts (band), 252
Kimber, Bryant "Beezo," 19
Kind of Blue (album), 109
King, B. B., 149
King, Martin Luther, Jr., 5, 85
Kitchen (club), 97
Knitting Factory (club), 21, 99
Komet, Reggie, 268
Kondo, Dorinne, 23, 101, 277n.1

"race music," evolution of, 149–50

Radio BRC (online show), 281n.3

radio stations and programming: black audiences for, 149–50, 280n.8; Hendrix's exposure on, 242–49; racial biases in, 91, 167–70, 278n.2, 281n.19. *See also* specific radio stations

Rainbows End (band), 201; discography, 270

Raincoats (band), 207

Raitt, Bonnie, 206, 214

Ramgortra, Satnam S., 130

Ramos, Sophia, 71, 184, 209, 212–16. *See also* Sophia's Toy (band)

rap music: independent producers of, 180; on MTV, 169; racialized marketing of, 166–70

Ravers magazine, 26, 214

Ravitch, Diane, 46, 276n.4

Reagan, Ronald, 17, 274n.14

Reagon, Toshi, 175, 206, 208

recording industry: Black Rock Coalition's focus on, 17–18, 26–32, 58, 70–75, 95–96, 132–34; black rock's difficulties with, 67–71, 195–99; Hendrix and, 242–49; independent producers in, 179–85, 189–92, 200–203; lack of black executives in, 166–70; postwar expansion of, 149–50; racialized marketing strategies in, 158–75; racialized political economy and, 26–27, 145–46; racism in, 145–54, 163–70, 281n.17

Redding, Noel, 234

"Red House," 252

Red Robin label, 280n.9

Reed, Lou, 204–5

reggae music: BRC connections to, 100–101; influence on Faith (band), 209

Reid, Fritz, 19

Reid, Ray, 38

Reid, Vernon, 2, 21, 30, 84, 86, 96; Black Rock Coalition and, 6, 14–15, 120, 122–23, 235, 257–58; BRC radio programs and, 188, 281n.3; criticism of, 159–60; discography, 270–71; with Family Stand, 157; Hendrix's influence on, 235–41; Hendrix tribute shows and, 251; identity politics and, 96, 159–62; Jagger and, 155; with Living Colour, 5–7, 128, 143–45, 191, 263–65; Los Angeles BRC chapter and, 98; in Masque (band), 99; music projects by, 105, 126, 129, 259; on racial politics and recording industry, 146. *See also* Living Colour (band)

representation: class structure and, 19–20; cultural politics and, 14, 17–21, 102–3, 275n.14

Res (musician), 261

research methodology, for Black Rock Coalition study, 21–26

Reynolds, Rhonda, 164–66

Rhone, Sylvia, 223

rhythm and blues (R&B): Hendrix's use of, 239–41; racialized marketing of, 166–70; rock 'n' roll compared with, 151–54; Sophia's Toy influenced by, 212–16

Rice, Thomas "Daddy," 247–48

Richards, Keith, 143, 155

Richie, Lionel, 163, 169

Righteous Babe Records, 260

Riot Grrrls, 207

ritual insult, in black rock lyrics, 131, 279n.9

Robey, Don, 280n.9

Robinson, Bobby, 280n.9

Rock City News, 94

"Rocket 88," 149

"Rock 'n' Roll," 261–62

rock 'n' roll music: black influences in, 91–92, 204–5; British invasion of, 154–58; cultural politics of, 7–8, 13–14; Hendrix's influence in, 239–49; local venues for, 99–103; racial issues and, 147–54; recording industry packaging of, 163–70; stereotypes in, 17–18; white appropriation of, 139–40, 150–54, 228–30, 248–49; women in, 206–30

"Rock 'n' Roll Nigger," 204

Rogers, Mark "Kumasi," 19

Rolling Stone magazine, 5, 94, 159, 178, 214, 248, 280n.5

Rolling Stones (band), 5–6, 143, 154–58, 234, 262, 282n.2

Ronettes (band), 207

Roots (band), 262

Rosaldo, Renato, 10, 23, 273n.3

Rosser, Felice, 2–4, 183, 209–12, 216. *See also* Faith (band)

Roxy Music (band), 37

Ruffin, Torrell "Tori," 129–34; discography, 269. *See also* Civil Rite (band)

Rufus (band), 212

"Run From the World," 183

Rykodisc, 179, 181

Saal, Jimmy, 63–64, 181–83, 187, 200

Sadownick, Daniel, 111, 126

Sae, Kellie, 48

St. Victor, Sandra, 208

Sandelbach, Rosalie, 171–72

Sanjek, Russell, 168–69

Santana (band), 28, 123, 162

Santoro, Gene, 94

Schwartzman, Helen B., 60

Scott-Heron, Gil, 28

Screaming Headless Torsos (band), 32, 99, 113; discography, 270; European concerts by, 199; independent recordings by, 202; live performances of, 104–5, 108–13; style and aesthetic of, 125–29

Screaming Headless Torsos Live (album), 129

Screamin' Jay Hawkins, 154

Seacor, Patrick, 3–4, 212

Seck, Cheick Tidane, 260

sexism: in Black Rock Coalition, 216–21; in rock music, 31–32, 206–16

Sex Pistols (band), 206

sexuality: in black women's music, 206–16; Hendrix's use of, 245–49; in NdegéOcello's music, 136–37; in rock music, 205–6, 215–30, 282n.1

"Shadow of Shadows," 184

Shakespeare, William, 266, 284n.2

Shank, Barry, 99

Sharp, Elliot, 202

Sharrock, Sonny, 28, 123, 126, 250

Shock Council (band), 30, 38, 105, 187, 202

"Should I Stay or Should I Go?," 145

Simon, Paul, 158

Simone, Nina, 4, 128, 262

Simpson, Lorna, 61

Simpson, O. J., 224, 226–27

Sinatra, Frank, 133

Sinclair, Tom, 137

Sinister Dane (band), 187

Sister Ax performances, 217

Skillings, Muzz, 6, 113, 146, 199. *See also* Living Colour (band)

Slick, Grace, 206

"Slow Ride," 263

Sly and the Family Stone (band), 28, 91, 123, 134, 162, 206. *See also* Stone, Sly

"Smile in a Wave," 128

Smith, Fred, 212

Smith, Mamie, 149

Smith, Patti, 204–6

Smith, R. J., 161

Smith, Susan, 226

Maureen Mahon is an assistant professor in
the Department of Anthropology at UCLA.

Library of Congress Cataloging-in-Publication Data
Mahon, Maureen.
Right to rock : the Black Rock Coalition and the cultural
politics of race / Maureen Mahon.
p. cm.   Includes bibliographical references and index.
Discography: p.
ISBN 0-8223-3305-8 (cloth : alk. paper)
ISBN 0-8223-3317-1 (pbk. : alk. paper)
1. Rock music—Social aspects. 2. African American musicians.
3. Music and race. 4. Black Rock Coalition. I. Title
ML3534.M31 2004   781.66'089'96073—dc22
2004002239